Alvin W. Gouldner

For Sociology

Renewal and Critique in Sociology
Today

Allen Lane

Allen Lane
A Division of Penguin Books Ltd
21 John Street, London WCIN 2BT

ISBN 0 7139 0446 1

Printed in Great Britain
by W. & J. Mackay Ltd, Chatham
Set in Monotype Garamond

*Dedicated with love, respect and wonderment
to my children*

*Andrew Ward Gouldner
Alessandra Walker Gouldner*

Contents

To create freedom and a reverent 'No' even in the face of duty:
for this, my brothers, the lion is necessary.
Friedrich Nietzsche, *Thus Spake Zarathustra*

The fact that a Veblen rather than a Weber gathers a school of
ardent disciples around him bears witness to the great
importance of factors other than the sheer weight of evidence
and analysis in the formation of 'schools' of social thought.
Talcott Parsons, *Essays in Sociological Theory* p. 117

. . . any new left in America must be, in large measure, a
left with real intellectual skills, committed to deliberativeness,
honesty, reflection as working tools.
The Port Huron Statement, of the Students for a
Democratic Society (S.D.S.)

Just as the sharpest critics of Marxism have usually been
Marxists, the keenest critics of sociology have usually been
sociologists and students of sociology. Often enough the men
whose rejection of such criticism is most vehement are those
who live off *sociology, while the most vehement critics are those*
who live for *it. Often, but not always.*
Alvin W. Gouldner, *The Coming Crisis of Western*
Sociology p. 15

Part One

Critiques of Sociology

Anti-Minotaur:
The Myth of a Value-Free Sociology

This is an account of a myth created by and about a magnificent minotaur named Max – Max Weber, to be exact; his myth was that social science should and could be value-free. The lair of this minotaur, although reached only by a labyrinthine logic and visited only by a few who never return, is still regarded by many sociologists as a holy place. In particular, as sociologists grow older they seem impelled to make a pilgrimage to it and to pay their respects to the problem of the relations between values and social science.

Considering the perils of the visit, their motives are somewhat perplexing. Perhaps their quest is the first sign of professional senility; perhaps it is the last sigh of youthful yearnings. And perhaps a concern with the value problem is just a way of trying to take back something that was, in youthful enthusiasm, given too hastily.

In any event, the myth of a value-free sociology has been a conquering one. Today, all the powers of sociology, from Parsons to Lundberg, have entered into a tacit alliance to bind us to the dogma that 'Thou shalt not commit a value judgement', especially as sociologists. Where is the introductory textbook, where the lecture course on principles, that does not affirm or imply this rule?

In the end, of course, we cannot disprove the existence of minotaurs who, after all, are thought to be sacred precisely because, being half man and half bull, they are so unlikely. The thing to see is that a belief in them is not so much untrue as it is absurd. Like Berkeley's argument for solipsism, Weber's brief for a value-free sociology is a tight one and, some say, logically unassailable. Yet it is also absurd. For both arguments appeal to reason but ignore experience.

I do not here wish to enter into an examination of the *logical* arguments involved, not because I regard them as incontrovertible but because I find them less interesting to me as a sociologist. Instead what I will do is to view the belief in a value-free sociology in the same manner that sociologists examine any element in the ideology of any group. This means that we will look upon the sociologist just as we would any other occupation, be it the taxi-cab driver, the nurse, the coal miner or the physician. In short, I will look at the belief in a value-free sociology as part of the ideology of a working group and from the standpoint of the sociology of occupations.

The image of a value-free sociology is more than a neat intellectual theorem demanded as a sacrifice to reason; it is, also, a felt conception of a role and a set of (more or less) shared sentiments as to how sociologists should live. We may be sure that it became this not simply because it is true or logically elegant but, also, because it is somehow useful to those who believe in it. Applauding the dancer for her grace is often the audience's way of concealing its lust.

That we are in the presence of a group myth, rather than a carefully formulated and well validated belief appropriate to scientists, may be discerned if we ask, just what is it that is believed by those holding sociology to be a value-free discipline? Does the belief in a value-free sociology mean that, in point of fact, sociology is a discipline actually free of values and that it successfully excludes all non-scientific assumptions in selecting, studying, and reporting on a problem? Or does it mean that sociology *should* do so. Clearly, the first is untrue and I know of no one who even holds it possible for sociologists to exclude completely their non-scientific beliefs from their scientific work; and if this is so, on what grounds can this impossible task be held to be morally incumbent on sociologists?

Does the belief in a value-free sociology mean that sociologists cannot, do not, or should not make value judgements concerning things outside their sphere of technical competence? But what has technical competence to do with the making of value judgements? If technical competence does provide a warrant for making value judgements then there is nothing to prohibit sociologists from making them within the area of their expertise. If, on the contrary, technical competence provides no warrant for making value judgements then, at least sociologists are as *free* to do so as anyone else; then their value judgements are at least as good as anyone else's, say, a twelve-year-old child's. And, by the way, if technical competence provides no warrant for making value judgements, then what does?

Does the belief in a value-free sociology mean that sociologists are or should be indifferent to the moral implications of their work? Does it mean that sociologists can and should make value judgements so long as they are careful to point out that these are different from 'merely' factual statements? Does it mean that sociologists cannot logically deduce values from facts? Does it mean that sociologists do not or should not have or express *feelings* for or against some of the things they study? Does it mean that sociologists may and should inform laymen about techniques useful in realizing their own ends, if they are asked to do so, but that if they are not asked to do so they are to say nothing? Does it mean that sociologists should never take the initiative in asserting that some beliefs that laymen hold, such as the belief in the inherent inferiority of certain races, are false even when known to be contradicted by the facts of their discipline? Does it mean that social scientists should never speak out, or speak out only when invited, about the probable outcomes of a public course of action concerning which they are professionally knowledgeable? Does it mean that social scientists should never express values in their roles as teachers or in their roles as researchers, or in both? Does the belief in a value-free sociology mean that sociologists, either as teachers or researchers, have a right to covertly and unwittingly express their values but have no right to do so overtly and deliberately?

I fear that there are many sociologists today who, in conceiving social science to be value-free, mean widely different things, that many hold these beliefs dogmatically without having examined seriously the grounds upon which they are credible, and that some few affirm a value-free sociology ritualistically without having any clear idea what it might mean. Weber's own views on the relation between values and social science, and some current today are scarcely identical. While Weber saw grave hazards in the sociologist's expression of value judgements, he also held that these might be voiced if caution was exercised to distinguish them from statements of fact. If Weber insisted on the need to maintain scientific objectivity, he also warned that this was altogether different from moral indifference.

Not only was the cautious expression of value judgements deemed permissible by Weber but, he emphasized, these were positively mandatory under certain circumstances. Although Weber inveighed against the professorial 'cult of personality' we might also remember that he was not against all value-imbued cults and that he himself worshipped at the shrine of individual responsibility. A familiarity with Weber's work on these points would only be embarrassing to many who today affirm a value-free sociology in his name. And should the disparity between Weber's own views and many now current come to be sensed, then the time is not far off when it will be asked, 'Who now reads Max Weber?'

What to Weber was an agonizing expression of a highly personal faith, intensely felt and painstakingly argued, has today become a hollow catechism, a password, and a good excuse for no longer thinking seriously. It has become increasingly the trivial token of professional respectability, the caste mark of the decorous; it has become the gentleman's promise that boats will not be rocked. Rather than showing Weber's work the respect that it deserves, by carefully re-evaluating it in the light of our own generation's experience, we reflexively reiterate it even as we distort it to our own purposes. Ignorance of the gods is no excuse; but it can be convenient. For if the worshipper never visits the altar of his god, then he can never learn whether the fire still burns there or whether the priests, grown fat, are simply sifting the ashes.

The needs which the value-free conception of social science serves are both personal and institutional. Briefly, my contention will be that, among the main institutional forces facilitating the survival and spread of the value-free myth, was its usefulness in maintaining both the cohesion and the autonomy of the modern university, in general, and the newer social science disciplines, in particular. There is little difficulty, at any rate, in demonstrating that these were among the motives originally inducing Max Weber to formulate the conception of a value-free sociology.

This issue might be opened at a seemingly peripheral and petty point, namely when Weber abruptly mentions the problem of competition among professors for students. Weber notes that professors who do express a value-stand are more likely to attract students than those who do not and are, therefore, likely to have undue career advantages. In effect, this is a complaint against a kind of unfair competition by professors who pander to student interests. Weber's hope seems to have been that the value-free principle would serve as a kind of 'Fair Trades Act' to restrain such competition. (At this point there is a curious rift in the dramatic mood of Weber's work; we had been listening to a full-throated Wagnerian aria when suddenly the singer begins to hum snatches from Kurt Weill's 'Mack the Knife'.)

This suggests that one of the latent functions of the value-free doctrine is to bring peace to the academic house, by reducing competition for students, and, in turn, it directs us to some of the institutional peculiarities of German universities in Weber's time. Unlike the situation in the American university, career advancement in the German was then felt to depend too largely on the professor's popularity as a teacher; indeed, at the lower ranks, the instructor's income was directly dependent on student enrolment. As a result, the competition for students was particularly keen and it was felt that the system penalized good scholars and researchers in favour of attractive teaching. In contrast, of course, the American system has been commonly accused of overstressing scholarly publication and here the contrary complaint is typical, namely, that good teaching goes unrewarded and that you must 'publish or perish'. In the context of the German academic system, Weber was raising no trivial point when he intimated that the value-free doctrine would reduce academic competition. He was linking the doctrine to guild problems and anchoring this lofty question in academicians' *earthy* interests.

Another relation of the value-free principle to distinctively

German arrangements is also notable when Weber, opposing use of the lecture hall as an arena of value affirmation, argues that it subjects the student to a pressure which he is unable to evaluate or resist adequately. Given the comparatively exalted position of the professor in German society, and given the one-sided communication inherent in the lecture hall, Weber did have a point. His fears were, perhaps, all the more justified if we accept a view of the German 'national character' as being authoritarian, that is, in Nietzsche's terms, a combination of arrogance and servility. But these considerations do not hold with anything like equal cogency in more democratic cultures such as our own. For here, not only are professors held in, shall I say, more modest esteem, but the specific ideology of educa-tion itself often stresses the desirability of student initiative and participation, and there is more of a systematic solicitation of the student's 'own' views in small 'discussion' sections. There is little student servility to complement and encourage occasional professorial arrogance.

When Weber condemned the lecture hall as a forum for value-affirmation he had in mind most particularly the expression of *political* values. The point of Weber's polemic is not directed against all values with equal sharpness. It was not the expression of aesthetic or even religious values that Weber sees as most objectionable in the university, but, primarily, those of politics. His promotion of the value-free doctrine may, then, be seen not so much as an effort to amoralize as to depoliticize the uni-versity and to remove it from the political struggle. The political conflicts then echoing in the German university did not entail comparatively trivial differences, such as those now between Democrats and Republicans in the United States. Weber's proposal of the value-free doctrine was, in part, an effort to establish a *modus vivendi* among academicians whose political commitments were often intensely felt and in violent opposi-tion.

Under these historical conditions, the value-free doctrine was a proposal for an academic truce. It said, in effect, if we all keep quiet about our political views then we may all be able to get on with our work. But if the value-free principle was suitable in Weber's Germany because it served to restrain political passions, is it equally useful in America today where, not only is there pitiable little difference in politics but men often have no politics at all. Perhaps the need of the American university today, as of American society more generally, is for more commitment to politics and for more diversity of political views. It would seem that now the national need is to take the lid off, not to screw it on more tightly.

Given the historically unique conditions of nuclear warfare, where the issue would not be decided in a long-drawn-out war requiring the sustained cohesion of mass populations, national consensus is no longer, I believe, as important a condition of national survival as it once was. But if we no longer require the same degree of unanimity to *fight* a war, we do require a greater ferment of ideas and a radiating growth of political seriousness and variety within which alone we may find a way to *prevent* war. Important contributions to this have been and may further be made by members of the academic community and, perhaps, especially, by its social science sector. The question arises, however, whether this group's political intelligence can ever be adequately mobilized for these purposes so long as it remains tranquillized by the value-free doctrine.

Throughout his work, Weber's strategy is to safeguard the integrity and freedom of action of both the state, as the instrument of German national policy, and of the university, as the embodiment of a larger Western tradition of rationalism. He feared that the expression of political value judgements in the university would provoke the state into censoring the university and would imperil its autonomy. Indeed, Weber argues that professors are not entitled to freedom from state control in matters of values, since these do not rest on their specialized qualifications.

This view will seem curious only to those regarding Weber as a liberal in the Anglo-American sense, that is, as one who wishes to delimit the state's powers on behalf of the individual's liberties. Actually, however, Weber aimed not at curtailing but at strengthening the powers of the German state, and at making it a more effective instrument of German nationalism. It would seem, however, that an argument contrary to the one he advances is at least as consistent; namely, that professors are, like all others, entitled and perhaps required to express their values. In other words, professors have a right to profess. Rather than being made the objects of special suspicion and special control by the state, they are no less (and no more) entitled than others to the trust and protection of the state.

In a *realpolitik* vein, Weber acknowledges that the most basic national questions cannot ordinarily be discussed with full freedom in government universities. Since the discussion there cannot be completely free and all-sided, he apparently concludes that it is fitting there should be no discussion at all, rather than risk partisanship. But this is too pious by far. Even Socrates never insisted that all views must be at hand before the dialogue could begin. Here again one might as reasonably argue to the contrary, holding that one limitation of freedom is no excuse for another. Granting the reality of efforts to inhibit unpopular views in the university, it seems odd to prescribe self-suppression as a way of avoiding external suppression. Suicide does not seem a reasonable way to avoid being murdered. It appears, however, that Weber was so intent on safeguarding the auton-omy of the university from politics, that he was willing to pay almost any price to do so, even if this led the university to detach itself from one of the basic intellectual traditions of the west – the dialectical exploration of the fundamental purposes of human life.

Insofar as the value-free doctrine is a mode of ensuring pro-fessional autonomy note that it does not, as such, entail an interest peculiar to the social science. In this regard, as a sub-stantial body of research in the sociology of occupations indi-cates, social scientists are kin to plumbers, house painters or librarians. For most if not all occupations seek to elude control by outsiders and manifest a drive to maintain exclusive control over their practitioners.

Without doubt the value-free principle did enhance the autonomy of sociology; it was one way in which our discipline pried itself loose – in some modest measure – from the clutch of its society, in Europe freer from political party influence, in the United States freer of ministerial influence. In both places, the value-free doctrine gave sociology a larger area of autonomy in which it could steadily pursue basic problems rather than journalistically react to passing events, and allowed it more freedom to pursue questions uninteresting either to the respectable or to the rebellious. It made sociology freer – as Comte had wanted it to be – to pursue all its own theoretical implications. In other words, the value-free principle did, I think, contribute to the intellectual growth and emancipation of our enterprise.

There was another kind of freedom which the value-free doctrine also allowed; it enhanced a freedom from moral compulsiveness; it permitted a partial escape from the parochial prescriptions of the sociologist's local or native culture. Above all, effective internalization of the value-free principle has always encouraged at least a temporary suspension of the moralizing reflexes built into the sociologist by his own society. From one perspective, this of course has its dangers – a disorienting normlessness and moral indifference. From another standpoint, however, the value-free principle might also have provided a *moral* as well as an intellectual *opportunity*. For insofar as moral reactions are only suspended and not aborted, and insofar as this is done in the service of knowledge and intellectual discipline, then, in effect, the value-free principle strengthened Reason (or Ego) against the compulsive demands of a merely traditional morality. To this degree, the value-free discipline provided a foundation for the development of more reliable knowledge about men and, also, established a breathing space within which moral reactions could be less mechanical and in which morality could be reinvigorated.

The value-free doctrine thus had a paradoxical potentiality: it might enable men to make *better* value judgements rather than *none*. It could encourage a habit of mind that might help men in discriminating between their punitive drives and their ethical sentiments. Moralistic reflexes suspended, it was now more possible to sift conscience with the rod of reason and to cultivate moral judgements that expressed a man's total character as an adult person; he need not now live quite so much by his past parental programming but in terms of his more mature present.

The value-free doctrine could have meant an opportunity for a more authentic morality. It could and sometimes did aid men in transcending the morality of their 'tribe', to open themselves to the diverse moralities of unfamiliar groups, and to see themselves and others from the standpoint of a wider range of significant cultures. But the value-free doctrine also had other, less fortunate, results as well.

Doubtless there were some who did use the opportunity thus presented; but there were, also, many who used the value-free postulate as an excuse for pursuing their private impulses to the neglect of their public responsibilities and who, far from becoming more morally sensitive, became morally jaded. Insofar as the value-free doctrine failed to realize its potentialities it did so because its deepest impulses were – as we shall note later – dualistic; it invited men to stress the separation and not the mutual connectedness of facts and values: it had the vice of its virtues. In short, the conception of a value-free sociology has had *diverse* consequences, not all of them useful or flattering to the social sciences.

On the negative side, it may be noted that the value-free doctrine is useful both to those who want to escape *from* the world and to those who want to escape *into* it. It is useful to those young, or not so young men, who live off sociology rather than for it, and who think of sociology as a way of getting ahead in the world by providing them with neutral techniques that may be sold on the open market to any buyer. The belief that it is not the business of a sociologist to make value judgements is taken, by some, to mean that the market on which they can vend their skills is unlimited. From such a standpoint, there is no reason why one cannot sell his knowledge to spread a disease just as freely as he can to fight it. Indeed, some sociologists have had no hesitation about doing market research designed to sell more cigarettes, although well aware of the implications of recent cancer research. In brief, the value-free doctrine of social science was sometimes used to justify the sale of one's talents to the highest bidder and is, far from being new, a contemporary version of the most ancient sophistry.

In still other cases, the image of a value-free sociology is the armour of the alienated sociologist's self. Although C. Wright Mills may be right in saying this is the Age of Sociology, not a few sociologists, and Mills included, feel estranged and isolated from their society. They feel impotent to contribute usefully to the solution of its deepening problems and, even when they can, they fear that the terms of such an involvement require them to submit to a commercial debasement or a narrow partisanship, rather than contributing to a truly public interest.

Many sociologists feel themselves cut off from the larger community of liberal intellectuals in whose spitty satire they see themselves as ridiculous caricatures. Estranged from the larger world, they cannot escape except in fantasies of post-humous medals and by living huddled behind self-barricaded intellectual ghettoes. Self-doubt finds its anodyne in the image of a value-free sociology because this transforms their alienation into an intellectual principle; it evokes the soothing illusion, among some sociologists, that their exclusion from the larger society is a self-imposed duty rather than an externally imposed constraint.

Once committed to the premise of a value-free sociology, such sociologists are bound to a policy which can only alienate them further from the surrounding world. Social science can never be fully accepted in a society, or by a part of it, without paying its way; this means it must manifest both its relevance and concern for the contemporary human predicament. Unless the value relevances of sociological inquiry are made plainly evident, unless there are at least some bridges between it and larger human hopes and purposes, it must inevitably be scorned by laymen as pretentious word-mongering. But the manner in which some sociologists conceive the value-free doctrine disposes them to ignore current human problems and to huddle together like old men seeking mutual warmth. 'This is not our job', they say, 'and if it were we would not know enough to do it. Go away, come back when we're grown up,' say these old men. The issue, however, is not whether we know enough; the real questions are whether we have the courage to say and use what we do know and whether anyone knows more.

There is one way in which those who desert the world and those who sell out to it have something in common. Neither group can adopt an openly critical stance toward society. Those who sell out are accomplices; they may feel no critical impulses. Those who run out, while they do feel such impulses, are either lacking in any talent for aggression, or have often turned it inward into noisy but essentially safe university politics or into professional polemics. In adopting a conception of themselves as 'value-free' scientists, their critical impulses may no longer find a target in society. Since they no longer feel free to criticize society, which always requires a measure of courage, they now turn to the cannibalistic criticism of sociology itself and begin to eat themselves up with 'methodological' criticisms.

One latent meaning, then, of the image of a value-free sociology is this: 'Thou shalt not commit a critical or negative value judgement – especially of one's own society.' Like a neurotic symptom this aspect of the value-free image is rooted in a conflict; it grows out of an effort to compromise between conflicting drives: On the one side, it reflects a conflict between the desire to criticize social institutions, which since Socrates has been the legacy of intellectuals, and the fear of reprisals if one does criticize – which is also a very old and human concern. On the other side, this aspect of the value-free image reflects a conflict between the fear of being critical and the fear of being regarded as unmanly or lacking in integrity, if uncritical.

The doctrine of a value-free sociology resolves these conflicts by making it seem that those who refrain from social criticism are acting solely on behalf of a higher professional good rather than their private interests. In refraining from social criticism, both the timorous and the venal may now claim the protection of a high professional principle and, in so doing, can continue to hold themselves in decent regard. Persuade all that no one must bell the cat, then none of the mice need feel like a rat.

Should social scientists affirm or critically explore values, they would of necessity come up against powerful institutions who deem the statement or protection of public values as part of their special business. Should social scientists seem to compete in this business, they can run afoul of powerful forces and can, realistically, anticipate efforts at external curbs and controls. In saying this, however, we have to be careful lest we needlessly exacerbate academic timorousness. Actually, my own first-hand impressions of many situations where sociologists serve as consultants indicate that, once their clients come to know them, they are often quite prepared to have sociologists suggest (not dictate) policy and to have them express their own values. Nor does this always derive from the expectation that sociologists will see things their way and share their values. Indeed, it is precisely the expected difference in perspectives that is occasionally desired in seeking consultation. I find it difficult not to sympathize with businessmen who jeer at sociologists when they suddenly become more devoted to business values than the businessmen themselves.

Clearly all this does not mean that people will tolerate disagreement on basic values with social scientists more equably than they will with anyone else. Surely there is no reason why the principles governing social interaction should be miraculously suspended just because one of the parties to a social relation is a social scientist. The dangers of public resentment are real but they are only normal. They are not inconsistent with the possibility that laymen may be perfectly ready to allow social scientists as much (or as little) freedom of value expression as they would anyone else. And what more could any social scientist want?

The value-free image of social science is not consciously held for expedience's sake; it is not contrived deliberately as a hedge against public displeasure. It could not function as a face-saving device if it were. What seems more likely is that it entails something in the nature of a tacit bargain: in return for a measure of autonomy and social support, many social scientists have surrendered their critical impulses. This was not usually a callous 'sell-out' but a slow process of mutual accommodation; both parties suddenly found themselves betrothed without a formal ceremony.

Nor am I saying that the critical posture is dead in American sociology; it is just badly sagging. Anyone who has followed the work of Seymour Lipset, Dennis Wrong, Leo Lowenthal, Bennett Berger, Bernard Rosenberg, Lewis Coser, Maurice Stein, C. Wright Mills, Arthur Vidich, Philip Rieff, Anselm Strauss, David Riesman, Alfred McClung Lee, Van den Haag and of others, would know better. These men still regard themselves as 'intellectuals' no less than sociologists: their work is deeply linked to this larger tradition from which sociology itself has evolved. By no means have all sociologists rejected the legacy of the intellectual, namely, the right to be critical of tradition. This ancient heritage still remains embedded in the underground culture of sociology; and it comprises the enshadowed part of the occupational selves of many sociologists even if not publicly acknowledged.

In contrast with and partly in polemic against this older tradition, however, the dominant drift of American sociology today is compulsively bent upon transforming it into a 'profession'. (Strangely enough, many of these same sociologists see nothing contradictory in insisting that their discipline is still young and immature.) This clash between the older heritage of the critical intellectual and the modern claims of the value-free professional finds many expressions. One of these occurred at the sociologists' national meeting in Chicago in 1958. At this time, the convention in a session of the whole was considering Talcott Parsons' paper on 'Sociology as a Profession'. After long and involved discussion, which prompted many members suddenly to remember overdue appointments elsewhere, Chicago's E. C. Hughes rose from the floor and brought a warm response by insisting that we were not a professional but, rather, a learned society. It was at this same meeting that the American Sociologist Society rechristened itself as the American Sociological Association, lest its former initials evoke public reactions discrepant with the dignity of a profession.

Another indication of the continuing clash between the critical intellectual and the value-free professional is to be found in the Phoenix-like emergence of Young Turk movements, such as S.P.S.S.I., the Society for the Psychological Study of Social Issues, which arose in response to the depression of 1929. When it was felt by Alfred McClung Lee and others that these Turks were no longer so young, they founded the S.S.S.P., the Society for the Study of Social Problems. Both these organizations remain ongoing concerns, each characteristically interested in value-related work, and each something of a stitch in the side of its respective parent group, the American Psychological Association and the American Sociological Association.

The tension between the older conception of sociologists as intellectuals and the newer drive to professionalization is also expressed by the differences between the current Columbia or Harvard outlook and the so-called 'Chicago tradition' which, with the change in that Department's character, is now either centred in Berkeley or is homelessly hovering. The difference between these two perspectives is most evident when they both embark on studies of the same institution.

A case in point can be found in the recent studies of medicine conducted by Columbia or Harvard and Chicago trained men. It is difficult to escape the feeling that the former are more respectful of the medical establishment than the Chicagoans, that they more readily regard it in terms of its own claims, and are more prone to view it as a noble profession. Chicagoans, however, tend to be uneasy about the very idea of a 'profession' as a tool for study, believing instead that the notion of an 'occupation' provides more basic guide-lines for study, and arguing that occupations as diverse as the nun and the prostitute, or the plumber and the physician, reveal instructive sociological similarities. Chicagoans seem more likely to take a secular view of medicine, seeing it as an occupation much like any other and are somewhat more inclined towards debunking forays into the seamier side of medical practice. Epitomizing this difference are the very differences in the book titles that the two groups have chosen for their medical studies. Harvard and Columbia have soberly called two of their most important works *The Student-Physician* and *Experiment Perilous*, while the Chicagoans have irreverently labelled their own recent study of medical students the *Boys in White*.

One of the most interesting expressions of resistance to the newer, value-free style of 'professional' sociology is the fascination with the *demi-monde* of a talented group of these ex-Chicagoans. For them orientation to the underworld has become the equivalent of the proletarian identifications felt by some intellectuals during the 1930s. For not only do they study it, but in a way they speak on its behalf, affirming the authenticity of its style of life. Two of the leading exponents of this style are Howard S. Becker, and Erving Goffman who may become the William Blake of sociology.

As a case in point, Goffman's subtle study, *Cooling the Mark Out*, takes its point of departure from an examination of the strategy of the confidence rackets. In the Con Game, Goffman points out, after the mark's loot has been taken, one of the con men remains behind 'to cool the mark out', seeking to persuade him to accept his loss of face rather than squeal to the police. Goffman then uses this strategem as a model to explore a great variety of legitimate groups and roles – the restaurant hostess who cools out the impatient customer, the psychoanalyst who cools out those who have lost in love. The point is insinuated that the whole world may be seen as one of marks and operators and that, in the final analysis, we are all marks to be cooled out by the clergy, the operator left behind for the job. This, it would seem, is a metaphysics of the underworld, in which conventional society is seen from the standpoint of a group outside of its own respectable social structures.

This group of Chicagoans finds itself at home in the world of hip, Norman Mailer, drug addicts, jazz musicians, cab drivers, prostitutes, night people, drifters, grifters and skidders, the cool cats and their kicks. To be fully appreciated this stream of work cannot be seen solely in terms of the categories conventionally employed in sociological analysis. It has also to be seen from the viewpoint of the literary critic as a style or *genre* and, in particular as a species of naturalistic Romanticism,[1] a term which I do not in the least intend opprobriously. That is, it prefers the offbeat to the familiar, the vivid enthnographic detail to the dull taxonomy, the sensuously expressive to dry analysis, naturalistic observation to formal questionnaires, the standpoint of the hip outsider to the square insider.

It may of course be asked, 'Is it any the less sentimentally Romantic to regard medical research on incurable patients as an "Experiment Perilous" ?' Possibly not. But it is at least much more *decorous* than seeing it as a process of 'cooling the mark out'. That, I suspect, is nearer the bone. The one thing that 'Classicists', whether sociological or literary, can never abide is a lack of decorum, even if the performance is in other respects brilliant. In sociology, objections to a lack of decorum as such are not made and, instead, often take the form of criticizing methodological deficiencies or moralistic proclivities. And, in truth, this Chicago group does betray persistent moral concerns, as evidenced, for example, by their readiness to focus on the degrading impact of the mental hospital on its inmates, or on the legal straitjacket in which the drug addict is confined.

The pathology characteristic of the *Classicist* is too well known to require much comment: theirs is the danger of ritualism, in which conformity to the formal canons of the craft is pursued compulsively to the point where it warps work, emptying it of insight, significant truth, and intellectually viable substance. Of the Classicist degenerating into neo-Classicism we might say, with Roy Campbell, 'They use the snaffle and the curb, all right, but where's the bloody horse?'

For its part, Romantic social criticism is vulnerable from two directions. The usual occupational hazard of the Romantic is, of course, excess, of the emotions or of the imagination. It may be guessed, however, that such excess stems not only from the personalities indigenous to those whom Romanticism attracts but, just as much, from the bitter attack upon them by the neo-Classicist and from their resultant polemic. Again, and perhaps more importantly, this Romantic standpoint is vulnerable to the crasser temptations of its own talent-earned success. Indeed, they have now learned to mute their jive to the point where they can communicate profitably with their stock-brokers. Perhaps the time will come when they will no longer have to pretend to be respectable and when they will, instead, have to work at seeming cool. But that time is not yet. Whatever the outcome, they have shown us still another facet of the resistance to the emergence of a value-free professionalism in sociology, and they have given us still another evidence of the intellectual vitality of a critical stance.

Despite the vigour of this and other groups, however, I believe that they are primarily secondary currents whose very visibility is heightened because they are moving across the main ebb. The dominant drift in American sociology is toward professionalization, the growth of technical specialists, toward the diffusion of the value-free outlook to the point where it becomes less of an intellectual doctrine and more of a blanketing mood. American sociology is in the process of accommodating itself.

In its main outlines, such efforts at accommodation are far from new. For the doctrine of a value-free sociology is a modern extension of the medieval conflict between faith and reason. It grows out of, and still dwells in, the tendency prevalent since the thirteenth century to erect compartments between the two as a way of keeping the peace between them. One of the culminations of this tendency in the Middle Ages is to be found in the work of the Arabian philosopher, Ibn Rochd, better known as Averroes. Averroes had believed that absolute truth was to be found not in revelation but in philosophy, which for him meant Aristotle. He felt that revelation, faith, and the work of the theologians was a kind of footman's philosophy necessary for those devoid of intellectual discipline and useful as a way of civilizing them.

Seeing theology as containing a measure of truth, albeit one inferior to that of philosophy, and being a prudent man, Averroes recommended that philosophers and theologians ought each to mind his own business and, in particular, that the philosophers, being intellectually superior, should show *noblesse oblige* to the theologians. He suggested that philosophers should keep their truth to themselves and write technical books which did not disturb or confuse simpler minds.

His disciples, the Latin or Christian Averroists, particularly at the University of Paris, accentuated this prudential side of their master's work; their strategy of safety was to define themselves as specialists, as technical philosophers. Their only job, said they, was to teach philosophy and to show the conclusions that flowed from it. These conclusions were 'necessary' but, when at variance with the truths of revelation, it was not their job to reconcile them, said the philosophers. From this developed the so-called Doctrine of the Twofold Truth – the truths of philosophy which were logically necessary and the divine truths of revelation. If there were contradictions between the two, the philosophers merely reaffirmed their belief in revelation, and let it go at that. This sometimes took a cynical form as, for example, in John of Jaudan's comment, 'I do believe that is true; but I cannot prove it. Good luck to those who can!' They thus built a watertight compartment between philosophy and faith, a separation which Saint Thomas continued and yet sought to transcend. To Saint Thomas, knowing and believing are distinct processes, each having its own separate and legitimate function and therefore not to be invaded by the other. In this view, there were two main classes of truths, both of which, however, derived from Divine Revelation. There were truths obtainable by natural reason alone, and there were truths of revelation, genuine articles of faith which eluded the grasp of reason and which were susceptible neither to proof nor disproof by reason.

With the development of modern science varying efforts to accommodate it to religion continued, often taking the form of some kind of separatist doctrine in which each is assigned a different function and each is chastened to acknowledge the authority of the other in its own sphere. Weber's doctrine of a value-free sociology, which creates a gulf between science and values, is in this tradition; it may be regarded as a Protestant version of the Thomistic effort at harmonizing their relations.

The core of Weber's outlook rested on a dualism between, on the one hand, reason or rationality, especially as embodied in bureaucracy and science, and, on the other hand, more elemental emotional forces, partly encompassed in his notion of Charisma. He regards each of these forces as inimical to the other. He himself is ambivalent to each of them, viewing each as both dangerous and necessary.

On the one side, Weber is deeply concerned to protect the citadel of modern reason, the university, and fiercely opposes the professorial 'cult of personality' which was the academic expression of the charismatic claim. This in turn disposes him to project an image of the university which is essentially bureaucratic, as a faceless group of specialists, each sovereign in his own cell and all sworn to foresake their individuality. Nonetheless he also hates bureaucracy precisely because it submerges individuality and dehumanizes men and is thus led to deny that he intended to bureaucratize the university in pleading for the doctrine of a value-free social science. (Yet while this was doubtless not his *intention*, his two-pronged polemic against the cult of academic personality and in favour of the value-free doctrine does seem to drive him toward such a bureaucratic conception of the university.)

If Weber is concerned to protect even the bureaucratic dwelling-places of rationality, he also seeks to confine bureaucracy and to circumscribe the area of its influence. In particular, he wishes to protect the highest reaches of statecraft from degenerating into a lifeless routine; he seeks to preserve politics as a realm in which there can be an expression of personal will, of serious moral commitment, a realm where greatness was possible to those who dared, persevered, and suffered, a realm so powerful that it could overturn the institutional order or preserve it. He wants to safeguard high politics as an arena of human autonomy, of pure value choices, at its finest.

Yet Weber also fears for the safety of rationality in the modern world. He knows that there are powerful forces abroad which continue to threaten rationality, that there are still untamed things in men which he, more than most, had had to face. Not unlike Freud, Weber was both afraid of and drawn to these unbridled forces, the passionate Dionysian part of men. While he believed that they were being slowly subdued by an onmarching rationalization, he continued to fear that they could yet erupt and cleave modern institutional life. Although fearing these irrational forces, he also felt their disappearance from the modern world to be a 'disenchantment', for he believed that they contained springs of vitality and power indispensable to human existence.

Weber is a man caught between two electrodes and torn by the current passing between them; he fears both but is unable to let go of either. He attempts to solve this dilemma by a strategy of segregation, seeking the exclusion of charismatic irrationality from certain modern *institutions*, such as the university, but admitting it into and, indeed, exalting its manifestations in the inward personal life of individuals. He wanted certain of the role structures of modern society to be rational; but he also wanted the role-players to be passionate and wilful. He wanted the play to be written by a classicist and to be acted by romanticists. Unusual man, he wanted the best of both worlds. Yet whatever the judgement of his intellect, his sentiments are not poised midway between them, but tend toward one of the two sides.

This becomes clear when we ask, if science cannot be the basis of value judgements, what then, according to Weber, was to be their basis? To answer this, we must go beyond his formal doctrine of a value-free sociology, to Weber's own personal profession of belief. Weber certainly did not hold that personal values should derive from the existent culture, or from ancient tradition, nor again from formal ethical systems which he felt to be empty and lifeless. Unless men were to become inhuman robots, life, he insisted, must be guided by consciously made decisions. If men are to have dignity, they must choose their own fate.

To Weber as a man, only those values are authentic which stem from conscious decision, from a consultation of the inner conscience and a wilful commitment to its dictates. From his *personal* standpoint, it is not really true that all values are equally worthy. Those consciously held by men are more worthy than those which are merely traditional and unthinkingly repeated. Those values that men feel deeply about and passionately long to realize are better than those which are merely intellectually appealing and do not engage their entire being.

In short, Weber, too, was seeking a solution to the competing claims of reason and faith. His solution takes the form of attempting to guard the autonomy of both spheres but, most especially I believe, the domain of conscience and faith. He wants a way in which reason and faith can cohabit platonically but not as full partners. The two orders are separate but unequal. For in Weber, reason only consults conscience and perhaps even cross-examines it. But conscience has the last word, and passion and will the last deed. Here Weber stands as half-Lutheran, half-Nietzschean.

If Weber thrust powerfully at traditionalism, nonetheless his main campaign here is waged against science and reason and is aimed at confining their influence. To Weber, even reason must submit when conscience declares, Here I stand; I can do no other! Weber saw as authentic only those values that rest on the charismatic core of the self and on its claims to intuitive certainty. Weber, too, was a seeker after certainty, the certainty that is more apt to come from the arrogance of individual conscience. For while much may be truly said of the arrogance of reason, reason always seeks reasons and is ready to sit down and talk about them.

To Weber as a Protestant, the individual's conscience is akin to the voice of revelation. He would have been dismayed at the implications of considering it as the echo of parental remonstrations. To him, individual conscience was transcendental while reason and science were only instrumental. Science is the servant of values and of personal conscience, which, like the heart, has reasons of its own. From Weber's standpoint, science and reason could only supply the means; the ends were to be dictated by values which, even if inscrutable, were to have the final voice.

I have therefore come to believe that the value-free doctrine is, from Weber's standpoint, basically an effort to compromise two of the deepest traditions of Western thought, reason and faith, but that his arbitration seeks above all to safeguard the romantic residue in modern man. I have personal reservations not because I doubt the worth of safeguarding this romantic component, but, rather, because I disagree with the strategy of segregation which Weber advances. *I believe that, in the end, this segregation warps reason by tinging it with sadism and leaves it feeling smugly sure only of itself and bereft of a sense of common humanity.*

The problem of a value-free sociology has its most poignant implications for the social scientist in his role as educator. If sociologists ought not to express their personal values in the academic setting, how then are students to be safeguarded against the unwitting influence of these values which shape the sociologist's selection of problems, his preferences for certain hypotheses or conceptual schemes, and his neglect of others. For these are unavoidable and, in this sense, there is and can be no value-free sociology. The only choice is between an expression of one's values, as open and honest as it can be, this side of the psychoanalytical couch, and a vain ritual of moral neutrality which, because it invites men to ignore the vulnerability of reason to bias, leaves it at the mercy of irrationality.

If truth is the vital thing, as Weber is reputed to have said on his death-bed, then it must be all the truth we have to give, as best we know it, being painfully aware and making our students aware, that even as we offer it we may be engaged in unwitting concealment rather than revelation. If we would teach students how science is made, really made rather than as publicly reported, we cannot fail to expose them to the whole scientist by whom it is made, with all his gifts and blindnesses, with all his methods and his *values* as well. To do otherwise is to usher in an era of spiritless technicians who will be no less lacking in understanding than they are in passion, and who will be useful only because they can be used.

In the end, even these dull tools will through patient persistence and cumulation build a technology of social science strong enough to cripple us. Far as we are from a sociological atomic bomb, we already live in a world of the systematic brainwashing of prisoners of war and of housewives with their advertising exacerbated compulsions; and the social science technology of tomorrow can hardly fail to be more powerful than today's.

It would seem that social science's affinity for modelling itself after physical science might lead to instruction in matters other than research alone. Before Hiroshima, physicists also talked of a value-free science; they, too, vowed to make no value judgements. Today many of them are not so sure. If we today concern ourselves exclusively with the technical proficiency of our students and reject all responsibility for their moral sense, or lack of it, then we may some day be compelled to accept responsibility for having trained a generation willing to serve in a future Auschwitz. Granted that science always has inherent in it both constructive and destructive potentialities. It does not follow from this that we should encourage our students to be oblivious to the difference. Nor does this in any degree detract from the indispensable norms of scientific objectivity; it merely insists that these differ radically from moral indifference.

I have suggested that, at its deepest roots, the myth of a value-free sociology was Weber's way of trying to adjudicate the tensions between two vital Western traditions: between reason and faith, between knowledge and feeling, between Classicism and Romanticism, between the head and the heart. Like Freud, Weber never really believed in an enduring peace or in a final resolution of this conflict. What he did was to seek a truce through the segregation of the contenders, by allowing each to dominate in different spheres of life. Although Weber's efforts at a personal synthesis brings him nearer to Saint Thomas, many of his would-be followers today tend to be nearer to the Latin Averroists with their doctrine of the twofold truth, with their conception of themselves as narrow technicians who reject responsibility for the cultural and moral consequences of their work. It is precisely because of the deeply dualistic implications of the current doctrine of a value-free sociology that I felt its most appropriate symbol to be the man-beast, the cleft creature, the minotaur.

NOTES
1. The problem of Romanticism in sociology is opened up here and is explored more systematically on pp. 323-366.

2

The Sociologist as Partisan: Sociology and the Welfare State

Sociology begins by disenchanting the world, and it proceeds by disenchanting itself. Having insisted upon the non-rationality of those whom it studies, sociology comes, at length, to confess its own captivity. But voluntary confessions should always be suspect. We should try to notice, when men complain about the bonds that enchain them, whether their tone is one of disappointed resentment or of comfortable accommodation.

In 1961, in an address to a learned society (reprinted here in chapter 1), I attacked what I took to be the dominant professional ideology of sociologists: that favouring the value-free doctrine of social science. Today, only six years later, I find myself in the uncomfortable position of drawing back from some who found my argument against the value-free myth so persuasive. I now find myself caught between two contradictory impulses: I do not wish to seem ungrateful towards those who sympathized with my position, yet the issue is a serious one and I also do not want to encumber discussions of it with considerations of personal tact or professional courtesy.

In a nutshell: I fear that the myth of a value-free social science is about to be supplanted by still another myth, and that the once glib acceptance of the value-free doctrine is about to be superseded by a new but no less glib rejection of it. My uneasiness concerning this came to a head upon reading Howard S. Becker's paper which boldly raises the problem, 'Whose Side Are We on?' Rather than presenting the storybook picture of the sociologist as a value-free scientist, Becker begins by stating that it is impossible for a social scientist to do research 'uncontaminated by personal and political sympathies'. We are told that, no matter what perspective a sociologist takes, his work must be written either from the standpoint of subordinates or superiors. Apparently one cannot do equal justice to both.

The most telling indication of just how large a change sociology has recently undergone, may be seen not so much from the position that Becker takes but from the way his position is presented. There is nothing defensive in the manner that Becker rejects the older, non-partisan conception of the sociologist's role. Instead, Becker presents his rejection of this position as if it needed no explanation; as if it were completely obvious to everyone; and as if there were nothing to argue about. His posture is not that of the cocky challenger but of a blasé referee announcing the outcome of a finished fight, and whose verdict must be obvious. More than anything else, this suggests that there has been a substantial change in the occupational culture of sociologists in the last decade or so.

Becker's conception of the partisan sociologist would be unimportant were it simply an expression of his own idiosyncratic individuality. The fact is, however, that there is every reason to believe that he is voicing the sentiments of a substantial and probably growing number of sociologists, and, in particular, those whose interests focus upon the study of social problems, or the sociology of 'deviant behaviour'. It is notable that the article in which Becker asks, 'Whose Side Are We on?', was delivered originally as his Presidential Address to the Society for the Study of Social Problems. This implies that Becker's constituency was at least large enough to have elected him to this modestly notable position in the structure of American social science. In short, Becker does not speak for himself alone.

That Becker's is a representative voice is further indicated by his own writings on deviant behaviour, especially his books *The Outsiders* and *Social Problems*, which are presently one of the two dominant standpoints in American sociology concerning the analysis of social problems. Becker, then, is a leading spokesman of a viable coterie of sociologists specializing in the study of social deviance, whose members include such able men as

Howard Brotz, Donald Cressey, John Kitsuse, Raymond Mack, David Matza, Sheldon Messinger, Ned Polsky and Albert J. Reiss; and this coterie in turn overlaps with a larger network that essentially comprises the 'Chicago School' of sociology. Becker's plea for a partisan sociology may be regarded as a weather-vane signalling that new winds are beginning to blow. Yet the direction from which they come is not altogether clear.

Since Becker forcefully entitles his discussion, 'Whose Side Are We on?', we might reasonably expect that he will, at some point, give a straightforward answer to his own straightforward question. Yet one reads it through and puts it down, only suddenly to notice that Becker gives no direct answer at all to his own question. Indeed, we pick it up once again to make sure that our first impression is correct and discover that this is indeed the case. If, in an effort to puzzle this through, we turn to Becker's earlier work, *The Outsiders*, we find that he does essentially the same thing there. In the culminating pages of that volume, he also asks: 'Whose viewpoint shall we present?' And once again we find that no straightforward answer is given. If there is a difference between this volume and Becker's Presidential Address, it is that, in the earlier volume, he states explicitly that there is no basis in terms of which an answer to the question can be formulated. That is, he holds that neither strategic considerations, nor temperamental and moral considerations can tell us 'to which viewpoint we should subscribe'.

It seems equally clear, however, that, although Becker refuses explicitly to answer his explicit question, he does have an answer to it. If instead of looking at the explicit formulations advanced by Becker or other members of his group, we look, rather, at the specific researches that they have undertaken, we find that they unmistakably do adopt a specific standpoint, a kind of *underdog* identification. As I have said elsewhere, theirs is a school of thought that finds itself at home in the world of hip, drug addicts, jazz musicians, cab drivers, prostitutes, night people, drifters, grifters and skidders: the 'cool world'. Their identifications are with deviant rather than respectable society. 'For them, orientation to the underworld has become the equivalent of the proletarian identifications felt by some intellectuals during the 1930s. For not only do they study it, but in a way they speak on its behalf, affirming the authenticity of its style of life.' Their specific researches plainly betray, for example, that they are concerned with and resent the legal straitjacket in which the drug addict is confined in the United States, or the degrading impact of the mental hospital on its inmates. In one part, this school of thought represents a metaphysics of the underdog and of the underworld: a metaphysics in which conventional society is viewed from the standpoint of a group outside of its own respectable social structures. At any rate, this is how it began; but it is not how it remains.

When Becker tells us that the world is divided into subordinates and superordinates, and that sociologists must look at the world from one side or the other, his implication seems to be that they should look at it from the standpoint of the deviant, of the subordinate, of the underdog. For these people, Becker says in his Presidential Address, are 'more sinned against than sinning'. The question arises as to why it is that, although Becker's leanings are clear enough, he chooses not to express them explicitly. Why is it that Becker does not declare openly for the standpoint of the underdog, since he clearly feels this way? If partisanship is inevitable, why doesn't Becker clearly state whose side *he* is on, rather than simply goading others to take a stand? There are probably both intellectual and practical reasons for Becker's failure to give a definitive answer to his own question – whose side are we on? First, I want to explore briefly some of the intellectual and practical factors that lead to Becker's reticence.

The Theory and Practice of Cool

In *The Outsiders*, Becker makes it plain that his own theoretical contribution leads to a focus, not merely on the rule-breakers or deviants, but also to a study of those who make and enforce the rules, and most especially the latter. Although much of Becker's concrete research has been on deviants, his own theory, which came later, has largely focused on rule-makers and rule-enforcers. A crucial stage, in what Becker calls 'the deviant career', occurs when someone declares that someone else's behaviour has violated the rules of their game. The deviant, in short, is made by society in two senses: first, that society makes the rules which he has broken and, secondly, that society 'enforces' them and makes a public declaration announcing that the rules have been broken. The making of the deviant, then, entails a process of social interaction. That being the case, the deviant-making process cannot be understood unless rule-making and rule-enforcing procedures or persons are studied.

The question then arises as to *whose* standpoint shall be adopted when rule-*makers* or rule-*enforcers* are themselves studied. Shall we describe their behaviour from their own 'over-dog' standpoint or from that of the 'underdog' deviants? One answer is given by Becker's more general theoretical position, the tradition of George Herbert Mead, which requires that men – even if they are 'overdogs' – be studied from the standpoint of their *own* conception of reality. The point here, of course, is that men's definition of their situation shapes their behaviour; hence to understand and predict their behaviour we must see it as they do. Becker's own specific theory of deviance, then, constrains him to look at the behaviour of rule-*enforcers*, while his Meadian tradition requires him to look at it from *their* standpoint, rather than that of the deviant rule-breakers.

But this, by itself, would still create no difficulties. For, if Becker were entirely comfortable with this position, he would simply recommend that studies be conducted from the standpoint of *whoever* is being studied, be they rule-enforcers, rule-makers, or deviant rule-breakers. If he were to be consistent, then, Becker would answer the question, whose side are we on?, simply by stating that we are on the side of whomever we are studying at a given time. In other words, he would advocate the devotional promiscuity of sacred prostitution.

The reason that Becker cannot adopt this fairly obvious conclusion, and why he cannot give any answer to his question, is a simple one: his *sentiments* are at variance with his theories. Becker is sentimentally disposed to view the entire ambience of deviance from the standpoint of the deviant persons themselves. It is this that makes him sit on a fence of his own construction. Caught in the divergence between his theories and his sentiments, he is unable to answer his own question, whose side are we on? His sentimental disposition to see the world of deviance from the standpoint of the deviant conflicts with his theoretical disposition to take the standpoint of whichever group he happens to be studying. Becker 'solves' this problem by raising the question, whose side are we on?, with such blunt force that makes the very question seem like an answer; and he evidences his own sentiments so plainly that he need not assert them and, therefore, need never take responsibility for them.

In suggesting that Becker has refused to answer his own question because of this conflict between his theories and his sentiments, I do not mean that this is the only reason for his reticence. For there are other, more practical, costs that would have to be paid were Becker (or anyone else) to announce such a position in a direct manner. A straightforward affirmation of sympathy with the underdog would, for one thing, create practical difficulties for Becker as a researcher. For he might one day wish access to information held by rule-enforcers and rule-makers who, in turn, might be dismayed to hear that Becker was disposed to view them from the standpoint of those whom they feel to be threats to society. Again, a straightforward affirmation of sympathy with the underdog or deviant might create a certain uneasiness among those who, either directly or indirectly, provide the resources which Becker, like any other research entrepreneur, requires. An outright expression of concern for or sympathy with the underdog thus conflicts with the sociologist's practical and professional interests. In other words: even genuine attachments to the underdog must be compromised with a tacit but no less genuine attachment to self-interest. We are, in short, also on our own side.

There is, I believe, still another reason why Becker fails to say whose side he is on. It has to do with the fact that he is not only on his own side and that, for all its underdog sympathies, his work is also on the side of one of the currently conflicting élites in the welfare establishment. But I must hold this for development at a later point. Becker's reticence about answering his own question, then, derives in part from a conflict between his sentiments and his interests, in part from a conflict between his theories and his sentiments, and, in part also, from a conflict within his sentiments.

There is still another way that Becker copes with the conflict between his sympathetic concern for the underdog and his equally human concern for more practical interests. We can see this if we notice the implicit irony in Becker's position, an irony that contributes importantly to the persuasiveness of his argument. Becker's central thesis is the impossibility of being value-free and the necessity of taking sides. In other words, he argues that real detachment is impossible. Yet one of the very things that makes Becker convincing is that he somehow manages to convey a sense of dispassionate detachment. This is largely accomplished through his *style*. Written in a non-polemical and flaccid style, Becker's rhetoric conveys an image of himself as coolly detached, despite his own explicit argument that partisanship and involvement are inevitable. The limp sobriety of his style projects an image of him as someone who has no axe to grind. It is through his style, then, that Becker invites us to believe that it is possible for a work to be biased without paying intellectual costs.

In effect, Becker appears to hold that emotional blandness is somehow an effective antidote to partisanship. Indeed, at various points, one suspects that Becker believes that blandness is also an effective substitute for analytic probing and hard thought. As I shall later develop, Becker believes that the real enemy of good social science is not a one-sided value commitment, but, rather, something that he calls 'sentimentality'.

Thus, while Becker invites partisanship, he rejects passionate or erect partisanship. In the very process of opposing the conventional myth of the value-free social scientist, Becker thereby creates a new myth, the myth of the *sentiment*-free social scientist. He begins to formulate a new myth that tacitly claims there is such a thing as a purely cerebral partisanship, which is devoid of emotional commitment and 'sentimentality'. Underlying this is Becker's tacit assumption that these entail intellectual costs, and costs *alone*. It seems equally reasonable to believe, however, that passion and sentimentality serve not only to produce costs and intellectual blindness, but may just as likely serve to enlighten, and to sensitize us to certain aspects of the social world. Indeed, it may be suspected that it is precisely, in some part, because there are certain intellectual gains derived from emotionally tinged commitments that it is possible for social scientists to sustain such commitments. In short, sentimentality does not seem to be the heartless villain that Becker makes it out to be. It is Becker who is being 'sentimental' when he fosters a myth that holds it possible to have a sentiment-free commitment.

To recommend that sociological researches be undertaken from the standpoint of subordinates or underdogs creates as many problems as it resolves. While such a standpoint expresses a sympathy that I share, I still feel obliged to ask: How do we know an underdog when we see one? Who and what are underdogs? What marks someone as an underdog? And we have to ask an even more difficult question: Why *should* we undertake our studies from the standpoint of the subordinate, the underdog?

Becker may recognize the intellectual bind in which he has placed himself by inviting research from the standpoint of the underdog. But he has only begun to glimpse it. Although acknowledging that a superior may be a subordinate to someone else, he fails to recognize that this works both ways: everyone who is a subordinate, *vis-à-vis* his superior, is also a superior in relation to some third party. If we regard every man as both superior and subordinate, overdog and underdog, how then do we know and on what basis do we select the underdogs whose standpoint we shall take? Clearly, Becker presents no logical solution to this quandary; he can intend it to be resolved only by the impulses of the very sentimentality that he deplores. It is also likely that Becker never confronts this problem – with *which* underdog shall he sympathize? – because he tacitly assumes that good liberals will instinctively know, and always agree, who the true underdogs are.

Let me acknowledge, once for all, that I share Becker's underdog sympathies. Yet I also believe that sociological study from an underdog standpoint will be intellectually impaired without clarifying the *grounds* for the commitment. A commitment made on the basis of an unexamined ideology may allow us to feel a manly righteousness, but it leaves us blind.

Sociology and Suffering

The question then is: Are there any *good* reasons to conduct research from an underdog standpoint? One such reason may be that a feelingful commitment to the underdog's plight enables us to do a better job as *sociologists*. Specifically, when we study a social world from an underdog standpoint, we elevate into public view certain underprivileged aspects of reality. These are aspects of social reality that tend to be comparatively unknown or publicly neglected because they are dissonant with conceptions of reality held by the powerful and respectable. To take the standpoint of the underdog in our researches, then, does two things. First, it gives us new information concerning social worlds about which many members of our society, including ourselves, know little or nothing. Secondly, it may give us new perspectives on worlds that we had thought familiar and presumed that we already knew. To that extent, then, taking the underdog's standpoint does indeed contribute to the successful fulfilment of the intellectual obligations that we have as sociologists. It helps us do the distinctive job we have.

I have acknowledged a sympathy with the underdog and with impulses to conduct researches from his standpoint. Yet in searching for the justification of my sentiments I must also candidly confess that I see no special virtue in those who are lacking in power or authority, just as I see no special virtue that inheres in those who possess power and authority. It seems to me that neither weakness nor power as such are values that deserve to be prized.

The essential point about the underdog is that he suffers, and that his suffering is naked and visible. It is this that makes and should make a compelling demand upon us. What makes his standpoint deserving of special consideration, what makes him particularly worthy of sympathy, is that he suffers. Once we see this, however, the nature of our relationship to the underdog changes; correspondingly, the nature of the obligation that we experience as *sociologists* may also change.

First, we can recognize that there may be forms of human suffering that are unavoidable, that cannot be remedied in some particular society or at some particular time. Correspondingly, however, there are also forms of suffering that are needless at particular times and places. I think that it is the sociologist's job to give special attention to the latter, while recognizing that it is no easy task to distinguish between avoidable and unavoidable suffering, and while fearing that some will all too easily categorize certain kinds of suffering as unavoidable so that they may disregard them with comfort.

Moreover, I would also insist that even when men experience needless suffering, a suffering which is unavoidable, tragic, and truly a part of the eternal human condition, they still deserve sympathy and loving consideration. It is vital for sociologists also to portray this unyielding part of the world. For this reason, I cannot imagine a humane sociology that would be callous to the suffering of 'superiors'. A sociology that ignored this would, so far as I am concerned, manifest neither a respect for truth nor a sense of common humanity.

But if all men suffer, and to some extent unavoidably, is there any reason at all to feel a special sympathy for underdogs? Is there any reason to make a special effort to conduct research from their standpoint? I think that there is.

For one thing, the suffering of some is still simply and literally unknown to many in society. This is a special and important part of reality which, I think, is one of our important responsibilities to understand and communicate. The problem is not simply that there exists what Becker calls a 'hierarchy of credibility' – in which men in power are presumably granted the right to declare what is real and true in the world around them. It is rather that these dominant conceptions of reality, sustained and fostered by the managers of society, have one common defect: they fail to grasp a very special type of reality, specifically the reality of the suffering of those beneath them. In failing to see this, what they must also fail to see is that those beneath them are indeed very much like themselves, in their suffering as in other ways.

This, in turn, implies that a sociology truly concerned with representing the standpoint of the underdog would most especially seek to communicate the character of his suffering, its peculiar sources and special intensity, the ways and degrees in which it is avoidable, the forces that contribute to it, and his struggle against it. The underdog's standpoint therefore deserves to be heard in sociology not because he has any special virtue and not because he alone lives in a world of suffering. A sociology of the underdog is justified because, and to the extent that, his suffering is less likely to be known and because – by the very reason of his being underdog – the extent and character of his suffering are likely to contain much that is avoidable.

Although Becker leans toward a sympathy and special consideration for the underdog's standpoint, and although the underdog's suffering is particularly visible, it is still one further paradox in Becker's discussion that we find him displaying no such concern for suffering. Rather, what we do find is a fear of such a concern, a fear that this concern will make us lose our cool. I would guess that it is in some part because of this fear that Becker makes such a point of rejecting 'sentimentality'.

Yet if it is not the suffering of the subordinate or the deviant that involves Becker – and others of his school – with the underdog, then what is it? It is my impression, from many years of reading their researches and of talking with them, that their pull to the underdog is sometimes part of a titilated attraction to the underdog's exotic difference and easily takes the form of 'essays on quaintness'. The danger is, then, that such an identification with the underdog becomes the urban sociologist's equivalent of the anthropologist's (one-time) romantic appreciation of the noble savage.

The Becker School's view embodies an implicit critique of lower-middle-class ethnocentrism, of small-town respectability, of the paradoxical superiority that one ethnic can feel toward another. Indeed, one might say that theirs is most especially a critique of the uneducated middle classes. Now this is no mean thing, for the piety of these strata is certainly pervasive in the United States. Becker's rejection of their smug narrowness is wholesome and valuable.

At the same time, however, Becker's school of deviance is redolent of romanticism. It expresses the satisfaction of the Great White Hunter who has bravely risked the perils of the urban jungle to bring back an exotic specimen. It expresses the romanticism of the zoo curator who preeningly displays his rare specimens. And like the zookeeper, he wishes to protect his collection; he does not want spectators to throw rocks at the animals behind the bars. But neither is he eager to tear down the bars and let the animals go. The attitude of these zoo-keepers of deviance is to create a comfortable and humane Indian Reservation, a protected social space, within which these colourful specimens may be exhibited, unmolested and un-changed. The very empirical sensitivity to fine detail, character-izing this school, is both born of and limited by the connoisseur's fascination with the rare object: its empirical richness is in-spired by a collector's aesthetic.

It is in part for this reason that, despite its challenging conception of a partisan sociology and its sympathy with the underdog, Becker's discussion is paradoxically suffused with a surprising air of complacency. Indeed, what it expresses is something quite different from the older, traditional sympathy with the plight of the underdog. Basically, it conceives of the underdog as a *victim*. In some part, this is inherent in the very conception of the processes by means of which deviance is conceived of as being generated. For the emphasis in Becker's theory is on the deviant as the product of society rather than as the rebel against it. If this is a liberal conception of deviance that wins sympathy and tolerance for the deviant, it has the paradoxical consequence of inviting us to view the deviant as a passive nonentity who is responsible neither for his suffering nor its alleviation – who is more 'sinned against than sinning'. Consistent with this view of the underdog as victim, is the more modern conception of him as someone who has to be managed, and should be managed better, by a bureaucratic apparatus of official caretakers. In short, it conceives of the underdog as someone maltreated by a bureaucratic establishment whose remedial efforts are ineffectual, whose custodial efforts are brutal, and whose rule-enforcement techniques are self-interested. While it sees deviance as generated by a process of social inter-action, as emerging out of the matrix of an unanalysed society, it does not see deviance as deriving from specified master insti-tutions of this larger society, or as expressing an active opposition to them.

The underdog is largely seen from the standpoint of the difficulties that are encountered when the society's caretakers attempt to cope with the deviance that has been produced in him by the society. Becker's school of deviance thus views the underdog as someone who is being mismanaged, not as someone who suffers or fights back. Here the deviant is sly but not defiant; he is tricky but not courageous; he sneers but does not accuse; he 'makes out' without making a scene. Insofar as this school of theory has a critical edge to it, this is directed at the caretaking institutions who do the mopping-up job, rather than at the master institutions that produce the deviant's suffering.

It is in some part for this reason that the kinds of researches that are undertaken from this standpoint tend to exclude a concern with *political* deviance, in which men do actively fight back on behalf of their values and interests. We thus find relatively few studies of people involved in the civil rights struggle or in the peace movement. For however much these deviant groups are made to suffer, no one could easily conceive of them as mere victims well under the control of bureaucratic officialdom. It is not man-fighting-back that wins Becker's sympathy, but rather, man-on-his-back that piques his curiosity.

What we have here, then, is essentially a rejection of unenlightened middle-class bigotry. And in its place is a sympathetic view of the underdog seen increasingly from the standpoint of the relatively benign, the well educated, and the *highly* placed bureaucratic officialdom: of the American administrative class. What seems to be a rejection of the standpoint of the superior is, I shall argue, actually only a rejection of the *middle-level* superior.

We may see this more clearly if we return to the problem that gives Becker his greatest uneasiness, the observation that every superior has his own superior, and, correspondingly, Becker's failure to observe that every subordinate has his own subordinate. (Lower than the prostitute is the pimp; lower than the pimp is the errand boy; and lower than the errand boy is the kid on the fringe of the gang who would like his job.) Now, since everyone may have someone or something above or below him, this does not make it more but less possible to know *which* subordinate's standpoint we should adopt. But this does not deter Becker for a moment. As he gaily says, 'I do not propose to hold my breath until this problem is solved.'

I, for my part, however, continue to be perplexed about the manner in which a specific stratum of underdogs comes to be chosen as the focus for an orienting standpoint. There is a hidden anomaly in any recommendation to look upon the world from the standpoint of underdogs. The anomaly is this: to a surprising degree, underdogs see *themselves* from the standpoint of respectable society; Negroes, in fact, often call one another 'niggers'. Thus, if we did study underdogs from 'their own' standpoint we would, inevitably, be adopting the standpoint of the dominant culture. It is precisely insofar as the deviant and subordinate do accept a role as passive victims rather than as rebels against circumstances, that they do view themselves from the standpoint of the dominant culture.

In the very act of viewing deviants and subordinates from *their own* standpoint, we are bound to see them from the standpoint of respectable society and its dominant institutions. We will also see deviants in terms of conventional categories not only when we look upon them as passive victims, but, also, to the extent that they are looked upon from the standpoint of the bureaucratic caretakers who are publicly chartered either to put them into custody or to correct their behaviour. Paradoxically, then, although Becker invites us to adopt the standpoint of the subordinate, and thereby presumably braves giving offence to respectable values, I believe that he himself is still using some version of the outlook of respectable society.

Ombudsman Sociology: Critique of the Middle Man

Becker seems to be adopting the position of the outcast. In point of fact, I believe that he is also embracing the position of 'enlightened' but no less respectable liberalism toward the outcast. Becker appears to be taking up arms against society on behalf of the underdog. Actually, he is taking up arms against the ineffectuality, callousness, or capriciousness of the caretakers that society has appointed to administer the mess it has created. Becker's argument is essentially a critique of the caretaking organizations, and in particular of the *low level* officialdom that manages them. It is not a critique of the social institutions that engender suffering or of the high level officialdom that shapes the character of caretaking establishments.

Much of deviant study today has become a component of the new style of social reform which is now engineered through caretaking public bureaucracies. The ideological standpoint implicit in Becker's School embodies a critique of the *conventional* welfare apparatus and of the *old* style welfare state, before it extricated itself from social movement reform. It is, as such, a critique of the ethnocentrism and the ineffectuality with which deviance is regarded and treated by certain of the local caretakers immediately responsible for it today. Becker's theoretical school is indeed taking sides; it is a party to the struggle between the old and the new élites in the caretaking establishments; between the welfare institutions inherited from the 1930s and those now promoted today; and between the 'locals' working in the municipalities and the 'cosmopolitans' operating from Washington D.C. His ideology is, in each case, injurious to the former and supportive to the latter. If this is seen, it can be better understood how certain of the other difficulties in Becker's discussion are to be resolved. We therefore need a temporary detour to obtain a view of these difficulties.

Becker makes a distinction between the conduct of research in two settings: in political and non-political situations. He is moved to make this distinction because he wants to hold that accusations of bias against sociologists, and reactions to them, differ, depending upon whether the situation studied is political or not.

Becker holds that in *non*-political situations sociologists are more likely to accuse one another of bias when their studies adopt underdog perspectives, than when they look at things from the standpoint of superiors. The reason for this, he says, is that in these non-political situations there exists an accepted 'hierarchy of credibility' which credits superiors with the right to define social reality in their spheres; since most sociologists, like others, tend to accept the established hierarchies of credibility, they therefore tend to view studies conducted from underdog perspectives as biased.

Now this is very curious. For what Becker is arguing is that most sociologists, who he says are liberal, will, despite this ideology, nonetheless identify with the overdog in their studies of non-political situations. In short, while most sociologists will presumably give free rein to their liberal ideologies when studying political situations, they will turn their backs on these same liberal ideologies, and act as if they were non-liberal, when studying non-political situations. If this is true, surely one must ask: How is this switch effected? What brings it about? Indeed, is it really a switch? We must consider the other side of the equation; that is, if we ask how some liberal sociologists come to identify with the underdog, we must also ask, how does it happen that others failed to do so?

Becker recognizes that *some* explanation is called for to account for sociologists' adoption of overdog viewpoints in their researches. He says that (in non-political situations) most sociologists tend to accept the dominant hierarchy of credibility. In other words, in these situations, most sociologists conduct their studies from the standpoint of responsible officials, says Becker, because they accept the standpoint of responsible officials. Becker's invocation of this tautology at least acknowledges that an explanation is in order. Yet when it comes to explaining why a minority of sociologists adopt an *underdog* standpoint in the same non-political situations, Becker does not even see that this, too, is a problem that needs explaining.

Bleak Hypotheses

What, indeed, are the sources of these sociologists' identification with underdogs? Clearly we cannot simply hold that such an identification with the underdog stems predominantly from the sociologist's liberal ideology. For Becker is quite right in stating that most sociologists are politically liberal. It is clear therefore that many, if not most, who adopt the overdog standpoint must share this liberal ideology. Thus, while the liberal ideology may be a necessary condition for adopting an underdog standpoint, it cannot be a sufficient condition for doing so. The question here, the most important question we ever confront in understanding how moralities and ideologies work in the world, is: By what specific mechanisms are men kept honest? In other words, how is it that they are made to conform to their ideologies or values?

It may be surprising, but there are actually many things that keep men – including sociologists – honest. First, remember, as Becker acknowledges, that an underdog standpoint is adopted by only a minority of sociologists. Being infrequent, a minority perspective is more likely to be visible in the larger professional community from whom sociologists seek recognition. Of course, such notice may take the form of hostile criticism. But while an underdog standpoint thus has its risks, it may also bring higher and quicker returns than the adoption of an overdog standpoint which, being common, tends to glut the market and to depress the price paid per individual contribution.

An underdog perspective may, then, be thought of as a career strategy more appealing to high variance betters who, in turn, are more likely to be found among the ambitious young. Bear in mind, however, that the larger professional audience to whom their work is addressed will for the most part conceive themselves as 'liberals' – on whose sympathy an underdog standpoint has some claim. Those adopting an underdog standpoint are, therefore, probably not engaged in as risky an undertaking as their minority position might imply. We are, in summary, suggesting a bleak hypothesis: sociologists with liberal ideologies will more likely adopt underdog perspectives when they experience these as compatible with the pursuit of their own career interests.

Implicit in this bleak hypothesis is the assumption that there is probably some positive relationship between the youth and low professional status, on the one hand, and the adoption of an underdog perspective, on the other. In brief, I would expect that younger intellectuals would, other things constant, be readier to adopt this high variance bet than older intellectuals. It may also be that older intellectuals who feel that they have been bypassed, or whose rewards have somehow not been appropriate, would also be more likely to adopt an underdog standpoint.

Correspondingly, I would also expect that as sociologists get older, as they become increasingly successful, more likely to live next door to or associate with those who are also successful, or themselves become involved in the practical management of public (including university) affairs, they too will come increasingly to adopt overdog standpoints despite their continued public professions of liberalism. Moreover, as sociologists become better established, recognized, and successful, they are – as they begin to move toward the zenith of their careers – risking more should they make a high variance wager on underdogs. The additional net advantage still possible to them is in this way diminished. In short, for the rising sociologist, identification with the underdog may mean greater risk than it does for the younger or less successful sociologists.

I would, however, suggest one important qualification concerning this disposition of older men toward increasing overdog standpoints. As they achieve (rather than merely approach) the zenith of their careers, the rewards that older sociologists are given for conformity to conventional overdog positions, are especially subject to a diminishing marginal utility; in the result some of them may be less subject to professional controls that dispose them to the conventional standpoints of their contemporaries. Thus some senior sociologists, beginning to think about the judgement of 'posterity' rather than the views of their contemporaries, may return to the underdog standpoints of their youth. Moreover, as their own age group thins out through death, they may receive more encouragement from the young with whom they are not in competition, than from the middle aged; and they may begin to feel that the future of their reputations will be more enduringly affected by the judgement of the relatively young. These, at any rate, are some of the ways in which the career and personal interests of some older sociologists may dispose them to defy the established hierarchy of credibility and to opt for the underdog. We might call it the 'Bertrand Russell Syndrome'.

But men are prompted to heed the voice of conscience and to abide by high principle by still other considerations. We can see some of these if we ask, how is it that the young, high variance betters are not brought under control by their elders in the course of their education, apprenticeship, and common research undertakings, and are in this way constrained to adopt the respectable overdog standpoints more congenial to the older? Here, again, things are not simple. In some part, the young men's underdog impulses will be protected by the academic ideology of collegiality, which nominally governs relationships. Thus even when working under the supervision of older men, the young men can lay claim for the protection of their underdog standpoints.

Once more, however, we must call attention to the role of bleak factors in keeping men honest. These essentially have to do with the ramifying and powerful role of the new funding structures in social science today which, in turn, are linked to the growth of the new welfare state and its new conceptions of social reform.

Nothing is more obvious than that these are plush times for American social scientists, and there is never any reason to underestimate the power of the obvious. So far as the older and better known men are concerned, they are often so fully funded that they may have little time to supervise their researches personally, to administer them with the continuing closeness that could effectively imprint their overdog identifications on the research. Sometimes the older men are so loosely connected with the researches they have funded that even basic research decisions are made by younger men from their different standpoints. Older men today are often constrained to surrender wide discretionary power to their juniors, if they are to keep them in today's seller's market in social research. The irony of the matter, then, is that the more successful the older man is in funding his research, the less successful he may be in having it conducted according to his lights: the research is less likely to be 'his'.

With the new funding situation and the greater ease of access to research money, it is now also much simpler for younger men to procure funds for themselves, for their own researches, and at an earlier age. Being their own masters, they can now more readily express their own underdog standpoint, insofar as they have one.

But it would seem that there should be a fly in this ointment. For the question that now arises is whether the new funding situation may simply mean that the younger men have only exchanged one master for another; for even if they are no longer subjected to the direct pressure of senior professors, they may now be subjected to the direct pressure of the funding agencies. In my opinion, this is exactly what has happened.

With growing ease of funding, younger men gain independent access to research resources at a time when their liberal underdog ideologies are still relatively strong and can shape their research. At the same time, however, the career gratifications of these funding opportunities, as well as the personal gratifications of being close to men of power, become vested interests that constrain to a dependency on the new sources of funding. Thus the younger man's more salient underdog identifications now need to be accommodated to his new-found 'appreciation' of overdogs. This is in part accomplished by submerging this 'appreciation' in a subsidiary awareness that is maintained by a collegial reciprocity: each tactfully agrees not to look the other's 'gift horse in the mouth'. (There are, alas, 'deviant' cases: e.g., those who make a career of denouncing Project Camelot and then themselves apply for a half-million dollar grant from the State Department.)

This accommodation of underdog identification to overdog dependencies is, quite apart from skilful rationalizing, not too difficult today. For the new funding agencies now desperately need information about underdogs; and these are not unreceptive even to researches conducted from the latter's standpoint, for much the same reason that colonial governments supported similar researches in anthropology. Overdogs in the welfare state – in Washington bureaucracies and New York foundations – are buyers of underdog research for much the same political reasons that the Johnson régime initiated the 'war on poverty'. To explore a few of the implications of this, I must revert to some of the larger institutional changes that come to a head in the welfare state.

Perhaps the crux here is the manner in which social reform in the United States has changed in character. What is new is not the 'plight of the cities', however increasing their deterioration, but rather that this becomes an object of a measured 'concern' rather than of 'shame'. What is new, in a somewhat larger historical perspective, is that the locus of reform initiatives and resources is increasingly found on the level of national politics and foundations, rather than in the political vitality, the economic resources, or the zealous initiatives of élites with local roots.

The reform of American cities was once a process that involved small businessmen, muckraking journalists, and local political machines, all of whom had some vital involvement and interest in their local communities. Today, however, with the changing structure, character, and ecology of the middle classes, many who might give leadership to urban reform live neither in the city itself nor in the still politically powerful rural areas, but live rather in suburbia and exurbia. The educated, bureaucratically employed, and highly mobile middle classes have a dwindling localistic attachment and a narrowing base of power on the *local* levels, which could provide them with the economic and political leverage to effectuate urban reform. They must, in consequence, seek a remedy not on the local but the national level.

As the locus of reform efforts moves upwards from the local to the national level, the conception and meaning of social reform changes. The urban reforms being sought by this new middle class are now aimed at the reform of a community to which they are less tied by complex interests, urbane pleasures, or by a round of familiarizing daily activities. It is not 'their' community that they now wish to reform – for their suburbs are decent enough as they view them. When they concern themselves with the plight of Negroes, it is not even 'their' Negroes whom they seek to help, but Negroes viewed abstractly and impersonally.

Social reform now becomes an effort largely motivated by bland political appraisal, removed economic calculus, prudent forecasting, or a sense of pity and sympathy that becomes increasingly remote as it loses rooting in daily experience and encounter. The community to be reformed becomes an object, something apart from and outside the reformer. The nature of the reform becomes less a matter of moral zeal or even of immediate personal interest and more of a concern prompted by a long range appraisal and prudence. Social reform now becomes a kind of engineering job, a technological task to be subject to bland 'cost-benefit' or 'system-analysis'. The rise of the welfare state then means the rise of the uninvolved reformer: It means the rise of reform-at-a-distance. Reform today is no longer primarily the part-time avocation of dedicated amateurs but is increasingly the full-time career of paid bureaucrats.

Today civil rights reforms and the war against poverty are pursued by many in a Bismarckian mood. Reform is no longer prompted by the twinge of conscience or the bite of immediate personal interest but, rather, by 'reasons of state', and on behalf of the 'national interest'. Personal liberalism becomes state liberalism. Liberalism changes in character from a matter of conscience, which had a penetrating claim upon private and daily decision, to electoral loyalty to the Democratic Party and to marginal differentiations in career strategies. The operational meaning of liberalism for the sociologist now tends to become calibrated in terms of the government agency for which he will work, or whose money he will take. From some current standpoints, for example, a truly 'liberal sociologist' is one who will reject money from the Defense Department but will seek and accept it from the State Department!

The funding agencies of social science today, whether government agencies or massive private foundations, are essentially the welfare state's purchasing agents for market research: they are the instrumentalities of this new reform movement. They express the 'detached concern' of educated but bureaucratically dependent middle classes who no longer have effective bases in localities; whose cosmopolitan sympathies are not personally and deeply engaged by a daily encounter with urban suffering; and whose fears are not deeply aroused by a close dependence upon the deteriorating urban community. Prodded partly by mild discomforts, vague forebodings, prudent extrapolations, partly by concern to maintain a decent image of themselves, and, not least, by the growing rise of the militant politics of public demonstrations, they approach the task of modern urban reform with a thin-lipped, businesslike rationality. This is the social context in which we can better understand some of the ramifying meanings of Becker's bland programme for an underdog sociology. It is the larger context which makes it possible for some sociologists today to stay honest: that is, to implement their liberal ideologies with an effort at underdog identification.

The superiors whose dominant 'hierarchies of credibility' are resisted by this underdog sociology are essentially those whose powers remain rooted in, and hence limited by, the local level. The sociology of the underdog is a sociology that rejects the standpoint of only the *local* officials: the head of the medical school, the warden of the prison, the city director of the housing agency. In short, the respectables who are being resisted, and whose hierarchy of credibility is disputed, are those local officials who, for the most part, do not control access to large supplies of research funds.

Toward a New Establishment Sociology

The new underdog sociology propounded by Becker is, then, a standpoint that possesses a remarkably convenient combination of properties: it enables the sociologist to befriend the very small underdogs in local settings, to reject the standpoint of the 'middle dog' respectables and notables who manage local caretaking establishments, while, at the same time, to make and remain friends with the really top dogs in Washington agencies or New York foundations. While Becker adopts a posture as the intrepid preacher of a new underdog sociology, he has really given birth to something rather different: to the first version of new Establishment sociology, to a sociology compatible with the new character of social reform in the United States today. It is a sociology of and for the new welfare state. It is the sociology of young men with friends in Washington. It is a sociology that succeeds in solving the oldest problem in personal politics: how to maintain one's integrity without sacrificing one's career, or how to remain a liberal although well-heeled.

The social utility of this new ideology is furthered by the fact that, for some while now, there has been a growing tension between the entrenched local welfare establishments and the newer and powerfully supported federally based agencies and programmes of the 'Great Society'. These new federal agencies, headed by personnel with substantially greater education than the local élites, are presently attempting to implement their new programmes against the resistance of the local notables. It is the ultimate function of the federally based programmes to win or maintain the attachment of urban lower and working classes to the political symbols and machinery of the American state in general, and of the Democratic Party in particular. While the local caretaking élites usually share these political aims, they also feel that their own local prerogatives and position are threatened by the growth of programmes over which they have less control, since they derive from national resources and initiatives. Becker's new underdog sociology functions to line up sectors of sociology against the 'backward' resistance, the officialdom on the municipal level, and in favour of the most powerful 'enlightened' sectors on the national level.

Essentially Becker's type of research does this because, in adopting the standpoint of the underdogs, it simultaneously shows how ignorant local caretakers are of this standpoint and how badly local caretaking officials manage their establishments. It must not be thought for a moment that Becker's work performs this ideological function through any intention to further the ambitions of the upper officialdom or by any intention to conduct his research in any narrowly conceived applied manner. It achieves its ideological consequences primarily by taking and revealing the standpoint of those for whom local caretaking officials are responsible and by 'unmaking' the ignorance of these officials. This is not an incidental or trivial byproduct; rather, this is exactly what carries the political payload. For it is this discrediting of local officials that legitimates the claims of the higher administrative classes in Washington and gives them an entering wedge on the local level.

Becker's readiness to sacrifice the middle dogs to the top dogs can be gleaned when he states that there is no point in attempting to adopt the standpoint of middle level officialdom. Looking at the situation from the standpoint of middle level officials – in other words, from the standpoint of the prison warden, the school principal, the hospital administrator – simply leads to an infinite regression, says Becker.

This has a seeming persuasiveness, but it is too glib by far. First, it is by no means certain that an 'infinite regress' problem is involved. Is it really true that every superior has a superior who, in turn, limits and prevents him from doing as he really would like? Isn't there some point at which the buck-passing ends? This would seem to be part of what C. Wright Mills had in mind when he spoke of the 'power élite'. We can, of course, maintain that even the highest officers of state in turn always require the consent of the governed. But this brings us back full circle; and we would then have to acknowledge that the very underdogs, who Becker says are more sinned against than sinning, are at least in part responsible for the sins against them; and why, then, should sociologists conduct their studies primarily from their standpoint?

It would seem that there is one way out of this impasse for Becker. He could say that it is not a matter of superiors and subordinates as such, but, rather, of the *institutions* governing their relationship. He might maintain that the need is not to study social situations from the standpoint of subordinates as an end in itself, but of conducting studies with a view to understanding how some are crushed by certain institutions, and how all alike are subjected to institutions that do not permit them to live as they wish. As I say, this position would be one way for Becker. But he neither sees it nor takes it. For this undercuts his 'infinite regress' gambit and leads research inevitably to the doorstep of power; it would force the research focus upward, fastening it on the national levels.

Parenthetically, but not irrelevantly, I think that *radical* sociologists differ from liberals in that, while they take the standpoint of the underdog, they apply it to the study of overdogs. Radical sociologists want to study 'power élites', the leaders, or masters, of men; liberal sociologists focus their efforts upon underdogs and victims and their immediate bureaucratic caretakers.

For all its difficulties, Becker's position does provide a vantage point for a criticism of local managers of the Caretaking Establishment, of the vested interests and archaic methods of these middle dogs. This is all to the good. But this vantage point has been bought at a very high price. The price is an uncritical accommodation to the national élite and to the society's master institutions; and this is all to the bad.

There is, I think, one other way in which Becker's position is too glib. It is premised upon a conviction (or sentiment) to the effect that, as he says in *The Outsiders*, while it may be possible to see a situation from 'both sides', this 'cannot be done simultaneously'. This means, explains Becker, that 'we cannot construct a description . . . that in some way fuses perceptions and interpretations made by both parties involved in a process of deviance. . . . We cannot describe a "higher reality" that makes sense of both sets of views.' I assume this means that although the sociologist can, at some point, present the views of one group and then, at another point, present the views of a different group, that nonetheless, the sociologist's own standpoint – when he speaks in an omniscient voice – tends inevitably to favour one of these sides more than the other, to present one side more attractively than the other. This frank confession of human fallibility is so appealing that it seems almost churlish to question it. But I do.

One reason that Becker sees no way out of this impasse is because he is committed to a kind of interpersonal social psychology which, with all its humanistic merits, fails to see that men – superiors as well as subordinates – may be powerfully constrained by institutions, by history, and indeed by biology. Becker's position is largely that of the undefeated, pragmatic, historyless and still optimistic American to whom 'everything is possible' in man-to-man, and manly encounter. If, however, we acknowledge that superiors no less than subordinates live within these limits – which may not be impossible to penetrate, but only costly to do so – we do not, I think, degrade their humanity but rather sensitize ourselves to it. We may then see that the issue not only entails a conflict between superiors and subordinates but a larger kind of human struggle. Such a perspective does not require us to restrain our sympathy for the underdog or ignore his special plight, but gives us a broader comprehension of it. To have a sense of man's common humanity does not demand a superhuman capacity to transcend partisanship. But a partisanship that is set within the framework of a larger humanistic understanding is quite different from one devoid of it. This is one difference between the merely political partisanship of daily involvements, and the more reflective and tempered partisanship which may well be such objectivity of which we are capable.

There are works of art that manifest this objective partisanship. The dramas of the great classical tragedians are a magnificent case in point. What makes them great is their objectivity; and what makes them objective is their capacity to understand even the nobility of their Persian enemies, even the dignity of their 'barbarian' slaves, even the bumbling of their own wise men. They do indeed express a viewpoint which in some sense does take the standpoint of both sides, and does so simultaneously. If great art can do this, why should this be forbidden to great social science? That it is not common is precisely what makes its accomplishment an expression of greatness.

Despite the inevitability of bias and the unavoidability of partisanship, the fact remains that two researchers may have the same bias but, nonetheless, may *not* be equally objective. How is this possible? Becker notes 'that our unavoidable sympathies do not render our results invalid' and that, despite them, research must meet 'the standards of good scientific work'. This does not clarify the issue as much as we might wish, for there never was any suggestion that partisanship impaired the 'validity' of research. There is also no doubt that partisanship does not necessarily impair the 'reliability' of a research. The validity and reliability of researches are matters quite apart from their *objectivity*.

And it is primarily this last concern which is engaged when the problem of partisanship is raised. The question here is only whether partisanship necessarily vitiates objectivity, and this in turn requires that at some point we clarify our conception of objectivity and of how it may be attained.

Once Again: The Problem of Objectivity

How, then, does Becker seek to enhance the objectivity of even partisan research? His views concerning this are sketchy in the extreme. Although he speaks of a need to maintain scientific standards, he quickly recognizes that there is no way in which we can be sure that sociologists will *apply* these standards 'impartially across the board'. He also expresses the qualified hope that, over the years, the accumulation of 'one-sided' studies will gradually produce a more balanced picture of a social situation; but he also recognizes that this does not help the individual researcher in the here and now.

The remedies in which Becker apparently reposes greater confidence consist rather of two other things. First, he recommends that we honestly confess the partisan position we have adopted, openly acknowledging that we have studied the problem from the standpoint of only certain of the actors involved and not of all. Considering that Becker has himself refused openly to acknowledge his own underdog standpoint, this solution to the problem of objectivity is not entirely confidence inspiring. Secondly, Becker also recommends – and it is this that he seems to feel most strongly about – the avoidance of 'sentimentality', whatever that may mean.

For my part, it seems to me that other things might be done.

For one, I would encourage a condemnation of complacency rather than of sentimentality. For it is complacency which allows us to think, à la Myrdal, that we have solved the problem of objectivity by good-naturedly confessing that, yes, we do indeed have a standpoint and by openly specifying what it is. Confession may be good for the soul, but it is no tonic to the mind. While the 'heart may have reasons of its own', when it simply chooses to assert these without critical inspection, then reason must condemn this as complacency. Of course, it is a good thing for sociologists to know what they are doing; and it is a good thing for them to know and to say whose side they are on. But a bland confession of partisanship merely betrays smugness and naïveté. It is smug because it assumes that the values that we have are good enough; it is naïve because it assumes that we know the values we have. Once we recognize that complacency is the mind's embalming fluid and once we move to overcome it, we are then forced to ask, what is it that is now making us so complacent?

The complacency of Becker and of his school of deviance derives in large measure from its own unexamined, comfortable commitment to political liberalism. It has wrapped itself in the protective covering of the liberal Establishment which dominates American sociology today, as well as American academic life in general. Becker blandly acknowledges, without making the least effort to explore its appreciable consequences, that 'it is no secret that most sociologists are politically liberal . . .' But it is complacency to allow ourselves to be appeased by a confession of the commonplace. To confess that most sociologists are politically liberal is like 'confessing' that men are conceived in sexual intercourse. The question is whether Becker sees any *consequences* in the thing confessed. Without considering these, confession becomes a meaningless ritual of frankness.

The important problem is the exploration of the ways in which the political liberalism of many sociologists today affects the worth, the scope, the bite, and the objectivity of their sociology. The very blandness of his confession implies that Becker fails to grasp that liberalism today is not simply the conscientious and liberating faith of isolated individuals. Political liberalism today instead verges on being an official ideology of wide sectors of the American university community as well as broader strata of American life. For many American academicians, liberalism has now become a token of respectability, a symbol of genteel open-mindedness, the fee for membership in the faculty club; in point of fact, liberalism is also an operating code that links academic life to the political machinery of the Democratic Party.

Far from being the conscientious code of isolated individuals, much of liberalism today is the well-financed ideology of a loosely organized but coherent Establishment. It is the dominant ideology of a powerful group that sprawls across the academic community; that is integrated with American politics; that has its opinion leaders in various publications; that has its heroes whose myths are recited. Liberalism, then, is the mythos of one of the dominating American establishments; it is not simply the hard-won faith of a happy few. As the ideology of an establishment, such official liberalism has things to protect. It has reasons to lie. It has all the social mechanisms available to any establishment by which it can reward those who tell the right lies, and punish and suppress those who tell the wrong truths. In its meaner moments, it is an intellectual Mafia. It is not only, therefore, as Becker says, that 'officials must lie because things are seldom as they ought to be'. Like any other member of an establishment, the sociologist who is a political liberal is expected to lie along with his fellow members of the Establishment, to feel the rightness of their cause and a responsibility for its success.

The bias of the sociologist, then, does not derive simply from the fact that it is inherent in the human condition or in sociological research. The sociologist also lies because he is a political person. It would seem, however, that sociologists have no right to be complacent about anything that they, more than others, should have good reason to know makes liars of them. They thus have no right to be complacent about the intellectual consequences of their own liberalism.

The complacency that oozes from Becker's discussion, the vapid frankness of its confessional style, rests upon a simple sociological condition: upon the fact that it is allied with official liberalism, is embedded in the liberal Establishment, and is supported comfortably by the welfare state.

This still leaves the question as to whether there is any road toward objectivity, and what direction it might take. In my view, the objectivity of sociologists is enhanced to the extent that they critically examine all conventional 'hierarchies of credibility', including their own liberal 'hierarchy of credibility', which is today as respectable, conventional, and conformist as any. Becker acknowledges that it is sometimes possible to 'take the point of view of some third party not directly implicated in the hierarchy we are investigating'. This would, indeed, he agrees, make us neutral to the contending groups in the situation under study. But, he adds, this 'would only mean we would enlarge the scope of the political conflict to include a party not ordinarily brought in whose view the sociologist has taken'. But isn't this precisely one possible meaning of an avenue toward objectivity?

Isn't it good for a sociologist to take the standpoint of someone outside of those most immediately engaged in a specific conflict, or outside of the group being investigated? Isn't it precisely this outside standpoint, or our ability to adopt it, which is one source and one possible meaning of sociological objectivity? Granted, all standpoints are partisan; and, granted, no one escapes a partisan standpoint. But aren't some forms of partisanship more liberating than others? Isn't it the sociologists' job to look at human situations in ways enabling them to see things that are not ordinarily seen by the participants in them? This does not mean that the sociologist should ignore or be insensitive to the full force of the actors' standpoints. But it does mean that he himself must have a standpoint on their standpoint. Objectivity is indeed threatened when the actors' standpoints and the sociologists' fuse indistinguishably into one. The adoption of an 'outside' standpoint, far from leading us to ignore the participants' standpoint, is probably the only way in which we can even recognize and identify the participants' standpoint. It is only when we have a standpoint somewhat different from the participants' that it becomes possible to do justice to their standpoints.

There are, it seems to me, at least three other possible conceptions of sociological objectivity. One of these can be characterized as 'personal authenticity' or 'awareness', another can be termed 'normative objectification', and the third may be called 'transpersonal replicability'.

To consider 'normative objectification' first: when we talk about the bias or impartiality of a sociologist we are, in effect, talking about the sociologist as if he were a 'judge'.[1] Now, rendering a judgement premises the existence of conflicting or contending parties; but it does not imply an intention to *mediate* the difficulties between them. The function of a judge is not to bring parties together but is, quite simply, to do justice. Doing justice does not mean, as does mediation or arbitration, that both the parties must each be given or denied a bit of what they sought. Justice does not mean logrolling or 'splitting the difference'. For the doing of justice may, indeed, give all the benefits to one party and impose all the costs upon another.

What makes a judgement possessed of justice is not the fact that it distributes costs and benefits equally between the parties but, rather, that the allocation of benefits and costs is made in conformity with some stated normative standard. Justice, in short, is that which is justified in terms of some value. The 'impartiality' or objectivity of the judge is an imputation made when it is believed that he had made his decision primarily or solely in terms of some moral value. In one part, then, the objectivity of the judge requires his explication of the moral value in terms of which his judgement has been rendered. One reason why Becker's analysis founders on the problem of objectivity is precisely because it regards the sociologists' value commitment merely as an inescapable fact of nature, rather than viewing it as a necessary condition of his objectivity.

Insofar as the problem is seen as one of choosing up sides, rather than a working one's way through to a value commitment, I cannot see how it is ever possible for men to recognize that the side to which they are attached can be wrong. But men do not and need not always say, 'my country right or wrong'. Insofar as they are capable of distinguishing the side to which they are attached, from the *grounds* on which they are attached to it, they are, to that extent, capable of a significant objectivity.

It should again be clear, then, that I do not regard partisanship as incompatible with objectivity. The physician, after all, is not necessarily less objective because he has made a partisan commitment to his patient and against the germ. The physician's objectivity is in some measure vouchsafed because he has committed himself to a specific value: health. It is this commitment that constrains him to see and to say things about the patient's condition that neither may want to know.

But in saying that the explication of the sociologist's value commitment is a necessary condition for his objectivity, we are saying little unless we recognize at the same time the grinding difficulties involved in this. For one, it is no easy thing to know what our own value commitments are. In an effort to seem frank and open, we all too easily palm off a merely glib statement about our values without making any effort to be sure that these are the values to which we are actually committed. This is much of what happens when scientists conventionally assert that they believe only in 'the truth'. Secondly, a mere assertion of a value commitment is vainly ritualistic to the extent that the sociologist has no awareness of the way in which one of his commitments may conflict with or exclude another. For example, there is commonly some tension between a commitment to truth and a commitment to welfare. Third, we also have to recognize that the values in terms of which we may make our judgements may not necessarily be shared by the participants in the situations we have studied. Our objectivity, however, does not require us to share values with those we study, but only to apply the values that we claim are our own, however unpopular these may be. In other words, this form of objectivity requires that we be on guard against our own hypocrisy and our need to be loved. This creates a problem because the values we may actually hold may differ from those we feel that we must display in order to gain or maintain access to research sites.

To come to another meaning of sociological objectivity, 'personal authenticity'. If the previous conception of objectivity, 'normative objectification', emphasizes that the sociologist must not deceive *others* concerning the value basis of his judgement, then personal authenticity stresses that the sociologist must not deceive *himself* concerning the basis of his judgement. By personal authenticity or awareness, I mean to call attention to the relationship between the sociologist's beliefs about the actual state of the social world, on the one hand, and his own personal wishes, hopes, and values for this social world, on the other hand. Personal authenticity or awareness exists when the sociologist is capable of admitting the factuality even of things that violate his own hopes and values. People do differ in this regard, some having a greater capacity and need for self-deception and others possessing less talent to attain the comforts born of such self-deception. Not all conservatives are equally blind to the fragility of the *status quo*; not all radicals are equally blind to its stability.

In this sense, then, one form of sociological objectivity involves the capacity to acknowledge 'hostile information' – information that is discrepant with our purposes, hopes, wishes, or values. It is not the state of the world, then, that makes information hostile, but only the state of the world in relation to a man's wants and values. Here, then, objectivity consists in the capacity to know and to use – to seek out, or at least to accept it when it is otherwise provided – information inimical to our own desires and values, and to overcome our own fear of such information.

Both forms of objectivity imply a paradoxical condition: namely, that one cannot be objective about the world outside without, to some extent, being knowledgeable about (and in control of) ourselves. In normative objectification, one of the central problems is to *know* our values, and to see that such knowledge is problematic. In personal authenticity there is a need for a similar knowledge of the self, but for a knowledge that goes beyond values into the question of our brute impulses and of other desires or wants that we may not at all feel to be valuable. In both forms of objectivity, also, it would be foolhardy to expect that the requisite knowledge is acquirable through a simple process of frictionless 'retrieval'. Rather, we must expect that either form of objectivity entails some measure of *struggle* in and with the sociologist's self and, with this, a need for courage. It now should be clear why I have taken up the cudgels against complacency, for it is the very antithesis of the kind of moral struggle required for objectivity.

Professionalism and Objectivity

Insofar as the pursuit of objectivity rests upon what I must reluctantly call 'moral character', we can also see another source from which sociological objectivity is deeply undermined today. It is undermined, from one direction, by a compulsive and exclusive cultivation of purely technical standards of research and of education, so that there is neither a regard nor a locus of responsibility for the cultivation of those very moral qualities on which objectivity rests. The truth is that to the extent that sociology and sociological education remain obsessed with a purely technical focus they have abdicated a concern with objectivity; it is merely hypocritical for those with such a standpoint to enter occasional accusations about others' lack of objectivity.

A second basic inner locus for our default with respect to the problem of objectivity is the growing transformation of sociology into a profession. This may seem paradoxical again, for surely professions profess value commitments, at least to client, if not public, welfare. Professions, however, do not tend to see value commitments as questions of personal commitment but tend, instead, simply to treat the values they transmit as non-problematic givens. Most civic professions tend to take the larger culture and institutions in their society as given. But it is precisely the peculiar nature of the sociologist's task to be able to take them as problematic. The development of professionalization among sociologists deserves to be opposed because it undermines the sociologist's capacity for *objectivity* in any serious sense. In effect, the growth of professionalization means the substitution of a routine and banal code of ethics for a concern with the serious kind of morality on which alone objectivity might rest.

A third specific conception of objectivity common to many American sociologists – and so common, in fact, that even C. Wright Mills agreed with it – is what has been termed 'transpersonal replicability'. In this notion, objectivity simply means that a sociologist has described his procedures with such explicitness that others employing them on the same problem will come to the same conclusion. In effect, then, this is a notion of objectivity as technical routinization and rests, at bottom, on the codification and explication of the research procedures that were employed. At most, however, this is an *operational* definition of objectivity which presumably tells us what we must *do* in order to justify an assertion that some particular finding is objective. It does not, however, tell us very much about what objectivity *means* conceptually and connotatively. It says only that those findings which are replicated are to be considered to be objective.

It is quite possible, however, that any limited empirical generalization can, by this standard, be held to be objective, however narrow, partial, or biased and prejudiced its net impact is, by reason of its selectivity. Thus, for example, one might conduct research into the occupational-political distribution of Jews and come to the conclusion that a certain proportion of them are bankers and Communists. Given the replicability conception of objectivity, one might then simply claim that this (subsequently verified) finding is 'objective', and this claim could be made legitimately even though one never compared the proportions of bankers and Communists among Jews with those among Protestants and Catholics. It might be said that, without such a comparison among the three religions, one would never know whether the proportion of bankers and

Communists among Jews was higher or lower than that among Protestants and Catholics. But this objection would simply indicate the technical statistical condition that must be met in order to justify a statement concerning the Jewish *differential*. Insofar as one happens not to be interested in making or justifying a statement about this, the objectivity of the original statement remains defensible in terms of the technical conception of objectivity as replicability. Thus it would seem that the replicability criterion falls far short of what is commonly implied by objectivity.

This technical conception of objectivity is in part, but in part only, reminiscent of the manner in which Max Weber conceived of it. We might say that the current conception is a kind of mindless corruption of Weber's. Weber essentially thought of scientific objectivity as something left over. It was a residual sphere of the purely technical, a realm in which decisions should and could be made without thought of their ultimate value relevancies. Weber's approach to objectivity comes down to a strategy of segregation – the conscientious maintenance of a strict separation between the world of facts and the world of values. Weber's emphasis here, therefore, is not on the manner in which scientific objectivity depends upon value commitments; this tends tacitly to be assumed rather than deliberately insisted upon. Weber's stress is placed, rather, upon the separation and discontinuity of facts and values. As a result, one may come away believing that, to Weber, the objectivity of research need not be coloured by the scientist's personal values or the manner in which these are arrived at and held. *En principe*, neither the sanity nor maturity of a scientist need affect his objectivity. The madman and the teenager can be as scientifically objective as anyone else in this view, so long as they adhere to purely technical standards of science, once having committed themselves to some problem. Weber's theory invites a fantasy that objectivity may, at some point, be surrendered entirely to the impersonal machinery of research.

The passionate artfulness with which Weber argues this case allows the world that he conjures in imagination to be mistaken for reality, and we may fail to notice just how *grotesque* this conjured world is. Actually, Weber's entire enterprise here is born of his attempt to overcome his conception of the world as grotesque by formulating a salvational myth of a value-free social science. Through this he strives to still his furious sense of uneasiness that the real world, in which science and morality do cohabit, is a world of mutually destructive incompatibles. Weber fantasies a solution in which facts and values will each be preserved in watertight compartments. The tensions and dangers of the conjunction of facts and values are to be overcome by a segregation of the sequential phases of research, so that: first, the scientist formulates his problems in terms of his value interests and, then, having done this, he puts his values behind him, presumably never again allowing them to intrude into the subsequent stage of technical analysis.

To overcome his experience of the world as grotesque, Weber formulates an incipient utopia in which the impure world is split into two pure worlds, science and morality. He then attempts to bridge the cleavage he has created by pasting these two purified worlds together, so that each is made sovereign in a different but adjacent period of time. The incongruity of the world has not so much been overcome as transcended in myth. The experienced unmanageability of the one world gives way to the promised manageability of the two worlds. The reality gives way to the myth, but the grotesqueness abides.

One central difference between Weber's and the current technical conception of objectivity is that Weber recognized that the technical sphere would have to be brought into some sort of alignment with the value sphere. The modern technical conception of objectivity, however, simply regards the value problem and its relation to the technical as either negligible or dull. It allows it to remain unclarified. The modern technical approach to objectivity also differs from the Weberian in a second way. The former takes it for granted that, somehow, social scientists will do the right thing. It assumes that, in some manner, there will be a mustering of motives sufficient to make social scientists conform with their technical standards and rules.

Commonly, the source of these motives is not explored. Sometimes, however, it is today held that the mutual inspection and the checks and balances of modern *professionalization* will suffice to keep social scientists honest. In short, it is assumed that the machinery of professionalism will make the machinery of science work.

This expectation underestimates the ease with which professionalism is corruptible as well as the power of the corrupting forces. Perhaps the most important example of this in the present generation was the work of the Warren Commission appointed by President Lyndon Johnson to investigate the assassination of President John Kennedy. Whatever one's conclusions concerning the substantive issues, namely, whether Lee Harvey Oswald was the assassin, and whether or not he alone or in conspiracy with others murdered President Kennedy, one miserable conclusion seems unavoidable: that there was scarcely a civic profession – the military, the medical, the police, the legal, the juridical – that was not involved in suppressing or distorting the truth, and which did not bow obsequiously to power. And I am far from sure that this was always motivated by a concern for the national welfare. The more that the respectable professions are transformed from independent vocations into bureaucratic and federally sponsored dependencies the more corruptible they will be in the future. Those who think that professional associations and universities will immunize the professions from the pressures and temptations of power have simply not understood the revelations about the C.I.A. penetration into these very associations and universities. For these show that they were willing and eager parties to their own corruption in the name of a well-financed patriotic devotion.

For his part, however, Weber never assumed that the technical machinery of science would be self-winding and self-maintaining. For Weber, the maintenance of objectivity at least required a persisting moral effort to prevent one's personal values from intruding into purely technical decisions. The machinery was really never thought of as operating successfully apart from men's characters. Weber premises that, even in the purely technical stages of later research, work will be subject to an ongoing superintendence by the social scientist's moral commitment to 'truth'. Since the continued force of this personal value is conceived to be compatible with the maintenance of technical standards, its significance is left unexplicated. It is only implicitly, therefore, that Weber indicates that the objectivity of research depends continuingly, and not only in the early problem-formulating stages, upon something more than the technical machinery of research.

The question arises, however, as to the meaning of this extra-technical, 'transcendental' commitment to the truth. Does it entail anything more than a commitment to the segregation of facts and values? Either it has some meaning beyond this or it does not. If it does not, then we are still left wondering how and why social scientists may be relied upon to adhere to this very segregation of facts and values: What endows it with binding force? If it does, and if the 'truth' that it demands is something more than the mere application of technical standards alone, then it must entail something more than a belief in reliability or validity. If 'truth' is not merely a summarizing redundancy for these terms it must be embedded with some conception that embodies or resonates value commitments that call for something more than pure truth alone.

The pursuit of 'truth for its own sake' is always a tacit quest for something more than truth, for other values that may have been obscured, denied, and perhaps even forbidden, and some of which are expressed in the quest for 'objectivity'. Objectivity expresses a lingering attachment to something more than the purely technical goods of science alone and for more than the valid-reliable bits of information it may produce. In this sense, 'truth for its own sake' is a crypto-ethic, a concealment of certain other substantive values through a strategy that, leaving them entirely in the open, diverts attention from them to another dramatically accentuated valuable: truth. The old Druidic sacred place is not destroyed; it is merely housed in an imposing new cathedral. In affirming that he only seeks the truth for its own sake, the scientist is therefore not so much lying as pledging allegiance to the flag of truth, while saying nothing about the country for which it stands.

What are the other values that lie obscured in the long shadows cast by the light of pure truth? In Western culture, these often enough have been freedom – the truth will set you free – and power – to know, in order to control. Underlying the conception of truth as objectivity there is, however, still another value, a faint but enduring image of the possibility of *wholeness*. One obvious implication of objectivity has commonly been to tell the 'whole' story. The longing here is to fit the partial and broken fragments together; to provide a picture that transcends the nagging sense of incompleteness; to overcome the multiplicity of shifting perspectives. Underlying the quest for objectivity, then, is the hope of dissolving the differences that divide and the distances that separate men by uniting them in a single, peace-bringing vision of the world.

In such a conception of objectivity there is, I suspect, the undertow of an illicit yearning that links science to religion. Perhaps this conclusion is an illusion. Worse still, perhaps it is 'sentimental'. Yet it will not seem so fanciful if it is remembered that the modern conception of an objective social science was born with early-nineteenth-century Positivism. This set itself the task of creating both an objective social science and a new religion of humanity, each informing the other and aimed at re-uniting society. The objectivity of the new sociology was, from its very beginnings, not an end in itself; it was clearly aimed at the enhancement of human unity and it then had the most intimate connection with an openly religious impulse.

The conception of objectivity has commonly projected an image of the scientist as linked to a higher realm, as possessed of a godlike penetration into things, as serenely above human frailties and distorting passions, or as possessed of a priest-like impartiality. The realm of objectivity is the higher realm of *episteme*, of *wahrheit*, of *raison*, of Truth, which have always been something more than sheer information. In other words, the realm of objectivity is the realm of the *sacred* in social science.[2] But why has the quest for this realm been encrusted under the defensive conception of truth for its own sake?

Essentially the fate of objectivity in sociology is linked with, and its fortunes vary with, the changing hopes for a peace-bringing human unity. Some power-tempted social scientists are simply no longer able to hear this music. Others may withdraw because their hope is so vital that they cannot risk endangering it by an open confrontation. For some, an open

admission would be dissonant with their conception of themselves as tough-minded and hard-headed. Still others have a
genuine humility and feel that the pursuit of this high value is
beyond their powers. There are also some who doubt the very
value of peace itself because, oddly enough, they want men to
endure and to live, and they suspect that the successful quest
for a peace-bringing unity spells death: they ask themselves,
after unity and peace, what?

Perhaps what has been most discrediting to the quest for
human unity is that, since its classical formulation, its most
gifted spokesmen have often had totalitarian proclivities; they
came to be viewed as enemies of the 'open society', who denied
the value and reality of human difference. In short, the plea for
human unity has often, and quite justifiably, been interpreted
as a demand for a tension-free society that was overseen by a
close superintendence of men from nursery to graveyard, and
was blanketed with a remorseless demand for conformity and
consensus. What has really been discredited, however, was this
chilling version of the dream of human unity, although it
remains extremely difficult to extricate the larger hope from the
nightmare form that it was given.

Whether objectivity is thought possible comes down then
to a question of whether some vision of human unity is believed
workable and desirable. It comes down to the question, as C.
Wright Mills once said, of whether there is still some vision of a
larger 'public' whose interests and needs transcend those of its
component and contending factions. In this sense, one possible
meaning of objectivity in social science is the contribution it
might make to a human unity of mankind. But to make such a
contribution the social sciences cannot and should not be
impartial toward human suffering; they must not make their
peace with any form of human unity that complacently accom-
modates itself to or imposes suffering.

At the same time, however, an empty-headed partisanship
unable to transcend the immediacies of narrowly conceived
political commitment is simply just one more form of market
research. A blind or unexamined alliance between sociologists
and upper bureaucracy of the welfare state can only produce
the market research of liberalism. It rests upon the tacit,

mistaken, but common, liberal assumption that the policies of this bureaucracy equitably embody the diverse interests of the larger public, rather than seeing that the bureaucracy is one other interested and powerful contending faction, and is more closely allied with some of the contenders rather than equally distant from all. It is to values, not to factions, that sociologists must give their most basic commitment.

NOTES

1. The next paragraph or so is indebted to the excellent discussion by Rostein Eckhoff, 'The Mediator, the Judge and the Administrator in Conflict-Resolution', *Acta Sociologica*, vol. 10, pp. 148–72.

2. It should be noted that this is not a 'call to religion' but a statement concerning the imputed meaning of 'objectivity' to conventional sociologists.

3

Remembrance and Renewal in Sociology

At the beginning of French sociology in the second quarter of the nineteenth century, after Henri Saint-Simon had died, his disciples began a series of lectures. Auguste Comte held forth on one street, and Barthélemy Prosper Enfantin and Saint-Amand Bazard competed on another. All three kept circling the same question, 'Who and what is the sociologist?' In the end, all of them made it clear that they were bent on establishing a new religion, a religion of humanity; sociologists would be the priesthood of the new faith in man.

This early priestly concept of the sociologist may now seem outlandish. But if the question is 'Who is the sociologist?' then the early French answer was more serious, and certainly more interesting, than the one sociologists conventionally give today. The usual answer now is that the sociologist is a person who studies group life, examines man in society, and does research into 'human relationships'.

This is a peculiarly superficial and narrow way for sociologists to define their role. Worst of all, it is lacking in an elementary self-awareness. It is as if a Congressman were to say he passes laws.

Pressed, the sociologist will acknowledge that what he does in the world is not adequately described by saying he studies it. He will admit that, like other men, he is influenced by and has an influence on his social surrounding; that sociological principles apply to sociologists as well as to other people; he may even acknowledge that there is, or can be, a sociology of sociology. But he will grant these things grudgingly, for reasons of logical consistency. He does not seem to find them deeply convincing, and he is not inclined to make them an operating part of his everyday work. The deepest source of trouble is that he has lost the habit of self-reflective thought.

What are sociologists – particularly social theorists – really up to? What happens when one begins with the assumption that social theory is made by men – and therefore by flawed men in a flawed society – and pursues that assumption seriously?

The conventional approach to social theory stresses the marriage between theory and research, the way research (the male element?) and theory (female passive?) interact happily ever after. But it is impossible to understand how social theory is actually made, or how it makes its way in the world, if one looks only at the role of rational and cognitive forces and especially if one operates with a tacit conception of theories of passive femininity.

Social theories are grounded in knowledge the theorist has gained through personal experience. Facts, rooted in personal reality, are of course utterly persuasive to the theorist. He becomes involved in, sees, experiences, such things as the French Revolution, the rise of socialism, the great Depression; and he never doubts the factuality of his experience. The theorist's basic conception of what is socially real and factual is thus rooted in the infrastructure of the man himself, in the local surrounding very close to his life.

Much theory work begins not as an effort to find or establish the facts but to make sense of experience, to resolve the part of it that is unresolved. Commonly, the theorist is trying to reduce the tension between a social event or process that he believes is real and some value that the event or process has violated. Thus theory-making is often an effort to cope with a threat to something in which the theorist is deeply and personally implicated.

For a theorist (as for others) there are two kinds of social worlds: permitted (or 'normal') worlds and unpermitted (or 'abnormal') ones. The theorist is likely to start work when he sees or suspects the existence of an unpermitted world, or a threat to a permitted world. A considerable part of his work is an effort to transform an unpermitted world into a permitted one, thus normalizing his universe. Most particularly he is attempting symbolically to re-establish a threatened or impaired equilibrium between power and goodness, for it is in terms of their relationship that a permitted or unpermitted world is defined.

Charles Osgood, in his work with the semantic differential, found that most words carry connotations of goodness or badness, and connotations of power or lack of power. We may postulate that these dimensions are also crucial in the world of social objects – that to assign meaning to social phenomena entails, among other things, judgements concerning both their goodness and their power.

It is extremely painful and threatening for a man to believe that what is powerful in society is not good, or that things of moral value lack power. When this happens he lives in and sees an unpermitted, abnormal world that needs a remedy. The theorist deposes the unpermitted world and readjusts the flawed relationship between good and power in various ways. He may, for example, affirm and accentuate the goodness of the powerful. This is essentially what the functionalist does by showing that those social objects that survive have an ongoing social usefulness (for in our world, to be useful is to be good). Or the theorist may affirm the power of the good, as Talcott Parsons does in emphasizing the social significance of shared moral norms. Or again, the theorist may deny, demean, or forbid the making of moral judgements while stressing the importance of evaluating the potency of objects. Machiavellianism or a realpolitik exemplifies this tendency in the political realm; a 'value-free' conception of social science does much the same in the realm of sociology. In a value-free social theory, however, it is not that the theorist fails to rate social objects on a goodness–badness scale but that the rating, having been defined as improper and irrelevant to his task, is done covertly, even unconsciously.

When a self-proclaimed value-free sociologist says that value judgements are improper, out of bounds, beyond his competence, he in effect avoids the tension between goodness and power by denying his responsibility for coping with the goodness-value side of the equation. Others may seek to redress an imbalance between power and goodness, in effect denying the existence of power apart from goodness. For example, the significance and prevalence of sheer power, brute force, raw coercion, conspiracy and violence in the world has long been ignored by Western sociologists, who to this day seldom confront the problem of war, either theoretically or empirically and scarcely even acknowledge the existence of something like imperialism.

It is appropriate at this point to enter the world of Talcott Parsons. Given the abstractness of Parsons' theory and the notorious obscurity of his prose style, it is not an easy world to enter. It is, however, a very reassuring one – for it is a world in which almost everything, including power, is basically good. Through Parsons' own writings and the work of his students, his vision of the world has had tremendous influence on sociology.

For Talcott Parsons the social world is, above all, a moral world. It is not what men actually do that is most important, for behaviour may include erratic departures of various sorts; the central issue is the values they share. Group values establish the perspective from which actual behaviour is viewed. As a result, there is a persistent pressure in Parsons' work to ignore social regularities that are not generated by moral codes – to neglect or see only as marginal, for example, technology, raw power, manipulation, imperialism or competition for scarce goods.

Parsons' stress on values requires systematic and repeated examinations of the social world in relation to its moral code, and Parsons performs such examinations endlessly. But the differences that he observes between reality and morality rarely disturb him and certainly never outrage him. For he sees them as temporary discrepancies, secondary aberrations, marginal deviations. In a 1953 paper on social stratification, for example, Parsons presents a picture of a happy, mobile and tolerant American society. He acknowledges that the actual state of affairs does diverge at some points from the ideal, but he is confident that through the inexorable workings of moral values such aberrations will be remedied.

The moralistic character of Parsons' work is related to several other characteristics of Parsonsian functionalism: to its stress on religion as the central source of social progress and solidarity; to its reluctance to confront issues of force and power; and to its fascination – one might almost say obsession – with the problem of social order.

The importance that Parsons characteristically attributes to religion in the modern world is expressed in two ways. First, he ascribes exceptional potency to religion: Parsons holds that it has brought into existence practically all of what he takes to be modern culture, including its uniquely powerful economy, technology and science. Second, he attributes great goodness to religion and its products, as substantiated by the presumably benign character of the welfare state it fosters.

Parsons resolves the problem of the split between power and goodness in the modern world by affirming that there is no such split. The social world is, instead, held to be both powerful and good, and both aspects have a common root in Christianity. To no other institution does Parsons attribute as much potency and goodness as he does to the Church – the rock and the light of modern civilization.

For all the talk about morality, however, the pursuit of stability is only contingently compatible with an emphasis on moral values. Those who demand social change, for example, customarily do so in the name of high moral values such as freedom, equality and justice. Those who reject the demands often do so in the name of an ostensibly higher value, social order. The exponent of order presents the issue as if it were a choice between order and anarchy. However, the goal of those who seek change is usually not *dis*order but a *new* order, one they consider more moral than the old. To make social order one's central concern is to exalt some moral values over some others. It is also to be conservative, not only metaphysically but politically.

When a theorist glimpses an unpermitted world in which the powerful and the good may not coincide, he can reduce the dissonance by avoiding the reality of power. This basic strategy is just as conservative as giving emphasis to those moral values that preserve social order. Parsons and other Western social theorists commonly avoid intellectual confrontation with the existence of sheer power. They usually stress that a world in which power exists without legitimacy will not long survive.

In 1961 and 1962 Parsons made a systematic re-examination of both force and power, apparently prompted by a conference called to discuss guerrilla and counter-insurgency warfare. Here we find that Parsons discusses only institutionalized power. The only power worthy of the name, in his opinion, is the power that involves conformity to legitimate obligations – legitimate because they contribute to collective goals. 'The threat of coercive measures, or of compulsion, without legitimation or justification, should not properly be called the use of power at all.' In mentioning justification, Parsons demonstrates that it is possible to be both empirically correct and intellectually absurd: empirically correct because even the most brutal exercises of coercion, such as the Nazi slaughter of the Jews or the American devastation of Vietnam are commonly *held* to be justified by those who commit them; intellectually absurd because Parsons does not specify *who* must regard coercion as justified before it can be defined as true, Parsonsian-type 'power'.

Parsons mentions another quality, legitimation, the possession of which can transform coercion into power. But he fails to see the literal sense in which coercion, violence, force, and all forms of might *make* right. For example, legitimacy may be born of a tacit trade-off between criminal and victim. The victim conceals his impotence by acknowledging the legitimacy of the claims made upon him, while the criminal conceals his brutality by forcing the victim to acknowledge the legitimacy of his claims. Precisely because power can be so brutal, men will strive to believe that it is not morally irrelevant. And like any other behaviour, the judgement that something is legitimate can be coerced.

Utopian as it frequently is, there are moments when Parsons' discussion of power and force threatens to be realistic. For example, he remarks that the obligations of power are always larger than it can fulfil at any one moment. If the demands made on it are too rapid, he says, it may resort to force. In maintaining that power *normally* fails to discharge some of its obligations, Parsons implies that there is usually some tension between power and morality – that they are far from being mutually adjusted. But since this implication contradicts his belief in the coextensivity of power and morality, it is not made explicit and the lapse into realism ceases.

What Parsons ignores is that it is their sheer power that allows the powerful to default on their moral obligations; that a lack of power constrains some to accept less than they can legitimately claim; and that these inequities are established as customary partly on the basis of the power distribution. Not all are able to default with equal impunity on their moral obligations. Some are hanged for stealing the goose from off the commons; others, however, steal the commons from under the goose without penalty. The level at which such immoralities come to be stabilized is determined, in large part, by the relative *power* of the groups involved.

In any given case, what is right or wrong, good or bad, is often uncertain, frequently disputed, and invariably resolved in a situation in which some have more power than others. If morality seems coextensive with power, it is partly because the powerful have the Procrustean ability to mould morality.

The ideological conservatism of functionalism is quiet rather than militant, and it has had to accommodate to functional theory's self-image as an objective, politically neutral discipline. Committed as it is to the value of order, however, functionalism can do little but accept the order in which it finds itself. This disposition to support established power makes it understandable that functionalism should begin to depart from its traditional neglect of the state and even move toward an alliance with it. Most American sociologists, although they are reluctant to engage in strong social dissent or criticism, are not unwilling to help solve social problems (and in the process further their careers) within the context of the *status quo*. Here it needs to be emphasized that, however much they talk of moral values, champions of social order are not in favour of just any moral beliefs. For example, functionalists prefer 'spiritual' to 'material' values. To want a car, a job, a clean apartment, may be just as expressive of a moral value as to want God, but what the champions of order vaunt above all are such 'transcendental, and non-empirical' values as temperance, wisdom, knowledge, and goodness and cooperation.

Freedom and equality, of course, are no less 'spiritual' than goodness and temperance, but freedom and equality can justify claims for a redistribution of material goods; they threaten property institutions and, indeed, the whole existing system of social stratification. For one who loves order, the highest values must be those that differ from freedom and equality and go on to *oppose* them. Thus the champions of order affirm only those moral values that have this interesting quality: a man may get more of them without taking anything away from someone else.

One might add, however, that the champions of order do not favour changes that would enhance privilege by further depriving the less privileged; indeed, they may even seek to ameliorate the lot of the unfortunate. While they counsel the have-nots not to demand too much too soon, they also urge restraint upon the haves: nothing too much, give a little, don't make pigs of yourselves. Underlying this apparent neutrality, however, is a fear that boat-rocking by either side will generate order-disrupting conflict. The counsel of moderation is not impartial to the dominant élites; it is a policy of prudence on their behalf.

For Parsons, there is a dilemma in holding that certain decencies of welfare are increasing on the one side, while moral standards are declining on the other. For me, there is no dilemma. Far from being incompatible with a general decline in attention to moral matters, an increase in the decencies of welfare is directly correlated with it. Both depend on increasing industrialization. As production becomes more efficient, men's tasks become more specialized, routine and mechanized; people are no longer required to be morally committed to their tasks in order to perform them effectively. Morality then becomes a private matter. Utilitarian culture, with its hardware embodiment in modern technology and its organizational embodiment in modern bureaucracy, can now fulfil its early promise to treat persons as *things*, while simultaneously advancing their health, longevity, literacy, and welfare.

As science, technocracy and bureaucracy become more autonomous and more powerful, men experience themselves as less potent, less in control of their own destinies. Their capacity to see themselves as moral actors is therefore threatened. In response, many are disposed either to reassert their potency *per se*, aggressively or violently and without regard for the moral character of the affirmation, or to relinquish the entire assumption that they are moral actors and capable of moral action. Everywhere in industrialized societies the decencies are growing and everywhere men are being indecently diminished.

The sociologist, like other men, is subject to social influence. He is shaped by domain assumptions (culturally derived beliefs and personal experience) as well as by the sentiments he has developed and the things he takes as real. And no more than other men is he ready to cast a cold eye on his own doings, to find out what he is really doing, and to distinguish this firmly from what he *should* be doing. Professional courtesy stifles intellectual curiosity; the teeth of piety bite the tongue of truth.

But our circumstances compel us to examine ourselves. We now require a 'sociology of sociology', a sociology that can deepen the sociologist's awareness of who and what he is as a member of a specific society at a given time, and of how his social roles and his personal life affect his professional work. This kind of sociology I have called Reflexive Sociology, and it is characterized by the relationship it establishes between being a sociologist and being a person – between the role and the man performing the role. The sociological enterprise, like others, becomes edged with a tragic sense when men suspect that they have wasted their lives. When they confine work to the demanding, misleading and unfulfillable paradigm of a value-free, high-science model, sociologists are wasting, indeed sacrificing, a part of themselves.

Since the 1920s, American sociology has viewed any involvement of the sociologist with his subjects as contamination and a danger to his objectivity. But the notion of contaminated research presupposes the existence of uncontaminated research, and this is pure folly. All research is contaminated, for all research entails relationships that may influence both sociologist and subject. The aim of the reflexive sociologist is not to remove his influence on others, but to *know* it.

While reflexive sociology denies the possibility of a value-free sociology, it also sees the dangers of a value-committed sociology. Men's highest values may make liars of them, as readily as their basest impulses do. But we must accept the dangers of a value commitment, because the risk of ending in distortion is better than beginning there, and a dogmatic and arid value-free sociology cannot be other than a myth.

Knowledge is moulded by a man's technical skills and by his intelligence but it also is moulded by all that he is and wants, by his courage no less than by his talent, by his passion no less than by his objectivity. If a man wants to change what he knows, he must change how he lives.

Reflexive sociology attributes importance to the theorist's infrastructure – his domain assumptions, his sentiments, the things that are real to him, and the way these things shape his theory. It emphasizes the manner in which such assumptions affect his perceptions of the larger society and provide the human grounding out of which social theory grows. Theory, I argue, changes with changes in the sociologist's infrastructure.

From this standpoint, then, the vital thing is not the wilful assertion of an alternative theoretical position. The decisive thing is to *establish* the human conditions that will nurture intellectual and theoretical alternatives, new technical paradigms, new middle-range theories, or even new epistemologies. 'Establish' here means that one wants a critically justified understanding of what kind of human conditions would be preferable and it also means putting this understanding into *practice*; it means an effort to *enact* these understandings in new communities and reconstructed institutions. Certainly, however, this is not a two-step activity, in which there is first understanding and only later *practice*. The last chapter of *The Coming Crisis of Western Sociology*, with its fuller discussion of 'Reflexive Sociology', contributes to such an effort.

Response to the book has moved me much further in this direction. Since social theory is grounded in social structure, the first task of sociology and social theory is to create the new *communities* – specifically, theoretical collectives – for rational discourse by social theorists. In my view, it is essential to establish – in the double sense of to *know* and to *institute* – the human and social conditions for the restriction of irrational and ideological components of discourse, for the control and exposure of false consciousness.

This task has two sides. One is oppositional, polemical, critical, isolating and combative. The theoretical collective must create a rift in the social world, separate itself from conventional and dominant definitions of social reality, and struggle against the institutions and conditions that maintain them, always taking care to protect itself against their inevitable backlash.

The other side, however, is *constructive*. Within any liberated social space that we manage to carve out, we can begin to design and construct theoretical communities that nourish and support rational discourse in sociology and social theory. As Jürgen Habermas has stressed, the most essential social condition for rational discourse is to eliminate all force and violence. Where force and violence remain possible, there will be an inescapable pressure that – openly and covertly, crudely and subtly – sets into motion a thousand inducements to false consciousness.

Rational theorizing means above all rational *discourse* in theory: it means dialectic and dialogue among truth-committed men joined in a community that speaks a common language. It is the rock-bottom foundation for the control of false consciousness and for the continuing critical development of social theory.

Such theoretical collectives are far more important to the development of social theory and sociology than all the technical instruments and rules, and all the courses on research methods and techniques.

The university's central problem is its failure as a *community* in which rational discourse about *social* worlds is possible. This is partly because rational discourse as such ceased to be its dominant value and was superseded by a quest for knowledge *products* and information *products* that could be sold or promised for funding, prestige and power – rewards bestowed by the state and the larger society that is most bent upon subverting rational discourse about itself. Indeed, theoretical communities need to protect themselves from impediments to rational discourse still growing within the university as much as from those in the larger society. In my view, the university provides a partially cleared but immensely threatened space in which such theory-generating communities might grow. The capacity of such theoretical collectivities to reach beyond the university, while maintaining a foothold there, is more than a way to express their relevance to the problems of the larger world; it is probably also a requisite for the maintenance of rational discourse in social theory.

My assumption, then, comes down to this: (1) the central problem facing all sociologies today is the interrelation between theory and practice, and (2) one can best enter this circle by community-creating efforts, and most particularly, by creating new theoretical collectives. In short, my assumption is that it is organization, social organization, that today provides the key mediation between social theory and social practice. Sociology today does not need a Karl Marx or an Isaac Newton; it needs a V. I. Lenin.[1]

To regard a reflexive sociology as only a negative critique of establishment sociology is, in my view, mistaken. Such a judgement ignores the fact that the criticism presents a design for the reorganization of sociology; it forgets that organization must mediate between theory and practice, establishing the social conditions necessary for rational discourse.

It is precisely on this organizational level that social theory attains its fullest reflexivity: here it establishes the conditions that enable it to establish itself and in establishing these conditions it tests and appraises the worth of the theory it has established. In this way social theory acts on behalf of the rest of the world, for the quest for rational discourse is not a sectarian need limited to social theorists but is a world need. Organization of new theoretical collectives then becomes the strategic, theory-yielding social methodology.

Social theorists cannot have truths about society without having truths about themselves. And they cannot have truths about themselves without knowing how to organize themselves in furtherance of rational discourse, and without enacting that knowledge. Once this is seen, then we cannot hold that the 'really important' part is first to understand and criticize *society* (as against theory), and it becomes clear that those who believe that the criticism and transformation of social theory is a secondary and separate task are hopelessly shallow. *A critique of social theory necessarily implies a change in the social organization of social theory in furtherance of rational discourse, and the knowledge that is required for this task, while crucial to theory, can transform the world.*

NOTE

1. If one actually reads what is said here it can be seen that the point is that sociology needs 'someone' to clarify its *own* organizational requisites, as Lenin had for Marxism. It is clearly not, as Lipset pretends (see pp. 141–2), an advocacy of activism versus scholarship. Anyone reading to the end will see this. This theme is then elaborated in our next essay; indeed, this essay can be regarded as a preview to the fuller development that follows.

4

The Politics of the Mind

The renewal of sociology is of course one aspect of the reconstruction of society. Clearly, we cannot have a reconstructed society without a critical revamping of our established ways of thinking about society. At the same time, I shall also argue that one of the reasons why we want a new society is that men may better live in it without lies, illusions and false consciousness. The new society we want is, among other things, a society that will enable men better to see *what is* and say *what is* about themselves and their social world. In other words, the very purpose of a new society is, in *some* part, to create a new sociology. A sociology then is not simply an instrument for creating a new society. It *is* that, vitally and importantly that, but that only in *part*. A sociology that says *what is* about man and society is also worth having in its own right and for its own sake, because it is in the nature of man to hunger after truth and to want to know who and what he is.

The renewal of sociology is something that not only entails a change of ideas. It also requires a reconstruction of how sociologists live as well as how they work. What we are involved in here is precisely an effort to contribute to the renewal of sociology, part of a collective effort.

Yet, as Marx says, men make their own history, but they do not make it under circumstances of their own choosing. What we must reckon with is history in all its 'heaviness'. There is the history of sociology to be reckoned with. There is the history of the societies in which sociology developed. And, yes, there is even our own individual history as persons. All these histories bring us to the watershed of the present. We do not then come to a task without a past. Which is to say, we come to it with both liabilities or limits, on the one side, and assets and opportunities, on the other. One of the ways in which my own past is similarly ambiguous is precisely through my past work and, most especially, my recent *Coming Crisis*.[1]

The Coming Crisis of Western Sociology was, despite its length, meant primarily to begin a discussion concerning the proper relation of sociology to society, and therefore of theory to practice. Its polemic against conventional, 'normal' sociology was meant to help clear a space within which an emancipatory sociology might arise in the United States. Certain discussions of *The Coming Crisis* – most especially those of Richard Flacks,[2] Alain Touraine and Maurice Zeitlin[3] – clearly recognize that this was its intention, and their sober and serious commentaries are often an exemplary contribution to the very discussion that the book had sought. What follows, then, is not at all an 'answer' to, and certainly *not* a polemic against these critics. What follows is a further exploration of certain problems that we all commonly recognize as vital. If I use *The Coming Crisis* as my point of departure it is not because I deem it to have special value but simply because I, like anyone else, must necessarily start with where I have been.

Five Basic Issues in *The Coming Crisis*

Flacks' discussion of *The Coming Crisis*, like most other responsible commentaries, deals most basically with four problems and revolves around four questions:

First, given my critique of the major theoretical positions held by most sociologists today, what alternative theoretical models do I endorse or see as preferable to those I criticized? For some who raise this question, there seems to be a feeling that I have not been 'constructive' enough. Thus Flacks speaks of my 'failure to offer a coherent alternative'.

A *second* question frequently raised in a critical vein is, why did I write a critique of *sociology* when it is a critique of *society* that is 'really' needed? 'Why doesn't Gouldner devote his energy developing a theory of society instead of a theory of social theory?' The implication is that sociology is a small part of the world and to concern oneself with it is to manifest a certain provincialism and narcissistic self-indulgence. According to Flacks, Tom Bottomore and Roscoe Hinkel a sociology of sociology is 'navel-gazing'. It may seem as if a proper reply to this is to say that a critic has no right to ask an author to have written a different book; for if the critic was not interested in the book the author wrote, then the critic should not have read it. But this response is shallow. For one thing, it premises that there exists only a very segmented relation between 'author' and 'critic', whereas I regard critics such as Flacks as members of my community, rather than as a mere 'audience'. As a fellow community member he may have the right to suggest that I should be working on something other than I have been.

Moreover, the 'don't read the book if you aren't interested in theory' reply is also a poor one because it ends the discussion where it should begin. That is, it tacitly accepts the false premise of the original criticism, namely, that there is a radical divorce between 'theory' and 'society'. This view mistakenly adopts an empiricistic/objectivistic position which wrongly assumes that 'society' exists apart from some theory about it. My own position, however, is that every society is a social reality in part constituted by a kind of everyday social theory, and that therefore the critique of society and of theory are inseparable. This was exactly Marx's supposition, too, as evidenced by the fact that his critique of modern society, *Capital*, is also subtitled 'A Critique of Political Economy' – which is to say, of economic *theory*.

Every society is in part a product of a social theory and every theory is in part a social product of the society. It is therefore impossible to make a critique of one without the other, although one may have a false consciousness and may think this possible. This particular kind of false consciousness, common to many theorists, is often called 'Objectivism'. My call for a Reflexive Sociology was, moreover, scarcely intended to confine sociology to a study of sociology. The goal was surely not to prevent studies of other parts of society but, rather, to enable them to be done more profoundly by sociologists with a deeper self-awareness, who had committed themselves and their work to human self-emancipation. But more on this later.

A *third* question has to do with Marxism and my relation to it. Flacks tells us that the positive alternative to normal academic sociology is and will be some variant of Marxism. '. . . the assimilation of neo-Marxism into American sociology is going to happen,' Flacks says. I also say this on p. 409 of *The Coming Crisis*: '. . . the future sociology of the New Left will seek . . . an economically sensitive neo-Marxism . . .'; on p. 444 I also speak of the 'emerging Marxist sociology'. We both agree, then, about what is *happening*; where we *may* disagree is in our views of what constitutes a *proper* relationship to Marxism, and between it and sociology. Flacks' criticism, like others, therefore emphasizes that I should have had more to say about Marxism in *The Coming Crisis*: '. . . it is a pity that Gouldner, who has wide first-hand contact with the Europeans, did not choose to incorporate their work into his book.'

In *The Coming Crisis*, however, I expressly maintain that world sociology is structurally differentiated into what I call 'academic sociology', on the one hand, and Marxism, on the other, and I devote most of my work to academic sociology, and do not there give equal attention to Marxism. In that volume I state that this is exactly what I intend to do; that given the size of the volume, I can do no other; moreover, I also expressly hold that the problem of analysing Marxism properly, in historical and analytic depth, is a very serious task indeed and that I am working on a separate study of Marxism[4] as a counterpart to *The Coming Crisis*.

Offhand, I can think of no reason why anyone should be expected to present his views on all the great questions of the world within the confines of a single volume, but I cheerfully wish good luck to those who think that they can do so.

The Coming Crisis was intended to focus on *academic* sociology, and I could not there give Marxism the fine-grained analysis it deserves. Still, almost any discerning reader will notice that Marxism is indeed discussed there, and at considerable *length*. I had to do so because Marxism comprises an important part of the cultural world that has shaped academic sociology, if only negatively. I recognized, however, that I could not do full justice to both Marxism and academic sociology in one volume. Yet one has but to look at the index to *The Coming Crisis*, and see the number of items referring to Marx and Marxism, to recognize that I in no way slighted Marxism.

A *fourth* question in Flacks' discussion is the problem of sociology's relation to the world, to practice, to efforts to transcend what we now have and liberate men from it. We must once again clarify our notion of who and what the sociologist is, what his job in the world is, and most pointedly, his relation to social movements, such as socialism, that share his emancipatory goals. More than anyone else, Flacks has specified a concrete and positive view of this relation, has done so on the basis of practice, and he deserves our very close attention when he speaks about this matter.

Objectivity versus Objectivism in Sociology

A *fifth* very basic problem is that posed by Zeitlin and Touraine concerning 'objectivity' in sociology. Both Zeitlin and Touraine are manifestly concerned to prevent deterioration of the boundary between 'mere ideology' and 'true' social 'science'. It is obvious that each feels that *The Coming Crisis* has threatened to overrun or blur this boundary.

Thus, Zeitlin: Gouldner 'verges on sociological solipsism, so that "ideology" seems to swallow up and absorb all valid knowledge of the objective world'.[5] I am alleged to have only 'verged' on this, and that ideology is alleged only to 'seem' to do this. This talk about 'verging' and 'seeming' stems from the fact that there is no evidence that I actually do what they allege that I do, namely, affirm that sociology is mere ideology and deny it truth value.

Touraine first commendingly remarks that my work opposes 'a pretension of objectivity [in American academic sociology] which had never been acceptable to many foreign observers, who have never ceased to see in most of American sociology a product of the American society. . . .'[6] Touraine then launches a set of nervous musings and hummings: 'If sociology is only [*sic*] ideology, the sociologist who critiques sociology is doing ideology, and sociological research is reduced to a debate of opinions.'[7] This formulation embodies a decisive conflation of issues that renders Touraine's judgement more confusing than clarifying.

Take the phrase 'debate of opinions'. Does Touraine wish to reduce the sway of *opinion* or the sway of *debate*? Does he think, specifically, that 'ideology' is the realm of debate, while 'science' is the realm of consensus devoid of debate? Obviously, what makes a view 'opinion' rather than knowledge is that there is an unresolved debate concerning it among members of some relevant group. Once that debate is resolved, the judgement reached defines what is knowledge. That is: knowledge is that belief which stands up under rational criticism and under the contention of rational debate. Science (including social science) thus never avoids the 'debate of opinions'. Whatever else it means, the doctrine of falsifiability insists that there can be no knowledge apart from dialectic, contention, debate; it insists that such debate is a *necessary* (not a sufficient) condition for the transformation of opinion into knowledge. Both 'knowledge' and 'opinion' are social realities; they are socially processed 'certifications' of the reliance that rational men may repose in certain beliefs.

The uneasiness, suspicion, and rejection of 'solipsism' and of 'attitudes' by Zeitlin and Touraine is indeed an attitude on their part. It has a meaning which, even if obscured, we are obliged to take seriously and seek to understand. My judgement is that it has something of the following meaning:

It means that their views are grounded philosophically in an *objectivistic* standpoint that does not understand the role of personal presence, or the propriety (because necessity) of this, and is therefore impelled to deny the reality and consequentiality of this personal presence/commitment. Objectivism thus cannot understand personal presence as a concealed and consequential thing in all efforts to know social worlds. Objectivism then is the very antithesis of reflexivity.

The objectivist thinks that 'objective' truth is that which exists apart from the men who constitute it, and thus as existing *apart* from their values, interests, or 'attitudes'. He assumes that truth is that knowledge of the world which would be cleansed of the impurities presumably brought by men's presence: their values, sentiments, attitudes, or interests. The objectivist therefore rejects knowledge as a social product, produced by himself as a social being in some social collaboration with others; he tacitly rejects the idea of knowledge as a social product, even if he himself happens to be a sociologist.[8]

In his effort to elude 'sociological solipsism' he thinks of *himself* in some correspondingly objectivistic manner: as a knowing machine, or a cognitive 'tool'. He thinks of himself as a 'mirror' held up to the merely 'reflecting' reality, or as a medium through which the world speaks. Others, in short, are viewed as Subject, and he now tacitly views himself as their Object. The objectivist's basic posture, then, is to deny and conceal his presence in the world and how this presence shapes it and what he says about it. In presenting his own work he seeks to expunge and edit out all traces of his personal presence and commitment.

Those, like myself, however, who reject such objectivism – and who believe that knowledge necessarily entails personal presence and commitment – wish to signal our presence in our work, to manifest and expose our projects and personal commitments and to make these fully obvious to all. In speaking, we try to alert others to the fact that our work must be understood as the outcome of a personal presence and commitment, no matter how else it is to be understood and no matter what else it is, lest we contribute to the deception and false consciousness of these others.

Objectivism, however, regards such a standpoint as a *submission* to a merely subjective and personal self whose only consequence, presumably, must be to distort knowledge of social worlds. Moreover, since the repression and denial of self is inevitably painful and hurtful to the denier, even though he is doing this on behalf of higher values, he feels a certain readiness to betray his own objectivistic commitment, and therefore a double distaste for those who, in rejecting objectivism openly, do not pay the costs that he has inflicted upon himself, and he punishes their work by denouncing it as solipsism, or mere 'attitudes', etc.

Touraine's and Zeitlin's standpoint is objectivistic, which is to say: *it is an ideology about 'objectivity'* that expresses a false consciousness. This is not to claim that they are mere empiricists, for doubtless they would acknowledge that 'theory plays a role in understanding the world'. But 'theory' too, can be implicated in objectivism. For before theory can 'play a role', theorists have to speak and enact it: which is to say theorists must make a *personal commitment* to the theory and to the goals on behalf of which they enact it. Indeed, the sense in which we can assume that theory is to be 'applied' to the understanding of some problems obscures the fact that the situation is not one in which there is, on the one side, theory, and, on the other, some 'thing' to which it is applied. In *both* cases what we are dealing with are different kinds of personally committed enactments: to say theory is 'applied' only means that a theory *held* by some theorists is being 'applied' by him to what he, the theorist, *defines* as relevant 'data', or to *his experience* of the social world, his *lebenswelt*.

Having failed in these crucial respects, neither Zeitlin nor Touraine understands that what is at issue is precisely: the nature, the meaning, the character of 'science', and therefore of social science itself. To counterpose a taken-for-granted 'social science' (or 'sociology') to 'mere ideology' is to obscure this elemental question and is thus to provide unreflective support to the conventional conception of the nature of a sociology. Which is to say, it provides support for the 'normal' sociology that exists.

Just as their position premises an unreflective, taken-for-granted conception of sociology and social science so, too, does their position correspondingly operate with an unreflective, taken-for-granted conception of *ideology*. They tacitly premise that there is only one, rather than several different conceptions of ideology, and there is only one critique rather than several different critiques of ideology. Having failed to clarify the alternative meanings of science, on the one hand, and of ideology, on the other, it is then most dubious for them to wring their hands in anguish about my supposed confusion of social science with ideology.

A reader of the reviews by Zeitlin and Touraine would never have guessed that I explicitly and forcefully rejected the views on which they insinuate I 'verge'. Far from verging on 'sociological solipsism', I actually oppose it. Let me quote from *The Coming Crisis*:

That the ideological implications and social consequences of an intellectual system do *not* determine its validity, for theory does indeed have a measure of autonomy, is *not* in the least denied here. Certainly the cognitive validity of an intellectual system *cannot* and should *not* be judged by its ideological implications or its social consequences. But it does not follow from this that an intellectual system should be (or, for that matter, ever is) judged only in terms of its cognitive validity, its truth or falsity. . . .[9]

. . . a critique of the ideology of professional autonomy, as of liberalism, must recognize that it does serve as a brake upon the sociologist's full assimilation into his society . . . yet such a critique does not make the most fair case if it merely affirms that autonomy is myth . . . rather the problem is that autonomy is too often given only ritualistic lip service by successful men comfortable within the *status quo,* and frequently is not pursued even to its achievable potentialities . . .[10]

. . . The object of a critique of the ideology of autonomy, then, is *not* to unmask the sociologist but, by confronting him with the frailty and ambiguity of his own professions, to stir his self-awareness. Its object is not to discredit his efforts at autonomy but to enable these to be realized more fully by heightening awareness of the social forces that, surrounding and penetrating the sociologist, subvert his own ideals.[11]
[Italics added. A.W.G.]

In view of unambiguous statements such as the above, it is wrong to claim or insinuate that I believe that sociology is only ideology and that I propose a return to personal tastes and opinions.

It is certainly true that *The Coming Crisis* does indeed deal critically with the conservative political ideology sedimented in various sociological theories, most especially Talcott Parsons'. Paradoxically, Zeitlin actually complains that I did not make a *fuller* critique of the ideology of social sciences *other* than sociology, while, at the same time, also complaining that my critique of sociology is one in which ideologies 'swallow up and absorb all valid knowledge of the objective world'. This is a contradiction. For would not the extension of my critique from sociology to all other social sciences have had the result of communicating an even greater sense of the potency of ideology in social theory? For Zeitlin, then, I am damned if I do disclose ideology in sociology, and damned if I do not expose the ideology in economics, history and political science.

Certainly I agree that an ideological analysis of other social sciences is most desirable. For my own part, however, I must confess to a certain personal scholarly inadequacy, and leave this task to others. I am simply not an Aristotle in total command of all social sciences and am not in a position, critically and responsibly, to evaluate history, economics and political science as well as sociology. I tried to write about and to limit myself to what I knew – to what I had studied and experienced – and I well know how very limited that is. Indeed, I said so in *The Coming Crisis*: 'Laborious though this effort will doubtless seem at times, let me repeat that I view it only as a very partial contribution to a critique of American sociology.'[12] It is precisely because I do not believe that sociology is only ideology that I did not attempt to pass judgement on four different scholarly disciplines in the course of a single book, let alone, as Zeitlin does, in the space of a single book review.

One of the more ironic parts of all this is that Maurice Zeitlin (Zeitlin of all people!) should defend sociology (sociology of all disciplines!) from the danger of being reduced to an ideology. This is ironic because it is sociology whose own efforts to ape the natural sciences have produced only the most pathetic results and whose own senior statesmen at times say as much. Thus even E. A. Shils, Talcott Parsons' longtime collaborator, candidly admits that

> Most of sociology is not scientific in the sense in which the term is used in English-speaking countries. It contains little of importance that is rigorously demonstrated by commonly accepted procedures dealing with relatively reproducible observations.[13]

But if sociology is not scientific in the sense commonly accepted by sociologists, then it is not Gouldner but sociology's own history that has failed to erect a sturdy barrier between sociology as science and sociology as ideology.

What then are Zeitlin and Touraine actually defending? In Touraine's case, it seems that all that is being defended is the possibility of a *future* sociology. Touraine says as much, once more spreading the glad tidings that sociology is again about to be born or reborn: 'The current crisis of sociology is really the birth of sociology.'[14] In the past, Establishment sociology defended its low-level achievements by heartrending stories about the vulnerable youth of their discipline. Now Touraine defends sociology on even more radical grounds. He declares that it has yet to be born, that it does not yet really exist, and has in fact all this while only been in a state of gestation. That being so, how could a non-existent sociology have a scientific component that is threatened with reduction to mere ideology?

As for Zeitlin, what is it that he is defending from my presumably insidious tendencies to ideologize? One can be sure that the one thing he is *not* defending is sociology. Zeitlin tells us at once that he does not believe that there can be 'such a thing as a "general theory" distinctive to sociology'.[15] (He does not clarify in what sense a sociology can exist *without* such a distinctive 'general theory'.) Then he adds, more generally: 'A substantive social theory that can be contained by departmental boundaries is worth little. . . .'[16] Note that this last statement does not simply deny the possibility of a general theory distinctive of sociology: it is an omnibus condemnation of *any* distinctively sociological theory and hence of a distinctive sociological perspective.

Leaving aside the countless questions that this attitude immediately suggests (such as, *what* is to be combined when social analysis seeks to overcome reified academic specializations and to make a holistic analysis of the social totality?), it is plain that it is not sociology as such that Zeitlin is defending from ideology. For it is clear that he denies the sheer existence of sociology as a distinctive discipline. What, then, is Zeitlin defending against sociological 'solipsism'?

Zeitlin replies plainly enough when he complains that I have ignored 'the emerging corpus of writing by young radical and Marxian scholars . . .' (much of whose work was published only after I had finished writing *The Coming Crisis*). It turns out, then, that the true science that Zeitlin is trying to protect from being tarred with ideology is Marxism, neo-Marxism, or some other 'radical' theory that 'compels us to stand outside our own society . . .'[17] I think these things very worth defending, but the question is *how*. Zeitlin's object is to protect *Marxism* (and not academic sociology) from an ideology-critique. My impression is that Zeitlin wants to defend Marxism by denying that Marxism lacks ideological dimensions, rather than by exploring what these might be. My impression is that Zeitlin actually believes that Marxism is devoid of a false consciousness, while I would want to find out what that was.

My impression – to sum it up briefly – is that Zeitlin's defence of a social science, his autistic need to defend it from non-existent attacks as mere ideology, actually derive from his anxieties about Marxism: it derives from his desire to protect an image of Marxism as a true, ideology-free, social science. His entire position, then, seems in general to be based upon an unreflective conception of what social science is, and in particular on a conception of Marxism that verges on positivism.

Zeitlin, after all, is the scholar who went to Cuba to study the Revolution, questionnaires in hand. His positivistic proclivities further manifest themselves in his complaint that I spent too much time studying *theory* and not enough time studying specific pieces of *concrete research*.

Thus he remarks, Gouldner 'neglects highly "important" standpoints embedded in empirical social research in sociology, and not merely in what is self-defined as "theory" '.[18] I suggest that Zeitlin tacitly conceives of a true, scientific, ideology-transcending social science, as: positivistic Marxism brought 'up to date' with survey research. This is his standard of ideology-free, true science. But this, it should hardly need saying, is just another unreflective version of Marxism. It is certainly not the only reading of Marx that can be made. If Zeitlin rejects a bureaucratized, academic social science, he does so, it seems, only so that he can support a technocratic conception of *Marxism*, a version of Marxism similar to Louis Althusser's structuralistic and bureaucratically congenial Marxism, rather than the more Hegelian Marxism so brilliantly exemplified by Georg Lukács in his *History and Class Consciousness*.

Let me end this section as I began, readily acknowledging that Zeitlin and Touraine have raised important problems.

Certainly, Zeitlin does so when he remarks that in *The Coming Crisis* 'Gouldner neglects the central problem of how we *do*, in fact, separate the *ideological* from the *truth* content in our theories of the world.'[19] This is a criticism of my work he shares with Touraine.

Both are correct if by this they mean that I had little to say about epistemological questions in *The Coming Crisis*. It is notable, however, that Zeitlin, in an unfortunately positivistic manner, does not really see that the issue that he has raised is an *epistemological* one. Rather, Zeitlin sees the problem in its primarily positivistic-empirical dimensions, saying that the central problem is *not* how we can rationally *justify* a distinction between ideology and truth, but how 'we do, in fact' distinguish the two. In other words, Zeitlin proposes an empirical study of how we customarily separate truth from ideology. But even if this could tell us how this is done, it cannot tell us whether it is being done *rightly*. In short, it does not really confront the central problem, namely, how to justify and how to understand such a distinction. After all, there are obviously different ways, some acceptable and some not, in which different persons make a distinction between truth and ideology. How can we determine which ways are acceptable and which ways are not, without epistemological analysis? Positivists commonly treat what men 'do' as the standard; which is exactly why positivism is a conservative standpoint, accommodating as it must to what 'is'.

Let me repeat: *The Coming Crisis* does indeed neglect epistemological problems. In working on *The Coming Crisis* I had been primarily concerned to clarify my mind about *onto-logical* issues and, to do so, I rather deliberately bracketed epistemological questions. But I have continued to work on epistemological problems and hope in time to have something of relevance to say about them. But until I can ask more than 'how we do, in fact' separate truth from ideology, I propose to keep my silence about epistemological problems.

On how the Coming Crisis is 'Positive'

Let me now return to the first question about the problem and need for a 'positive' theoretical position. What would a positive position look like if it were to be a consistent outgrowth of my own assumptions? Consider the central assumptions of *The Coming Crisis*. These, after all, insist on the special importance of the theorist's 'infrastructure' – his domain assumptions, sentiments and the things he personally defines as 'real' – and how it shapes his theoretical performances and theoretical products. The basic emphasis is on the manner in which such an infrastructure mediates between the theorist and the larger society and provides the human grounding out of which social theory grows. Theory, I argue, changes with changes in such an infrastructure.

From this standpoint, then, the really vital thing is not the voluntaristic, merely wilful, assertion of an alternative theory or a 'positive' position. This would be a kind of 'methodological utopianism'. Rather, the decisive thing is to 'establish' the human conditions – the infrastructure – that can nurture various intellectual alternatives, new technical paradigms, new middle-range theories, or new epistemologies. 'Establish' here means a critically justified understanding of the kind of infrastructure it would be *preferable* to have; it also means to put this understanding into *practice* by building it into new communities and institutions. (Certainly, however, there is no implication that this is a two-step activity, in which the two steps are separated, so that there is first understanding and only later praxis.) The last chapter of *The Coming Crisis*, 'Toward a Reflexive Sociology', is just such an effort. It attempts to sketch out certain aspects of the social structure, the kinds of role relations and the kind of moral code that might provide an infrastructure superior to that which now exists and which could provide the social basis for the natural emergence of various new theories.

Fundamental to my entire position concerning the question of a positive alternative are three things: (1) my rejection of the assumption that it is a moral imperative to be 'positive' and to provide 'solutions' as a kind of ransom that one pays for the right to criticize; (2) my resistance to Methodological Utopianism and (3) my belief that the important thing is not only the literary stipulation of new social theories but, rather, the creation of new *communities* – such as the Santa Barbara collective – for social theorists. (For a preliminary statement of my position on this see Chapter 3.)

In my view, the essential reflexivity of sociology and social theory is based upon the fact that its first task, prerequisite to all else, is to establish – in the double sense of to *know* and to *institute* – the human and social conditions requisite for the control and exposure of 'false consciousness', for the control of the irrational and ideological components of discourse. Put positively, an emancipatory sociology's first task is to establish the social and human conditions required to *sustain* rational discourse about social worlds: *logos*. I regard this as the *minimal* task, not the full, long-range programme.

This task has two sides: on the one hand, there is a need to *create* tension, conflict, criticism and struggle against conventional definitions of social reality, to extricate oneself from them, and to undermine their existential foundations by struggling against the social conditions and institutions that sustain them. In other words, there is a need to create a rift in the social world, to separate ourselves from the dominant definitions of social reality, and to struggle against the institutions that maintain them. (There is also a need to protect ourselves against their inevitable backlash.) This is the oppositional, polemical, critical, isolating and combative side of the process.

On the other side, however, there is a constructive process in which, within whatever liberated social space is carved out, we begin at once to design and create new communities that support rational discourse in sociology and social theory. As Jürgen Habermas has stressed, the most elemental social condition of rational discourse is to eliminate all use of force and violence. Where force and violence remain possible an inescapable pressure is set up in which, openly and covertly, crudely and subtly, a thousand inducements to false consciousness are set in motion.

I will return to the question of the general importance of community for social theory. For the moment, however, I want simply to stress the sheer primordiality of establishing a community and the priority of a theoretical collectivity for all efforts at rational theorizing. Rational theorizing means above all rational *discourse* in theory; it means dialectic and dialogue among committed men joined in a common-language-speaking community. This is the indispensable requisite for the control of false consciousness and for the ongoing critical development of social theory. The establishment of such theoretical collectives is far more important to the development of social theory and sociology than all the technical instruments and rules, all the books and seminars on research methods and techniques, put together. These technicalities are trivial in comparison to the need to establish theoretical collectives.

My assumptions here, then, come down to this: (1) the central problem facing all sociologies today, both academic and Marxist, is the interrelation between theory and *praxis*, and (2) that one can best enter this circle by community-creating efforts. In short, my assumption is that it is organization, social organization, that today provides the key mediation between social theory and social praxis. It is in *this* sense that what sociology needs today is not so much its first Newton and another Karl Marx but, rather, a V. I. Lenin who can formulate its organizational requirements. For neither theory nor praxis is possible without social organization.

At any rate, perhaps enough has been said to make clear why those who criticized *The Coming Crisis* for not having offered a 'positive' alternative may have been led to this judgement simply because they were looking for it in the wrong place. They were not considering the question of how social organization must mediate between theory and praxis, and how it is necessary to establish a group structure necessary for rational discourse in social theory.

It is precisely on this level that social theory attains its fullest reflexivity: social theory must determine, evaluate, critique the conditions that enable it to organize itself; in *enacting* these conditions it tests and appraises the worth of the theory it has established. In establishing and testing these conditions for itself social theory also acts universalistically, on behalf of the rest of the world. For the quest for rational discourse is not a sectarian need of social theorists alone but a world need. The theorist's collective then becomes a strategic, theory-generating, theory-consolidating, theory-critiquing social matrix.

To hold that the first task of sociology is to establish – in theory and in practice – the conditions of its own existence as a practical rational discourse, and that these conditions are of universalistic relevance, implies that knowledge about society cannot be established without *re-creating at once* a part of society, and that what we learn about re-creating that one part of society has implications for all of society. Once this is seen, then it becomes transparently clear that *we cannot and should not contrast a criticism of sociology invidiously to a criticism of society, or separate the two tasks.*

There are certain dilemmas here, however, for we cannot equate the common sense – or consensus – of a community with truth; for consensus must be arrived at in *certain* ways if it is to be regarded as true; most especially it must be tested dialectically as the condition of its acceptance. If, on the one hand, we cannot believe something to be true simply because it is the consensus of a group, neither can we believe something to be true if we alone believe it and have failed in our efforts to win the consensus of our group. Community is *not* a sufficient condition of truth, but it is assuredly a *necessary* one. Only when this community has a special structure and culture, however, can its consensus be trusted to embody truth. Among the elements of its culture there must be the use of the dialectic, which is to say, a tensionful form of social interaction in which conformity to the rules of logic comprise some of the norms of social interaction; where conformity to these rules of discussion alone constitute one basis for esteem and self-esteem; where all other things that a person is or has, or other statuses he occupies, are formally excluded from the judgement of the *worth* and *truth* of his speech, even as it is fully recognized that they are continuously and *consequentially* present in the speaker and his speech.

Quite apart from the language used, and certainly apart from all matters of technique and instrumentation, a vital requisite of the theoretical collective within which rational discourse is possible, is the commitment of its members to truth and the high value they assign to it. There must be a commitment to true speaking, for without this there can be no believable consensus, and without this there can be no truth established.

Without commitment to truth there can be no reliance upon claimed reports about the world or the self, and no way of avoiding the cheat. Minimally, this means that group members must have or cultivate certain kinds of motives and characters – e.g., non-dogmatic, non-authoritarian, open. It means that all social arrangements, cultural commitments, institutions, within the group and in the larger society, that inhibit true speaking and rational discourse must be opposed, exposed, criticized and struggled against.

There is a fundamental paradox in the role of the community as the ground of knowledge. There can be no knowledge without community and without membership in a community of men speaking the same language. At the same time, however, community membership constitutes a security, if not an advantage, a source of gratifications such as incomes or jobs; and these give men a motive to retain their membership quite apart from the collective's or their own contribution to truth. In short, sheer membership in a community gives a man motives to lie, to become a 'rip-off', and to hang on as useless 'deadwood'. He will be tempted to tell the community what it wants to hear – or to maintain a tactful silence – so that he may retain membership in it, rather than risk ostracism or expulsion for telling it what it does not want to hear but which he may nonetheless believe. This, of course, is precisely the familiar dilemma of the Party intellectual, theorist or ideologue; but it is by no means peculiar to him alone. One finds much the same process of expulsion and ostracism employed in universities against those whose intellectual models are too far outside the average community member's tolerance of difference.

Truth must in the end be sifted by the contestful friction of minds within the community; in short, through the dialectic. In the end, the 'truth' must always prevail because only that is true which prevails in the contest of minds, and which survives criticism and efforts to falsify it. Only that is true which is judged by members of the theoretical community to have survived the baptism of criticism, and thus only those who have a capacity to bear conflict and tension have a calling for the theorist's office.

While dialectic seeks to protect the group's commitment to

knowledge, it is not the only way in which the commitment to knowledge is protected by a commitment to 'method'. In the last analysis, method is an explication and objectification of the procedures the group believes are required before any item of belief may properly be certified (by members of the group) as true. 'Method', therefore, creates obstacles to the yea-saying impulses of our own conviviality, mutual affection or dependence, our personal biasses and our movement loyalties or involvements. The essence of method is constraint, self-imposed constraint. Without it, it is unlikely that the individual can find his way to conclusions that will ever differ from those with which either he or his community began. At the same time, however, it must be stressed that the decision concerning the validity of any method, not to speak of the enforcement of its use, is entirely a decision of the community. The judgement that something is true is a judgement made by the common-language-speaking members of the community on the basis of their application of methods, which also depend upon the decision and consensus of the community. Knowledge, then, depends as much on community consensus concerning method, as on consensus concerning the particular belief held true.

While by no means eliminating the threat that community membership represents to truth-speaking, the conditions outlined above may, with others, help to curtail this threat. The organization of theoretical collectives on these nuclear principles is the strategic condition for the emergence, and for the support once emerged, of a new emancipatory sociology, and is *a* fundamental way in which organization mediates between social theory and social practice. For it is the special reflexive task of such a social theory to search for the conditions within its own special community, and within the *larger* society, that will inhibit false consciousness and foster rational discourse. This, then, bears most directly on the distinctive *nature* of the knowledge that the theory should aim at, and, in this, I concur largely with the Critical School in general and Jürgen Habermas in particular. In short, what is sought is truth as *practical* reason; practical because relevant to the understanding and transformation of our daily lives and the historically shaped society in which we live. We want to understand our social world and ourselves and others in it, so that we may change it in ways that enable us to understand it still better, to have fuller rational discourse in it, so that we may be better able to change it, and so on.

Man as Person: Man as Object

We want to change the world so that we can be more rational men. We want to strengthen our rationality so that we can act more effectively to build a world that protects rational men. There is then an irreducible and intrinsic value to the sheerly rational. But to insist that rational discourse is an *end* no less than a means, is *not* to say that it is our *only* end. The ultimate end of our social theory and social praxis is human fulfilment and liberation, and we certainly cannot conceive of this simply as a liberation of reason alone, for man is a good deal more than reason.

I assume that all men are capable of reason, and that through this they are capable of some understanding of themselves and other men. At the same time, however, men also participate in a variety of other conditions, they are moved by a variety of forces – biological, ecological, psychological and historical – which invisibly control their behaviour in the form of irrational, compulsive, or purely 'natural' forces or laws.

The manner in which these other forces mould men's behaviour is not always known to them, partly because they may have *motives* for not knowing them, and partly because they simply may not have ways of perceiving them, given the ordinary languages with which they relate to the world. In some part, men are capable of autonomy, capable of a full humanity in which they are 'persons' and the subjects of history. In another part, however, they are *dependent* objects, not essentially different from lesser animals or even inanimate objects which cannot be moved by an appeal to reason or by self-examination, or even led astray by symbolic manipulation. *Men thus simultaneously dwell in two worlds, they exist as both subject and object; as creatures of triumphant reason and of reason baffled; as linguistical creatures capable of a unique responsiveness to symbols of their own emission and as dumb creatures moved by pre-symbolic forces; whose behaviour is often patterned by invisible ecological scarcities, by bone structure, by hormones, by brawn and brain, and evolutionarily implanted imperatives.*

It is a function of the emancipatory social sciences to liberate man's reason from any force, in or out of himself, symbolic or not, in the psyche and in the society, that cripples and confuses reason. It is the special function of these social sciences continuously to dissolve man's opaqueness to himself; to help him understand those forces that act upon him that he ordinarily finds unintelligible; and to help him transform these natural forces that use him as an object into humanly controllable forces under his control. There are, then, certain forces that act upon men symbolically and through their understanding. There are, however, other forces, like blind obsessions, hunger, hormones, anxiety, scarcities, bombs dropped, guns used, available energy supplies, disease and ill health, all of which may have their patterning effect upon men, without a word being spoken, heard or understood.

Different men, men from different cultures, doubtless respond differently to a toothache, to hunger or to a bullet wound. But a bullet wound slows everyone down. All will work somewhat less efficiently, and attend somewhat less sensitively to others when they are in pain; and when pain grows great, we retain only the faintest hold on our membership in society. At some point the sheer humanity of all men can be broken by nature's torture and our 'persons' may be engulfed by the vulnerabilities of our dumb objectness. Men then are exposed to a very complex, 'exquisite' kind of suffering, the suffering to which the civilized and human are exposed; but we are also capable of the suffering of dumb animals. Being objects, we can literally be broken.

A humane sociology seeks to liberate men from *both* forms of suffering and from the suffering as such, not simply from the lack of 'fulfilment' of man's unique potentialities as a creature of reason; for our problems are not simply rooted in the failure of understanding. Man's peasant anguish has at least as vital a claim on a humane sociology as his urbane *angst*. These are the most elemental value commitments of an emancipatory sociology. To fulfil them, it must turn in two different directions simultaneously:

On the one hand, sociology requires and has ready to hand a developing tradition of hermeneutics whose function it is to engage men's understanding, to ask for and interpret the *meaning* of events, and to mediate between the world and man in his quest for meaning. Essentially emerging in the seventeenth-century interpretation of sacred texts, partly rooted in the philologists' experience in interpreting alien languages, and in the interpretation of human objectifications such as art, a more generalized hermeneutics emerges in association with the *Geisteswissenschaften* (the human disciplines) and as its methodology, until its most recent and most generalized development in the phenomenologically concerned hermeneutics of Hans Georg Gadamer's *Wahrheit und Methode*. For those who must have science, the interpretations of an hermeneutics will not suffice. But a cultivated and disciplined hermeneutics that can fortify and deepen men's practical reason already exists, while it is very questionable whether a sociology exists in any serious sense as a 'science'.

The pursuit of hermeneutic understanding, however, cannot premise that men as we find them, with only their ordinary language and understanding, will be capable of understanding and liberating themselves. At decisive points, the ordinary language and understanding fails and must be transcended. It is essentially the task of social theory, and the social sciences more generally, to create new and 'extraordinary' languages, to help men learn to speak them; to mediate between the deficient understandings of ordinary language and the different and liberating perspectives of the extraordinary languages of social theory.

So long as man participates in the being of objects and has an opaque objectness, so long does he participate in a world of nature subject to characterization, *en principe*, by natural laws. From this perspective there is a place for a positivistic study of men as natural objects subject to natural laws. It is the aim of a liberative social science to diminish man's objectness, to liberate his reason and understanding from diminution by it, and thus to limit man's control by natural laws. Man's subjection to natural law is continually dwindling, but this is an asymptotic development that will never be finally consummated. There is an irreducible core where man remains sunk in objectness, where he is, in effect, at one with all the world.

What we think of this depends in part on how prideful we are of man and how contemptuous we are of the rest of the cosmos. It is only those who will settle for nothing less than being the absolute lords of the cosmos who hold objectness in secret contempt. But objectness is the ground of our being even if not its culmination. To hold objectness in contempt is to hold our primordial parent-being in contempt. It is to be ashamed of a part of ourselves.

The liberation that a humane social theory should seek, then, is not the liberation of man's reason and understanding *alone*, but the proper treatment and enjoyment of his total embodied being as well, rather than nourishing a Platonic fantasy of escape from its confines. Whether man can respect the animal and object side of himself depends on his ability to respect other dumb objects and feel his kinship with them, too. It is only through man's union of dumb energies and rationality that man transforms the object world *more* than symbolically. In other words, through work and thought, which respects the alien objectivity of the world without seeking to dominate the cosmos.

Sociology as World-creating

I have repeatedly insisted that knowledge of society is not something simply found or 'discovered'. Rather it is something forged, constructed in the community of common-language-speaking men – from their experience, their labour, their talk, their reflection. It is the product of a speech community, of men whose speech is mutually intelligible because it is based on a shared experience that leads them to use and construe their language in the same manner. Indeed, their commitment to this common language and their capacity to employ it skilfully is what marks them as members – and in part entitles them to be members – of the community. No common language, no community, no truth.

Here we come upon a central misunderstanding concerning

the nature of a sociology and social theory. The conventional assumption of academic sociologists is that the aim of sociology is to discover and validate 'knowledge' about human relations, about social interaction, or about human groups; and, further, that the way to do this is through the use of a proper *methodology*, construed primarily in its cognitive character. The social world is often treated as a given, as an 'objective' 'thing' constituted in separation from the enterprise of social theory and sociology. The assumption is that this world is an *object* external to the social theorist, and that *knowing about* this world-apart is best achieved by visitations and forays out into it, and by slicing off and bringing back samples from it.

What I have suggested in *The Coming Crisis*, however, is that such a standpoint deeply misconstrues and, indeed, misdescribes, what sociology is doing. If one looks at what sociologists actually do – but do with a distorted, false consciousness – it may be seen they do not simply 'study' society but *conceptualize* and *order* it. That is why much of sociology, from its most elementary textbooks to the work of Talcott Parsons, consists of developing and arranging sets of *concepts*, rather than primarily establishing 'laws' or empirically verified propositions about the relations between 'things'.

To say that sociologists are in the business of creating concepts means that they are in the business of proposing and fashioning ways of looking at, thinking, and talking about – and hence contributing to the *very constitution* of – social objects and social worlds. They are not simply *studying* a social world-apart, but are contributing to the construction and destruction of social objects. To say social theorists are concept-creators means that they are not merely in the *knowledge*-creating business but, above all, in the *language*-reform and language-creating business. In other words, they are from the beginning involved in creating a new *culture*.

Sociology's conceptualizing drive expresses and embodies its effort to build at once a culture within which a deepened understanding of the larger social world may be built. In other words, sociology starts by creating a small social world in order to gain leverage on a larger one. The ultimate task of sociology, then, is achieved not in studying a given ordinary, everyday culture and community. Its task is, rather, the *creation* of an *extraordinary* new language, a new culture, and a new community, in part, by establishing sociology's own requisites in language, culture, and community. In a crippled and falsely conscious way, sociology is already a 'counter-culture' and parallel-culture. It can begin to overcome its flawed condition only by recognizing itself for what it really is and truly does, which is to say, as a world-*creating* effort. Sociology's *transcending* objective is not, and never has been, to create a 'science'. This was at first an aim subsidiary to its true task, which is to create a new culture and a new community, and without which a new science of man is impossible. In time, however, the subsidiary aim replaced the true task and sociologists became ritualistically committed to knowledge for its own sake alone, and the true-community-creating task of sociology was repressed.

Sociology aims, then, not simply to conduct 'empirical researches' but also to create a new language and thus intrinsically a new community. Historically speaking, the classical Positivism of the nineteenth century, which gives rise to one kind of sociology, always assumed that its *ultimate* task was to bind the social cleavage that gaped wide in post-revolutionary France, to provide a new basis of consensus, and to discover – through the use of a science that would provide 'positive' results – a set of beliefs in which all men might concur and thereby restore community. The *Geisteswissenschaften* that emerged in Germany, and in particular its hermeneutic methodology, had a similar transcendental aim of mediating among diverging historical traditions. Both sociologies, however different in other respects, conceived of 'knowledge' about social worlds, and the social disciplines that would produce it, as aiming at the *reconstruction* of society. Where they lacked clarity, however, was in the understanding that sociology, in its turn, had its own organizational and community requisites which it must establish at once as the pre-condition of its own knowing.

Sociology and the Movement

This brings us to the problem of the relationship between the sociologist and the 'Movement', sociology and socialism, the

role of the radical intellectual, or, most generally, the theory /
praxis problem. It is understood that this vital problem deserves
far more analysis than I can bring to it here.

As I understand Flacks' position on this, he sees 'sociology'
as contributing to the Movement, and especially to socialism,
in two ways: first, by providing the Movement with various
forms of *information*, and by doing (or evaluating) various
researches of possible use to it. Secondly, he also sees sociology
as contributing to the Movement in quite another way, by
fostering its awareness of what I had called 'bad news'; in other
words by strengthening its ability to forgo rationalization and
to be realistic. These are, I suggest, two profoundly different
ways in which sociology can contribute to the Movement. In
the first case, the sociologist is in effect a kind of technician,
supplying the Movement with data useful for the realization of
goals that the Movement may take as given. In the second, the
sociologist, in helping strengthen the Movement's awareness of
its situation and its very goals, serves more nearly as a kind of
clinician.

I concur with Flacks that both are important. But I would
add that the former role as technician should be subordinate to
the latter role as clinician. The reason for this is that how information is appraised and used and the consequences of its
employment, depend importantly on the awareness and goals
of the people using it. Sociologists should under no conditions
become the market researchers of the Revolution, helping
Movement people or socialists realize any goals that they might
wish. Instead, I believe that sociologists should help the Movement and socialists only to the extent that they are judged as
contributing to *human emancipation* and to the extent that they
pursue this goal with *awareness* of the difficulties and dangers
of possible costs and unanticipated consequences. Without such
awareness there is an ever-present and real danger that the
Movement can degenerate into various forms of unfreedom and
neo-Stalinisms, and that the slogan 'power to the people' can
come to serve as a disguise for the power of a new élite.

Yet if, on the one hand, sociologists reject a role as mere
technicians, refusing to help the Movement realize any goals it
wishes, still, on the other hand, sociologists must not arrogate

to themselves the right to set goals for the movement, or to set themselves above the Movement as a new élite and, in effect, use their position as a way of acquiring power for themselves.

Either of these two tactics, that of the dependent technician passively 'obeying orders' or of the arrogant élite trying to garner power and to give orders, either of these tactics is pathological. Both pathologies must be avoided and efforts should be bent to establish Movement relations with sociology in ways that avoid them for the beginning. But how?

Here we can see exactly why the question of a Reflexive sociology is not an academic question but a practical and urgent question. Here we can clearly see why the strengthening of the sociologists' *self-awareness* is not a matter of navel-gazing self-indulgence or an escape from the world. For there will be no avoidance of these pathologies unless the sociologist can achieve some insight into and control over his own false consciousnesses. What seems at first a narcissistic 'navel-gazing' turns out, I submit, to be an indispensable and necessary condition for a politically effective and healthy involvement of sociology. But more on this question later.

Fundamental to Flacks' conception of the relation between sociology and the Movement is a tacit and deeply questionable conception of sociology. Flacks does not seem to think that there is anything intrinsically wrong with sociology as it is. He certainly acknowledges that sociology now is politically conservative, but he assumes that this ideological character of sociology can be shed like a snake sheds its old skin and dons a new one over the same old flesh and bones. In other words, Flacks assumes that sociology's political conservativism is not intrinsic to its intellectual character. Flacks assumes that sociology's conservative ideology is extrinsic to it, an accidental aspect of its existence in a capitalist society, but not intrinsic to its essence. Flacks thus apparently believes that one can make sociology work for the Movement more or less as it already works for the Welfare–Warfare State, but now sociology will simply have a new master, or a new goal. Presumably this is just a question of the old, essentially unchanged sociology being harnessed to different, more humane goals. In other words, survey research is survey research, but instead of using it to learn how to accommodate the poor to their lot, one now 'turns the guns the other way around' and uses it to learn how to win people to socialism. Thus while Flacks is sensitive to a need to have sociology be something more than market research for the Movement, I do not think he yet sees what would be necessary for this.

Flacks' conception of the relation between sociology and the Movement is based upon a supposition or hope that sociology is really at bottom value-free or neutral and that it can be made useful for different goals, whether emancipation or domination. But an objectivistic sociology that seeks to establish natural laws and which views men as objects in exactly the same way as a natural science does, already rests upon a thingified conception of man that is inherently antithetical to the goal of human emancipation. What is also needed is an understanding of how men do indeed act in countless ways to reproduce and maintain the very 'system' that blocks their own liberation, and how this system is not only some alienated thing apart from and rising above them, but is also rooted in their own daily doings, myriad mundane enactments, countless tiny comings and goings. What is needed is a sociology that will do more than record what is, but which will also confront what is with critique. What is needed is something more than a sociology that will provide an abstracted perspective of the 'sociological' side of society, but a holistic social science that allows a view of the historically situated concrete society as a totality – in its economic, political, linguistic, psychodynamic, no less than its sociological 'sides'. I do not believe that normal sociology as we know it now can be the foundation of such an effort or that the task is simply to 'apply' it to new and higher goals, any more than I believe that a flight to Marxism is the answer.

One vital reason why sociology cannot simply be harnessed unchanged to new liberative goals is that it is profoundly lacking in reflectiveness. Normal sociology inherently embodies the very kind of mindless activism, a drive for control and power, and a narrow stress upon the instrumental and useful, which are fundamentally antithetical to the very goals of an emancipatory sociology. When the normal sociologist encounters a problem his first impulse is to put on his hat, shoes, and coat, and to leave at once, to go somewhere, anywhere, as long as it is somewhere else, to go into the 'field', and to probe and prod the 'out there'.

The normal sociologist's deepest dogma is fundamentally *externalizing*. Interested in something, he immediately mounts a 'research' and, in precisely that invidious sense, he 'commits' a social science. Obviously, what he should do first, and do with careful thoroughness, is to *think* about the thing, and to talk with colleagues and comrades. Higher and prior to research, there is *reflection*. The sociologist should first conduct a dialogue with himself and with others to see what he already knows/ believes about the matter at issue and to evaluate critically the results this produces.

This hardly seems worth saying, some will say, because this is obviously what was always intended by those who long stressed the importance of the theoretical dimension in the proposed marriage between theory and research. My own impression, however, is that more often than not, that is not done even by those respectful of the claims of sociological theory'. This is so because of the limited and technical conception of theory used by most sociologists. Specifically: a sociological 'theory' is believed to be problematic and worth thinking about only in its specifically *sociological* character. In a theory about 'anomie', for instance, the sociologist might think about a few of the 'key' terms – for instance, 'anomie', 'ritualism', 'innovation', etc. Usually, however, he will pass over and say little about other terms that he also uses, for instance, 'social', or 'cultural'; he will say still less (or nothing) about words like 'structure', or 'process'. And there is absolutely no case on record in the history of sociology in which a sociologist is known to have systematically pondered the meaning of 'is'.

All these are simply not 'his job', he says. There is, of course, a sense in which he must take some things as 'given', otherwise he will never get on with the special interests that he has. After all, the sociologist will tell you, he is not a philosopher, almost as if he believed that ignorance of philosophy was the beginning of sociological wisdom. Our central point is, however, that the way the sociologist gets on with his work, the quality of the results he produces, often reveals the unreflective haste with which he has gotten on with his job.

It reveals something else, too. It reveals his conception of the *nature* of an 'investigation'. The sociologist tacitly assumes that it is the task of his investigation to produce something like a 'product'. A product being something separable from the *process* preceding it and having utility, worth, and meaning apart from it. Driving hard for the production of a demonstrable, separable product that has meaning and value apart from the prior process from which it derived, it is inevitable that this process becomes devalued. But this 'process' is nothing else than *rational discourse* itself, and the focus on a separable intellectual product must inevitably lead to the degradation of rational discourse. It is in a utilitarian culture, where science is viewed primarily as a source of utilities to revolutionaries and reactionaries alike – particularly, of power and control – that it comes to assume a character as a technology whose value is in its usable product.

The sociologist's very conception of the 'theoretical' is crippled fundamentally by the division of labour he accepts. It is distorted by his conception of himself as a technical specialist or 'professional' who has no responsibility except for a very narrow band of his activities, whether these are conceived as his 'technical' task or as the 'product' it produces. Which is why it is *not* correct to say that those who have advocated the 'marriage' of theory and practice have long engaged in the kind of reflection called for here.

In effect, the concern for 'theory' and the commitment to 'theory' is paradoxically a retreat from the important thing: *thought*. What we have been talking about, then, is *shallowness*. Shallowness is the belief that one can practise an intellectual discipline such as sociology without practising philosophy. Shallowness is the assumption that it is possible to do serious work without serious thought. Shallowness is the idea that technique suffices. Like others, I have been guilty of shallowness.

It may be objected, however, that sociology has not entirely forsaken philosophy. Look, we will be told, at its 'methodology' and methodologists. What other scientific discipline has methodologists, it may be asked. True, there is no other, except perhaps psychology. But methodology is only the bad conscience of sociology. It is a token concession to thought. It is the attempt to provide for reflexivity, self-awareness, by the creation of a specialized discipline; and that is like attempting to provide for sanity in a madhouse by declaring the hours between 11.30 a.m. and noon to be the 'sane time'.

The problem with sociology is the very nature of its specialization, which inevitably leads to shallowness. By establishing methodology, sociology hoped to overcome the limitations born of a crippling specialization by further intensifying it and by declaring that it is the responsibility of this specialization to do the serious thinking. Still, a bad conscience is a sign of hope; sociology may yet prove vulnerable to philosophy. But lately there has been talk of doing away with methodology in sociology.

At any rate, it should be clear that a shallow, philosophically unreflective sociology cannot be successfully harnessed to the goal of helping men rid themselves of their false consciousness and emancipating themselves.

Another major consideration here is that I do not believe that the important thing is to bring sociology as such, as a distinct and separate intellectual discipline, into any relationship with the Movement or with socialism. Indeed, and as a corollary, I do not think that collectives of *sociologists*, of specialists in *sociology alone*, should be organized. What are needed, I believe, are collectives composed of people experienced in different and various technical specialities. Here we see another side and another basic reason for the collectives of 'social theorists' discussed earlier.

Practical reason in the service of human emancipation cannot rest on sociology, anthropology, economics, or political science alone, or on any one intellectual specialization now academically established. An understanding of the concrete social *totality*, which is what we require, cannot derive from such disconnected specializations. Moreover, it is impossible for any one person today to combine all of these 'behavioural' or social sciences within himself. Yet to return to an earlier, unreconstructed Marxism that does not incorporate the reworked and re-analysed accomplishments of the various social sciences in the last half century is a form of sectarian fundamentalism.

Aside from the problem of combining the technical social sciences there are questions of history and of historical knowledge. And then there is linguistics. To make matters worse, the understanding of the social totality sought here is obviously not intended to proceed positivistically, with concern only for the isolated facts, the data, the specialized empirical researches. What is also needed is a *philosophical* no less than an historical and empirical perspective. What is also needed is the conceptualizing sensitivities of the philosophically 'musical', not to speak of their viable tradition of logic, epistemology, ontology, and of the philosopher's special horizon which knows that it is not a separable end-product that alone counts but the entire texture of the discussion, for rationality dwells in that discussion and not in any one of its products. Theoretical analysis of the social totality, then, requires the integration of the various 'empirical' disciplines under the aegis of philosophy, of history, of linguistics, and hermeneutics. Brought together, not with a view to superseding any one of these as separate disciplines, not to create a new 'specialization' that will transcend them, but brought together within the framework of a concern for the concrete social totality, with an ultimate interest in human emancipation approached on the level of *practical reason*. The aim then is to *understand* our concrete social totality, not to create new laws or theories of social science. The aim is to 'apply' *critically* those 'empirical' specializations that have already been developed, this 'critical' application deriving from their subordination within an overarching framework of: historicality, linguisticality, hermeneutics, and philosophy.

There is only one 'subject' within which this intellectual enterprise can be housed and only one that can command the variety of scholarship envisaged; that 'subject' of course is an organization, the organized theoretical community, and not the individual person. A newly organized intellectual community, a new theoretical collectivity, becomes the subject and dwelling place for the integrated understanding of the concrete social totality.

The integration sought is not one in which there is produced, say, a single volume, with one chapter on the economics of the totality, and another on its politics, its sociology, its history, and so on. The significant expression of the collectivities' unity is not in such editorial ritualism but, rather, develops within each of the member specialists who is transformed by his dialogue with the others. The work that he does is then no longer done as it had been; it is no longer that of the traditionally isolated and intellectually narrow specialist.

The 'plan' here, then, is quite different from the usually insipid multi-disciplinary projects in the 'behavioural' sciences. For one thing, what is premised is a group of men who have come together not to pursue careers, but to foster rational discourse aimed at understanding their society as a totality. It is not bits and pieces of knowledge or of theory that are sought but the cultivation of a *practical reason* that contributes to the emancipation of man.

The men coming together are not technicians hierarchically linked in a bureaucratic chain of command, with each working in isolation at his own specialized bit of the research. They are, rather, scholars, in open and intense contact with others in his collective, each working on problems of his own choosing and as he pleases, but within the common commitment to understand the concrete totality of modern society. What is envisaged is an ongoing group, not one brought together for the conduct of a single 'study', but maintaining its unity by reason of its shared critical position toward the specialized disciplines, by a common philosophical, linguistic, historical, and hermeneutic method and liberative conception of its mission. Its maintenance of itself as a community and the achievement of its liberative mission, not the conduct of a single study, are its primary tasks. Here, then, is a project, a plan, a design for a 'community' of scholars organizationally consistent with George Lukács' call for the study of the social totality. (Actually, however, it is more than a 'plan', it is also a *description* of the Critical School of Theory as it first developed in Frankfurt. By tracing out the *organizational* implications of Lukács' theory we have been led to 're-invent' the Critical School. But this is another story and cannot be explored here.)

Theory and Ideology

It seems to me that theorists, intellectuals, or scholars who engage in *some* form of a political praxis that brings them into abrasive opposition to established society, and who attempt to change some part of the social world in an emancipating way, achieve a different and penetrating understanding of their social world. Other things being equal, they can, I believe, see certain things not seen by other scholars whose political praxis differs. The value of a radical political praxis, then, is not problematic here, so long as it is understood that this value is not simply the automatic 'response' to an action-stimulus but must be mediated by reflection upon that experience. As Flacks says also, '. . . activist modes of knowing are themselves limited.'

The problem, as I see it, is a two-sided one: of enhancing the value of theory for practice and, no less, of practice for theory. Flacks has spoken of the first side of the equation; let me now say a few things about the second. That is, under what conditions is political practice more intellectually and theoretically productive? This brings us to the problem of how the relations of radical theorists and of political groups ought to be arranged so as to ensure that the theorists' work will be deepened.

Jürgen Habermas has suggested that we might conceive of 'ideology' as arising when rational discourse breaks down and, indeed, that it is a way of concealing (and accommodating to) this breakdown. A prior question is also relevant: Why does rational discourse break down? Here we will mention only that this may happen when interests stifle discourse. That is, rational discourse is disrupted when it threatens the interests of the speakers, and it needs to be understood how very diverse these interests may be. Ideology, then, may be related to rational discourse on two levels: first as a kind of *fraudulent* discourse, a kind of counterfeit rationality that conceals the breakdown of rationality, on the one hand, and, also, as a concealment of the very forces that led to this breakdown, on the other. Ideology is thus both *discourse*-relevant and *interest*-relevant.

In contrast to ideology we counterpose 'theory'. Social

theory is rational discourse about the social world in that, on one level, it is deliberately seeking to advance certain interests in the world; it knows the interests that it advances, and provides an extraordinary language for rational discourse concerning these interests. On another level, social theory provides – as do Marxism or Freudianism – an *extraordinary* language with which men can become aware of the *ideological* usages of *ordinary* languages, and of the interests that these obscure and conceal. Theory, then, always has two sides: an establishing and affirming side, and an unmasking and polemical side. In one part, social theory seeks to say what is about the social world and, in another, it relates to ideologies about the social world, disclosing their meaning. A proper relation between theory and praxis, then, is not only one that advances praxis, but one that also advances theory as distinct from ideology.

The political praxis and involvement open to a social theorist will differ substantially with the kind of political groupings and organizations with which he is involved and to which he allows himself to be attached. In this connection, Paul Breines has made an interesting suggestion, namely, that *ideology* 'seeks to legitimate a particular organization, sect, or state power' and presumably, that social 'theory' does not. Here the point seems to be whether the intellectual's attachment has a *particularistic* character. In other words, it is one thing to be attached to, say, the interests of the working class and, quite another, to be committed to a particular political party or grouping which is always one among a number claiming to represent this larger interest.

We might formulate the issue by saying that there is a difference between 'partisanship' and 'commitment', partisanship being attachment to a *party* or 'part' of the larger interest, while commitment is an attachment to the larger interest itself and lends support only contingently to the various parties, depending on their policies and positions, rather than being an unqualified commitment to the organization itself.

The formulation of the *Communist Manifesto*, on the question of the attachment of Communists, is relevant to this issue: 'The Communists are distinguished from other working-class parties by this only: they point out and bring to the fore the common interests of the entire proletariat, independently of all nationality . . . they always and everywhere represent the interest of the Movement as a whole . . .' This suggests clearly that, in Marx's and Engels' view, the Communists were *not* a party like others, precisely in that theirs was not a partisan attachment to any organizational form, but only to the working class beyond it and to that class as a whole.

One of the things that happened in the history of the working class and of Communism is that this soon ceased to be the case. It had been true of Marx and Engels themselves, in part because their own organizational partisanship and party involvements were relatively peripheral. Marx and Engels never played a role as full-time *political* leaders of party organizations (successful or not), in the manner of say, Kautsky, Lenin or Mao. In large measure, they themselves were *not* primarily active leaders of mass working-class organizations or élite vanguards. For the most part, they served as intellectual 'consultants' to the emerging German Social Democrats and other working-class parties in Europe. Doubtless the only thing that today protects Marx and Engels from being denounced by certain misguided activists as hypocritical 'professors, intellectuals and idealists' whose political praxis is at variance with their theory, is that such activists are often unaware of how Marx and Engels actually spent most of their days and years, and, indeed, of how many of these were spent in the libraries of Europe, or at home, reading and writing, and for great stretches at a time, doing 'merely' theoretical work.

Today there are few or no Communists, in the sense intended by Marx and Engels, precisely because most of those who think themselves such are deeply implicated in political groups that demand primary loyalty to themselves rather than to the working class, and whose definition of what is in the interest of the working class as a whole turns out, conveniently and marvellously, never to be at variance with the interests of their own political party.

It is my general view that the theoretical and intellectual creativity of Marxists increase, other things equal, if they have made commitments rather than partisan attachments, if their primary commitment is to values rather than factions, to the broader Movement rather than to sectarian Party, if they have attached themselves to certain larger social strata, such as the working class or peasantry, to whose interests and whose 'Movement' they are primarily committed, and if they do not submit to the discipline of a particular party, sect or organization, *in arriving at a definition of what the common interest of this social stratum is*. Frequently, 'editorial boards' have served as *de facto* collectives of theorists that have insulated their members from party pressures. Parties or sects require loyalty primarily to themselves quite apart from their furtherance of a larger social stratum's interest and quite apart from the group's loyalty to rational discourse. And parties and sects will, with uncontrollable false consciousness invariably, vigorously, and bitterly deny that this is what they do.

It is precisely because a political organization has an interest that is invariably distinct and special, and is not reducible to the interests of the strata that it claims to represent, it is because it acquires a *special* interest even as it claims that it has no special interests, that such groups invariably foster an ideologization – a false consciousness – that undermines the rationality of discourse within them. It is this interest that generates ideology and undermines theory in political groups. Not that this is the only source of ideology in such political groups, but it is a necessary, inevitable and irreducible source of it. Which is another reason why theorists must have their own collectives.

In general, then, the creative development of theory is more likely to occur when the theorists are related primarily to a diffuse movement rather than to a sharply boundaried loyalty-demanding organization. This is exactly why the Critical School of Frankfurt was such a creative turning for Marxist theory. For, despite ambiguities in the political involvements of its members, the very existence of the Critical School itself served, if nothing else, as a counterbalance to whatever Leninist party attachments existed. That the Leninist tradition came to insist that 'its' intellectuals be tightly involved in the party structure and come under party discipline has been a major source of the ideologization of the Marxist movement, of the false consciousness of Marxist culture, and one of the fundamental organizational obstacles to the theoretical development of Marxism. Stalinism was only the grotesque intensification of the development that had preceded it.

One of the most common sources of false consciousness in all modern radical movements is the distortion of the *actual* relations they have with theorists and intellectuals. On the one hand, activists often tend to deprecate the worth of the intellectual's performance and the authenticity of his political practice, and they seek to expose his intellectual work to the ideologization of organizational interest. In other words, to what they call 'discipline'. While some activists may deprecate the importance of theoretical work – in contrast to really 'practical' contributions – at the same time they seek to bring theory under control, thus contradicting that very deprecation. Much of the critique of theory and of intellectuals in such movements essentially consists of a critique of *open* intellectuals by *covert* intellectuals who play the role of party leaders and organizational functionaries. In other words, it is often to be understood as a conflict among different kinds of intellectuals. In particular, it is an attack on those intellectuals who have a political and intellectual base in some segment of the larger intellectual world, and who are therefore less controllable by those lacking this outside base. One recurrent technique for the control of the outside intellectual by the functionary is the latter's call for the 'unity of theory and praxis', which may sometimes only mean the *subordination* of theory to praxis, and of the theorist to the functionary.

Most falsified of all is the relation between intellectuals and the larger social strata they claim to represent. It is precisely because of the self-hatred and suspicion – partly pathological, partly realistic and justified – directed toward intellectuals, by themselves and by others, and partly because they are *not supposed* to be acting on their *own* behalf but only on behalf of some larger social stratum, that it becomes enormously difficult for anyone to see the role that intellectuals actually do play. In *some* part, intellectuals are involved in a radical politics not only – and sometimes, not primarily – because they want to further the interests of some *other* social strata, but, also, because intellectuals need a 'client-group' in order to further their *own* special interests.

Intellectuals and theorists do have certain special interests, among them are interests in furthering *culture*. They also have a vital interest in extending rational discourse and in establishing the social conditions that foster this. That they may seek to further the interests of larger social strata is sometimes simply because they assume that these strata will, by 'abolishing' themselves, abolish all impediments to culture and to reason. For radical intellectuals, even the interest of a larger social stratum such as the working class, is *not* an end in itself but a means to rationality and culture.

Marx said, 'Philosophy is the head of emancipation, and the proletariat is the heart.' But it takes a great deal of fancy theoretical footwork – in short, of ideology and false consciousness – to assume that the head and heart of politics are always integrated and have identical interests.[20] Indeed, much of the discussion among Marxists today, concerning the failure of the proletariat as an historical force thus far, is in effect a discussion about the possibility of a 'heart-transplant'; that is, of replacing the proletariat with another historical actor: e.g., students, blacks, third-world forces, etc. Intellectuals are capable of being an autonomous political force and when one social group does not play the role they have assigned to it, when it fails in its 'historical responsibility', intellectuals will often shop around for another client group to 'represent'. False consciousness is generated when the special, vested interests of intellectuals are deemed illegitimate and are therefore concealed, and when intellectuals feel they must pretend to be representatives of another group's interests.

Stated positively, what follows is a conception of the role of the radical social theorist (I am not speaking of intellectuals in general) and of his relation to a radical politics that I, at any rate, would encourage.

(1) The theorist as theorist should commit himself to the establishment of *his own* social collectivity, to know intellectually and to create practically the conditions requisite for rational discourse and human liberation, and within whose protection he and his fellows work toward the understanding of the concrete social totality with which they are historically faced. A

'theorist' is simply one who takes this as his primary human and political commitment, and his own primary way of contributing to human fulfilment. (An 'intellectual' we might say is a theorist who is actively interested in mobilizing and wielding power.)

(2) Theorists should positively seek out involvements with and on behalf of specific social strata and contribute to them and to social movements representing them in practical political ways, especially (and indeed, only) insofar as these strata are evolving in directions compatible with human emancipation.

(3) Theorists should engage themselves politically in ways that bring them into tension, conflict, opposition and resistance to established authority, institutions and culture, for these help them to escape from conventional definitions of social reality.

(4) The relations between theorists, on the one hand, and movements or parties, on the other, should be governed by the principle that each is *autonomous* of the other organizationally, but collaborate on the basis of their common commitment to human emancipation. Theorists should not wait to be asked for intellectual work or assistance by these groups, but should take initiatives in providing them. This should be done, however, without insisting on the political group's use and, acceptance of, or commitment to, the theoretical collectives' work. Theorists should seek no power, no office and no leadership in political groups, and they should reject full-time political roles. Their primary engagement should be to their own *theoretical* collectivities, and if they undertake practical leadership roles in political groups they should resign their membership in their theoretical collectivity.

(5) Whatever their other political attachments, theorists should never submit to the discipline of any specifically political party or organization that believes itself entitled to discipline him on the basis of his intellectual products or work – that is, to control him as theorist, or to expel him from membership, on the basis of disagreement with his intellectual or theoretical work. That judgement should reside only in his own theorists' collective.

It is assumed that if theorists are doing work of value to

movements, the latter will inform themselves about it, will use it as far as possible, and will have valuable critical reactions to their experiences with its use. It must also be assumed, however, that if political movements take no interest in the theoretical work being produced by the theoretical collectivity it is either because this work is not or is not seen as relevant, or because such political movements have been corrupted by anti-intellectualism or irrationalism. In the first case, it is the responsibility of the theoretical collectivity to re-examine the character of its intellectual work. In the second case there is a fundamental conflict of interest between the political movement and the theoretical collectivity. In this event the theoretical collectivity should consider modifying its political associations, withdrawing from political interaction with such irrational groups, and in any event making public its critique of them. But under no conditions should the theoretical collectivity enter into an internal struggle within the political group to correct the line it has taken.

My insistence on the maintenance of institutionalized distance between theorists and party activists may seem very un-Marxist to some Marxists. Actually, it is not un-Marxist; it is merely un-*Leninist*. If one acknowledges that Engels was no less a Marxist than Lenin, then it is important to note that Engels insisted on the maintenance of the theorist's intellectual autonomy from Party controls. Thus in a series of letters to August Bebel (*Briefe an Bebel*, Berlin, D.D.R., 1958) Engels complained about the effort of the party press to suppress an article he had written for it; warned them that 'no party can condemn me to silence if I have decided to speak', insisted that 'socialist science' cannot exist without 'freedom of discussion', expressed resentment at intellectual dependence on even a worker's party; and acknowledged that 'it is a barren position for anyone with initiative to be the editor of a party journal. Marx and I always agreed that we would never accept such a position and could only work for a journal financially independent even of the Party itself' (18 November 1892). Engels, then, had no doubts about the importance of maintaining the autonomy of socialist theorists and he recognized that their autonomy, and the value of theory they produced, was threatened not merely by 'capitalist society' but also by the socialist party itself. For Engels, then, the 'unity of theory and practice' clearly entailed the *rejection* of any idea that this meant the subordination of theory to party activists or party committees.

The Critique of 'Navel-Gazing' as a Defence of False Consciousness

Oddly enough (as it will doubtless seem to some), I believe that the most serious question raised about *The Coming Crisis* is that which calls into question its critique of social theory and sociology, which therefore deprecates the importance of deepening the self-awareness of theorists, and which holds this critique up to ridicule as a form of 'navel-gazing'. This criticism has been made, interestingly enough, both by conventional academicians and also by their seeming opposites, highly politicalized activists. In my view, this is the most far-reaching and wrongheaded criticism made of *The Coming Crisis*; for it is at the heart of the issue of the relations between theory and practice and it implies a doctrine that demeans the role of consciousness and reason in life and in politics.

Behind the snickers about a critique of social theory as a form of 'navel-gazing', there is a more general suspicion of intellectuals and thinkers and of ideas and theory. Those who regard a critique of theory as a waste of time must, also, regard theory itself as a trivial factor in politics and life. This invidious judgement is I believe still another evidence of the continuing power of *bourgeois* society, of its preference for the practical and the useful, and of its corresponding contempt for theory and intellectuals. To view a *critique* of theory as trivial rests on a view of theory itself as trivial. This, in turn, rests on the bourgeois preference for the 'practical'. In short, the charge that a critique of theory constitutes 'navel-gazing' rests on certain bourgeois *theories*, another reason why a critique of theory is indispensable. Those misguided activists who hold a critique of theory, and theory itself, in suspicion and ridicule are in the grip of an uncriticized bourgeois theory. In the end, therefore, no one should be surprised if the new social order they seek turns out to be all too similar to the old régime they oppose.

The secret source of the revolutionary intellectual's self-hatred – his contempt for what he is and does – is his bourgeois father's Philistine values.

At bottom, the ridicule of 'navel-gazing' expresses an uneasiness with all efforts at self-knowing and self-*reflection*. It is false consciousness's effort to protect itself from change.

The critique of theory and theorists stands in a direct historical line with all efforts that assign value to consciousness and self-consciousness and that go back to the venerable inscription on the Temple at Delphi which enjoined man to: Know Thyself. This ancient injunction still contains the most powerful of political implications. Black Power, Women's Liberation and the Student Rebellion are not simply involved in knowing and changing the world outside but are just as profoundly involved in changing and knowing themselves and their own identities. Black Power, for example, does not only want more power for Blacks but it also wants to transform Blacks; it wants Blacks with a new identity – with a new awareness and knowledge of self.

What needs to be stressed, then, is both the venerability and the ongoing relevance of a concern with self-knowledge in Western civilization. What is possible for us, what we can do and how we can act depends on what we are and on knowing what we are. Men are not sticks of wood who may be used without their knowing themselves. They are not 'masses' to be shaped by élites like a sculptor shapes clay. Knowing who you are in our society is in part knowing that you are part of a tradition in which knowing who you are is important and which is committed to this quest. A sociology of sociology and a critique of social theory is simply a part of this tradition and an effort to enact it under special contemporary conditions.

Those rejecting such a quest must inevitably fall prey to a false consciousness and to a destructive smugness. For they must feel that it does not matter if they do not know who they are, or that they already know this. Those who believe that their selves are not worth knowing, or are already known, can only make history with a false consciousness; they will inevitably produce political catastrophes and political monstrosities. The more that men hold self-knowing (in its various forms) in contempt, the more we may be absolutely certain that they are prepared to be used by forces they do not comprehend. To that extent they are the activist brothers of the unreflective 'externalizers' in normal sociology. Being unable to search themselves, they prefer to 'go out of their minds' – to externalize.

The Reflexive Sociology called for in *The Coming Crisis* is a way of reconstructing how we think and learn about society, and changing the *people* who do the thinking-learning. In other words: this project for the reconstruction of sociology, the change of sociology, of social theory and of the social theorists is not something of merely instrumental value. It is not something we seek only as a means to bring about something else in the future. The reconstruction of sociology is a part of a reconstruction of society that begins at once, here and now. We cannot have a new, reconstructed larger society without a critical revamping of our established ways of thinking, of our theories about society.

We want a new society so that men can live better in it – e.g., without lies, illusion and false consciousness. It is a society which, *among other things*, will also enable men better to see and to say what is about the human condition, about man and society and their history. An emancipatory sociology then is *not* simply a *means* to a better world. It is something worth having in its own right; it is in itself part of what would make a better world better. Theory, in short, is not 'merely' a tool to action or a means to a better practice. Good theory, like sanity, is worth having in its own right.

Sociology and social theory are worth having for their own sake and in their own right – *as well as for their help in emancipating men* – because it is in the nature of men to want truth and to want to know what is. Knowledge is not simply a hammer with which to make the world yield; knowledge of world and of self-in-the-world is an aspect of our very humanness and a fulfilment of that humanness.

Flacks is therefore correct in saying that 'Gouldner seems to wish that sociologists could be a band of morally committed, intellectually courageous persons . . . of brilliant insight and deep compassion, alert to the potentialities of corruption in their environment . . .'

This is indeed my conception of what sociology and sociologists *should* be. And why not? When pursued according to my understanding of it, sociology should be, on the one side, instrumental to the furtherance of human emancipation. On the other, such a sociology would be an end in itself, embodying the ancient human aspiration for self-knowledge. If that is not a high calling, then none is. If that is not a 'sacred' work, then none is.

The *Communist Manifesto* rightly holds that 'the bourgeoisie has stripped of its halo every occupation hitherto honoured and looked up to with reverent awe'. There is, however, no reason to allow the world (or sociology) to remain as the bourgeoisie left it. *The Coming Crisis* does not call for the restoration of routine sociology, but for a new and extraordinary one. This sociology's dedication to human fulfilment and self-knowledge would indeed justify viewing it, not with 'reverent awe', but as a humane way to live and to help others live humanely. And it is this sociology of which I speak when I speak 'For Sociology'.

NOTES

1. *The Coming Crisis of Western Sociology*, A. W. Gouldner, Basic Books, 1970.

2. *Social Policy*, 1972.

3. *American Journal of Sociology*, vol. 77, no. 2.

4. The papers in the third part of this volume are *not* the separate study of Marxism mentioned here, although they do give *some* indication of its developing direction and concerns.

5. ibid., p. 312.

6. ibid., p. 318.

7. ibid., p. 318.

8. Ironically, a specific school of Marxism adapts this very position, despite Marxism's own stress on the *ideological* character of political economy and other 'bourgeois' theories. These, of course, are the Althusserians, one of whom, Paul Q. Hirst, had this to say in his critique of *The Coming*

Crisis: '. . . the subject's social experience is not the source of knowledge but an epistemological obstacle to it . . . No social relations, whatever their character, feudal, capitalist, or socialist, can constitute the real conditions of existence of a science.' Paul Q. Hirst, 'Recent Tendencies in Sociological Theory', *Economy and Society*, May 1972; pp. 216–27.

9. *The Coming Crisis,* p. 12.

10. ibid., p. 59.

11. ibid., p. 60.

12. ibid., p. 14.

13. E. A. Shils, *Daedalus,* Fall 1970.

14. *American Journal of Sociology,* p. 319.

15. ibid., p. 315.

16. ibid., p. 315.

17. ibid., p. 317.

18. ibid., p. 313.

19. ibid., p. 313.

20. It is one of the falsifying functions of such an organismic metaphor – about 'head and heart' – to imply, without claiming it responsibly, that this identity of interests exists.

5

For Sociology

Now, soberly considered, how does this matter stand?
George Santayana

By July 1972, a full two years after the publication of *The Coming Crisis*, it might seem that all that was going to be written about it by professional sociologists would have already been published. Certainly, one might have thought that the *American Journal of Sociology*, having previously published a full-scale symposium on *The Coming Crisis*, with major reviews by Maurice Zeitlin and Alain Touraine, had had its say about the *Crisis*. Apparently, however, these reviews did not deal with the book as the editors of the *A.J.S.* had wished. For in July 1972 the *American Journal of Sociology* once more returned to *The Coming Crisis* and this time unleashed a full-scale critique.

It is evident that the *Journal* did not mean to confine itself to a critique of the *Crisis* alone, but sought to bring all of radical sociology under critical inspection. Nonetheless it is also clear that it regarded the *Crisis* as the decisive work of radical scholarship with which it had to reckon. While speaking of the '*Varieties* of Political Experience in Sociology' it is plainly not the variety that comes in for sustained criticism but, more narrowly, the 'radical', and, still more narrowly, it is *The Coming Crisis of Western Sociology*. Under the banner of 'objective' scholarship it mounts a vigorous critique; while criticizing the radicals for their politicalization of sociology, the editors of the *Journal* themselves execute a deeply politicalized incursion into the sociological community.

In other words: in the very act of denying the radicals' charges concerning the political character of Establishment sociology, this issue of the *Journal* tacitly confirms them. This issue of the *A.J.S.* really resolves the differences between the radicals and the Establishment; for, as we will see, the Establishment actually *admits* the major charges made by the radicals. If one views this issue of the *A.J.S.* as an inadvertent manifestation of the politics, morality, and, above all, of the *intellectual quality* of the sociological establishment, one may once again see what it was that so deeply disturbed the radicals. What the July 1972 issue of the *A.J.S.* presents us with, then, is not another discussion *about* the nature of normal sociology; it is rather a definitive and concentrated *exhibition* of its flawed *being*.

Even in the most superficial way, as a sheer act of publication, the July 1972 issue was no ordinary issue of the *Journal*. For example: this issue of the *A.J.S.* was published *simultaneously* as a magazine and as a book, and, indeed, as a clothbound and as a paperback book. When was the last time that this happened in American sociology? This was a concerted, and well supported, effort to 'turn people's heads' around, in the community of sociologists.

The radicals have, of course, long attacked the liberalism of normal sociology as hypocritical sham. While I believe this an overstatement, consider the following: it took the *Journal* one month to reply to two cables I had sent from Amsterdam, immediately after receiving this issue in mid-September 1972, each asking (quite politely) how many words I could have to answer their *sixty* pages of direct attack on *The Coming Crisis*. I put the question in that way because C. A. Anderson had several months earlier refused to publish my reply to Zeitlin and Touraine on the ground that it was too long, and he intimated that I had wished to reply simply to get more publicity for *The Coming Crisis*. I answered that the *Crisis* scarcely needed more publicity, without then knowing that, even as he was refusing to publish my reply (of a few thousand words), Anderson was already planning to give *The Coming Crisis* a great deal more of the very publicity that he claimed that I was seeking.

Such a reply is quite normal in most professional journals and intellectual magazines. In fact, editors who are concerned to be fair-minded will often invite those whose work is to be criticized in their pages to prepare a reply that can be published at the same time as the criticism. But not editors Anderson, McFarland and Schwartz.[1] Such behaviour, of course, belies in practice the very 'liberalism' they vaunt in principle. It suggests that this issue of the *A.J.S.* did not aim only to understand the radicals, but to *control* them.

A final point about the nature of this issue as a publication: someone might well think that the editor of the July issue of the *A.J.S.* is Tom Bottomore, a leading Marx scholar at the University of Sussex. If so, he would be well advised to look again. The way in which the *Journal*'s Table of Contents is organized, the very first item being an Introduction by Tom Bottomore, creates the illusion that Bottomore is the issue editor. In point of fact he is *not*. Bottomore actually had nothing to do with the selection of the contributors, as an editor normally would have. Bottomore was asked only to write some general comments about the manuscripts. (These, one must assume, were actually selected[2] by the *Journal*'s usual editors, C. A. Anderson, D. McFarland and Barry Schwartz.) Indeed, Bottomore was not even allowed to see all of the magazine's articles prior to their inclusion, and some were sent him too late for him to give them serious scrutiny; he wrote what was to be called his 'Introduction' to an issue whose contents were not altogether known to him.[3]

Let us now get on with it and see what their criticisms amount to. Clearly, I cannot here reiterate the theses of the *Crisis* and I will be fortunate if I have space enough to reply to the arguments of my critics. It is only their main arguments, rather than their quick thrusts, to which I must devote the limited space here. For this reason, I shall say little about Professor Rhoads' comments concerning my *Crisis*. I believe him profoundly mistaken about most matters of substance he raises. He is clearly right only once, when he asserts that I was wrong in holding that Parsons did not term technology an 'evolutionary universal'. Parsons had so *termed* it, but he dismissed it there with only a very brief discussion. And that brevity was the substance of the matter I had raised. Still, whether of substance or not, any such error is regrettable. While discussing my own errors, I should also add that, shortly after the publication of the *Crisis* I discovered (from Robert Merton) that my assertion that C. Wright Mills had never been made a Professor at Columbia was in error. Having discovered this, I immediately had this statement removed from the Avon paperback edition of the *Crisis*, which was then in production.

To the best of my knowledge these two are the only errors of fact to have been identified in *The Coming Crisis*' 528 pages, despite the hostile scrutiny to which they have sometimes been subjected.[4] In dealing with critics such as these, I confess there is a temptation to overstate one's own case and to deny one's own errors. I have made every effort to resist this temptation; I invite the reader to judge whether the critics of *The Coming Crisis* have done the same.

The Lipset–Ladd Critique

The central arguments against *The Coming Crisis* are mustered by Seymour Lipset and Everett Ladd, whose joint work I shall simply speak of as 'Lipset'. Let me summarize them: *The Coming Crisis*, they hold, has two main theses; that 'the theoretical orientations fostered by Talcott Parsons carry conservative implications and have been dominant within the field' (*A.J.S.*, p. 67) at least since the end of the Second World War. There are then two distinct points that Lipset will challenge; first, that bearing on Parsons' *dominance* within sociology and, secondly, that bearing on his ideological *conservatism*. Moreover, Lipset further generalizes his argument and adds a defence of the ideological character of functionalism more broadly, and of sociology, still more broadly.

The Dominance Problematic

Radical critics of sociology, says Lipset, 'contend that the dominant theme of sociology since World War II has been functional analysis . . .' (*A.J.S.*, p. 71). Lipset adds that the 'largest single . . . survey of American sociologists was conducted by Gouldner and his then doctoral student, J. T. Sprehe, in 1964'. He then holds that 'Gouldner relies heavily on the responses to one of the 89 attitude items [in that survey] to justify his contention that the work of Talcott Parsons has been predominant' (*A.J.S.*, p. 72). This item indicated that the great majority of American sociologists then agreed that 'Functional theory was still of great value for sociology'.

It is correct that I referred to this survey item and to the answers it elicited; it is simply not true, however, as Lipset claims, that I 'rely heavily' on it for any reason, let alone for the specific reason of substantiating Parsons' dominance in post Second World War sociology. I do *not* rely heavily on it; I merely mention it (*Crisis*, pp. 167–9) toward the end of a two-page discussion of why I believe Parsons to have been the dominant theorist of the period. Indeed, some five or six reasons were given.

I began by suggesting that Parsons' influence rests *first* on 'his own prolific writings . . .'; that it is exerted also through the *writings* of such students as Robert Merton, Wilbert Moore, Kingsley Davis, Robin Williams and others, all of whom I hold to be important 'because of their intellectual work . . .', 'their dominant roles as officers of the A.S.A. . . .', 'and as editors of its journals'. I go on to note that 'the work of Parsons and his students is widely known and translated throughout the world, being read in London, Cologne, Bologna, Paris, Jerusalem, Tokyo, and Buenos Aires'. It is only at this point that I mention that the survey data *also* indicates the esteem in which many sociologists hold Parsons. I also go on to state emphatically that he *deserves* concentrated attention, not only because of his world influence, but also because of 'the intrinsic significance of Parsons' theory as theory . . .'.

At this point Lipset changes course. Instead of holding on to the dominance point he conflates it with the conservatism point. He does this by passing on to a lengthy and totally irrelevant examination of Sprehe's doctoral dissertation, which reports on the survey. Lipset is quite right in saying that Sprehe shows that many 'sociologists hold leftish positions', especially if 'leftish' is left unexamined. But in invoking Sprehe's dissertation, Lipset fails to make it clear that there is absolutely nothing in it that refutes my contention concerning *Parsons' dominance*. Instead the dissertation explores the political *ideology* of sociologists in *general*, their liberalism or conservatism, rather than either the ideology or the specific dominance of *Parsons* himself. In other words, Sprehe's dissertation is wrongly used to convey the *impression* that I was mistaken in judging Parsons to be dominant and conservative. More on this later.

Sprehe's survey is also the occasion for a number of quick thrusts concerning subsidiary issues intended mainly to suggest that I was being contradictory in using survey data (why, I cannot imagine), and to raise strange intimations (twice repeated!) concerning Sprehe's study; for example, mentioning that, although the largest such study, 'very little from it has been published' (*A.J.S.*, p. 72). Though trivial and irrelevant, this sounds sinister. Since it is not uncharacteristic of Lipset's critique, let us ventilate the matter. First: it is not true to say that Sprehe's thesis was never published. To 'publish' is to make things publicly accessible – not to 'print' in a book. To the best of my knowledge Sprehe's thesis was microfilmed by, is in the microfilm collection at, and is purchaseable from, the University of Michigan. Secondly: inter-university library loan makes even the original typed copy available. Lipset knows all this.

When last I spoke with Sprehe about his plans, he said that he first wished to do further analysis of this data before publishing. I strongly concurred in believing this desirable. Some time later Sprehe wrote me, telling me of his plans to change jobs and to move to a new locale. Did I want the original data, I was asked. I quickly said yes, jumping at the chance; but I was later shocked to learn from Sprehe that his data had all been tragically thrown out by a janitor! Yet the truth is that I do not actually *know* if any of this is relevant to why Sprehe's dissertation was not published. I am sure that if Lipset had really wanted to know, he would have asked Sprehe directly. Indeed, I would be greatly surprised if Lipset had not long since done just that.

Still in the same vein of vague insinuations: in a footnote (5, p. 76, *A.J.S.*) Lipset justifies his 'identifying me with the survey' on the ground that, in the *Crisis*, I had spoken of it as having been *conducted* by both Sprehe and myself. Lipset is correct in his facts, faulty in his inferences. While I did *conduct* the survey with Sprehe, I did *not write* it up. Sprehe's writing, his dissertation, is of course *his*. The initial impetus and idea for this survey happen to be mine. Moreover, I also wrote a great many of the questionnaire items and, in a general way, suggested approaches to data-analysis. Neither of us, however, was satisfied with the analysis, on which Lipset relies so heavily; in truth, it was suspended to let Sprehe complete the formalities of his dissertation, in the expectation that he would later return to it.

But to reiterate: this dissertation write-up, and the findings it reports, are Sprehe's work; no one has ever said or should say otherwise. In consequence, while Lipset is correct in saying I helped *conduct* this survey, I cannot be imputed to have responsibility for Sprehe's write-up and the data or analysis it presents. Lipset, therefore, is profoundly *wrong* in identifying me with Sprehe's written manuscript.

Indeed, some things of special interest to me in the survey are not even reported in his dissertation. Some were only subsequently run at my request and, so far as I know, appear only in me *Crisis*, but not in the dissertation. This is true of some of the noteworthy findings that I use in the *Crisis*. See, for example, footnotes 1 and 23, p. 285 of the *Crisis*, where I state this *explicitly*. These further document that Lipset was mistaken in identifying me with Sprehe's dissertation.

To refute my contention that Parsons' functionalism was the dominant theoretical standpoint, Lipset denies that its adherents had any special influence on the organizational life of professional sociologists. He thus denies the special influence of the Parsonians on the publications of the American Sociological Association, and denies that they were dominant as officers of the A.S.A. (*A.J.S.*, p. 77). Lipset ignores the fact that the editors operate under the tutelage of the A.S.A.'s Council, where functionalists have been present in ample number; under the guidance of the A.S.A. Presidents, who have often been functionalists; and under the guidance of the A.S.A.'s Publication Committee. What Lipset refrains from telling us is that after the Second World War, Parsons long held the decisive role on the A.S.A. Publication Committee, which was influential in selecting editors of the A.S.S. Moreover, Parsons always had considerable influence on the Council, as well as on the full-time executive director who worked closely with the *Review*'s editor. Lipset fails to mention that for a period of five years, from 1961–5, Parsons himself occupied the strategic office of secretary of the A.S.A., which was then passed on to Parsons' former student and fellow functionalist, Robin Williams Jr, who held it for another three years.

The *A.S.R.* editors were also under influence from the A.S.A. presidents, among whom there were Parsons himself and Robert Merton, Robin Williams, Kingsley Davis and Wilbert Moore. My point is, first, that almost all of the first generation of Parsons' students of any prominence have been A.S.A. president and, secondly, that their political influence on the A.S.A. was strong enough to get themselves and their friends nominated *repeatedly*. In recent years, functionalists such as W. J. Goode and Mirra Komarovsky have also been A.S.A. president.

In the end, however, and despite all his marching back and forth, Lipset capitulates completely; he actually *concurs* in my judgement of Parsons' dominance in world sociology. Lipset invokes various surveys, not only in the U.S., but also in Britain and Japan, which plainly indicate that Parsons and Merton are, indeed, the most highly reputed of American sociologists. 'All such surveys indicate that Parsons and Merton are invariably the two most cited modern sociologists' (*A.J.S.*, p. 77).

Webster's *Third New International Dictionary* (unabridged) defines 'dominance' as the 'dominant position in order or forcefulness . . . the relative position of an animal in the social hierarchy of its kind' (p. 671). As Lipset conclusively states: 'there can be no question that Parsons has had more impact on sociology than any other modern scholar' (*A.J.S.*, p. 78). Thus the dominance problematic is resolved, and on the basis I had asserted. We will soon see that Lipset also capitulates on the 'conservatism' problematic in much the same way.

The Conservatism Problematic: Toward a New Lev Parsons

It is fundamental to the Establishment's critique of *The Coming*

Crisis to deny that Parsons' theoretical orientation is socially conservative in character, and this is the second of Lipset's main contentions. Lipset makes it clear from the very beginning of his article that he intends to challenge the radicals' view that 'the theoretical orientations fostered by Talcott Parsons carry conservative implications . . .' (*A.J.S.*, p. 67). He seeks to refute this in several ways: by a new revelation of Parsons over-looked radical youth; by attempting to refute critically my discussion of Parsons in relation to the Pareto Circle at Harvard, accusing me of a policy of 'guilt by association'; by emphasizing the *generally* liberal character of academic sociology, and by counterposing this to the 'radical's' view of it as conservative. I shall discuss these issues *in seriatim*.

On Parsons' radical youth: 'Far from being an apolitical or conservative student at Amherst College, Parsons was a member of the Student League for Industrial Democracy (S.L.I.D.), a direct ancestor of *Students for a Democratic Society* . . .' (*A.J.S.*, p. 78). In fact, Lipset tells us, Parsons once actually wrote an article with a fellow student who later became a Communist! All this, recited with a straight face, presumably establishes Parsons' radical credentials. Although Lipset will later accuse me of convicting Parsons of 'guilt by association', in linking him to Harvard's Pareto Circle, he sees nothing contradictory in attempting to *redeem* Parsons' politics by linking him to *S.L.I.D.* My alleged 'guilt by association' is presumably shoddy thinking; Lipset's *own* 'redemption by association' only indicates what a careful scholar he is! So much for the virtues of Lipset's objective, non-politicalized sociology.

It is sadly obvious that the entire issue of Parsons' youth is an irrelevant red herring. I had never mentioned *anything* about Parsons' student politics, but Lipset insinuates that I *did*, when he says, 'far from being an apolitical . . .'. The radical past of Parsons that Lipset talks of is a fiction. The League for Industrial Democracy, to which Parsons is linked, was, in fact, 'a Cold War Socialist Organization'.[5] It never bore any resemblance to the confrontational S.D.S. (from which it arose) but was, rather, more nearly a genteel group of Social Democrats. Moreover, Parsons' student article dealt with a matter of civil liberties, the firing of Amherst's liberal president,

Alexander Meiklejohn, and was by no means a call to invade and occupy his office!

Far more important (and characteristic of Lipset's thought) is his allegation that in analysing Parsons' first scholarly article, it was my purpose 'to show that Parsons was always fighting socialism' (*A.J.S.*, p. 79). As usual, Lipset conflates intellectual issues. Surprisingly, Lipset fails to see that my critique of Parsons as an anti-*Marxist* is one thing, and a critique of him as an anti-*socialist* is quite another. Moreover, Lipset also assumes that being a socialist automatically precludes one from being a 'conservative'. I, however, had repeatedly held that speaking of Parsons or of functionalism as 'conservative' was *not* equivalent to saying they were necessarily *anti-socialist*.

Let me quote the decisive statement on this. In *The Coming Crisis* (p. 331), I expressly make the meaning of 'conservatism' problematic and seek to define it explicitly. Indeed, I discuss it for six pages. I suggest there that functionalism's conservatism is, in part, manifested by its stress on the problem of social 'order', previously discussed intensively on pp. 251–4. I then go on to say (p. 331):

> this same concern with order has commonly made Functionalism uneasy about demands for a basic reallocation of social advantages, thus allowing it to work within and for the particular form of industrialism under which it first came into existence: until recently this has been essentially capitalist in character. Yet this is not equivalent to saying that Functionalism is inherently and necessarily *capitalistic* in its ideological commitments, for . . . I also believe Functionalism to be congenial to *socialist* forms of industrialization, at a certain level of their development. In holding that Functionalism is not *inherently* procapitalist or prosocialist, however, I am not saying that it is neither conservative nor radical. I am, in fact, maintaining that its very adaptability to both capitalism and socialism . . . is precisely what makes it essentially conservative in character. In this regard, Functionalism is at one with the Positivism that Comte earnestly promised would 'consolidate all power in the hands of those who possess the power – whoever they may be.' . . . Functionalism's essential posture . . . is not necessarily antisocialist or even procapitalist. But it is nonetheless conservative . . . it will work to conserve either form of industrialism, once it is established . . . Functionalists are not Pollyannas who see no fault in the *status*

quo. But neither do they see the possibilities of a future significantly different from the present (*Crisis*, pp. 331–3).

In a similar vein, and at the very beginning of *The Coming Crisis* (p. 9), I speak of American sociology more broadly. There I point to the logical difficulties encountered by some (not all) radicals who,

out of a rote Marxism, have concluded that American Academic Sociology is an instrument of American corporate capitalism. For clearly the conservative character of American sociology cannot be attributed to its subservience to corporate capitalism if an essentially similar sociology has emerged where, as in the Soviet Union, there is no corporate capitalism.

My intention clearly was to show that Parsons' work was in part to be understood as a response to *Marxism*; that it was anti-*Marxist*; that it initially emerged out of an effort to generalize the anti-Marxism of Sombart and Weber; and that it was a response to or an expression of anxiety concerning *Communism*, in short was anti-Communist, rather than anti-*socialist*. I had thus sought to emphasize the anti-*Communist* and anti-*Marxist*[6] (but not the anti-*socialist*) inspiration of early Parsonianism. It is, after all, well known that some socialists are anti-Marxist and that many are violently anti-Communist.

I should add, however, that I have never found anything in the slightest pro-socialist in Parsons' *theoretical* work – which is what interests me – despite Lipset's marvellous intimations about Parsons' flaming youth. (In reading his account of the young Parsons' revolutionary past there were moments when I felt that Lipset's revolutionary nostalgia might run away with him and that he would end by invoking an image of Parsons as that indomitable 'grey eagle of the Revolution' and would cap his reminiscences by speaking of his Harvard colleague with respectful affection, as Lev Parsons, 'the old man'.)

Lipset implies that I misinterpreted Parsons' first scholarly papers and mistakenly held that 'Parsons was always fighting socialism'. My foregoing remarks have shown that Lipset is profoundly confused about the difference between fighting socialism and fighting Marxism. In discussing these early articles, which were critical appraisals of Sombart's and Max

Weber's critique of capitalism, published by Parsons in 1928–9, I had held that Sombart's and Weber's work was to be understood as anti-Marxist, stressing as they did the role of ideas and of religious ethics in the origin of capitalism. I added that 'while Parsons concurred in their anti-Marxism he was much perturbed by their pessimism and anti-capitalism' (*Crisis*, p. 180). I also held that Parsons' *Structure of Social Action* 'stems in important part from his earlier interest in these anti-*Marxist* theories of capitalism' (*Crisis*, p. 181). I went on to argue that Parsons' position was then essentially a kind of cautious Protestant perfectionism, that he was then more *optimistic* than Durkheim had been and I later argued that his was also a more *liberal* functionalism than Durkheim's (*Crisis*, p. 182 and p. 195–9).

In that context, I held that Parsons believed that modern society could be 'gradually perfected within the framework of capitalism . . .'. Lipset denies this, wishing us to believe that when Parsons says we might build a more ideal society, on the basis which we now have', he has in mind the *transcendence* of capitalism by *socialism*. Actually, I myself did in fact state that Parsons was then 'prepared to entertain the thought that capitalism itself might one day be superseded . . .' (*Crisis*, p. 184). But I also noted that by 1965 Parsons had declared that capitalism was on the verge of being transcended and had said that 'calling [the United States] "capitalistic" in anything like the classical Marxian sense is increasingly forced.' In brief, Parsons makes it perfectly clear here that it is not the advent of *socialism* to which he is referring, but rather, of democracy, the welfare state, trade unionism, education, science and humanistic culture. It is clear, then, that it was correct to hold, as I had, that Parsons believed in the perfectibility of modern society within the framework of *capitalism*.

The tendentious character of Lipset's interpretations of *The Coming Crisis* are once again evident in his interpretation of my treatment of Parsons' membership in the Pareto Circle. As I mentioned, this was a seminar that met at Harvard from 1932 to 1934. There is no question but that the leading spirits of the group, L. J. Henderson and Crane Brinton, and a young follower such as George Homans, clearly viewed Pareto's import as conservative. Homans has said, '. . . I felt during the thirties that I was under personal attack, above all from the Marxists. I was ready to believe Pareto because he provided me with a defence.'

Similarly, Crane Brinton makes it plain, in his own commentary, that I am not unusual in regarding the seminar as anti-liberal. Brinton acknowledges that even 'mild American-style liberals' on campus *at the time* were critical of the seminar's politics. Speaking of the seminar's conservatives, Lipset holds that Gouldner 'attributes their supposed motivation to Parsons as well' (*A.J.S.*, p. 79). In point of fact, I do no such thing. Actually, Parsons was not even central to my discussion of the Pareto Circle. Rather, this was written to clarify how social conditions during the Great Depression of the thirties impinged on social theory in the U.S., and, in particular, how they shaped the 'internationalization' of academic sociology at that time. In fact, far from one-sidedly emphasizing the *connection* between Parsons and the Pareto Circle I had actually indicated his *distance* from it: 'Parsons seems not to have been quite nuclear to the circle . . . [and] his own anti-Marxist position [anti-*Marxist*, Professor Lipset, please not, not anti-*socialist*] was therefore somewhat different from – less parochial and earlier than – that of other members of the circle' (*Crisis*, p. 149–50).

Lipset attempts to argue that the seminar's character was politically indifferent, presumably because both conservatives and liberals were involved. This might be more convincing, however, had Lipset made a distinction between its central and peripheral members. The central members were likely to be the more conservative. In any case, Lipset errs in repeatedly asserting that I made inferences about Parsons from *his membership in the Pareto Circle* when, in fact, I did *not*. There is absolutely no basis for his charge that I had engaged in a 'quick imputation of political orientation by affiliation . . .'. This, alas, is exactly what we have seen Lipset doing, in reverse, by appealing to Parsons' membership in the Student League for Industrial Democracy as evidence of youthful radicalness!

But in the end, Lipset once again capitulates on the issue at hand, i.e., with respect to Parsons' and functionalism's *conservatism*. He acknowledges, tacitly but clearly, that they are indeed conservative. This emerges in his discussion of the urgency of 'activism', when he goes on to stress that functional theory, in particular, emphasizes an opposite style:

> Stressing interrelationships and the fact that, in the absence of a key factor theory of change, harmful 'unanticipated consequences' may result from 'purposive social action', functional analysis implicitly argues for some caution in radical social changes. The functionalist, in effect, tells the young (or old) activist that he should move carefully. And his course of 'action' is usually a request for more research . . . (*A.J.P.,* p. 97).

That Lipset does not understand these remarks as a surrender, on the question of Parsons' conservatism, would be difficult to credit. In truth, they repeat some of the *Crisis'* central arguments quite closely. It should have been added, however, that functional analysis's conservatism was at first manifested by its 'caution' concerning New Deal reforms, and not by its opposition to 'radical social change'.

Even in his surrender on the question of Parsons' conservatism, Lipset seems to have no time or taste for complexities or careful distinctions. For the truth is that the *Crisis* actually never charged Parsons and functionalism with having a *general* and *universally conservative* character, as Lipset mistakenly formulates it. The *Crisis* actually held that Parsons' theory did *not* have a conservative but a *liberal* implication for *Soviet*-controlled societies. In the *Crisis*, I spoke of Parsons' work as being 'compatible with the more liberal initiatives' of East European societies. For, as I pointed out (see *Crisis*, p. 454), Parsons' social systems theory focused on self-regulation, and this 'means the relaxation of the massive centralized controls which they have established.'

Lipset on Lenin

There is one distortion of my work, in Lipset's discussion, that is trivial but particularly shameless. Lipset is speaking of the conflict between scholarship and activism. Most especially, he says,

in an effort to defend himself from the radical attacks on *The Coming*

Crisis of Western Sociology [and now who is imputing motives to whom? – A.W.G.] Gouldner has made it clear that the issue is largely one of a commitment to basic scholarship versus activism . . . He states explicitly: 'Sociology today does not need a Karl Marx or an Isaac Newton; it needs a V. I. Lenin', that is, a theorist concerned with political action (*A.J.S.*, p. 96).

My entire point, in referring to Lenin, however, was to suggest the Lukácsian thesis that *organization* is required to mediate between theory and practice. This seems a point that a sociologist should be expected to grasp. And the social organization of which I was speaking here was, as I made amply plain, the organization of social *theorists*, not political activists. More than that, my discussion also made it perfectly clear that one function of such an organization of theorists is precisely to *prevent* them from being dominated by political activists.

My reference to Lenin, then, was a reference to someone whose special genius is commonly understood to be organizational. I was saying that we need to focus time and thought on clarifying the requisites of the community life of social theorists. This is shown by the fact that, after referring to Lenin, I then went on to say that

the organization of new theoretical collectives then becomes the strategic, theory-yielding social methodology. Social theorists cannot have truths about society without having truths about themselves. And they cannot have truths about themselves without knowing how to organize themselves in furtherance of rational discourse.

It is therefore perfectly plain that I did not invoke Lenin for the sake of political action but with a view to fortifying *social theory*. I might also add that I did not in the least want the organizational problems of sociology solved in terms of anything like (Lenin's specific concept of) an instrumentalizing vanguard party. The ironic thing about all this is that Lipset should so flagrantly misread me in the midst of his campaign to protect scholarship from political activism!

Such a shameless misrendering of my views should make it clear that this issue of the *A.J.S.* was more nearly an act of war than of justice. Establishment critics have done just about everything, short of a book-burning, to discredit the *Crisis*. Indeed,

one of them, Jackson Toby, who is quoted by Lipset, scurri-
lously suggests that my motive in writing the *Crisis* was money.
I am accused of having shifted from an 'earlier respectful view
of Parsons to the current hostile view influenced by a shrewd
assessment of what would "resonate" in the marketplace . . .'
(*Contemporary Sociology*, November 1972, p. 110).

Toby attempts to fortify this effort at character assassination
by arguing that, in an earlier book, I had made fifteen 'respectful references to Parsons'. (Lipset quotes this on *A.J.S.*, p. 100.)
'Respectful references' is, to understate, an exaggeration. If
either Lipset or Toby had taken a little trouble to look up the
fifteen references to which they refer, they would have seen
that almost all were *footnotes* merely mentioning Parsons' work.
Indeed, some of the allegedly 'respectful references' to Parsons
are actually citations of Max Weber's *Protestant Ethic*, which
Parsons only translated. So the fifteen 'respectful references' to
Parsons, those miserable fifteen references that supposedly
document my intellectual opportunism and venality, turn out on
inspection to be: the blandest *mentions*; are not *'respectful'* at all;
are sometimes not even references to *Parsons* but rather to
Weber's writings; and sometimes they are not even made by
me, in my section of the book to which Lipset and Toby refer,
but are in sections written by others.

Had I in truth suddenly changed from a Parsonsophile to a
Parsonsophobe for the love of lucre? There was no such change
and no such motive. From the very beginning I was highly
critical of Parsons' work. In my contribution to L. Gross's
Symposium on Sociological Theory, which Lipset cites, I speak of
Parsons' theory in the following 'respectful' reference: 'To a
Malinowski, it might well seem that this is a form of academic
monasticism in which men are cleansed of their baser passions
for sex, food, and material possessions by theoretical purification.' This was written in 1959, four years before the *Modern
Sociology*, with its allegedly respectful references!

Perhaps Lipset and Toby merely meant to say that I took
Parsons seriously. In truth, I have always respected the seriousness of his intellectual dedication and the creativity of his
speculative gift. Indeed in *The Coming Crisis* I affirm the
theoretical importance of Parsons, not because of what citation

surveys find, but because of his intrinsic significance for theory (see *Crisis*, p. 456). In fact, I have taken Parsons seriously since my very first article on general theory, 'Some Observations on Systematic Theory, 1945–55', in Hans Zetterberg (ed.) *Sociology in the United States of America*, Unesco, 1955, reprinted here in Chapter 6. In this paper the reader can also see that I there *lay out almost every one of the main criticisms adumbrated in The Coming Crisis* some seventeen years later. There has been no change in my judgement of Parsons' theory in that time, but primarily a deepening and development of it. That Lipset of all people does not know of this continuity is strange considering that he himself wrote the article directly after mine in the Zetterberg volume.

The Conservatism of Sociology-in-General

Lipset goes to great lengths to cite every survey he can muster – apparently believing that only in surveys is there truth – to demonstrate that sociologists as a *group* tend to be more liberal than many other academicians. As ever, he is a master at driving home the uncontroversial point. Indeed, sociology's liberalism is precisely one of its redeeming features. Better liberal than reactionary. So far as I am concerned, it is not bad news but good that the polls 'showed sociology to be among the liberal fields in academy.' Certainly I would much prefer this to the opposite.

What Lipset conceals, however, is that this is exactly what I, too, had said in characterizing the ideological position of sociologists: 'It is often said, and truly, that most American sociologists today regard themselves as liberals' (*Crisis*, p. 501). Much earlier in the *Crisis* I had insisted that 'liberalism is the politics toward which the conventional professional ideology of autonomy is disposed to drift.' (See *Crisis*, p. 59.) Indeed, one of the *central* points I make in discussing the history of American functionalism is that, after the Second World War, it increasingly sought ways to ally itself with and serve the Welfare State. A large part of the *Crisis* deals extensively with functionalism's and academic sociology's 'Shift toward the Welfare State'.

Lipset rather cleverly conceals the extent to which it is I

who emphasized that sociology is not only conducive to conservative political behaviour but may also be conducive – not only to liberalism – but to *radicalism*. It is I who gave extended treatment to the manner in which many in the student rebellion of the sixties were students of sociology. It is therefore not simply, as Lipset says, that I 'noted' this; I *stressed* the role of young sociologists in this rebellion throughout the world 'from Nanterre to Columbia Universities' (*Crisis*, p. 9), and I went on to emphasize that 'sociology may produce, not merely recruit, radicals; that it may generate, not merely tolerate, radicalization.' (See *Crisis*, p. 11.) *The Coming Crisis* stressed how paradoxical it is for radical sociologists to denounce sociology as conservative. That 'the keenest critics of sociology today have usually been sociologists', testifies, I held, 'both to the profound flaws and to the continuing value, to the painful predicaments and to perduring potentialities of the sociological perspective' (*Crisis*, p. 15).

All right, so there never was any question in anyone's mind that sociologists were more liberal than most other academics; that they will vote for democratic candidates and civil liberties and against the war in Vietnam more than others; and that sociology students were in the vanguard of the student revolt. *The Coming Crisis* clearly, fully, and repeatedly said all that. On what, then, do we differ?

Well, for one thing, we differ on what this might *mean*. Lipset is far too ready to call sociologists 'liberal' and let it go at that; eager to pin a medal on sociology, he does not want to read the citation too closely. He does not want to be bothered with complexities that may require him to make this interpretation problematic. For example, Lipset emphasizes that many studies of religious belief have 'shown that, among Americans, religious unbelief is associated with liberal to left political values' (*A.J.S.*, p. 81). If that is so, what inferences can be drawn from the religious dispositions of American sociologists in general, and functionalists in particular, that are reported on in *The Coming Crisis* from our survey data? These data show that, as late as 1964, almost 28 per cent of the members of the American Sociological Association had once thought about becoming clergymen (*Crisis*, p. 24). Again I show (*Crisis*, pp. 258–9) that 'functionalists' – whom Lipset assures us are *not* conservative – were more likely than *anti*-functionalists to manifest a greater religiosity and stronger religious affiliations. Lipset never even discusses these findings, let alone challenges them. Yet does it not follow that, if unbelievers are more politically liberal than believers, and since functionalists are more likely to be believers, they are *less liberal* than *anti*-functionalists? Which is exactly what we all along maintained!

Moreover, we might well ask how this aspect of their religious belief system is connected with their liberal politics? It needs to be remembered that what is usually referred to as their 'liberal' politics is an inference from verbal replies to very limited survey inquiries about which candidates they would vote for in national elections, which parties they favour, what ideological labels they put on themselves, etc. In short, it may well be that in their public (political) behaviour they may be more ready to opt for a liberal position than in their more private beliefs.

That something like this may be at work is suggested by data that Lipset mentions, but buries, in a footnote. This is the fact that, while sociologists with greater publication records and funding 'were to the left' of those with less,

many who are liberal or leftish on national and international issues, and who reject the idea that social science can be neutral, are not supportive of student activism or the demands for intramural student power – correlations between academic achievement and left views do not hold up for campus issues (*A.J.S.*, p. 84).

In short, one may well wonder how 'left' or 'liberal' sociologists are, or would be, if their 'liberalism' meant they would no longer get funded by the welfare state? In short, how 'liberal' are sociologists if being liberal is costly?

Granted that most sociologists today are 'liberals', Lipset completely misses the fact that the character of liberalism today has changed – as I discuss extensively in the *Crisis*. Liberalism today, I indicate, is no longer the conscientious faith of a brave minority fighting a callous establishment. Liberalism today is itself a powerful establishment. Senator McGovern's ability to seize control of the Democratic Party from the party professionals during the 1972 elections is only one of the latest and most obvious indications of this. Liberalism today is not an 'outsider's' politics; it is a central part of the governing political apparatus. It has a powerful press whose pages distort the truth just as systematically as do other ideological groups. What does it mean to say that Daniel Patrick Moynihan is a 'liberal' when he works for, and has power in, both the Democratic and Republican administrations?

Consider the matter in terms of Lipset's insistence on the mutually contradictory nature of scholarship and activism: '. . . the two roles, scholarly analyst and political actor, must be separated . . .' and be kept 'as distinct as possible' (*A.J.S.*, p. 98). The reason for this, he holds, is that the requisites of the two are opposed. Activists or politicians, Lipset says, are inherently advocates and must make decisions under pressure; the scholar's tempo should be more reflective and careful. The problem, of course, is that insofar as this is true, and represents a contradiction between the two – which it does – it is a contradiction that is no less true for a *liberal* than for a radical sociologist.

Liberalism is as much of a politics as radicalism and it is a politics that has no less need for prompt decision and forceful advocacy. My point, then, is not that Lipset is wrong, but profoundly one-sided, in seeing contradictions between theory and activist practice. He fails to see that these contradictions are *inescapable* and apply to all sociologists. For, in one way or another, in one degree or another, all are political men and must cope with the dissonance between their politics and their scholarship.

This dissonance between scholarship and politics arises as much for the liberal sociologist as for the radical. The point to note, however, is that – as we all agree – radicals are only a tiny minority of sociologists; liberals are the great majority. That is exactly the rub that Lipset persistently avoids. Lipset employs a double standard, criticizing the radicals for the way in which *their* politics threatens *their* scholarship, but says nothing of the same threat from the *liberalism* of sociologists.

One must also insist that, if theory and practice, scholarship and activism, are invariably in contradiction, for *all* politics and ideologies, it is also true that their relationship is *not only* a relation of contradiction, in which politics serves *only* to corrupt scholarship. One's politics often serve to energize one's scholarship; they often sensitize us to considerations that those of a different politics may ignore. So our politics blinds us in some cases but illuminates our work in *other* ways.

In both cases, our scholarship is shaped by our politics as *one* aspect of our total human existence. I tried repeatedly in *The Coming Crisis* to indicate the *variety* of social forces that impinge on our scholarship, suggesting its linkage even with interpersonal and sexual ties, rather than reducing the question to one of politics alone. I therefore held, very early in the *Crisis* (p. 40), that 'if every social theory is thus a tacit theory of politics, every theory is also a personal theory, inevitably expressing, coping, and infused with the personal experience of the individuals who author it'.

The central thesis of *The Coming Crisis* – the central reason for which it was written – is expressed in the very next sentence:

Every social theory has both political and personal relevance, which, according to the technical canons of social theory, *it is not supposed to have*. Consequently, *both the man and his politics are commonly screened out* in what is deemed the proper presentation of presumably 'autonomous' social theory (*Crisis*, p. 41, italics added).

If there is any point to *The Coming Crisis*, if it can be reduced to a single theme, it is precisely this: that social theorists commonly work with a false consciousness; thinking that *their* theory is the product of an 'immaculate' theoretical conception, they fail to see that it is not only their political *enemies'* theory that is corrupted by their politics, but also their *friends'* and their *own* theory. They fail to see, even when they are sociologists, how *their* own theory is not only the product of a technical tradition, of logic or of evidence, but of *their whole social existence*. It is this that is the heart of *The Coming Crisis*. *The Coming Crisis* is *not* only a study in the 'sociology of knowledge'; it is above all a struggle against the false consciousness of social theorists today who, paradoxically, fail to see how their theory is shaped by their whole social being.

A simple point, some may say, and surely 'known' by every

sociologist. Indeed, Talcott Parsons himself wrote essentially the same thing more than thirty years ago. He then put it in a somewhat limited way, but its general implications are clear:

The fact that a Veblen rather than a Weber gathers a school of ardent disciples around him bears witness to the great importance of factors other than the sheer weight of evidence and analysis in the formation of 'schools' of thought. (T. Parsons, *Essays in Sociological Theory*, p. 117.)

Yet even while saying this he *exhibits* a certain readiness to *forget it*, or at least to attribute only subsidiary significance to it: Parsons put it in a *footnote*. More than that, Parsons emphasizes that *Veblen*'s school arose for reasons *other* than its intellectual substance and implies that Weber's failure to win ardent disciples was a kind of injustice. But one gets the impression that if Weber *had* won such a following, then Parsons, thinking it well earned, might have said nothing about the 'great importance of factors other than the sheer weight of evidence and analysis . . .', at least so far as Weber's popularity was concerned. Such a failure exemplifies the false consciousness against which the whole of *The Coming Crisis* was written.

The 'reflexivity' and awareness called for by the *Crisis* is exactly the feature of the *Crisis* that brought the most unanimous criticism from sociologists of all political persuasions, left as well as right. 'Navel-gazing', they commonly said in amused contempt. The 'real' job, all agreed, is not the criticism of sociology but the criticism of society, as if the two tasks are separable. But in this critique we can once again see that what they say, and what they exhibit, are profoundly different. In mounting a critique of *The Coming Crisis* and of radical sociology more generally, their self-understanding is that they are undertaking this out of a love and respect for sociology, out of a wish to foster a 'good' sociology. In particular, they conceive themselves as seeking to *protect* sociology from *politicalization*. Yet what they *exhibit* is quite different. In condemning *The Coming Crisis*'s struggle against the sociologist's false consciousness as 'navel-gazing' they must, in the end, give support to an unexamined existence, to a life exempt from critical inspection.

In snidely condemning the examined life as 'navel-gazing', it is they who voice a suspicion of reason; it is they who reject self-criticism; it is they who imply a certain contempt for sociology, as something hardly important enough to critique.

Perhaps that is how men of affairs feel about sociology; perhaps that is how consultants to the State Department feel about ideas; perhaps that is how political activists think about the life of the mind. They all agree with Horowitz and Becker who tell us: 'Sociology in itself means very little apart from the larger social tasks . . .' (*A.J.S.*, p. 65). But some of us think otherwise. Those of us who live a more modest existence; we who do not cut such a great swath in the larger world; we who have lived our lives *for* sociology, we impractical intellectuals and dusty scholars, are convinced that sociology is terribly important; and it is therefore greatly worthy of the most profound criticism of which we are capable. We believe that self-criticism is indispensable. Not simply because it helps to make a better society or a better sociology, but also because a life unexamined is simply not worth living. Yes, this *has* been said before . . .

It is because the lives of all serious sociologists are profoundly linked with their sociologies; it is because this is as true for a Lipset, for a Parsons, for a Horowitz and Becker, as it is for myself, that a criticism of sociology is inevitably a criticism of our *existence*, and not simply of our writings and lectures. It is exactly because of this that we sociologists must experience a criticism of sociology as a challenge to our lives. It is the anguish felt when our work is criticized, the tart or vicious reply made by all of us, that reveals the man underneath the theorist, the life behind the theory. In the very act of saying sociology is important and that we want to protect *it* (from politics and other things), what we are also saying is that our *lives* are important to us and we do not want to *waste* them. If *The Coming Crisis* drew blood, this was only because there were indeed *men* behind the theories it criticized and this, after all, was (with all its implications) the central thesis of the book. In responding to the *Crisis* with some anguish, exasperation, and even fury, the critics of the *Crisis* provide the best evidence of its essential validity.

A Note on Becker and Horowitz

In this connection it is appropriate to say a few words about the article by Howard Becker and Irving Horowitz in the same issue of the *Journal*. They conclude their article by invidiously counterposing the criticism of sociology to the criticism of society, 'calling us back again *first* to the criticism of society and only second to the criticism of other sociologists' (*A.J.S.*, p. 65). This critique of 'navel-gazing', this invidious juxtaposition of the critique of sociology with the critique of society, is *not* at all a mere personal attack; it is, rather, greatly revealing of the deepest difficulties of their intellectual position.

For what it is worth, it is my view that Becker and Horowitz's paper is easily the most substantial and far-ranging contribution to this issue of the *A.J.S.* Their effort to characterize a radical sociology is one of the more probing I have seen. Frank in its understanding of the political commitments it entails, it also properly insists on the *special* values that a sociology, any sociology, must also sustain. While sceptical about a radical sociology, their understanding of it is far more sensitive than most. And at the same time, their criticism of conventional sociology, while scattered, is nonetheless serious and probing. If one is to believe what one reads, their disentanglement from normal sociology is continuing. Yet their analysis retains very serious problems, most especially in their ideas about *how* ideology enters sociological analysis.

This is given a rather limited discussion and only one point is made. They think that bias or ideology enters sociology primarily through the 'causes' that the sociologist elects to consider, and through which he attempts to account for the problem he is examining. In selecting causes, they suggest, the sociologist tacitly assigns *blame* to some groups or institutions, and he fosters the belief that the problem may be solved in one way rather than another, or even that it is not solvable at all.

I think that they are correct in describing this assignment of causes as a port of entry for the sociologists' ideology. But it is only *one* of many such, others of which strike me as more fundamental. It might seem from their account that ideology would not enter analysis if the sociologists did not assign causes. Yet well before the assignment of causes, even in the very formulation of the problem, the sociologist's ideology and values enter, and, as Max Weber said, quite properly so. More than that: even if one is engaged in a limited ethnographic description of events, without assigning causes and even without formulating a problem, even here the sociologist's ideology and values penetrate the very description itself, being sedimented in the total linguistic structure with which he 'terms' his description, problems, and causes.

But let this lie. Return to the idea that ideological bias enters sociology through the sociologist's selection of causes and the blame that this tacitly assigns. Clearly, what have been omitted here are the *categories* in which these causes are formulated or 'termed'. This world of categories is taken by them as a given, which, in effect, means that a large part of the sociologist's *social reality* is being taken as 'given'. Which is to say, it is being taken *uncritically*.

Since the world of the theoretical and categorical is taken as a given, and because it is, it may then *seem* as if one need only make selections *from* these givens. Indeed, one can only *select* from something already pre-formed and given. Essentially, then, Horowitz and Becker view sociologists as selecting causes from a 'box' of causes, in which they have somehow already been placed. It is only thus that they can and do accept the world of *sociology* as a given, while stressing that one must criticize *society*.

But if society has had a hand in shaping sociology, and if, as Becker and Horowitz say, 'every group in power is bent on the protection of privilege' (*A.J.S.*, p. 54), surely one form this takes is the support of sociologies conducive to their power and privilege. Again, Becker and Horowitz affirm: 'Whenever someone is oppressed, an "establishment" sociologist seems to lurk in the background, proving the facts which make oppression more efficient and the theory which makes it more legitimate to a larger constituency' (*A.J.S.*, p. 48). Well then, if sociologists do indeed serve to support power and oppression in the way Becker and Horowitz suggest, it would seem impossible for them to use sociology, as they call upon us to do, to criticize *society* without criticizing sociology. It is simply impossible to undertake the criticism of society without first (or simultaneously) criticizing sociology, with a view to making sociologists aware of how the very society and élites they seek to criticize have lodged themselves in their own thought and being. In the end a fettered criticism of sociology, and a contempt for *self*-criticism, inevitably cripple the criticism of society.

On a Certain Quality of Mind

It is one of Lipset's main theses that I had wrongly condemned sociology-in-general (and not only Mr Parsons) as 'conservative'. In his view, sociology is one of the most liberal of academic disciplines. One central thesis of the *Crisis* is that modern academic sociology, directly implicated as it is in the Welfare–Warfare State as consultants, contractors, and client-recipients, and *in*directly through the university as a training/ channelling system, and saturated by theories stressing the importance of social order and morality, that this sociology's *dominant character* is predominantly 'conservative'. This judgement on normal, conventional sociology is, it would seem, seconded by Becker and Horowitz in their contribution to this issue of the *A.J.S.*:

. . . social scientists have undertaken research designed to further the interests of the powerful at the expense of those powerless . . . Prison research has for the most part been orientated to problems of jailers rather than those of prisoners; industrial research, to the problems of managers rather than those of workers; military research, to the problems of generals rather than those of privates (*A.J.S.*, p. 4).

The *Crisis's* position about this is, however, rather more complicated than the simple assertion that sociology is 'conservative'. I fear that I shall again have to invoke one of those 'tiresome' scholarly distinctions to clarify the argument, and it is this: there is a substantial difference between saying that sociology is conservative (the position Lipset attributes to the *Crisis*), and the position actually taken by the *Crisis*, namely that sociology's *dominant* ideological characteristic is conservative.

Lipset mistakes the part for the whole, and the head for the entire organism. The distinction, as usual, eludes him.

My thesis in the *Crisis*, then, was not that sociology-in-general was wholly conservative, but was the rather different contention that its *controlling* character is conservative. This, of course, implies the existence of a controlled underside that is *not* conservative. My central point, to be still more specific, has long been that sociology is a divided (minotaur-like) beast, internally *contradictory* in character, being partly liberative at the same time that it was repressive. It is precisely this former aspect that has made and has attracted radicals to sociology. It is precisely the latter that disappointed and repelled them.

That my judgement on academic sociology has *always* had this complexity is visible in various ways. In one, it may be seen in my long-held interest in integrating functionalism with Marxism, acknowledged quite clearly in the *Crisis* (p. 482). Again, it is perfectly explicit in the *Crisis* where, in the very first chapter (p. 11), I held that sociology has a *liberative* dimension that both attracts and generates radicals:

> I believe that there are aspects of the character of and outlook intrinsic to Academic Sociology itself that sustain rather than tame the radical impulse . . . in the normal course of working as a sociologist, there are things that happen that may radicalize a man . . . I believe that sociology has its own 'internal contradictions' which despite its powerful link to the *status quo* and its deepgoing conservative bent, have the unwitting but inherent consequence of fostering anti-establishment and radicalizing tendencies, particularly among young people (*Crisis*, p. 11). . . . sociology is by no means totally repressive or uniformly conservative in character, but also possesses a liberating or radicalizing potential, susceptible to further growth (*Crisis*, p. 12).

I have thus repeatedly said – no, insisted, emphasized, and stressed – that 'sociology has a dialectical character and contains both repressive and liberative, dimensions' (*Crisis*, p. 12). I have made it perfectly clear that a transcending objective of the *Crisis*, one of its fundamental reasons, was to help sociologists and others to extricate sociology's liberative dimension:

> For the extrication and further development of its liberative

potential will depend, in important part, on the penetration of an historically informed critique of sociology as a theory and as a social institution. Sociology today is akin to early nineteenth-century Hegelianism, especially in the ambivalence of its political implications . . . The extrication of the liberative potential of modern Academic Sociology from its encompassing conservative structure is a major task of contemporary cultural criticism (*Crisis,* p. 12).

In a later section (pp. 437–43), I developed an analysis of three major contradictions of academic sociology from which I concluded:

there are powerful contradictions within sociology which provide leverage for the transformation of sociology itself. These suggest that radicals are not justified in viewing sociology in the way that Rome looked upon Carthage . . . [and that] Academic Sociology, even with its profoundly conservative structure, still retains politically liberative potentialities that can be useful in transforming the community (*Crisis,* p. 442).

I had already said much the same in an article in *Social Policy* for May/June 1970. Indeed, it was precisely because I *rejected* a view of sociology as unregeneratively conservative, that this article aroused the ire of a *small* sector of the left; of the nihilists who shortly revealed their programme to be nothing less than the *destruction* of sociology as a whole; and not only of conventional academic sociology but of 'radical sociology' as well.[7]

In short, neither the nihilist fraction nor the alleged 'friends of rationality' in the sociological establishment can see academic sociology as a contradictory whole. Both insist on a one-sided, totalizing judgement; both demand that sociology be viewed as either all corrupt or all good. The nihilist fraction blew its mind when I insisted that academic sociology retained a liberative potentiality; the 'friends of rationality' did the same when I held that sociology's dominant character was conservative. Both were incapable of acknowledging the *contradictions* of academic sociology and of seeing their importance. In the end, the academician who waves the banner of scholarship to exorcize the evils of political activism converges with the nihilist who holds scholarship in contempt.

Professor Rhoads' Critique of the 'Crisis'

In reading his commentary, my eye was first caught by Professor Rhoads' striking claim that he would 'disclose' my errors from the 'original works' of the theorists I discuss. In fact, he twice claims (*A.J.S.*, pp. 136, 273) that his reply is based upon 'original' sources. How marvellous, I thought; at last I would have the judgement of a true scholar. Nonetheless (being from Missouri), I turned to his list of references. Sure enough, not one of the foreign sources he uses is cited in the original language! In point of fact, Rhoads uses only *English translations*. One of them, Émile Durkheim's *Socialism*, was in fact made available to English readers in a volume that I edited – which Professor Rhoads' reference fails to mention. So much for Professor Rhoads' claim to original scholarship.

There is a certain difficulty in responding to Rhoads' criticism that, I believe, derives from its vague and meandering statement. Lacking a central nervous system, his is not a critique that can be dispatched with a single blow. To clarify Rhoads' intention, I found it helpful to refer to the *abstract* (*A.J.S.*, p. 273) of his article, written, I presume, in his own words. This abstract reveals that Rhoads makes one major contention and several auxiliary arguments:

A *Major contention* Rhoads 'disputes Gouldner's principal conclusion that there is a crisis in academic sociology . . .'

B *Auxiliary arguments*
(1) Rhoads contends, allegedly at variance with Gouldner, that 'sociological positivism took a broader perspective than that toward the utilitarianism of the middle class . . .'

(2) 'The functional theory of classical sociology appeared elsewhere than in contexts characterized by the supremacy of the middle class over the aristocracy . . .'

(3) 'Parsons' theory is not an anti-deterministic defence of capitalism . . .'

(4) Parsons' theory 'does recognize the autonomy of the individual'.

As for the major contention: essentially, Rhoads disputes

my argument 'that academic sociology is now in the early stages of a crisis'. He immediately makes a fundamental mistake, however, in failing to see the decisive distinction (that is made in the *Crisis*) between arguments that document the sheer *existence* of this crisis and those that *explain* the crisis. In other words, Rhoads conflates two different things: the physician's report that the 'patient' is seriously ill (dying, or dead) with the 'medical pathologist's' autopsy which seeks to explain what had happened.

On page 410 of my *Coming Crisis* this distinction is made central to the argument. I emphasize that one must distinguish the way in which the coming crisis is 'manifested' from the forces 'contributing' to this crisis. Under the first heading, the factors manifesting the crisis, I mention no less than *six* distinct points, only one of which is considered by Rhoads; in footnote 17 on page 151, he mentions my reference to the decline of interest in functionalism among young sociologists. Rhoads replies, quite irrelevantly, that 'there is no way of knowing what proportion of young sociologists will not accept functionalism in the future' (*A.J.S.*, p. 151). Fair enough. But after all, I had not 'prophesied' that all young people, now and forever, would reject functionalism. If I believed that to be true, then I would have spoken not of the 'crisis' of academic sociology, but, rather, of its impending *death*.

Perhaps Rhoads has confused the nature of these two claims. Still, I cannot see how this is possible because I explicitly stated that 'the central implication of a crisis is *not* of course, that "the patient will die"' (*Crisis*, p. 341). Moreover, Rhoads also fails to mention the specific statistical evidence that I present (*Crisis*, p. 377) demonstrating that 'the youngest [sociological] respondents tend to be more hostile toward Functionalism and, indeed, more than twice as much so as the oldest.' I also add that 'when a theoretical viewpoint manifests a declining ability to attract the young, there are solid grounds for asserting that a crisis is impending for it' (*Crisis*, p. 377).

It should now be thoroughly clear why Rhoads' principal reply to the *Coming Crisis*, namely that there is no crisis, fails entirely. It fails because Rhoads does not understand the elementary distinction between the forces 'manifesting' the sheer existence of this crisis and those 'contributing' to it.

Rhoads focuses his arguments entirely on the latter question, seeking to discredit the reasons that I had advanced to *explain* the crisis. But all his arguments against my account of the *origin* of the crisis *might* conceivably be correct; the findings of my 'autopsy' might be demonstrated to be wrong, but that would still not disprove my argument about the sheer *existence* of a crisis in sociology. In other words: the pathologist's autopsy might be disputed; but *that* would not change the fact that the patient was dead (dying, or in crisis).

A further word about the question of the crisis in sociology: it would seem evident that what we are presently witnessing is not simply the routine cumulation and working out of the implications of 'normal' sociology's established paradigms. As Thomas Kuhn makes plain, a crisis is upon an intellectual discipline when its established paradigms are challenged and when radically different ones are advanced and found attractive.

Among the clear indications that it is just this that is happening are the following: the growth of the 'radical' sociology whose impact is amply evidenced in the very issue of the *A.J.S.* to which this is a reply; the resurgence and renewed vitality in sociology of various models of Marxism and neo-Marxism; the elaborated development of Erving Goffman's unique social dramaturgy; the spread of Harold Garfinkel's ethno-method-ology and its growth from programmatic statement to concrete studies such as those of David Sudnow, Harvey Sacks and others; the very important new meta-theoretical work by Alan Blum; Peter Winch's provocative sociological version of Wittgenstein; and the powerful work and great growth of interest in the 'newer' generation of the Frankfurt School – Jürgen Habermas, Alfred Schmidt and Albrecht Wellmer, to mention a few. Surely the emergence or crystallization of all these developments, within the space of a decade, is evidence of the major upheaval – in intellectual paradigm, no less than in mood – that amply justifies speaking of a *crisis* in academic sociology.

If one wishes to make a special point of linking such a crisis to epistemological shifts, as Robert Friedrich stresses,[8] then certainly the accelerated development of a phenomenological sociology, as in the work of a Garfinkel, a Peter Berger, an

Aaron Cicourel and a Jack Douglas, is of major importance in providing further evidence. Indeed, one wonders what point there was in the American Sociological Society having recently given its major award to Robert Friedrich's excellent *A Sociology of Sociology*, if the awarding committee did not concur in that study's main theses, among which is its central contention of the existence of exactly such a *crisis*. (Friedrich himself fully acknowledges the similarity of our theses about the crisis in an issue of the *Louisiana State University Journal of Sociology*: '. . . the convergence is too self evident to deny . . . Each centers about the issue of "*crisis*", views that "crisis" (my "revolution") without trepidation . . .'.)

Let me consider Rhoads' auxiliary contentions briefly. Insofar as B1 and B2 are concerned, Rhoads conflates the following possible contentions: (1) that Comte *aimed* at winning the support of the middle class; (2) that his theory tacitly but unintentionally *expresses* middle-class assumptions; (3) that his theory was found interesting and was *accepted* by middle-class persons; (4) that it was *functional* to them.

Rhoads is unclear as to which of these four different theses *he* wants to assert, and he also is not clear as to which of them I asserted, which I presume is why he formulates his point so vaguely. The one clear statement that he makes about this issue is precisely the one which I never asserted: 'There is little doubt Comte intended to resonate his theories in the mind of the middle class individuals . . .' (*A.J.S.*, p. 139). It would also seem obvious that one must distinguish what Comte 'intended' at different times in his life. For instance, I think that, whatever his earlier intent, there is considerable evidence to show that Comte did not 'intend' this *after* his break with Saint-Simon. Further, I point out (*Crisis*, p. 92) that it was because Saint-Simon and Comte's sociology *opposed* middle-class individualistic utilitarianism that they 'then *failed* to win stable support from the emerging middle class' (italics added). In other words, I did *not* say that when born sociology was an expression of middle-class assumptions. I also fully acknowledge that 'sociology appeared elsewhere than in contexts characterized by the supremacy of the middle class over the aristocracy' – whatever that may mean! I state expressly that 'sociology was born, then, as the counterbalance to the political economy of the middle class . . .' (*Crisis*, p. 92). Again (on p. 100), I further emphasize that positivists then 'resented the middle class failure to appreciate and support them'. On page 106 I indicate that positivism did *not* then simply resonate middle-class values but that 'it was *critical* of their narrowly economic and individualistic version of utilitarianism' (italics added). Moreover, I could not have made this more emphatic than by saying (*Crisis*, p. 106),

the positivistic sociology of the early nineteenth century was *not* the intellectual creation of the propertied middle class. Its ground work, rather, was initially laid by the dispossessed *aristocracy* . . . marginal social strata . . . [and] these men were commonly viewed with profound *discomfort* by the propertied middle class [italics added].

Finally, I plainly state that it was only *later*, when 'the middle class were secure, that it subsequently became friendlier to sociology, contributing to its institutionalization' (*Crisis*, p. 107).

It should thus be perfectly clear that I did *not* at all narrowly link the emergence of sociology to the middle class; that I did *not* claim that Comte's theories were formulated to be particularly attractive to the middle class; I certainly did not hold that Comte's theories tacitly expressed the then dominant middle-class ideology. I expressly *rejected* the idea that Comte's theories were accepted by the middle class, or that they were then even *functional* to them. Rhoads' position concerning the relations between social theory and social structure is cast on the level of an introductory text, and that is quite bad enough. But I really must protest when Rhoads alleges to be describing my position when he is, in point of fact, only betraying his own. For example: Rhoads mentions my discussion of the larger historical context out of which, I suggest, Talcott Parsons' theory at first emerged; briefly, the First World War, the Soviet Revolution, the rise of Fascism-Naziism, the Great Depression of 1929. Concerning this, Rhoads first holds that I argue that 'these events made the international middle class anxious . . .' (*A.J.S.*, p. 143). The simple truth is that I did *not* say that *these* events 'made' the middle classes anxious because, while some did, others, such as the advent of Naziism-Fascism, were clearly the *outcomes* and not the *sources* of middle-class anxiety.

Rhoads then contends: 'Gouldner argues that it became Parsons' task [*sic*! – A.W.G.] to create a theory that would restore their confidence in the traditional social order and, more specifically, in capitalism (*A.J.S.*, p. 143). This is simply not so, and nowhere do I argue any such thing. Here, once more, Rhoads succumbs to intellectual vertigo and here, once again, he conflates aims and functions and blurs intentions with results. It is precisely because I insisted on such distinctions that even Rhoads must admit (*A.J.S.*, p. 139) that I made a cognate distinction between the 'class position of the theorist and the class whose domain assumptions the theory resonates'. (Here, as in other places, Rhoads characteristically buries dissonant material in a footnote.)

But the very idea that I had held that Parsons *knowingly undertook to use his social theory to restore confidence in capitalism* is a naïve caricature of my position. To suggest this is a vulgarity totally alien to the *Coming Crisis* and which I resent having attributed to it. I ask the readers of Rhoads' work to notice that he cannot and, indeed, *does not* document that contention. The truth is that the *Crisis* had *expressly* held that Parsons' anti-Marxism, one of the groundings of his subsequent theory, actually *precedes* the Great Depression: '. . . Parsons had already been familiarized with the European critics of Marxism . . . during his European studies, which were *prior* to the Depression' (*A.J.S.*, p. 150; italics added).

Rhoads' penny-dreadful vulgarity is irrepressible. He writes as if I had treated Parsons as a paid propagandist for the Chamber of Commerce. For example, he (*A.J.S.*, p. 150) maintains that I had held that 'Parsons created an antideterministic theory to restore [*sic*! – A.W.G.] capitalism's vitality'. No, I had held no such thing. Again, it is important to notice that nowhere does he quote me as saying anything that substantiates that allegation.

Rhoads generally wants to deny that Parsons' theory is an anti-deterministic defence of capitalism. To do so properly, he would have to distinguish between the two separate problematics involved in this contention. There is the first question of whether the Parsons of *The Structure of Social Action* was, indeed, anti-deterministic; there is, secondly, the different question of whether, or how, this anti-determinism, is linked to a 'pro-capitalism'. (It is vital to remember that the first issue revolves entirely around my critique of Parsons' early *Structure*.) Generally, Rhoads is not terribly neat about such distinctions, and he is hardly ever clear about which of these different points he is disputing. He misses the major point, previously discussed in responding to Lipset, that I had held that functionalism is not necessarily more pro-capitalist then pro-socialist – it is pro-*status quo*.

Rhoads' contention about my thesis concerning Parsons' anti-determinism hinges on two questions, first, the implications of Parsons' 'voluntarism', and, secondly, the implications of his *system* paradigm. In connection with the first, Rhoads holds that 'the only proof he [Gouldner] offers for his interpretation [of early Parsons as an anti-determinist] is a simple quotation from Parsons' (*A.J.S.*, p. 144), in which Parsons formally defines the meaning of an 'end'. But this is totally wrong.

Far from being the only proof I offer of Parsons' early anti-determinism, the quotation to which Rhoads refers is only a very *secondary* point, whose merely auxiliary significance I signal by burying it in a footnote at the end of that chapter. The real argument that I advance for the anti-determinism of Parsons' voluntarism cannot rest, and was never made to rest, on any single quote from Parsons. This proof was, rather, grounded in an analysis of the total structure of Parsons' most basic argument.

Remember that Parsons starts *The Structure of Social Action* with a central critique of philosophical positivism and *utilitarianism*, which he contrasts to his notion of 'voluntarism'. Parsons stresses that a central issue between these two models has to do with whether values are reduced to other social conditions. Parsons holds that a major inadequacy of positivism is that it tends to do this, while a major virtue of voluntarism is that it does not. Parsons stresses that voluntarism is distinguished by the fact that, in it, value-generated efforts are not reduced to other social forces; that values remain orthogonal to all other factors affecting social outcomes. As I mention in the *Crisis*: 'That men's values cannot be reduced to other social conditions implies that they cannot be predicted from other social conditions . . .' (*Crisis*, p. 190). Specifically, Parsons' voluntarism implies that it will never be possible to account for all the variance in social values in terms of other social factors. But if this is so, and if there is always a (mysterious?) core of human values that defies prediction (and hence explanation?) in terms of other social factors, then it is not correct to conclude that Parsons' value-focused voluntarism does indeed serve 'to undermine the entire possibility of any kind of determinism' (*Crisis*, p. 190).

The second argument Rhoads seeks to refute concerning Parsons' anti-determinism is grounded in the latter's 'multi-factor' *systems* model. Here I will merely reaffirm that mine was a reasonable interpretation of the metaphysical and political implications of *that* systems model. The thesis that Parsons' and functionalism's system model is, at bottom, anti-determinist is also accepted by Parsons' colleague and protector, Lipset himself. Indeed, in that very issue of the *American Journal of Sociology*, Lipset forcefully asserts that functional analysis, by 'stressing inter-relationship . . . in the absence of a key factor theory of change, [also implies that] harmful "unanticipated consequences" may result from "purposive social action" ' (*A.J.S.*, p. 97). In short, Lipset agrees that Parsons' systems model *does* have an anti-determinist bent insofar as it accents 'unanticipated consequences'. More than that, Lipset also indicates, in the same place, that Parsons' system model has anti-radical consequences – exactly what Rhoads denies – when he ends this remark with the low-key understatement, that 'functional analysis argues for some caution in radical social change' (*A.J.S.*, p. 97). Certainly this is dissonant with Rhoads' contention that Parsons' system model is *not* pro-*status quo*.

At this point there is a danger of obscuring an important issue. Rhoads approaches my contention, concerning the early Parsons' voluntarism, as if I single-mindedly opposed it as a sin to be extirpated. No such thing. Rhoads fails totally to notice that I had held that, in his voluntarism, the 'young Parsons' vision converges with that of Marx, and particularly the young Marx of alienation' (*Crisis*, p. 185). Indeed, I made reference to such convergences on more than one occasion. Both Lipset and Rhoads have, I fear, failed to see the point of them, perhaps because I had not hammered it home hard enough.

The central implication of this point bears on the nature and direction of Parsons' anti-Marxism which, be it remembered, was not developed on the basis of any serious, first-hand knowledge of Marx. For instance, there is not one citation in his *Structure of Social Action* (which views Marx as intellectually obsolescent) to any of Marx's own writing; nor is there any citation of Marx's own writing even in Parsons' 1965 paper on Marx. (Parsons, unlike Rhoads, had not used 'original' sources.) In general, Parsons seems to have been especially ignorant of Marx's pre-1847 work, in short, of the young Marx. Parsons' anti-Marxism was largely based on his reading of secondary German sources – the Weberian and Sombartian critique of Marxism.

The essential point to which these several considerations lead is this: Parsons largely conceived of Marxism as its German academic critics (of the classical period) had conceived of it; as a wooden, evolutionary, materialistic determinism; as a 'scientific Marxism', rather than as a *critical* Marxism. In short, Parsons' polemic against Marxism 'in general' was really a polemic against only one dimension of Marxism. This is one of the central implications of having indicated, as the *Crisis* does, that the young Parsons converges with the young Marx. It is now obvious that, far from holding Parsons to be uniformly and unqualifiedly anti-Marxist, I had actually held that his work had primarily developed in opposition to *one side* of Marxism; in terms of a very incomplete and defective reading of Marxism; and that this distorted polemic had led Parsons into a tacit and partial convergence with another side of Marxism, critical and voluntaristic Marxism – which, by the way, Lewis Coser discusses most ably in that same issue of the *A.J.S.*

This, at any rate, now enables us to clarify quite precisely *how* Parsons' anti-determinism is also anti-Marxist. It is because Parsons had no glimmer of the young, more voluntaristic Marx, and because he had one-sidedly interpreted Marxism as determinist, that Parsons was led to emphasize the anti-determinism of his own voluntarism and, indeed, to affirm his own voluntarism against (his one-sided reading of) Marxism.

But there is still more to the origins of Parsons' theory; these go beyond Parsons' grounding in an anti-Marxism of *any* sort. Parsons' early theory was not just grounded in a polemic against 'scientific' Marxism, and Rhoads (and others) are mistaken in holding that this was the sum and substance of my position. For it is not just *Marxism* that the early Parsons wishes to refute but, also, the *anti-Marxism of Sombart and Weber*. In the *Crisis* I repeatedly emphasized that Parsons' early theory was rooted in his opposition to Sombart's and Weber's *critique* of Marxism, and most especially in Parsons' opposition to the *deterministic* implications of *their* work. For example:

Parsons took exception to two aspects of their position: the deterministic metaphysics and the pessimistic structure of sentiment which suffuse their work. In their determinism both Sombart and Weber viewed capitalism as Marx had, says Parsons (*Crisis*, p. 181).

Let me now return to Rhoads' other argument, namely, that I was wrong in defining Parsons' theory as *deterministic*, because Parsons 'does recognize the autonomy of the individual'. Here Rhoads claims that I was being contradictory; for, he says, to speak of a 'deterministic cast to Parsons' theory contradicts Gouldner's previous attempt to reveal an anti-determinism within it' (*A.J.S.*, p. 147). I can only hope that Rhoads enjoyed a warm sense of triumph in having uncovered this 'contradiction', for it can only be temporary. This is only a *seeming* 'contradiction' and just a bit of careful reading would have shown that the contradiction was not real but only apparent.

One trouble with Rhoads is that elementary distinctions continually elude him. His point about a contradiction fails because he has missed the elementary distinction between the *early* Parsons and the *later*, between the young and the older Parsons. To say that a man can hold different positions in different periods of time is a trivial distinction, but vital to the case at hand. My point about Parsons' *anti*-determinism was clearly related to my analysis of Parsons' *early*, pre-Second World War phase and, still more specifically, to his 1937

Structure of Social Action. Rhoads does not acknowledge, perhaps he saw no significance in it, that the question of Parsons' *anti*-determinism arises in my *Crisis* only in the chapter on 'The Early Parsons'. My references to Parsons' more 'deterministic' formulations, however, refer clearly to Parsons' *later* work. Indeed, Parsons *himself* has characterized his own later position as cultural determinism. (See *Societies: Evolutionary and Comparative Perspectives*, Prentice Hall, Englewood, N.J., 1966, p. 113.) '. . . I am a cultural determinist, rather than a social determinist'.

It is, therefore, in no way contradictory for me to have emphasized the more deterministic features of Parsons' work, for this was a reference to his later work, most especially his development of social systems analysis, while my discussion of his *anti*-determinism bore on Parsons' early work, and, most especially, on his voluntarism. Frankly, it had not occurred to me that a reference to a shift in Parsons' metaphysics (notice his increasing use of mechanistic models) was in any way especially noteworthy or original.

In common with (what I had taken to be) a fairly wide understanding of it, I had indicated that Parsons' work had, over time, changed from *The Structure of Social Action*, where he had stressed that outcomes are shaped by the value-generated strivings of persons, to *The Social System* where he emphasizes the degree to which (and the mechanisms by which) these strivings are implanted in persons and shaped by the social system. These differing characterizations of these two works, and the general development of Parsons described here, are essentially accurate. They constitute the core of my argument in this connection; they are the concrete referent of Rhoads' argument about the anti-determinism–determinism 'contradiction'. But if there is any 'contradiction' here it is in Parsons, although I do *not* see it that way. As far as I am concerned, Parsons simply changed his mind or his early emphasis – for reasons, by the way, that I discuss in the *Crisis*.

Once again, it is evident that Rhoads' account is saturated with textbookish oversimplifications, by an almost self-destructive insistence on overlooking the most elementary distinctions; defects in no way compensated by his great use of 'original' sources. I could go on, and on and on; but surely everyone must by now have had enough of this.

'How Does This Matter Stand?'

I have earlier shown that Lipset could not support (indeed, surrendered) his two main contentions, namely that Parsons' sociology was neither conservative in character nor dominant in influence. He contradicts himself, finally acknowledging that Parsons was, indeed, the most influential of American sociologists and that his sociology was, in truth, conservative in character.

Throughout, we have also found that Lipset's case against *The Coming Crisis* is based upon his failure to make certain elemental distinctions. For example: he fails to distinguish between anti-Marxism, anti-socialism, and anti-Communism; and he fails to see that it was the *first* that I had principally asserted concerning Parsons; fails to see that I had expressly stated that functionalism should *not* be understood as being anti-*socialist* but is, despite this, to be understood as being *conservative*; fails to see the important distinction between saying that sociology-in-general is conservative (which he alleges is my charge), and what I actually said, namely that sociology's *controlling* character is conservative and that sociology also has important *radicalizing* potentialities. In speaking of Sprehe's dissertation, Lipset similarly fails to understand the simple distinction between the *conduct* of a survey and its *write-up*, and he thus fails to see why he was wrong in identifying me with Sprehe's writing. Lipset fails to see that it is contradictory to accuse me of attacking Parsons by a process of 'guilt by association', and for him to *defend* Parsons by 'redemption by association'.

It is precisely this simplism that characterizes both critiques of the *Crisis*. One objects not only to their politics or establishmentarianism, but, *most deeply*, to the quality of reason that they exhibit; to their inability to face complexity; to the failures of sensitivity and intellectual nerve they manifest; to the textbook level of discourse, to its lack of reflectiveness and wonder, and – one hates to say this to professionals, but – one must also object to a certain evident amateurism. In the end, it is the quality of *mind*, not politics, that confronts us with the deepest abyss.

In concluding, let me stress that these bare-bones comments of mine have a deliberately 'negative' intention: simply to *reply* to the criticisms levelled against *The Coming Crisis*. My remarks are *not* intended to expound, defend, or reaffirm the theses of the *Crisis*. The reader is warned that if he has read only my critics' criticisms, and my replies, his knowledge of what the *Crisis* actually *affirms* is most severely limited. But if I had thought there an easier and shorter way of saying what I had in mind than writing the *Crisis*, I would have chosen it.

Concerning the specifically ideological character of functionalism against which I argue in the *Crisis*, in contrast to the ideological position that I affirm there, each of these – the opposed and the affirmed positions – exemplify the basic logical possibilities that arise and express themselves systematically when men come to believe that there is a fundamental disparity between what the social world *should* be and what it *is*. It is precisely because sociological functionalism is an exemplar of one such basic possibility that makes its critique a very basic need, and not a matter of the sociologist's navel-gazing.

Nicolas Lobkowicz, attempting to portray Hegel's critique of the ought, characterizes these two different world views with subtle brilliance; I will quote him at length for that reason, even though the response that I criticized is here affirmed, and the response I favoured is here criticized:

Confronted with a reality which fails to satisfy the norms of reason, man can maintain two quite different attitudes. On the one hand, he can dream of another reality, long for a more perfect world, or call for action and eventually proceed to transform the reality in question. On the other hand, he may become suspicious of his own judgement, and instead of trying to transcend it he may look at the given reality long enough and close enough to discover its hidden rationality. Someone who does not understand, who is intellectually blind, will feel that there always remains something to be done. He never will be satisfied; his life will be an endless longing for improvement. In the end, he will urge change for the sake of change alone. In opposition to this attitude, the wise man will realize at a certain moment that all longing for another world and all calling for action are due to a lack of knowledge. He will realize that it is no longer his task to teach the world how it ought to be, but rather to show the world's own rationality. (*Theory and Practice*, University of Notre Dame Press, 1967, p. 154.)

I am inclined here to follow William James' advice to call our intellectual adversaries by the nobler names. Let us then say that the functionalists and Parsonians (and the conservative import attributed to them in the *Crisis*) are, in the sense of the above quotation, the 'wise men'. In effect, *The Coming Crisis* had described them as the modern sociological counterpart of Hegel's wise man. From this standpoint, then, their 'functionalism' and my own more 'critical theory' are to be understood as *metaphors* of the most fundamental reactions possible to the split in the world between the is and the ought.

Essentially, this is how the *Crisis* views functionalism – as the 'wise man's' conservatism – as 'priestly', not as 'propagandist'. Whatever else, such a view does not slight functionalism's significance and does not trivialize it. Seeing this, but missing the larger meaning, others have in fact complained that I attributed *too* much significance to it. In the end, however, no one can impair the seriousness with which functionalists deserve to be taken except they themselves. If theirs is the 'wise man's' conservatism, they will behave as wise men; they will not be content to score debater's points merely to deny their conservatism. Let them be 'wise' not only about the world but, also, about *themselves*. Wise men will no more dream about pursuing another reality concerning their *own* nature than they would seek to deny social reality. They will best persuade us to become reconciled to the world as it is by setting a good example, and becoming reconciled to their own character. A failure of nerve at this late hour ill-befits their dignity and that of the world-view they exemplify and enact.

NOTES
1. I am indebted to the following friends and colleagues for having helped, in quite various ways, to make possible the publication of the present article: Noam Chomsky; Rose Loeb Coser; Herbert Gans; Joan Huber; Harvey Molotch; Paul Piccone; Frank Riessman; Charles Willie. Because

of limitations of space, this is only part of the reply that was written. I am now told that this reply may be published in March 1973, *A.J.S.*

2. One of the advisory editors of the *A.J.S.* states that the articles in this issue were not selected in the usual competitive way.

3. The above account is based on a telephone conversation with Professor Bottomore on the morning of 10 October 1972, when he was at his home in Sussex and I at my office in Amsterdam.

4. While writing this I was re-reading Rodney Needham's 'Introduction' to Émile Durkheim's and Marcel Mauss's *Primitive Classification*, University of Chicago, 1963. In this book of ninety-six pages Needham found 'there were no fewer than sixty-nine bibliographical errors . . . there are a number of places at which Durkheim and Mauss misrender their sources, and at one point they cite a non-existent publication' (pp. xlvi–xlvii). In citing these errors I mean neither to compare myself with these great sociologists, nor to excuse my own errors.

5. James Weinstein, 'The Left, Old and New', *Socialist Revolution,* July–August 1972, p. 41.

6. These two are scarcely identical!

7. This is explicit in a leaflet ('Seize the Time!') distributed at the caucus of Radical Sociologists at the August 1970 convention of the American Sociological Association in Washington, D.C.

8. See R. W. Friedrich's 'Dialectical Sociology: toward a resolution of the current "crisis"', *British Journal of Sociology*, September 1972, pp. 263 *et seq.*

Part Two

Backgrounds to Sociology

6

Some Observations on Systematic Theory, 1945-55

Systematic sociologists in post-war America have enjoyed a productive era;[1] in less than a decade P. A. Sorokin produced his culminating *Society, Culture and Personality* (1947),[2] Florian Znaniecki published his *Cultural Sciences* (1952),[3] George Homans completed his pathbreaking and lucid volume on *The Human Group* (1950),[4] while Talcott Parsons and his associates have issued a series of volumes (Parsons 1949, 1951; Parsons and Shils, 1951; Parsons, Bales and Shils, 1953),[5] the most important of which is *The Social System* (Parsons, 1951). It is noteworthy that all of the above theorists, with the exception of Znaniecki, have done their work at Harvard University and it is quite conceivable that this has contributed to the important convergence found in their books.

It should be unnecessary to preface the following comments with the *caveat* that, in the space allotted, this writer can scarcely hope to describe systematically the contributions of any one of these complex volumes, let alone formulate a critical and synthetic appreciation of them all. The reader is therefore warned that he will be exposed to only the smallest fragment of their contents. In particular, attention will be given primarily to the more complex and extensive theoretical work done by Parsons.

It is a kind of poetic justice that some of the key difficulties of systematic theorists may be regarded as stemming from problems involved in integrating two strategic *empirical* generalizations.[6] These empiric generalizations might be formulated as follows: (a) some human behaviour is *normatively* oriented, being shaped by values, symbols, signs, etc.; (b) most human beings live in groups at any given time in their life cycles, and their behaviour is influenced by their *interaction* with others. The recurrent use of these propositions as key postulates in almost all systematic sociological theory derives, we suggest, not only from the powerful range of implications to which they lead, but also from their substantial empirical basis.[7]

Of the four theorists mentioned, only Homans has tended to organize his system around the second generalization, although he has by no means neglected the role of normative elements. Despite the fact that the second empirical generalization is the better validated, most current theory has been based upon the almost polemic affirmation of the first generalization.[8] In part, this derives from the fact that the merely social or group level is, as anthropologists have long since noted, also pre-human, ants and other creatures living a social existence. This is regarded as a potent disqualification of generalization (b) as a basis for systematic theory by those who maintain that an analytically independent science requires a distinctive subject matter. If, however, the first empirical generalization (a) is taken as the primary point of departure, it is at least justifiable on the grounds that it utilizes a distinctively human characteristic, normatively oriented, meaningful behaviour. In certain places, Znaniecki (1949) seems to have advanced a conception of sociology as a study of 'social' phenomena, while systems of knowledge, language, or religion were to be the foci of distinct cultural disciplines. In a rejoinder Sorokin (1947),[9] remarked that without cultural values 'human interaction would be purely biophysical . . . and sociology would lose the basis of its existence'. This, however, is an overstatement because Znaniecki had said that sociology was distinctively, not exclusively, concerned with social phenomena. Parsons retains a trace of Znaniecki's original formulation in his proposal that anthropology become a 'science of culture', in which the focus would be on cultural phenomena treated as an independent system of symbols (Parsons and Shils, 1951, p. 20; Parsons, 1951, pp. 553–4).[10] So far, however, anthropologists give little indication of finding this an acceptable charter for their discipline; this may be due to the fact that most anthropologists, in contrast with some sociologists, are much less interested in establishing the independence of their discipline, and are much more interested in working out the relations between their researches and those of psychologists, geographers, and biologists in concrete empirical contexts.

The problem of the distinctive subject matter of sociological analysis can be explored on at least three different levels of generalization (Levy, 1952, p. 18).[11] The theorist can elect to work on (a) the level of 'social action', the highest plane of generalization, which is concerned with the theories and concepts required to analyse *any* social action; (b) on the level of 'social systems', which, in Parsons' terms, refers to any system of social action involving a number of interacting individuals; this includes, but is not exhausted by, another level (c) that of 'societies'. In short, all social systems involve social action, but not the reverse; all societies comprise social systems, but not all social systems are societies.

In his earlier work, Parsons had defined social action in terms of the means–ends schema. This meant that the study of action had to focus on the standpoint of the actor; the actor's behaviour had to be understood as a function of the ends he was pursuing, the norms which shaped these ends, his resultant definition of the situation. This is convergent, but not identical, with what Znaniecki has called the 'humanistic coefficient' (1934, esp. pp. 36–9).[12] In part, then, ends or goals were conceived of as temporally prior to and partially determinative of behaviour. Many difficulties resulting from this model have been extensively explored by both Sorokin and Znaniecki, both of whom regard it as an inadequate approximation to human behaviour.

Sorokin, for example, has stressed that many social actions are not purposive means to an end, for example, the alcoholic's inability to resist liquor, or the soldier's cowardice despite his earlier resolution to be brave (1947, pp. 44–6).[13] Znaniecki's objections to the means–ends schema have even greater theoretical cogency. If behaviour is shaped by prior ends, asks Znaniecki, how can one account for the development of new ends, or for changes in the ends by which behaviour is presumably shaped? Despite his philosophical training, Znaniecki is extremely sensitive to the constraints imposed by empirical data, even the data provided by daily observation. He notes that social action is not a homogeneous entity, but that there are heterogeneous types of social action – creative, habitual, or imitative actions – and suggests that the means–ends schema is at best adequate for dealing with the latter two varieties. 'Creative' social action is that in which ends change or in which new ends emerge; this is an ideal type which, of course, is more or less present in almost any concrete social action. Znaniecki (1952)[14] therefore proposes that purposes or ends cannot be conceived solely as the prior regulators of action, but that 'an action in its total course manifests a gradual formation of a purpose which becomes gradually realized as it is being formed' (1952, p. 198).[15]

In short, ends and, by implication, values also, must be seen as partially modified and shaped in the very process of action and interaction and not as some ontologically superior entities. This two-way avenue between values and interaction patterns is systematically developed by Homans, with both sides of the equation, interaction as well as sentiments or values, being taken as problematic (1950, esp. pp. 125–7).[16] In part for these reasons, it may be supposed, Parsons' most recent statements of the action schema have been partially, though not radically, revised. The salience of the means–ends schema has been reduced in the recent formulations. Parsons now tends to conceive of 'action' as requiring a focus on an actor in a situation, and a concern with his orientation to a situation which is composed of social, physical and cultural objects. 'Action is a process in the actor-situation system which has motivational significance to the individual actor' (1951, p. 4),[17] which is to say that it has a 'bearing on the attainment of gratifications or the avoidance of deprivations' (ibid.) for the actor. Obviously, however, motivation may be analysed on a purely biological or pre-symbolic level, in terms of reflexes, drives, or instincts; Parsons is therefore compelled to specify further his conception of social action in order that it may be distinguished from 'behaviour' on the purely biological level.

He does this by stating that action is oriented by a system of 'expectations' which the actor develops about objects in his situation. These objects, moreover, come to have 'meaning' for the actor; when the meanings evoked by signs or symbols are shared by a number of actors there are the beginnings of a culture (Parsons, 1951, p. 5).[18] Both Sorokin and Znaniecki agree that social action is behaviour-oriented toward meaningful objects. The question remains, however, whether Parsons' re-conceptualization of the action schema enables it to escape the earlier objections which the former theorists have lodged against it. Furthermore, is all behaviour equally anticipatory and shaped by expectations? How do variations in the degree of the anticipatory orientations affect subsequent behaviour? Is there not an undue preoccupation with orientation to the future implicit even in the revised version of the action schema?

Even in its present form, the action schema focuses on behaviour as anticipatory, not as retrospective, as oriented to the future, not as oriented by the past. To be sure, Parsons acknowledges that orientations to the future are an outcome of past experience; but the implications of this are barely explored. There is also a real question here of the extent to which this conception of the action schema is a culture-bound approximation to behaviour in Western societies, whose rationalistic cultures place a premium on an orientation to the future. The action schema may, however, be a less adequate approximation to behaviour in tribal or traditionalist cultures, where greater value is placed on reverence for and preservation of old, received patterns (cf. Smith, 1952).[19]

Stated differently, there seems to be some need for a new concept analogous to that of the 'reference group', but in which the actor's orientation to a time period, rather than to a group, is taken as problematic. A generalized concept such as this, which may be called the 'reference period',[20] would withhold commitment to the dubious assumption that all social action is equally anticipatory and future-oriented. It would seem sufficient to stress that men do have some time orientations which affect their behaviour, and to submit the question of the degree of their past- or future-orientation to empirical examination.

In contrast to Parsons' detailed formulation, one of Parsons' former students, Marion Levy, very candidly defines social action as behaviour which is not determined either by heredity or by the non-human environment. Levy indicates that social action is a residual concept and suggests that it is required principally to assert the analytic independence of sociological analysis (Levy, 1952, pp. 7–8).[21]

It may well be that much of this problem can be obviated by taking the empirically concrete human organism as the centre of attention, and by defining the problem as one of accounting for the variance in anything that it does or that happens to it individually or in association with others. From this standpoint, some variances in human functioning or structures will be more or less accounted for by variations in values, interaction patterns, and by other conceptual tools which sociologists have traditionally employed or will introduce. Other parts of the variance will be accounted for by concepts utilized in biology, psychology, and other disciplines. The vital problem, in terms of the needs of an empirical discipline, is to formulate and operationalize concepts which can account for empirically detectable variance.

Even if one sets aside questions of the logical niceties of Parsons' analysis of 'social action', there still remain important empirical issues. A specification of the elements of social action is no more attainable by formal definition alone than are the attributes of 'life', which the biologist regards as the 'subject matter' of his discipline. Znaniecki, almost alone among the systematic theorists who have raised the question, has stressed that the characteristics of social action cannot be taken as *a priori* data but are also to be inductively sought and empirically validated.

The conflict between the two empirical generalizations, as to which should become the point of departure for theory-building, has now largely been resolved by combining the two foci into a single unit. Sorokin's conception of the generic properties common to all 'socio-cultural' phenomena had led him, rather early, to a fully explicit combination of normative-meaningful and interactional foci, as his very use of the unit concept 'socio-cultural' implies. 'The most generic model of any socio-cultural phenomenon', Sorokin writes, 'is the meaningful interaction of two or more human individuals . . . a meaningful interaction is any interaction where the influence exerted by one party over another has a meaning or value superimposed upon the purely physical and biological properties of the respective actions' (Sorokin, 1947, pp. 44–6).[22]

Parsons' later discussion of the 'social system' closely converges with this. 'A social system,' writes Parsons, 'consists of a plurality of individual actors, interacting with each other in a situation . . . and whose relations . . . [are] defined and mediated in terms of a system of culturally structured and shared symbols' (Parsons, 1951, pp. 5–6).[23] In other respects, Parsons' formulation develops and extends Sorokin's. First, Parsons makes explicit that the interacting actors are performing 'roles' which, as he puts it, are orientations 'organized about expectations in relation to a particular interaction context . . .' (1951, pp. 38–9).[24] Even in this respect, however, Parsons' and Sorokin's formulations are still not greatly different, for Sorokin (1947) also stresses 'role' as a key component of the social system (pp. 70–71).[25] More distinctive, however, is Parsons' conception of the social system in terms of the ego-alter model. 'Ego' and 'alter' are the generalized terms which Parsons uses for any pair of interacting and reciprocal social roles. The value of this model is that it focuses attention on social relationships without necessarily obliterating the component units who are interacting, and without focusing on these actors merely as biological organisms. Thus, the social system is analytically differentiated and is not treated as a homogeneous, undifferentiated entity as Durkheim did when he stressed the concept of 'association'.[26]

In analysing these role relations, Parsons speaks of the actors' mutual orientation to a set of shared expectations, rather than of 'rights' and 'obligations' which would be subsumed under 'expectations'. If such a reconceptualization results in a loss of precision, it gains by raising the level of abstraction. This, in turn, facilitates the formulation of certain generalized propositions relevant to any social or ego–alter system. Specifically, Parsons is now able to state cogently the conditions under which the system will remain in or lose equilibrium. The system is postulated to be in equilibrium when ego and alter conform to each other's expectations and when each rewards such complaint behaviour (Parsons, 1951, p. 205).[27] It is at this point, where Parsons' analysis is firmly founded in a generalized analysis of social order and social control, that it clearly transcends Sorokin's formulations.

Several comments might be made at this juncture concerning the ego–alter schema and its postulated equilibrium conditions. It is noteworthy, though not in itself a cause for alarm, that the schema utilizes an underlying model at variance with those successfully employed in the physical sciences, in which entropic tendencies toward 'disorder' are postulated. This, of course, is at the centre of the cybernetics-information theory model, where it is assumed that messages have a 'natural' tendency toward disorganization (Wiener, 1954).[28] In contrast, Parsons writes:

It is certainly contrary to the common sense of the social sciences, but it will be nevertheless assumed that the maintenance of the complementarity of role-expectations, once established, is not problematical . . . No special mechanisms are required for the explanation of the maintenance of complementary interaction-orientation (Parsons, 1951, p. 205).[29]

Here there seems to be an echo of the classic Durkheimian polemic against the Marxist notion of 'internal contradictions', in which Durkheim insisted that the normal division of labour did not produce anomie. In short, the system is not conceived as possessing *internal* sources of conflict and tension. If it is assumed, as Parsons (1951) does, that once a stable system of interaction is established it 'tends to continue unchanged' (p. 251),[30] then we must expect changes to arise from pressures *external* to the system as such. As Parsons writes, 'Let us assume that, from whatever source, a disturbance is *introduced into* the system . . .' (Parsons 1951, p. 262, our emphasis – A.W.G.).[31]

Parsons fails to weigh the possibility that a system's tendency to retain its equilibrium may change its adaptation to a changing environment, human or non-human. Thus the very stability of a social system may generate maladaptations to an environment which, in turn, generate internal tensions for the system. In general, Parsons' theory has tended to focus on the system itself, and has given little attention to the problem of inter-system relations.

Parsons also seems to bypass the possibility that ego's rewarded conformity with certain of alter's expectations may cumulatively generate a neglect of other of alter's expectations. These may go unnoticed for a period, only suddenly to become perceived and to emerge as a source of tension. For example, the wife who expects and encourages her husband to be 'successful' and a 'good provider' may gradually discourage the husband's participation in the family until a point arrives where this is suddenly perceived and defined as a problem. In general, there seems to be little place in Parsons' work for sudden shifts in the definition of a situation, or in anything else for that matter (with the exception of his peripheral discussion of charisma). This is partly attributable to Parsons' effort to link his social theory with a psychology of motivation and his neglect of psychologies which centre on problems of *perception*.[32]

There are two points here: (a) gradual and, at first, imperceptible deviant tendencies are possible precisely because conformity is a range or a zone of behaviour, not a pin-point (cf. Homans, 1950, p. 295).[33] In short, gradual, hence undetected deviance is possible because of a feature of a stable social system, namely its built-in toleration of some range of behaviour as permissible. No stable social system is possible without a range of acceptable conformity and yet, because of it, every social system is vulnerable to a 'creeping' kind of transformation which may, at some point, be defined as threatening and may unstabilize the system. (b) No stabilized social system is possible without some standardized system of priorities for conformity to varying expectations, so that decisions may be made among competing options. Yet, given such a system of priorities, cumulative compliance with top-priority expectations may lead to a cumulative neglect of low-priority expectations which can suddenly become a focus of disorganization. For example, the newly married bride's sudden discovery that the 'romance' has gone out of her marriage. In short, certain tendencies toward deviance seem to stem from some of the very features which are requisite for system stability.

One fundamental consequence of Parsons' conception of the social system in terms of this equilibrium model is its inability to cope adequately with social process and change, and seriously to integrate such problems with his basic conceptual scheme. In Parsons' approach, as one writer has put it, 'processes of social becoming, currents, and eddies of mass behaviour, rapidly evolving social structures, fads, fashions and other elementary forms of collective behaviour simply do not fall significantly within his scope of analysis' (Habenstein, 1955, p. 237).[34] It is noteworthy that this criticism, by a somewhat sceptical member of the Chicago school of sociology, is echoed almost word for word by a well-disposed critic from the Cornell school: Parsons' 'position minimizes the importance of interaction which is not culturally structured . . . crowds, mobs, panics, etc.' (Martel, n.d., p. 56).[35]

There are two implications of this critique which deserve to be distinguished. The first is that 'collective behaviour' as a form of highly transient, fluidly changing behaviour escapes through the larger mesh of Parsons' conceptual net. In brief, focus on the equilibrium model makes it difficult to cope with dynamic processes. The second and equally important implication of the above critique is that Parsons' preoccupation is with culturally shaped social structures, regardless of their rate of change. This, in turn, leads Parsons to an almost exclusive concern with 'institutionalized' structures and to a concomitant neglect of structures which are stable but not institutionalized. These need not refer to structured patterns of deviance or the unrecognized and unintended mechanisms of defence which restore the equilibrium of a threatened ego–alter system. Some structured deviance or defence mechanisms can be regarded as sub-cases of a larger realm of phenomena which may be termed 'latent structures'[36] (Levy, 1952, pp. 7–8) by analogy with the concept of 'latent functions' (Merton, 1949).[37] Latent structures would be the culturally unprescribed patterns which subserve some social function; if they are patterns of belief they may be termed latent culture structures,[38] e.g., the belief in luck, rather than 'hard work', as the vehicle for upward mobility; if they are patterns of interaction and relations, they may be called latent social structures, e.g., a most important set of such latent social structures are those referred to by the Chicago school of ecology in such concepts as 'dominance', 'concentration', or 'centralization'. Other examples of latent social structures would be oligarchical power patterns and social classes in a democratic culture, or 'informal groups' in a factory. It is noteworthy that Parsons places little emphasis upon the latter despite their importance in recent empirical studies of formal and especially industrial organization.

The abiding problem of Parsons' conceptual scheme remains the task of coping systematically with questions of change. Parsons' pessimism concerning the possibilities of a theory of change is surprisingly profound:

. . . a general theory of the processes of change of social systems is not possible in the present state of knowledge . . . We repeat we do not have a complete theory of the processes of change in social systems . . . When such a theory is available the millennium for social science will have arrived. This will not come in our time and most probably never.

It is perhaps superfluous to note, as Parsons himself would surely acknowledge, that there is no science which has been 'complete' in any respect, and no science ever expects to be.

A significant feature of even Parsons' partial statement of the available canons for analysing social change is the degree to which it is characterized by *ad hoc* concepts and assumptions. Above all, there is an elaboration of the Veblenian concept of 'vested interest', around which resistances to change are organized. Parsons (1951) holds that almost all change occurs in the face of resistance and by overcoming it (p. 491),[39] a key postulate of Freudian therapy[40] as well as of Marxism. Indeed, the extent to which Parsons' efforts at theoretical and empirical analysis of change suddenly lead him to enlist a body of Marxist concepts and assumptions is nothing less than bewildering considering that Parsons is one of the few truly profound critics of Marxism writing today. It almost seems as if two sets of books were being kept, one for the analysis of equilibrium and another for the investigation of change. This is particularly evident in Parsons' analysis of 'The Problem of Controlled Institutional Change' (Parsons, 1949, pp. 310–48),[41] which attempted to develop a sociologically sophisticated strategy for coping with conquered Germany. Similar tendencies seem evident in another penetrating article on McCarthyism (Parsons, 1955).

Parsons stresses that '. . . the conception of a completely integrated social system is a limiting case. Every at all complex society contains very important elements of internal conflict and tension' (Parsons, 1949, p. 317).[43] Though one of the sides to a conflict may impede change, the other party may be enlisted as 'allies'. While the equilibrium model denies internal tension, the analysis of change apparently requires that it assume central importance. Moreover, the statement involves what is practically a Marxist conception of the strategy of social change. Further: '. . . it is probably best to attack the Junkers at their most vulnerable point – their economic bases . . . it can above all be attacked as a case of exclusive class privilege' (p. 325).[44] Moreover, the German civil service's conservative patterns are held to depend on 'the class basis of recruitment of the higher personnel' (p. 326).[45] Finally, Parsons remarks that, even though ideas are interdependent with other parts of the social system, 'it is one of the most important results of modern psychological and social science that, except in certain particular areas, ideas and sentiments, both on the individual and mass levels, are dependent manifestations of deeper-lying structures – character structures and institutional structures . . . than independent determinants of behaviour' (p. 336).[46] This formulation is strongly reminiscent of the Marxist formula that 'it is not the consciousness of men that determines their being, but, on the contrary, their social being that determines their consciousness.' This is noteworthy only because it indicates the extent to which Parsons has had to draw upon *ad hoc* models, concepts, and assumptions peripheral to his own systematic analysis to handle the problem of change. This formulation also seems at variance with Parsons' own formalized conception of the general nature of social systems. Here Parsons (1951) states that 'there are no one or two inherently primary sources of impetus to change in social systems . . . The central methodological principle of our theory is that of the interdependence of a plurality of variables' (p. 493).[47] There seems to be some unresolved conflict between this statement and those in which he de-emphasizes the role of ideas and underlines the role of class factors and, in particular, where he remarks, 'The economic-occupational structure seems to be the most promising lever of institutional change . . .' in post-war Germany (Parsons, 1949, p. 334).[48]

Parsons' focus on the social system as a system of mutually interdependent variables has, of course, long been a cardinal doctrine of functionalists. The indications seem to be, however, that Parsons is constrained to revise this formal postulate when he undertakes a concrete socio-historical analysis of change. Indeed, it may be that the divergence between theories conceiving of behaviour in terms of social systems, and theories which stress the importance of certain factors, is not so radical as is often assumed. The factor theories can be viewed as having taken the system as a datum, and focusing on the problem of identifying and weighing certain parts of the system.[49] A single-factor theory being, in this view, a limiting and unsophisticated case of such theories. As a reaction to the empirical difficulties which resulted, the functionalists counterposed a stress on the system as a whole, taking it as problematic. In turn, they neglected or took as given the question of the differential significance attributable to varying parts of the system.

In some measure, the earlier functionalists neglected the problem of factor-loading, because they lacked the statistical tools to secure an empirical resolution of the problem. Today, however, mathematical and statistical developments seem to be on the verge of making this possible and have therefore re-opened this long dormant issue among functionalists. For example, Paul Lazarsfeld has attempted to develop a statistical model which

provides a procedure for discovering which of the interacting elements proponderate . . . It will be agreed, I suppose, that such provision for discovering which outcomes predominate *under specified conditions* moves an appreciable step beyond the mere assertion of interdependence. (Lazarsfeld and Merton, 1954, p. 59, emphasis by A.W.G.).[50]

In his discussion of the relations between theories of equilibrium and of change, Parsons (1949) assumes the logical priority of equilibrium analysis. 'The essential point is that for there to be a theory of change of pattern . . . there must be an initial and a terminal pattern to be used as points of reference'

(p. 483).[51] A serious question concerns the possibility of determining whether a system is in equilibrium, and what this entails, without temporal analysis which focuses on the changes the system has undergone. Two systems, for example, may both be in equilibrium, in the sense that ego and alter are complying with each other's expectations in any given time-unit. It is quite possible, however, for one of these systems to be entering the equilibrium phase and for the other to be leaving it. It would seem very difficult, if not impossible, to differentiate these two equilibrium situations, and to develop different prognoses for them, by a cross-sectional analysis alone. From this standpoint, the analysis of change is fundamental to the analysis of equilibrium. It is clear that the problem of integrating diachronic and synchronic analyses, genetic/historical methods with cross-sectional research, remains one of the most urgent strategic tasks of modern systematic theory.

NOTES

1. I should like to express my appreciation to Florian Znaniecki, Oscar Lewis, Martin Martel and Howard S. Becker for reading this paper and for their suggestions; needless to add, they cannot be held responsible for the conclusions which this writer advances.

2. New York, Harper, 1947.

3. Urbana, University of Illinois, 1952.

4. New York, Harcourt Brace, 1950.

5. T. Parsons, *Essays in Sociological Theory*, Glencoe, Free Press, 1949 (enlarged edition 1954) and *The Social System*, Glencoe, Free Press, 1951; T. Parsons and E. A. Shils, eds., *Toward a General Theory of Action*, Cambridge, Harvard U.P., 1951; T. Parsons, R. F. Bales, and E. A. Shils, *Working Papers on the Theory of Action*, Glencoe, Free Press, 1953.

6. cf. Robert K. Merton, esp. pp. 11, 86, 91–6 for a discussion of his notion of 'empirical generalization', *Social Theory and Social Structure*, Glencoe, Free Press, 1949.

7. It is particularly necessary to raise questions concerning the empirical status of even key postulates in a theoretical system, and to treat this as an independent problem, when the system is not a truly deductive one, as for example, in the case of Parsons' theory. For when the system is not genuinely deductive, the lower level propositions are not true 'theorems' the

validity of which necessarily lends confirmation to the higher level propositions.

8. This, however, is not true of many English anthropologists. Much of the theoretical conflict between them and American anthropologists derives from the English anthropologists' stress on the first proposition, and the Americans' accent on the second, in the form of concern with cultural patterns. 'While I have defined social anthropology as the study of human society (i.e. the forms of association to be found amongst human beings) there are some who define it as the study of culture.' – A. R. Radcliffe-Brown.

9. P. A. Sorokin, *Society, Culture and Personality*, New York, Harper and Row, 1947.

10. op. cit., p. 20; *The Social System*, op. cit., pp. 553–4.

11. M. J. Levy, jr, *The Structure of Society*, Princeton U.P., 1952, p. 18.

12. F. Znaniecki, *The Method of Sociology*, New York, Farrar and Rinehart, 1934, esp. pp. 36–9.

13. P. A. Sorokin, op. cit., pp. 44–6.

14. F. Znaniecki, *The Cultural Sciences*, Urbana, University of Illinois Press, 1952.

15. ibid., p. 198.

16. G. C. Homans, *The Human Group*, New York, Harcourt Brace, 1950, esp. pp. 125–7.

17. T. Parsons, *The Social System*, op. cit., p. 4.

18. ibid., p. 5.

19. M. W. Smith, 'Different Cultural Concepts of Past, Present and Future', *Psychiatry*, 15, 1952, pp. 395–400.

20. cf. Karl Mannheim's concept of the 'paradigmatic experience', which focuses on the orientation of behaviour to the past, in his *Diagnosis of Our Time*, New York, Oxford U.P., 1947.

21. op. cit., pp. 7–8.

22. op. cit., pp. 44–60.

23. *The Social System*, op. cit., p. 4.

24. ibid., pp. 38–9.

25. P. A. Sorokin, op. cit., pp. 44–60.

26. Durkheim: 'May not sociology feature an idea which might well be

the basis not only of a psychology but also of a whole philosophy - the idea of association.'

27. *The Social System*, op. cit., p. 205.

28. N. Wiener, *The Human Use of Human Beings*, New York, Doubleday, 1954.

29. *The Social System*, op. cit., p. 205.

30. ibid., p. 251.

31. ibid., p. 262.

32. Most particularly, a neglect of Gestalt psychology.

33. op. cit., p. 295.

34. R. Habenstein, 'From Secular to Sectarian', *Midwest Sociologist*, 17, 1955, p. 237.

35. M. U. Martel, 'The Theory of Action of Talcott Parsons, 1937–51', n.d., p. 56.

36. op. cit., pp. 7–8.

37. R. K. Merton, *Social Theory and Social Structure*, Glencoe, Free Press, 1949.

38. cf. Claude Lévi-Strauss' discussion of 'unconscious models' in his *Social Structure* in A. L. Kroeber (ed.), *Anthropology Today*, University of Chicago, 1953. Strauss, it seems, blurs the distinction between models of culture and social structure, tending to reduce the latter to the former. See also the cognate concept of the 'projective distance' of a model in P. F. Lazarsfeld and A. H. Barton, 'Qualitative Measurement in the Social Sciences', in D. Lerner and H. D. Lasswell (eds.), *The Policy Sciences*, Stanford University Press, 1951.

39. *The Social System*, op. cit., p. 491.

40. This is lucidly developed in Anna Freud's *The Ego and the Mechanisms of Defense*, New York, International Universities Press, 1946. The key to psychoanalytical discussion of resistance and its role in therapy is probably that found in some of Wilhelm Reich's earlier work, an English translation of which is available in his *Character Analysis*, New York, Orgone Institute Press, 1945.

41. *Essays in Sociological Theory*, op. cit., pp. 310–48.

42. T. Parsons, 'McCarthyism and American Social Tensions; a Sociologists View', *Yale Review*, 1955, pp. 226–45.

43. *Essays in Sociological Theory*, op. cit., p. 317.

44. ibid., p. 325.

45. ibid., p. 326.

46. ibid., p. 336.

47. *The Social System*, op. cit., p. 493.

48. *Essays in Sociological Theory,* op. cit., p. 334.

49. There are even biographical data that can document this in the case of Marxism; in fact, Bukharin later made the concept of 'social system' focal and integrated it with orthodox Marxism. For example, a society 'may be considered as a whole consisting of parts (elements) related to each other; in other words, the whole may be regarded as a system' (N. Bucharin, *Historical Materialism: A System of Sociology*, New York, International, 1925, p. 75), or we 'define society as a system of interaction' (p. 87).

50. P. F. Lazarsfeld and R. K. Merton, 'Friendship as Social Process,' in M. Berger, T. Abel, and C. H. Page (eds.), *Freedom and Control in Modern Society*, New York, Van Nostrand, 1954, p. 59.

51. *Essays in Sociological Theory*, op. cit., p. 483.

7

Reciprocity and Autonomy in Functional Theory

The intellectual fundament of functional theory in sociology is the concept of a 'system'. Functionalism is nothing if it is not the analysis of social patterns as parts of larger systems of behaviour and belief. Ultimately, therefore, an understanding of functionalism in sociology requires an understanding of the resources of the concept of 'system'. Here, as in other embryo disciplines, the fundamental concepts are rich in ambiguity.

The recurrent use of organismic models by leading contributors to functionalism, such as Durkheim and Radcliffe-Brown, has its major intellectual justification in the fact that organisms are *examples* of systems. To the extent that the organismic model has proved fruitful in sociological analysis it has been so because the organism was a paradigmatic case of a system. It has been easier to unravel the implications of system-thinking by the direct inspection of a concrete case of a system, such as an organism or, for that matter, a machine, than it has been to analyse formally the implications of the concept of a system treated in full abstraction.

Yet the occasional vulgarities of those using organismic models clearly indicated the hazards of this procedure.[1] Indeed, we might say that the organismic model has been misleading in sociological analysis precisely in so far as it led to a focus on characteristics which were peculiar to the organism but not inherent in a generalized notion of a 'system'. Thus the need to distinguish between the concrete case, namely the organism, and the thing it was a case of, namely a 'system', became increasingly evident to functional theorists.

Yet in one sense the organismic theorists were correct. That is, if social behaviour is to be understood by application of system models, a generalized concept of a system alone is insufficient. For there is always a question of the *kind* of system model that shall be employed in the understanding of social behaviour. There are at least two ways of approaching this problem. One is the strategy of the organismic theorists, namely to take a concrete case of a system and use it as a guide. But even this is ambiguous because biological organisms vary enormously and there remains the difficult problem of stipulating *which* organism is to be used as a model. A second route, to be followed here, is to make explicit the most generalized dimensions in terms of which systems, formally construed, may vary and then to stipulate the conjunction of formal system dimensions which are to be applied to social behaviour.

From a sociologist's standpoint the two most important aspects of a 'system' are the 'interdependence' of a number of 'parts' and the tendency of these to maintain an 'equilibrium' in their relationships. Consequently, much of system analysis and functional theory resolves itself into questions about 'interdependence' and 'equilibrium'. As shall be indicated later, equilibrium necessarily implies interdependence, but interdependence does not necessarily imply equilibrium. Agreeing with Parsons that 'the most general and functional property of a system is the interdependence of parts or variables', this paper shall therefore focus on the concept of interdependence, leaving the equilibrium problem for later analysis.[2]

There is another problem to be considered here. It is implicit in the concept of system, and becomes manifest as soon as an effort is made to apply it to any given subject matter. This is the problem of identifying the interdependent parts. That is, what elements shall be held to constitute the system and on what grounds shall a decision be made to include certain elements in the system?

System Models in Merton and Parsons

It has been suggested above that system analysis is central to sociological functionalism. This will be documented by examination of the two leading American contributors to functional theory in sociology, Robert K. Merton and Talcott Parsons. As shall be seen below, system concepts play a pivotal role in both their formulations of functional theory. It will also be noted, however, that the nature of their commitment to a system model differs, Parsons' being what may be called a total commitment, while Merton's can be regarded as a strategy of minimal commitment.

With characteristic cogency, Robert Merton has stated his conception of the 'central orientation of functionalism'. This he finds is 'expressed in the practice of interpreting data by establishing their consequences for larger structures in which they are implicated. . . .'[3] It is instructive to contrast this with the more extended formulation by Talcott Parsons:

> The most essential condition of successful dynamic analysis is continual and systematic reference of every problem to the state of the system as a whole. . . . Functional significance in this context is inherently teleological. A process or set of conditions either 'contributes' to the maintenance (or development) of the system or it is 'dysfunctional' in that it detracts from the integration and effectiveness of the system. It is thus the functional reference of all particular conditions and processes to the state of the total system as a going concern which provides the logical equivalent of simultaneous equations in a fully developed system of analytical theory.[4]

Without doubt, there is substantial convergence in these two statements concerning the fundamentals of functional analysis. Both Merton and Parsons agree that in accounting for any social or cultural pattern an effort must be made to relate this to the context in which it occurs, so that it may not be understood in isolation but must be analysed in its relation to other patterns. In short, both postulate a system model in dealing with social and cultural phenomena.

There is, however, a notable difference in emphasis in Merton's and Parsons' formulations. This is expressed in Parsons' stress on the notion of a 'system' while Merton persistently avoids explicit use of this concept. In fact, there is but one reference to it in the index to Merton's volume on *Social Theory and Social Structure*. More importantly, Merton's avoidance of the system concept is above all suggested by the architecture of his basic paradigm of functional analysis.[5] This does not begin with an analysis of 'social systems', but, rather, with a directive to identify the 'units' which are problematic in any given case. For Merton, the first step in functional analysis involves stipulation of 'some standardized (i.e., patterned and repetitive) item, such as social roles, institutional patterns, social processes, cultural patterns . . .'.[6] In brief, for Merton functional analysis is focused on some delimited unit of human behaviour or belief, with a view to accounting either for its persistence or change by establishing its consequences for environing social or cultural structures.

System analysis could have entered into Merton's directives for functional analysis in at least two major ways: either by treating the structural context to which the unit is linked as a system, and/or by analysing the unit itself as a sub-system composed of interdependent parts. Neither of these courses is explicitly stressed in Merton's formulations.

When Merton does take up the structural context in his paradigm, his comments are primarily devoted to a consideration of the ways in which this context generates constraints, limiting the range of variation in the problematic pattern with which the functional analyst is directed to begin. He does indicate that social structures are composed of interdependent elements, and to this extent acknowledges their systemic character, but this never becomes an object of formal analysis.

Furthermore, the problematic unit pattern with which Merton's paradigm of functional analysis begins is not itself explicitly identified as subject to system analysis. In the operational protocols which follow the paradigm, Merton states that the unit pattern on which the analysis focuses must be seen as implicated in the behaviour of people who are differently located in the larger social structure. He indicates also that it is necessary to locate 'these people in their interconnected social statuses'. The emphasis here, however, seems to involve a structural location of the component elements rather than a focus on the systematic character of the structure itself.

For example, Merton does not require that the problematic unit be related to any postulated 'need' of the contextual structure *as a system*. Indeed, while Merton concedes that 'in every functional analysis [there] is some conception of the functional requirements of the system under observation', he goes on to insist that the notion of functional requirements or needs of the social system 'remains one of the cloudiest and empirically most debatable concepts in functional theory'.[7]

For Parsons the central theoretical and empirical problems are those which involve a social system as such, and which explain how it is maintained as a going system. Empirically delimitable units become important for him primarily as they enter into the maintenance of the social system, in the satisfaction of its needs, or in their resolution of its problems. In contrast to Merton, Parsons does not focus on the explanation of empirically delimited units of social behaviour or belief, but instead centres attention directly on analysis of the contextual structure as a system.

The Selection of System Parts

Parsons' assumption is that it is impossible to understand adequately any single pattern except by referring it to some larger systemic whole. He therefore assumes that the *whole* system must be conceptually constituted prior to the investigation and analysis of specific patterns. In consequence, Parsons is led forthwith to the analysis of the *total* anatomy of social systems in an effort to identify their constituent elements and relationships. This presumably makes it possible to refer any given problematic pattern in a systematic manner to all the component structures constituting the system. The theoretical strategy here requires that all the constituents of the whole system be *immediately* constituted in an *ex cathedra* manner.

But whether or not a given structure in the social anatomy is in fact there, or whether it is useful to postulate it, is an important part resolvable only by empirical research. The specification of the component elements of social systems is, in principle, no more attainable by theoretical postulation alone than are the attributes of 'living' systems, which the biologist regards as the systems with which his discipline deals. What seems to have been neglected is that the elements of social systems cannot be merely constituted *a priori*, but must also be inductively sought and empirically validated.

It is in large measure because of their differing orientations to the role of empirical operations not in science in general, but in theory construction in particular, that Parsons and Merton differ in this regard. That is, part of the problem here is how one identifies and provides a warrant for the elements held to be constitutive of a social system. In large measure, Merton differs from Parsons because he feels that *empirical* operations are necessarily involved in the very admission of elements as part of a social system. He does not regard this problem as solely resolvable by theoretical postulation. Although he has not committed himself on this specific point in any extended manner, Merton's emphasis on theories of the 'middle range', which he counterposes to Parsons' stress on systematic, all-encompassing theories,[8] indicates that he takes a much more empirical and heuristic approach to the process of constituting a social system.

Pursuing Merton's strategy of middle-range theories, no commitment would be made to any variable which could not pay its way empirically. The expectation is that cumulative research would, through successive approximations, sift out a battery of explanatory variables and establish their interrelations.[9] This is by no means a new species of empiricism, nor a new espousal of the prerogatives of research against those of theory. It is simply an insistence that theoretical considerations alone cannot provide scientifically legitimate grounds for the admission of elements to a social system.

Objection may be lodged against this approach on the grounds that, not having staked out in advance *all* the constituent elements of the social system, the problematic pattern cannot then be related to the system as a whole. The procedure can therefore yield only incomplete explanations of any particular pattern. This is quite true, but it is an objection just as applicable to Parsons' strategy. For although Parsons takes cognizance of the 'total' social system, this is by no means a closed and complete system, but an open and partial one. Many of the things accounting for variance in particular patterns of social behaviour will also fall outside of its jurisdiction and it, too, can account for no more than part of the variance.

The basic gain of the Mertonian strategy is that it prevents either premature commitment to, or premature exclusion of, any given structure as an element in the social system. The latter, the exclusion of structures from the social system, is as vital a decision as that of inclusion, and would seem no more susceptible to a purely theoretical resolution.

As Parsons formulates his conception of the social system, elements in the biological constitution and physiological functioning of man, as well as features of the physical and ecological environment, are excluded. So, too, seems to be the historically developing cultural complexes of material artifacts. To a Malinowski it might well seem that this is a form of academic monasticism in which men are cleansed of their baser passions for sex, food, and material possessions by theoretical purification.

Among other tendencies, Parsons' theory of the social system leads research attention away from *systematic* efforts to develop and validate generalized propositions concerning the manner in which ecological and other properties of the physical environment of groups structure patterns of social organization. In exiling these from the social system, Parsons at best derives a purely formal advantage, namely that of establishing a distinct class of systems which may form the object of an independent social science. But in doing this he fails to make a systematic place for numerous cogent researches which, if lacking in formal elegance in this sense, do illuminate the important ways in which social behaviour is structured by ecological forces. To constitute the social system thusly may well accomplish the objective of establishing a charter for an independent social science. But it may be a Pyrrhic victory bought at the cost of a scientific ritualism, where logical elegance is substituted for empirical potency.

The systematic omission of such ecological forces from models which seek to account for variance in social and cultural behaviour would, moreover, seem to have varying degrees of appropriateness, depending on the society under study. Evans-Pritchard's[10] and Steward's[11] studies of primitive groups clearly demonstrate the potency of ecological forces in shaping social organization in folk societies. In societies with advanced technologies and urban centres, however, these forces are patently less powerful in structuring social behaviour. Thus Parsons' model of a social system may have an *unequal* capacity to account for variance in social behaviour in different social systems. It may, because of its exclusion of ecological elements, be a more powerful tool in dealing with industrially advanced urban societies than with 'underdeveloped' primitive groups which have much less control over nature.

While it is for this reason tempting to think of Parsons' model as essentially one of an industrially developed social system, we cannot do so because no systematic provision is made for some of the very elements which characterize these. In particular, Parsons' model of the social system excludes all 'material' elements, including tools and machines. This would seem dubious on several interlocking grounds: first, precisely because these are man's own unique and distinctive creations, the very products of his social interaction. Secondly, because they enter intimately as mediating instruments of communication and hence of symbolic social interaction. Thirdly, because they are also instruments of transportion, often making possible the very interchanges among social parts which enable them to establish interdependences. Fourth and last, because modern electronic and cybernetic devices have developed to the point where the distinction between human thinking and machine operation is no longer so radical as was assumed in the organismic tradition from which functionalism grew.[12]

The line between the interaction of man with man, on the one side, and the interaction of men with machines, on the other, has begun to grow wavery. Parsons holds that 'a social system consists of a plurality of individual actors, interacting with each other in a situation . . . and whose relations . . . [are] defined and mediated in terms of a system of culturally structured and shared symbols'.[13] If this is so, then it may well be that modern machinery qualifies, not simply as the environment in which social interaction occurs, but as a *party* to the interaction itself, as a member of the social system, as well as a cultural artifact which, like shared symbols, mediates communication.

Here again it is necessary to insist that the matter cannot be decided by *a priori* postulation alone. Whether we want to constitute a model of the social system as a man-man system or, instead, as a men–machine system, depends in important part on the empirical consequences stemming from the inclusion or exclusion of machines. Internal consistency and parsimony, such as they are in modern social theory, are necessary but not sufficient criteria of the postulate sets of an empirical sociology. One might well remember Ruskin's sarcasms about a fictitious science of gymnastics which postulated that men had no skeletons.

In one respect, Parsons' work manifests a fairly widespread tendency among sociologists, namely an inclination to rest content with a demonstration that some sociological variable 'makes a difference'. If a variable can be shown to control even the smallest proportion of variance in a problematic pattern it is all too readily regarded as a memorable contribution to sociology and all too ceremoniously ushered into its theoretical hall of fame. It is surely no treason to theory to suggest that, in the last analysis, not only empirical researches in general, but mathematical ones in particular, will have a voice in legitimating conceptual innovation. For unless sustained interest is manifested in the *degree* of variance which a variable controls, and unless, further, we can identify sociological variables that certifiably control *substantial* proportions of variance in specified patterns of human behaviour, sociology will remain scientifically immature and practically in effectual.

The Principle of Functional Reciprocity

It would seem clear from the foregoing that the ways in which Merton and Parsons seek to apply the notion of a 'system' to sociological analysis differs and, particularly so, with reference to the manner in which constituents shall be identified and admitted to or excluded from the system. Yet it needs to be stressed that this involves no necessary difference in principle with respect to the strategic place of the concept of a system, especially as an *explanatory* tool.

This can be documented by reference to Merton's analysis of

the latent functions of political machines in the United States.[14] He opens this by inquiring how it is that political machines manage to continue operating, despite the fact that they frequently run counter to both the *mores* and the law. In the more generalized terms of his paradigm of functional analysis, Merton begins by identifying a social pattern, the political machine, and seeks to explain its persistence by establishing its consequences for the larger social structures in which it is implicated. The *general* form of his explanation of the persistence of the political machine is to demonstrate that it performs 'positive functions which are at the same time not adequately fulfilled by other existing patterns and structures'.[15]

Among these are (1) the organization and centralization of power so that it can be mobilized to 'satisfy the needs of diverse subgroups in the larger community', including (2) personalized forms of assistance – jobs, legal aid, food-baskets, for deprived, lower-class groups, (3) political privileges and aid to business groups, (4) channels of social mobility for disadvantaged groups in the society, and (5) 'protection' for illicit rackets.

Now in so far as the objective of the above analysis was to provide an *explanation of the persistence* of the political machine, then the mere establishment of the consequences of the machine for the larger structures in which it is involved provides only a partial and one-sided answer. The explanation is incomplete in so far as the analyst has not explicitly traced the manner in which the groups or structures, whose needs have been satisfied, in turn 'reciprocate' and repay the political machine for the gains it provides them. In this particular case, the patterns of reciprocity are so largely evident and well documented that it would be belabouring the obvious to dwell upon them, and were perhaps for this reason omitted. The reciprocities involved are all too clearly implied in the notion of the 'corruption' of the machine.

Ordinarily, however, the formal adequacy of a functional *explanation* of the persistence of a social pattern would seem to require that the analyst demonstrate not merely the consequences of A for B, but, also, the reciprocal consequences of B for A. The only logically stable terminal point for a functional analysis is not the demonstration of a social pattern's function for others, but the demonstration of the latter's reciprocal functionality for the problematic social pattern.

In short, functional analysis premises the operation of a 'principle of functional reciprocity', a principle variously employed by Marx,[16] by Mauss,[17] by Malinowski,[18] by Lévi-Strauss,[19] and by Homans[20] in different empirical contexts. This underlying functionalist assumption might just as well be made explicit and could be stated in the following generalized form: (1) Any one structure is more likely to persist if it is engaged in reciprocally functional interchanges with some others; (1.1) the less reciprocal the functional interchange between structures, the less likely is either structure, or the patterned relation between them, to persist – (1.2) *unless compensatory mechanisms are present*.

Essentially, the principle of reciprocity implies a system of interdependent parts engaged in mutual interchanges. It is in this sense that the notion of a system is necessarily involved in Merton's analysis of the political machine as, we think, it must be in any functional analysis.

It needs to be stressed, however, that 'mutual interchange' does not necessarily imply that the relations among parts of a social system are invariably those of symmetrical functional reciprocity. It does, however, imply either that such functional reciprocity exists, or that there has developed some compensatory mechanism for coping with the lack of or breakdown in it. It is, we suspect, precisely because Merton saw that the relations between parts were not invariably those of symmetrical functional reciprocity that he did not commit himself to a generalized principle of reciprocity. Nonetheless, it is implied by his analysis. It is only by chancing an explicit formulation of the assumption and laying it open to critical examination, that it can be tempered and refined, or invalidated and rejected.

There is something of a tactical dilemma here which needs to be resolved. It seems evident, on the one hand, that to cease analysis before attempting to *establish empirically* the reciprocal functionality of B for A, and to explain the persistence of A by demonstrating its functions for B, is to substitute postulation for research. On the other hand, there are substantial empirical grounds for rejecting an unqualified principle of reciprocity.

For this would involve the dubious assumption that structures which derive gains from others are invariably 'grateful' and that power-constrained services, with little or no reciprocity, are not merely unstable but totally impossible.

An unqualified principle of reciprocity diverts attention from the specific social or cultural mechanisms which may compensate for the lack of functional reciprocity. Among such compensatory mechanisms may be culturally shared prescriptions of unconstrained 'generosity' such as the Christian notion of 'turning the other cheek', the feudal concept of *noblesse oblige*, or the Roman notion of 'clemency'.[21] There may also be cultural prohibitions banning the examination of certain interchanges from the standpoint of their reciprocity, such as the sociologically wise cliché, 'It's not the gift but the sentiment that counts.' Again, power arrangements may serve to compel continuances of services for which there is little functional reciprocity. Although these may be expected, from the present standpoint, to be less stable than those where functional reciprocity motivates continued performances, they are certainly not for that reason sociologically unimportant.

Another arrangement which may serve to prevent or control failures in functional reciprocity is the mutual sharing of structures A and B, of some third structure C. To use Lévi-Strauss' terminology[22] in a broader sense, we would say that a situation of 'generalized interchange' – where A supplies B's needs, B supplies C's, and C supplies A's needs – may be more stable than that of a 'restricted interchange' between A and B alone. This case is relevant to Parsons' discussion of the basic equilibrium model of the social system. The minimal social system, comprised of two role players, Ego and Alter, is postulated by Parsons to be in equilibrium when each conforms to the other's expectation and is rewarded by him for such compliant behaviour. It is clear, first, that this model implicitly utilizes the principle of reciprocity and may be regarded as a special case of it. More to the point here, however, note that Ego may in fact continue to comply with Alter's expectations, not because Alter reciprocates or rewards such compliances, but because Ego's compliances are expected and rewarded by a third role player. In short, the system may be maintained, and guarded against defaults in functional reciprocity, through the intervention of 'third' structures which perform what may be termed a 'policing' function.

It is impossible to do justice here to the question of whether this implies that the minimal model of a social system should be constituted of three rather than two role players. As a conservative inference from the foregoing, however, it would seem that an important focus of functional analysis couched in role terms should be centred on the stabilizing activities of such 'third parties' as the witness, *amicus curiae*, police, friend of the family, arbitrators, or ritual adjudicators such as 'old men of the earth'.[23] In complex social systems it may be expected that such third-party roles will be structurally specialized and differentiated from others; in simpler social systems it may be that such policing functions will be conjoined with others.

It is clear from all this, then, that in explaining any social pattern it cannot be merely assumed that functional reciprocity will operate in any given case, but it is necessary to establish empirically its occurrence. Failing in this, it is necessary to search out compensatory arrangements which provide a functional substitute for reciprocity.

There are important connections between the principle of functional reciprocity and the older anthropological concept of a vestigial 'survival'. A social pattern was commonly regarded as a 'survival' if it could not be established that it made any contributions to the adaptation of a going system in which it was *presently* implicated. The polemical opposition of the earlier functionalists to this concept logically rested on the tacit assumption of an *unqualified* principle of reciprocity. That is, they premised that a structure which persisted was obviously securing satisfaction of its needs from others, and, if it continues to receive these, this can only be because this structure somehow reciprocally contributed to the others' adaptation. The anthropological functionalist was therefore enjoined to exercise his ingenuity to search out what were, in effect, hidden reciprocities.

The early functionalists' polemical opposition to the notion of a survival, however, tended to obscure the significance of varying *degrees* of functional reciprocity, and to neglect the mechanisms which might control the instabilities resulting from a breakdown in functional reciprocity. The early functionalist neglected the fact that a 'survival' was simply a limiting case of a larger class of phenomena, much deserving of study, namely, relations between structures in which there is little functional reciprocity. Essentially, the early functionalists' opposition to the concept of a 'survival' now has unwarranted survival in the neglect of the problem of asymmetrical patterns of functional reciprocity.

Interdependence as Problematic

It is one of the central implications of these comments that the notion of interdependence, so crucial to the concept of a system, needs to be taken as problematic rather than as given, if a system model adequate to the analysis of social behaviour is to be developed. One of the reasons why this has not been systematically done in Parsons' analysis is related to the distinction which he makes between a 'theoretical' and an 'empirical' system. The former refers to a logically interrelated conceptual scheme or a set of propositions. An empirical system, on the other hand, 'has to do with the criteria for coherence and harmony to be applied to some specific body of subject matter'.[24]

There are, it would seem, two meanings which might be attributed to Parsons' use of the term 'empirical system'. One is that it unwittingly retains vestiges of eighteenth-century usage, referring to a 'natural' system which is somehow there 'in itself' in a realistic sense, that is, apart from any particular conceptualization. Despite the fact that this would be radically at variance with Parsons' methodological position, which is predominantly constructionist, there are uneasy moments when a reader may feel that such an inference is not altogether outlandish. In so far, however, as an 'empirical system' is held to consist of 'criteria' to be applied to some subject matter, it is clear that the empirical system cannot be the referent of the theory, but must instead be a set of assumptions in terms of which these referents are to be studied.

A second and by far the most acceptable interpretation, therefore, is that what Parsons means by an 'empirical system' is, perversely enough, what philosophers of science commonly term a 'formal system'. Purely formal systems, as in mathematics and logic, are those devoid of any kind of empirical content, and this is much the way in which Parsons uses the notion of an empirical system. When a formal system is applied to a specific subject matter it is said to be 'interpreted'; some formal systems have many interpretations, others have none. The nub of the issue here is the nature of the interpretation to be given to the formal and empty notion of a 'system' when it is applied to human relations. In order for a formal system to be successfully applied, it would seem necessary that the interpretation to which it is subjected be explicitly examined.

The significant point, however, is that the notion of a theoretical system denotes what Parsons regards as analytically problematical, while the formal concept of an 'empirical system' is largely unexplored or taken simply as setting the terms within which the theoretical system must develop. As a result of this, the notion of 'empirical system' does not become systematically problematic for Parsons, and he fails to explore the alternative interpretations which are possible even within such a commitment.

We, on the contrary, would stress that even on a formal level of system analysis, there are different elements involved in the conception of an 'empirical system' and, combined or interpreted differently, they may constitute different types of empirical systems.[25] It is therefore necessary to choose among competing formal models and to identify those that constitute a better 'fit' for the known, relevant data.

As mentioned above, the two key elements involved in the concept of system are first, 'interdependence', and secondly, 'self-maintenance' or equilibrium. It makes a good deal of difference whether interdependence and equilibrium are treated as undifferentiated attributes, or whether they are viewed as dimensions capable of significant variation in degree.

Unless the latter procedure is followed and unless, further, it is clearly seen that interdependence and equilibrium are not synonymous terms but are independently variable, then there is a compelling tendency to by-pass the possibility that there are significantly different types of empirical systems even on the most formal level of analysis. Mere use of the concept of an empirical system is much as if a mathematical physicist were to commit himself only to the use of 'geometry' in general, without stipulating the specific system of geometry he proposes to employ in solving his particular problems.

Viewed in Parsons' way,[26] the concept of an empirical system is essentially an 'ideal type' and is subject to the liabilities inherent in all such concepts. That is, it obscures the underlying continua involved in its constituents, and focuses attention on particular, and especially extreme, values of the dimensions. To speak of systems as characterized by an interdependence of parts and their equilibrium tends to obscure the fact that these are things which can vary in degree. Moreover, it tends to create a presumption that they universally co-vary in the same direction.

One may find, however, a conjunction of low interdependence with high equilibrium, where the low interdependence permits a localized absorption of externally induced trauma, thus guarding the remainder of the system elements from ramifying damage. It is this kind of a conjunction which would seem to be implied in the notion of 'insulation', which Parsons, along with other functionalists, regards as a 'defence mechanism' of social systems. In brief, the lowering of the degree of interdependence may contribute to an increase in the degree of equilibrium, or in restoring it to a higher level.

Conversely, an instance of a conjunction of high interdependence and low equilibrium would seem to be implied in the notion of a 'vicious cycle'. Here, the very interdependence of elements enables negative feedback cycles to develop with cumulative impairment of the system's equilibrium. From these considerations it seems clear that equilibrium and interdependence may vary independently and, consequently, conjunctions of different values of these two variables may be postulated concerning the character of social systems.

Functional Autonomy and Degrees of Interdependence

A crucial assumption of the analysis here is that there are *varying degrees* of interdependence which may be postulated to exist among the parts of a system. At one extreme, each element may be involved in a mutual interchange with all others; at the opposite extreme, each element may be involved in mutual interchanges with only one other.[27] The former may be regarded as defining maximal interdependence and 'systemness', the latter as defining minimal interdependence or 'systemness'.

Still another way of viewing interdependence is from the standpoint of the parts' dependence upon the system. The parts may have varying amounts of their needs satisfied by, and thus varying degrees of dependence upon, other system elements. A number of parts which are engaged in mutual interchanges may, at one extreme, all be totally dependent on each other for the satisfaction of their needs. In this case the *system* they comprise can be said to be 'highly' interdependent, while these *parts* can be said to possess 'low' functional autonomy. Conversely, a system may be composed of parts all of which derive but little satisfaction of their needs from each other; here the system would be minimally interdependent and the parts would be high on functional autonomy. Operationally speaking, we might say that the functional autonomy of a system part is the probability that it can survive separation from the system.

A conceptualization of 'systemness' in terms of functional autonomy has been suggested here because the notion of mutual interdependence commonly used in definitions of systems tends toward a focus primarily on the 'whole' or on the relations between parts, and on their functionally reciprocated need for each other. 'Functional autonomy', however, focuses on the *parts*, albeit in their relation to each other; it directs attention to the possibility that any part may have little, as well as great, need for another, and that the mutual need of parts need not be symmetrical. In short, it focuses attention on interchanges where functional reciprocity may not be symmetrical, and thus directs analysis to tension-producing relationships.

In these terms, the question becomes, 'What can be predicated about the functional autonomy of the parts of social systems, and in what ways does the problem of the functional autonomy of the parts enter into the analysis of social systems?' In the following comments, which explore several of these implications, it will be emphasized that the problem of functional autonomy is of considerable significance for the analysis of tension within social systems, and thus for the analysis of social change.

Functional Autonomy and System Tension

To the degree that parts possess some measure of functional autonomy, they must be expected to seek to maintain this. In short, the equilibrium assumptions, applied to a social system as a whole, would seem equally applicable in principle to its parts. Thus, the parts of a social system should be expected to 'maintain their boundaries'. It must then be assumed that parts with some degree of functional autonomy will resist full or complete integration into the larger system. Conversely, the system itself, straining towards integration, can be expected to seek submission of the parts to the requirements of the position they occupy. Consequently, there may be some tension between the part's tendency to maintain an existent degree of functional autonomy and the system's pressure to control the part.

It would seem that this or some similar model underlies various theories, such as the Freudian, which postulate an endemic conflict between the individual and the society or group. Essentially, these have been answered by formulations counter-stressing the malleability of the individual organism, the potency of the socialization process, and the inability of the organism to become a full 'human being' apart from society.

Actually, however, the very malleability of the organism which makes it susceptible to socialization by one social system also allows it to be resocialized by another; its malleability is thus actually a condition of its functional autonomy. Furthermore, the relevant question here is the ability of the already socialized individual to remain such after separation from any given social system, not merely to become such without involvement in some society.

More pointedly, it would seem that, once socialized, many individuals do have a capacity to generate an 'escape velocity'; and that human beings are not invariably characterized by a total dependence upon any one social system.[28] *Socialized* individuals have some measure of mobility, vertical and horizontal, among the social systems within their society, moving with varying degrees of ease or stress from one to another. They may and do also migrate to, or sojourn in, societies different from those in which they were originally socialized. They have, in our terms, considerable, if varying, degrees of functional autonomy in relation to any given social system. Consequently, if we think of the 'socialized individual' as in some sense a 'part', and not merely as the raw material, of social systems, it would seem necessary to eschew models which overstress the interdependence of the parts and to select those which systematically include concern with their functional autonomy. To fit the data of social behaviour the system model required must be such as to facilitate not only the analysis of the interdependence of the system as a whole, but also the analysis of the functional autonomy of its parts, and the concrete strains which efforts to maintain this autonomy may induce.

Two lines of sociological analysis which have recently been developed are highly relevant to these assumptions about functional autonomy. One stems from the study of occupations made by E. C. Hughes and his students, in which the repeated observation of diverse occupations – both noble and profane – indicates that their occupants typically strive to maintain a degree of functional autonomy. As Hughes puts it, they seek to maintain a degree of social distance or freedom, not merely from all in the same social system in which they operate but, most particularly, 'from those people most crucially concerned with [their] work'.[29]

A second and more generalized direction from which the problem of functional autonomy has been approached in sociological terms is that developed by Erving Goffman. Utilizing materials from his study of a mental hospital, Goffman distinguishes between two types of deference behaviour, that is, the expression of appreciation of one person to and for another. One type, 'avoidance rituals', refers to those forms of deference stipulating what one may *not* do to another, and which leads actors to maintain social distance from each other. The second, 'presentational rituals', specify what *is* to be done and involve expressions of positive appreciation and regard. Goffman sums up his analysis as follows:

I have mentioned four very common forms of presentational deference: salutations, invitations, compliments, and minor services. Through all of these the recipient is told that he is not an island unto himself and that others are, or seek to be, involved with him and with his personal concerns . . . avoidance rituals, taking the form of proscriptions, interdictions, and taboos . . . imply acts the actor must refrain from lest he violate the right of the recipient to keep him at a distance. . . .

In suggesting that there are things which must be said and done to a recipient, and things that must not be said and done, it should be plain that there is an inherent opposition and conflict between these two forms of deference. . . . There is an inescapable opposition between showing a desire to include an individual and showing respect for his privacy. As an implication of this dilemma, we must see that social intercourse involves a constant dialectic between presentational rituals and avoidance rituals. A peculiar tension must be maintained, for these opposing requirements of conduct must somehow be held apart from one another and yet realized together in the same interaction; the gestures which carry an actor to a recipient must also signify that things will not be carried too far.[30]

It would seem that a system model which focused solely on the 'wholeness' of the system and neglected the functional autonomy of the parts would be unable to fit the kind of data obtained in either Hughes' or Goffman's researches. Nor, above all, would it systematically cue the analyst to the tensions which result in social systems by virtue of the parts' strain toward functional autonomy, or to the analysis of the ways in which they maintain their functional autonomy. From the standpoint of the kind of system model which Parsons favours, the emphasis on interdependence would conduce to a one-sided focus – in Goffman's terms – on the 'presentational rituals'. That is, it conduces to a preoccupation with the mechanisms of social integration, and to a neglect of the avoidance rituals which constitute proper ways in which socialized individuals are enabled to resist total inclusion in a social system and total loss of their functional autonomy.

In Parsons' system model, concern is largely focused on the needs of the system as a whole, and the stability of this system is viewed as dependent upon their satisfaction. The implication here, however, is that there is a sense in which the very striving of the system to satisfy its needs may generate tension for it, in so far as this impairs the functional autonomy of the parts. This means that a need of systems, which possess parts having degrees of functional autonomy, is to inhibit its own tendencies to subordinate and fully specialize these parts. In short, it must inhibit its own tendencies toward 'wholeness' or complete integration if it is to be stable. The system model thus indicated for the analysis of social behaviour is not one in which the system is viewed as a 'plunger' playing an all-or-none game, but as a mini-max player seeking to strike a federalizing balance between totalitarian and anarchist limits.[31]

It is commonly assumed that the 'organization' of the system, that is, the particular arrangement of its parts, provides primarily for the avenues of integration among them. In our terms, however, 'organization' not only serves to link, control, and interrelate parts but also functions to separate them and to maintain and protect their functional autonomy. Organization is seen then as shaped by a conflict, particularly by the tensions between centripetal and centrifugal pressures, as limiting control over parts as well as imposing it, as establishing a balance between their dependence and independence, and as separating as well as connecting the parts.[32]

Social organizations, in so far as they involve role systems, manifest the dualism indicated above. It is of the essence of social roles that they never demand total involvements by the actors, but only segmental and partial involvements. To say that a person is an actor in a social system and that he plays a role there implies, on the one side, that he is subject to some system controls and to the requirements of the role, and that he has obligations to the collectivity of which his role is a part. On the other side, however, it also implies that his obligations to that system are somehow limited. Even when the actor is involved in a primary social system, where the role obligations are diffuse and numerous, he is never exposed to unlimited obligations.

One of the most common ways in which consideration of the functional autonomy of parts has implicitly entered into current sociological analysis has been as an element in the generation of system tension. The drive of the subpart to maintain or to extend its functional autonomy has been frequently understood as a source of tensions for the system. In 'organizational analysis', in the technical sociological sense, the tensions between the 'field offices' and the 'main office', between the various departments within an organization, as well as in the commonly noted oscillation between centralization and decentralization, all imply cognizance of the significance of functional autonomy. Similarly, concern with the development of 'organized deviance' and its potentially disruptive impact on the system again betokens a tacit appreciation of the tension-provoking potential of functionally autonomous parts.

Because parts have or strive to maintain different degrees of functional autonomy, it cannot be assumed that all have an equal role in the generation of tensions for the system. It would seem reasonable to suppose that those parts in a social system with most functional autonomy can more readily become loci of organized deviance and of effective resistance to system controls.

If it is reasonable to assume that some system parts have a greater role as loci of system tension, it would also seem consistent to maintain that not all have an equally deep involvement in the resolution of the tensions of the system, or in the mobilization of defences against these. That is, those parts with least functional autonomy, those which cannot survive separation from a social system, are more likely to be implicated in its conservation than those which can.

Contrariwise, those with most autonomy are most able to press for or to accept changes, when these are consistent with their own autonomy. For example, it is evident that the eighteenth-century French nobility had a greater involvement in the maintenance of the *ancien régime* than did the French *bourgeoisie*, which could and did survive separation from the older social system and acted as a stimulant to its basic reorganization. It would seem, then, to put the matter differently, that not all parts of a system have an equal 'vested interest' in its maintenance. The concept of the differential functional autonomy of parts directs attention to the need to distinguish between parts having a greater or lesser vested interest in system maintenance.

The Strategies of Parts and Systems

Among other things, the functional autonomy of a part implies that it is not totally contingent upon the parasystem for the satisfaction of its own needs. There are at least three importantly different strategies with which this situation can be played, from the standpoint of the part. One is the strategy of withdrawal. The part can, so to speak, go into business for itself and resist such a high degree of specialization that it loses power to service its own minimal metabolic needs. A second strategy is to spread its risks, so that its needs may be normally satisfied by a number of systems in which it is involved.

Both of these strategies for the maintenance of the functional autonomy of a part present difficulties and sources of tension for the parasystem. The functional autonomy of a part, whichever strategy it employs, allows it a degree of refractoriness to the imposition of controls from the system. This may be exemplified by the case of bureaucratic resistance to higher-echelon policy decisions.

A special source of tension derives from the part's involvement in multiple systems. To the degree that two systems share a part then the laws of both will affect the behaviour of the part. This means not only that such a functionally autonomous part will be refractory to system steering, but that it will tend to oscillate and initiate changes for either system.

For example, it is not simply that the socialized human being may be refractory to the controls of a social system because he is involved in a biological system and is consequently required to eat, sleep, or breathe. But being involved in a biological system, the human being is also subject to various mundane liabilities such as illness, injury, and death. These are far from entirely governed by the laws of any social system and thus their occurrence is random relative to the functioning of social systems. Although social systems may develop mechanisms for cushioning their effects, for example, through 'understudies' or prescribed rules of succession,[33] these effects must always, in some measure, be actively disruptive to the social systems, even if only to the personalized relations within them.

While we have here stressed the sharing of a part between a

social and a biological system, the point is much the same in the case of parts shared between two or more social systems. The shared parts are more likely to engage in oscillations disruptive to one or both systems. In sociological analysis, this has been recognized in the concern with multiple-role involvements in general, and 'cross-pressure' situations in particular.

There is a third strategy which a functionally autonomous part may adopt, in addition to withdrawal and spreading the risk. That is, it may undertake a reorganization of the entire system in which it finds itself, so that it may secure fuller satisfaction of its distinctive needs and so that these are now higher on the schedule of priorities to which the new system orients itself. In short, functionally autonomous parts may have a 'vested interest' in changing the system. Here, again, is an important source of tension for the system.

There is, from this standpoint, an inherent ambiguity in a conflict between a part and its encompassing system. Such a tension may signify one of two different things: either (1) that the part generating the tension has not yet been controlled by or excluded from the larger system, but that it ultimately will, or (2) that the friction-generating part is the harbinger of a new reorganization of the whole system.

There seem to be at least three empirically important strategies which a system can adopt to cope with the potentialities of tensions thus induced. One is to insulate itself and withdraw its parts from the environing system, excluding or 'alienating' parts possessing significant functional autonomy, admitting only those it can highly control, and refusing to share parts with other systems. Demands for deep occupational involvement, separation between family and work life, and highly selective programmes of recruitment would be examples of such a strategy as practised by many modern businesses. A second strategy is that of expansion, in which the system attempts to engulf others which share its parts and thereby tighten control over them. This is also exemplified by the tendency of certain modern industries to develop an interest in the employee's personal life, to concern itself with the character of his wife, and to influence and regulate his residential living.[34] A third strategy is that of 'selective risk'. That is, the system will maximize its security by delegating its basic metabolic needs to structures within it which have minimal functional autonomy. This statement, however partial, of the specific and diverse strategies by means of which systems may respond to tensions is, it would seem, a formulation appreciatively more determinate than the mere assertion that systems attempt to 'maintain their boundaries'.

On the level of social systems, these considerations imply that distinctions will be made between core functions and peripheral ones,[35] and between 'reliable' and 'unreliable' or disloyal personnel,[36] the former functions being allocated to the former personnel. One would also look for tendencies of limited purpose organizations to transform themselves into 'total institutions', or for total institutions to be transformed into limited purpose organizations by functional differentiation, specialization, and insulation of parts. Finally, the above considerations of system strategy would imply that it is necessary for the sociologist to identify and examine the particular policy which a social system has adopted in its relations to environing systems. It is to be expected that all social systems, not merely governments, but families, schools, or factories, will also develop some kind of a 'foreign policy', tacit or explicit, which regulates its relations with surrounding social systems.[37]

It may be noted in passing that the threats to which the system is seen here to be variously responding derive from the defences of its functionally autonomous parts. In this connection what is a threat from the system's standpoint is a defensive manoeuvre from the part's standpoint. Conversely, the system's defences against these are, in turn, threats to the part's defences.[38] Consequently, it is to be expected that efforts to reduce the threatening behaviour of either the part or the system will be resisted. In short, not only efforts to change the system, but also those directed at *maintaining* it are likely to entail conflict and resistance.

Functional Autonomy and Structural Dedifferentiation

In so far as a system is composed of some parts which have a degree of functional autonomy, it possesses potentialities for certain types of changes, or responses to tensions, which would not exist if it had no functionally autonomous parts. A system with no functionally autonomous parts would have only one of two dodges when confronted with powerful disruptions. It could either dissolve and be completely destroyed or it would have to undergo radical structural reorganization.

However, given a system some of whose parts have a measure of functional autonomy, there is a third response available to an extremely disruptive stimulus, namely dedifferentiation. That is, the system can surrender higher levels of integration and permit its functionally autonomous parts to regroup on a lower level of complexity. Sociologically speaking, this means that when a complex social system's defensive mechanisms do not permit it to cope adaptively with threats, it may destructure itself into component primary groupings, surrendering its sovereignty to the parts.

Julian Steward's theory of 'levels of sociocultural integration' is, in effect, a statement of this possibility. As he remarks,

> In culture, simple forms such as those represented by the family or band, do not wholly disappear when a more complex stage of development is reached, nor do they merely survive fossil-like. . . . They gradually become specialized, dependent parts of new total configurations. . . .[39]

Steward holds that it is useful to look upon the larger, more complex, social systems, such as the nation state, as a distinctive level of organization but one which is, nonetheless, composed of parts – families and communities – which continue to retain a significant measure of functional autonomy. In the event that the larger more complex system is dissolved, they may survive separation from it.

Steward has analysed several anthropologically interesting cases in which this happened, one of the best documented of which is that of the Cuna-Cueva Indians of the Isthmus of Panama. The evidence indicates that at the time of the Hispanic conquest, this tribe had a fairly complex state structure, with a ruling class of nobles and priests. The conquest, however, destroyed these national and state institutions of the Cuna. Neither Spanish governance nor Catholic religion effectively substituted for these, as the Cuna moved back into regions to which the Spanish were unwilling to follow. There Cuna life reorganized itself on a simpler communal basis, with the village becoming the largest unit of political life. It is clear, however, that such dedifferentiations of social structure are not peculiar to primitive peoples and have not infrequently occurred in historical European societies, most notably following the fall of the Roman Empire.

The phenomenon of dedifferentiation indicates that the functional autonomy of system parts may not only be *conducive* to system tensions, but can also provide a basis for responding to them. Indeed, the functional autonomy of the parts of a *social* system, allowing as it does for structural dedifferentiation, may be functional to the maintenance of the integrity of the *cultural* system. For the cultural system, the historically accumulated heritage of beliefs and skills may be maintained at least in some part in the smaller units into which the larger one has been dedifferentiated. To make this possible, however, the part must always be invested with more of the culture than it requires for the performance of its distinctive system function. In short, the part must not be overly specialized. It can be thus seen from another perspective why the parts of social systems *must be allowed* measures of functional autonomy by the system. The functional autonomy of parts then is not an unmitigated source of difficulty for the system, but may provide a basis for a defensive strategy of last resort, structural dedifferentiation.

Sociologists have, of course, long been aware of processes of structural dedifferentiation. In thinking of this, however, they have tended to focus primarily on the level of the atomization of the anomic individual, and to regard this as a purely pathological phenomenon. The existence of masses of men who are anomically cut adrift from larger social systems does, of course, imply that these systems are experiencing serious difficulty in maintaining themselves.

But such anomic dedifferentiation can also be seen as a desperate expedient through which the system is striving to maintain itself. As Merton states,

some [unknown] degree of deviation from current norms is probably functional for the basic goals of all groups. A certain degree of 'innovation', for example, may result in the formation of new institutionalized patterns of behaviour which are more adaptive than the old in making for realization of the primary goals.[40]

Tensionful as it may be, the anomic dedifferentiation of a social system need not be a requiem of its total dissolution, but a necessary prelude to its reorganization. For anomic disorder may make possible a ferment of innovation which can rescue the system from destruction.[41] When a system has exhausted its routine solutions for an important problem and when these have failed, then, at that point, anomic randomness is more functional than the treadmill and orderly plying of the old structures. The anomic individual may not merely be an uncontrolled 'social cancer', but a seed pod of culture which, if only through sheer chance, may fall upon fertile ground. In short, *limited* increases in randomness, by way of structural dedifferentiation, may be the ultimate defence of systems in the face of extremity.

It has been suggested that the discrimination of functionally autonomous parts within a social system is significant because these aid in identifying possible loci of strain within the system, as well as marking out the boundaries along which dedifferentiation may occur. In the role terms so central to social system analysis, then, it would seem that the identification of the most and least functionally autonomous roles within the system may be a valuable point of departure for the analysis of strains within the system. We may speak of roles which have relatively great functional autonomy as 'cosmopolitans' while those having little can be termed 'locals'. I have, in another connection, attempted to develop the thesis that certain important strains in social systems can be analysed as an outcome of tensions between cosmopolitans and locals.[42] Not merely roles, however, but other kinds of parts within social systems can be examined from the standpoint of their functional autonomy, and systematic consideration of these can aid in the analysis of system tension and change.

System Theories versus Factor Theories

In the analysis of system changes, a distinction is commonly made between endogenous and exogenous sources of change, that is, between forces internal and external to the system. Our emphasis here on *degrees* of functional autonomy and *degrees* of system interdependence may be linked up with this distinction between exogenous and endogenous forces, and seen in its further ramifications for the analysis of change.

In noting that the functional autonomy of parts and system interdependence are matters of degree we, in effect, state that exogenous and endogenous factors are not qualitatively but quantitatively different. That is, they are simply at opposite ends of the same continuum of interdependence and functional autonomy. Hence, specific system parts may be both *partly* exogenous and *partly* endogenous. Thus, if exogenous forces are peculiarly important to the understanding of system change, as they are commonly held to be in Parsons' and other system models, *any* element *in* the system may be important in understanding system change to the extent that it possesses a degree of exogenousness, though all need not be equally so.

In some measure this may be regarded as a partial resolution of the classical tension between two lines of sociological theory. One of these, the position stemming from Comte and passing through Durkheim to Parsons, stresses that system change has to be thought of as deriving from exogenous forces, the system *model* itself not being conceived of as possessing internal sources of disequilibrium. The other, deriving from the Marxian tradition, stresses that the system can change due to its 'internal contradictions', that is, endogenous forces. Here the point stressed is that social systems may be looked upon as composed of parts having varying degrees of functional autonomy and interdependence; thus the difference between the external and internal, the 'inside' and 'outside' of the system, is not an absolute distinction, and the thickness or permeability of the system boundaries varies at different zones.

It is in this sense that some system parts can be thought of as having relatively greater *independence* than others, *vis-à-vis* the system under study, and may thus be of strategic importance in accounting for system changes. In *Structure of Social Action*, Parsons has stressed that independent parts are also interdependent, but he has tended to treat both independence and interdependence as 'constants' rather than as variables.[43] We, on the contrary, have emphasized that they are variables. To say that two parts are interdependent is not to imply that they are *equally* so and thus, even within a system of interdependent parts, various parts can have *varying* degrees of independence or freedom.

Having gone this far, it is now evident that a stress on the 'web of interdependence' within a system by no means relieves the analyst of the problem of factor weighting or loading. The analyst must still cope with the task of determining the differential contribution made by different system parts to the state of the system as a whole. In short, different system parts make different degrees of contribution to either the stability or the change of the system, and these need to be analytically and empirically distinguished.

As a matter of fact, this tends to be done, even by Parsons, with respect to the analysis of system stability when he utilizes the notion of 'defence mechanisms'. In effect, this constitutes an effort at the qualitative analysis of components of the system which play a particularly important role in enabling it to maintain its integrity. Logically, a parallel analysis of those system elements which make more important contributions to system *change* would seem to be equally desirable. It may be that the notion of the differential functional autonomy of system parts may provide an analytic tool for the qualitative discrimination of factors contributing importantly to system change.

It is one implication of these comments that the divergence between analytic models conceiving of social behaviour in terms of social systems of interdependent parts – long a cardinal doctrine of functionalists – and models stressing the importance of certain 'factors' is not so radical as is often assumed. Although there are general grounds for believing that there are 'no one or two inherently primary sources of impetus to change in social systems', there are equally plausible grounds for asserting that not all elements of a social system contribute to its change. There is nothing inherently incompatible between an effort to develop a *generalized* theory of social change along these lines and one which stresses, as does Parsons, 'the plurality of possible origins of change'.[44]

Historically speaking, it seems that as a result of the empirical difficulties which older and methodologically unsophisticated factor theories encountered, functionalists polemically counterposed a stress on the system as such. In taking systemness as problematic, and focusing solely on the question of an unclarified 'interdependence' of elements, they were led to neglect the problem of the *differential* significance which various parts of the system had in determining changes in the system.

Although the methodological position of earlier functionalists commonly affirmed an amorphous interdependence of parts within a social system, it does not follow that the specific empirical analyses in which they engaged actually utilized this principle. In particular, the classic contributors, from Comte to Parsons, have often gone out of their way to stress the significance of 'shared value elements' in maintaining the equilibrium of social systems.[45]

Contrariwise, some of the early 'factor' theories can be regarded not as having denied, but as having taken system interdependence as given, and as having focused their analysis on the problem of identifying and weighting the various parts within it.[46] If this view of the matter is correct, it may be that the distinction between social theories has not so much been between system and factor theories, but rather between overt and covert factor theories, or between implicit and explicit system theories.

Factor theories are intrinsically difficult to demonstrate rigorously without the use of mathematical tools. For they imply a quantitative difference between two or more elements in determining a given outcome. In so far as system models simply make a vague affirmation of the 'interdependence' of parts they are more readily given empirical application in a purely quantitative manner.

It may be, therefore, that earlier functionalists neglected the problem of weighting system parts, because they then lacked the mathematical tools requisite for a rigorous resolution of the problem. Today, however, mathematical and statistical developments may be on the verge of making this possible and have, therefore, demanded that this dormant issue be reopened.[47]

NOTES

1. Many of the early users of the organismic analogy were well aware of its difficulties and by no means deluded themselves into believing that society *was* an organism. Indeed, some of the classic organismic theorists were far more methodologically astute than some who reject the organismic analogy with the banal and irrelevant criticism that it does not seem intuitively fitting. For a methodologically wise use of the organismic analogy see A. R. Radcliffe-Brown, *Structure and Function in Primitive Society*, Glencoe, Ill., Free Press, 1952, ch. IX.

2. For a tentative and partial statement of my views on the problematics of the equilibrium model see 'Some Observations on Systematic Theory, 1945-55', Chapter 6 in the present volume.

3. R. K. Merton, *Social Theory and Social Structure*, Glencoe, Ill., Free Press, rev. ed., 1957, pp. 46-7.

4. T. Parsons, *Essays in Sociological Theory Pure and Applied*, Glencoe, Ill., Free Press, 1949, p. 21.

5. Merton, ibid., p. 50 *et seq.*

6. Merton, ibid., p. 50.

7. Merton, ibid., p. 52.

8. Merton, ibid., p. 4 *et seq.*

9. cf. Merton's critical appreciation of the method of 'successive approximations' in P. F. Lazarsfeld and R. K. Merton, 'Friendship as Social Process', in M. Berger, T. Abel and C. H. Page, eds., *Freedom and Control in Modern Society*, New York, Van Nostrand, 1954, pp. 60-62. Contrast this with Parsons' statement that 'In a system of interdependent variables . . . the value of any one variable is not *completely* determined unless those of *all* the others are known.' T. Parsons, *The Structure of Social Action*, New York, McGraw-Hill, 1937, p. 25. (Our emphases – A.W.G.)

10. E. E. Evans-Pritchard, *The Nuer*, Oxford, Clarendon Press, 1940.

11. J. H. Steward, *Theory of Culture Change*, Urbana, University of Illinois Press, 1955, especially chs. 6-10.

12. Among a spate of recent literature on this see W. R. Ashby, *Design for a Brain*, New York, Wiley, 1952; N. Wiener, *Cybernetics*, New York, Wiley, 1948; L. A. Jefress, ed., *Cerebral Mechanisms in Behavior*, New York, Wiley, 1951; H. Von Foerster, ed., *Cybernetics, Transactions of the 6th, 7th, and 8th Conferences*, New York, Josiah Macy, Jr, Foundation, 1950, 1951, 1952; perhaps the most cogent popular account is that of W. Sluckin, *Minds and Machines*, Penguin Books, 1954.

13. T. Parsons, *The Social System*, Glencoe, Ill., Free Press, 1951, pp. 5-6.

14. Merton, ibid., p. 71 *et seq.*

15. Merton, ibid., p. 73.

16. The principle of reciprocity enters Marx's theoretical analysis not in peripheral but in central ways; it is most importantly implicated in his concept of 'exploitation'; this is rendered technically specific in the manner of nineteenth-century political economy in his analysis of 'surplus value'. If one puts aside Marx's moral condemnations of exploitation and considers only its sociological substance, it is clear that it refers to a breakdown in reciprocal functionality. It is a basic implication of Marx's analysis that exploitation in class societies induces social instabilities. Characteristically, however, Marx is interested in the sources of instability and change and thus focuses on the contrary of functional reciprocity. Marx is also concerned to analyse the compensatory mechanisms in modern society which conceal the the breakdown in functional reciprocity and, in this connection, his concept of 'fetishism' is clearly relevant. See especially K. Marx, *Capital*, vol. I, tr. by Eden and Cedar Paul, New York, Dutton, 1930, pp. 43–59.

17. See M. Mauss, *The Gift*, Glencoe, Ill., Free Press, 1954. Mauss stresses that there is a universally recognized obligation to reciprocate gifts which have been accepted. In his last chapter, Mauss also seems to be verging on a concept of 'exploitation' when he comments that people have 'a strong desire to pursue the thing they have produced once they realize that they have given their labour without sharing in the profit', p. 64.

18. This comes out most clearly in Malinowski's discussion of Trobriand society concerning which he remarks that its whole structure is arranged into 'well-balanced chains of reciprocal services'. Discussing the exchanges between the coastal fisherman and the inland gardeners, of fish and vegetables, respectively, he notes that such *reciprocity is a mechanism which underlies and induces conformity with the obligations they have to each other*. B. Malinowski, *Crime and Custom*, Paul, Trench, Trubner, 1926, pp. 46, 23 *et seq.* There is no doubt that Radcliffe-Brown also assumed a principle of reciprocity which he called 'the principle of equivalent return'. This he held was expressed in the *lex talionis*, in the principle of indemnification for injury, and in the principle that those who give benefits should receive equivalent benefits. From his Chicago University seminar, 'The Nature of a Theoretical Natural Science of Society', 1937.

19. C. Lévi-Strauss, *Les Structures élémentaires de la parenté*, Paris, Presses Universitaires, 1949. In this volume, which owes so much to Mauss and Durkheim, Lévi-Strauss presents his now near-classic theory of the 'exchange' of women.

20. G. C. Homans and D. M. Schneider, *Marriage, Authority, and Final Causes*, Glencoe, Ill., Free Press, 1955. This represents a criticism of particulars of Lévi-Strauss's theory. Homans' forthcoming work on a

systematic theory of 'exchange' is also fundamentally based on the principle of reciprocity.

21. For a discussion of such a mechanism in a modern industrial setting, see the analysis of the 'indulgency pattern' in A. W. Gouldner, *Wildcat Strike*, Yellow Springs, Ohio, Antioch Press, 1954, pp. 18–26.

22. Lévi-Strauss, ibid., p. 548.

23. See the discussion in Max Gluckman, *Custom and Conflict in Africa*, Glencoe, Ill., Free Press, 1955.

24. T. Parsons and E. A. Shils, eds., *Toward a General Theory of Action*, Cambridge, Harvard University Press, 1951, p. 49.

25. For systematic efforts pointing in this direction see J. Feibleman and J. W. Friend, 'The Structure and Function of Organization', *Philosophical Review*, 54 (Jan., 1945), pp. 19–44, and A. Angyal, 'The Structure of Wholes', *Philosophy of Science*, 6 (Jan., 1939), pp. 25–37.

26. cf. Parsons and Shils, ibid., p. 107. 'The most general and fundamental property of a system is the interdependence of parts or variables. . . . This order must have a tendency to self-maintenance, which is very generally expressed in the concept of equilibrium. . . .'

27. For an excellent discussion of this by a sociologist see G. Shapiro, *The Formulation and Verification of a Theory of Primary Social Integration*, unpublished doctoral dissertation, Cornell University, 1954, especially ch. 2.

28. In this connection, the significance of Asch's experiments on the effects of group influence on perception would not only be that some 33 per cent of his subjects distorted their perception to conform with the pressures of others in their group, but also that 67 per cent of them did *not* do so. See S. E. Asch, *Social Psychology*, New York, Prentice-Hall, Inc., 1952, ch. 16.

29. E. C. Hughes, 'Work and the Self', in J. H. Rohrer and M. Sherif, eds., *Social Psychology at the Crossroads*, New York, Harper and Brothers, 1951, p. 322.

30. E. Goffman, 'The Nature of Defence and Demeanor', *American Anthropologist*, 58 (June, 1956), pp. 486–8.

31. The philosophic posture here parallels that developed in E. Cassirir, *An Essay on Man*, New Haven, Yale University Press, 1944.

32. For discussion of some of the problems here from a philosopher's viewpoint see R. B. Winn, 'The Nature of Relations', *Philosophical Review*, 50 (Jan., 1941), pp. 20–35.

33. On the problem of succession in social systems see A. W. Gouldner,

Patterns of Industrial Bureaucracy, Glencoe, Ill., Free Press, 1954, pp. 59–104.

34. A stimulating if impressionistic account of this pattern is to be found in W. H. Whyte, *Is Anybody Listening?*, New York, Simon and Schuster, 1952.

35. For a case of this see the discussion in A. W. Gouldner, *Wildcat Strike*, ibid., p. 24.

36. This is more extensively developed in A. W. Gouldner, 'The Problem of Loyalty in Groups Under Tension', *Social Problems*, 2 (Oct., 1954), pp. 82–7.

37. cf. K. Mannheim, *Man and Society in an Age of Reconstruction*, New York, Harcourt, Brace, 1941, p. 245.

38. For fuller discussion see A. W. Gouldner, ibid., ch. 10, and especially p. 171.

39. J. H. Steward, 'Levels of Sociocultural Integration', *Southwestern Journal of Anthropology*, 7 (Winter, 1951), p. 379.

40. Merton, ibid., p. 182.

41. Of similar import are Morris Ginsberg's comments in his essay on 'Moral Progress': 'There is no reason, it seems to me, for believing that the men of this age are suffering from a weakening of moral fibre.' Again, some of modern man's bewilderment 'is a sign not of moral decay but rather of moral ferment'. M. Ginsberg, *Reason and Unreason in Society*, Cambridge, Harvard University Press, 1948, pp. 317–18.

42. A. W. Gouldner, 'Cosmopolitans and Locals: Toward an Analysis of Latent Social Roles', *Administrative Science Quarterly*, 2 (Dec., 1957), pp. 281–306 and (March, 1958), pp. 444–80.

43. T. Parsons, *The Structure of Social Action*, ibid.

44. T. Parsons, *The Social System*, ibid., p. 494.

45. See the cognate analysis of Parsons' theory in the excellent piece by David Lockwood, 'Some Remarks on *The Social System*', *British Journal of Sociology*, 7 (June 1956), pp. 134–45, where the nub of the criticism is the neglect of structured but non-normative elements in Parsons' work.

46. One of the most interesting cases of this is, of course, that of Marxism, which is commonly interpreted as a factor theory. It is clear, however, if not from Marx himself then at least from Engels, that they were deeply concerned about system analysis. Among Engels' frequent references to the matter are the following: 'Marx and I are ourselves partly to blame for the fact that younger writers sometimes lay more stress on the economic side than is due it. We had to emphasize this main principle in opposition to our adversaries, who denied it, and we had not always the time, the

place, or the opportunity to allow the other elements involved in the inter-action to come into their rights.' Again, 'According to the materialist conception of history the determining element in history is *ultimately* the production and reproduction in real life. More than this neither Marx nor I have ever asserted.' Finally, 'In nature nothing happens alone. Every-thing has an effect on something else and vice versa. . . .' K. Marx and F. Engels, *Selected Correspondence, 1846–1895*, tr. by D. Torr, New York, International Publishers, 1942, pp. 477, 475, 114. N. Bukharin was one of the first of later Marxists to develop formally the use of system analysis on a sociological level. For example, a society 'may be regarded as a whole consisting of parts (elements) related to each other; in other words, the whole may be regarded as a system'. N. Bukharin, *Historical Materialism: a System of Sociology*, New York, International Publishers, 1925, p. 87.

47. For example, Paul Lazarsfeld is developing a statistical model which 'provides a procedure for discovering which of the interacting elements preponderate . . .' Lazarsfeld and Merton, ibid., p. 59.

8

The Norm of Reciprocity: A Preliminary Statement

'There is no duty more indispensable than that of returning a kindness', says Cicero, adding that 'all men distrust one forgetful of a benefit'.[1] Men have been insisting on the importance of reciprocity for a long time. While many sociologists concur in this judgement, there are nonetheless few concepts in sociology which remain more obscure and ambiguous. Howard Becker, for example, has found this concept so important that he has titled one of his books *Man in Reciprocity* and has even spoken of man as *Homo reciprocus*, all without venturing to present a straightforward definition of reciprocity. Instead Becker states, 'I don't propose to furnish any definition of reciprocity; if you produce some, they will be your own achievements.'[2]

Becker is not alone in failing to stipulate formally the meaning of reciprocity, while at the same time affirming its prime importance. Indeed, he is in very good company, agreeing with L. T. Hobhouse, who held that 'reciprocity . . . is the vital principle of society',[3] and is a key intervening variable through which shared social rules are enabled to yield social stability. Yet Hobhouse presents no systematic definition of reciprocity. While hardly any clearer than Hobhouse, Richard Thurnwald is equally certain of the central importance of the 'principle of reciprocity': this principle is almost a primordial imperative which 'pervades every relation of primitive life'[4] and is the basis on which the entire social and ethical life of primitive civilizations presumably rests.[5] Georg Simmel's comments go a step further, emphasizing the importance of reciprocity not only for primitive but for all societies. Simmel remarks that social equilibrium and cohesion could not exist without 'the reciprocity of service and return service', and that 'all contacts among men rest on the schema of giving and returning the equivalence'.[6]

Were we confronted with only an obscure concept, which we had no reason to assume to be important, we might justifiably consign it to the Valhalla of intellectual history, there to consort eternally with the countless incunabula of sociological ingenuity. However convenient, such a disposition would be rash, for we can readily note the importance attributed to the concept of reciprocity by such scholars as George Homans, Claude Lévi-Strauss and Raymond Firth,[7] as well as by such earlier writers as Durkheim, Marx, Mauss, Malinowski and von Wiese, to name only a few masters.

Accordingly, the aims of this paper are: (1) to indicate the manner in which the concept of reciprocity is tacitly involved in but formally neglected by modern functional theory; (2) to clarify the concept and display some of its diverse intellectual contents, thus facilitating its theoretical employment and research utility; and (3) to suggest concretely ways in which the clarified concept provides new leverage for analysis of the central problems of sociological theory, namely, accounting for stability and instability in social systems.

Reciprocity and Functional Theory

My concern with reciprocity developed initially from a critical re-examination of current functional theory, especially the work of Robert Merton and Talcott Parsons. The fullest ramifications of what follows can best be seen in this theoretical context. Merton's familiar paradigm of functionalism stresses that analysis must begin with the identification of some problematic pattern of human behaviour, some institution, role, or shared pattern of belief. Merton stipulates clearly the basic functionalist assumption, the way in which the problematic pattern is to be understood: he holds that the 'central orientation of functionalism' is 'expressed in the practice of interpreting data by establishing their consequences for larger structures in which they are implicated'.[8] The functionalist's emphasis upon studying the *existent* consequences, the ongoing functions or dysfunctions, of a social pattern may be better appreciated if it is remembered that this concern developed in a polemic against the earlier anthropological notion of a 'survival'. The survival, of course, was regarded as a custom held to be unexplainable in terms of its existent consequences or utility and which, therefore, had to be understood with reference to its consequences for social arrangements no longer present.

Merton's posture toward the notion of a social survival is both pragmatic and sceptical. He asserts that the question of survivals is largely an empirical one; if the evidence demonstrates that a given social pattern is presently functionless then it simply has to be admitted provisionally to be a survival. Contrariwise, if no such evidence can be adduced 'then the quarrel dwindles of its own accord'.[9] It is in this sense that his position is pragmatic. It is also a sceptical position in that he holds that 'even when such survivals are identified in contemporary literate societies, they seem to add little to our understanding of human behaviour or the dynamics of social change. . . .'[10] We are told, finally, that 'the sociologist of literate societies may neglect survivals with no apparent loss'.[11]

This resolution of the problem of survivals does not seem entirely satisfactory, for although vital empirical issues are involved there are also important questions that can only be clarified theoretically. Merton's discussion implies that certain patterns of human behaviour are already known to be, or may in the future be shown to be, social survivals. How, then, can *these* be explained in terms of functional theory? Can functional theory ignore them on the grounds that they are not socially consequential? Consequential or not, such social survivals would in themselves entail patterns of behaviour or belief which are no less in need of explanation than any other. More than that, their very existence, which Merton conceives possible, would seem to contradict the 'central orientation' of functional theory.

Functionalism, to repeat, explains the persistence of social patterns in terms of their ongoing consequences for existent social systems. If social survivals, which by definition have no such consequences, are conceded to exist or to be possible, then it would seem that functionalism is by its own admission incapable of explaining them. To suggest that survivals do not help us to understand other patterns of social behaviour is beside the mark. The decisive issue is whether existent versions of functional theory can explain social survivals, not whether specific social survivals can explain other social patterns.

It would seem that functionalists have but one of two choices: either they must dogmatically deny the existence or possibility of functionless patterns (survivals), and assert that all social behaviour is explainable parsimoniously on the basis of the same fundamental functionalist assumption, that is, in terms of its consequences for surrounding social structures; or, more reasonably, they must concede that some social patterns are or may be survivals, admitting that existent functional theory fails to account for such instances. In the latter case, functionalists must develop further their basic assumptions on the generalized level required. I believe that one of the strategic ways in which such basic assumptions can be developed is by recognizing the manner in which the concept of *reciprocity* is tacitly involved in them, and by explicating the concept's implications for functional theory.

The tacit implication of the concept of reciprocity in functional theory can be illustrated in Merton's analysis of the latent functions of the political machine in the United States. Merton inquires how political machines continue to operate, despite the fact that they frequently run counter to both the *mores* and the law. The *general* form of his explanation is to identify the consequences of the machine for surrounding structures and to demonstrate that the machine performs 'positive functions which are at the same time not adequately fulfilled by other existing patterns and structures'.[12] It seems evident, however, that simply to establish its consequences for other social structures provides no answer to the question of the persistence of the political machine.[13] The explanation miscarries because no explicit analysis is made of the feedback through which the social structures or groups, whose needs are satisfied by the political machine, in turn 'reciprocate' and repay the machine for the services received from it. In this case, the patterns of reciprocity, implied in the notion of the 'corruption' of the machine, are well known and fully documented.

To state the issue generally: the demonstration that A is functional for B can help to account for A's persistence only if the functional theorist tacitly assumes some principle of reciprocity. It is in this sense that some concept of reciprocity apparently has been smuggled into the basic but unstated postulates of functional analysis. The demonstration that A is functional for B helps to account for A's own persistence and stability only on two related assumptions: (1) that B *reciprocates* A's services, and (2) that B's service to A is *contingent* upon A's performance of positive functions for B. The second assumption, indeed, is one implication of the definition of reciprocity as a transaction. Unless B's services to A are contingent upon the services provided by A, it is pointless to examine the latter if one wishes to account for the persistence of A.

It may be assumed, as a first approximation, that a social unit or group is more likely to contribute to another which provides it with benefits than to one which does not; nonetheless, there are certain general conditions under which one pattern may provide benefits for the other despite a *lack* of reciprocity. An important case of this situation is where power arrangements constrain the continuance of services. If B is considerably more powerful than A, B may force A to benefit it with little or no reciprocity. This social arrangement, to be sure, is less stable than one in which B's reciprocity *motivates* A to continue performing services for B, but it is hardly for this reason sociologically unimportant.

The problem can also be approached in terms of the functional autonomy[14] of two units relative to each other. For example, B may have many alternative sources for supplying the services that it normally receives from A. A, however, may be dependent upon B's services and have no, or comparatively few, alternatives. Consequently, the continued provision of benefits by one pattern,[15] A, for another, B, depends not only upon (1) the benefits which A in turn receives from B, but also on (2) the power which B possesses relative to A, and (3) the alternative sources of services accessible to each, beyond those provided by the other. In short, an explanation of the stability of a pattern, or of the relationship between A and B, requires investigation of mutually contingent benefits rendered and of the manner in which this mutual contingency is sustained. The latter, in turn, requires utilization of two different theoretical traditions and general orientations, one stressing the significance of power differences and the other emphasizing the degree of mutual dependence of the patterns or parties involved.

Functional theory, then, requires some assumption concerning reciprocity. It must, however, avoid the 'Pollyanna Fallacy' which optimistically assumes that structures securing 'satisfactions' from others will invariably be 'grateful' and will always reciprocate. Therefore it cannot be merely hypostatized that reciprocity will operate in every case; its occurrence must, instead, be documented empirically. Although reciprocal relations stabilize patterns, it need not follow that a lack of reciprocity is socially impossible or invariably disruptive of the patterns involved. Relations with little or no reciprocity may, for example, occur when power disparities allow one party to coerce the other. There may also be special mechanisms which compensate for or control the tensions which arise in the event of a breakdown in reciprocity. Among such compensatory mechanisms there may be culturally shared prescriptions of one-sided or unconditional generosity, such as the Christian notion of 'turning the other cheek' or 'walking the second mile', the feudal notion of *noblesse oblige*, or the Roman notion of 'clemency'. There may also be cultural prohibitions banning the examination of certain interchanges from the standpoint of their concrete reciprocity, as expressed by the cliché, 'It's not the gift but the sentiment that counts.' The major point here is that if empirical analysis fails to detect the existence of functional reciprocity, or finds that it has been disrupted, it becomes necessary to search out and analyse the compensatory arrangements that may provide means of controlling the resultant tensions, thereby enabling the problematic pattern to remain stable.

A Reconceptualization of 'Survivals'

Thus far reciprocity has been discussed as a mutually contingent exchange of benefits between two or more units, as if it were an 'all or none' matter. Once the problem is posed in this way, however, it is apparent that reciprocity is not merely present or absent but is, instead, quantitatively variable – or may be treated as such. The benefits exchanged, at one extreme, may be identical or equal. At the other logical extreme, one party may give nothing in return for the benefits it has received. Both of these extremes are probably rare in social relations and the intermediary case, in which one party gives something more or less than that received, is probably more common than either of the limiting cases.

Having cast the problem of reciprocity in these quantitative terms, there emerges an important implication for the question of social survivals. The quantitative view of reciprocity now enables us to reconceptualize the notion of a survival. It may now be seen that a survival was tacitly treated as one of the limiting cases of reciprocity, that is, one in which a pattern provides *nothing* in exchange for the benefits given it.

The polemical opposition of the earlier functionalists to this view of a survival rests implicitly on an unqualified principle of reciprocity. These functionalists made the cogent assumption that a social pattern which persists must be securing satisfaction of its own needs from certain other patterns. What was further and more dubiously assumed, however, was that if this pattern continues to be 'serviced' this could only be because it reciprocally provided *some* gratifications to its benefactors. In the course of the polemic, the question of the degree of such gratification – the relation between its output and input – became obscured. To the early functionalists, the empirical problem became one of unearthing the hidden contributions made by a seeming survival and, thereby, showing that it is not in fact functionless. In effect, this enjoined the functionalist to exert his ingenuity to search out the hidden reciprocities, for it was assumed that there must be some reciprocities somewhere. This led, in certain cases, as Audrey Richards states, to 'some far-fetched explanations. . . .'[16]

If, however, it had been better understood that compensatory mechanisms might have been substituted for reciprocity, or that power disparities might have maintained the 'survival' despite its lack of reciprocity, then many fruitful problems may well have emerged. Above all, the early functionalists neglected the fact that a survival is only the limiting case of a larger class of social phenomena, namely, relations between parties or patterns in which functional reciprocity is *not equal*. While the survival, defined as the extreme case of a *complete lack* of reciprocity, may be rare, the larger class of *unequal* exchanges, of which survivals are a part, is frequent. The tacit conception of survivals as entailing no reciprocity led the early functionalists to neglect the *larger class of unequal exchanges*. It is this problem which the functionalist polemic against survivals has obscured to the present day.

The 'Exploitation' Problem

It was, however, not only the functionalist polemic against the concept of survivals that obscured the significance and inhibited the study of unequal exchanges. A similar result is also produced by the suspicion with which many modern sociologists conventionally regard the concept of 'exploitation'. This concept of course is central to the traditional socialist critique of modern capitalism. In the now nearly-forgotten language of political economy, 'exploitation' refers to a relationship in which unearned income results from certain kinds of unequal exchange.

Starting perhaps with Sismondi's notion of 'spoliation', and possibly even earlier with the physiocrat's critique of exchange as intrinsically unproductive, the concept of exploitation can be traced from the work of the Saint-Simonians to that of Marx and Proudhon.[17] It is also present in Veblen's notion of the Vested Interest which he characterizes as 'the right to something for nothing' or, in other words, as *institutionalized* exploitation. Even after the emergence of sociology as a separate discipline the concept of exploitation appears in the works of E. A. Ross,[18] von Wiese and Howard Becker.[19] As it passed into sociology, however, the concept was generalized beyond its original economic application. Ross and Becker–von Wiese, for example, speak of various types of exploitation: economic, to be sure, but also religious, 'egotic', and sexual.

However, just as the concept of exploitation was being generalized and made available for social analysis, it almost disappeared from sociological usage.

'*Almost* disappeared' because there remains one area in which unabashed, full-scale use of the concept is made by sociologists. This is in the study of sexual relations. As Kanin and Howard remark, 'It has been the *practice* to speak of exploitation when males were found to have entered sexual liaisons with women of comparative lower status.'[20] Kingsley Davis also uses the notion of exploitation implicitly in his discussion of the incest taboo, remarking that '. . . father–daughter incest would put the daughter in a position of subordination. While she was still immature the father could use his power to take advantage of her.'[21] What Davis is saying is that one function of the incest taboo is to prevent sexual exploitation. He goes on to add that 'legitimate sexual relations ordinarily involve a certain amount of reciprocity. Sex is exchanged for something equally valuable.'[22] This is an interesting commentary, first, because Davis is quite clear about treating exploitation in the context of a discussion of reciprocity; and second, because he explicitly uses a notion of reciprocity in a strategic way even though it is not systematically explored elsewhere in his volume, once again illustrating the tendency to use the concept and to assume its analytic importance without giving it careful conceptualization.[23]

The continued use of the concept of exploitation in sociological analyses of sexual relations stems largely from the brilliant work of Willard Waller on the dynamics of courtship. Waller's ambivalent comments about the concept suggest why it has fallen into sociological disrepute. 'The word exploitation is by no means a desirable one,' explains Waller, 'but we have not been able to find another which will do as well. The dictionary definition of exploitation as an "unfair or unjust utilization of another" contains a value judgement, and this value judgement is really a part of the ordinary sociological meaning of the term.'[24] In short, the concept of exploitation may have become disreputable because its value implications conflict with modern sociology's drive to place itself on a value-free basis, as well as because it is a concept commonly and

correctly associated with the critique of modern society emphasized by the political left. But the cocnept does not simply
express an ideological judgement; it also refers empirically to
certain transactions involving an exchange of things of unequal
value. It is important to make sure that distaste for the term, for
ideological reasons, does not obscure its sociological viability.
If it is important to recognize the term's ideological implications,
it is also vital to see that a compulsive rejection of it is no less
ideological.

The ideological implications of the concept of exploitation
have *not* excluded it from studies of sexual relations, although
almost all other specializations in sociology eschew it. Why this
is so remains a tempting problem for the sociology of knowledge, but cannot be explored here. In the present context, the
important implications are the following: if the possible sexual
exploitation of daughters by fathers gives rise, as Davis suggests,
to mechanisms that serve to prevent this, then it would seem
that other kinds of exploitation might generate other kinds of
mechanisms. These may be no less important and universal
than the incest taboo. If the exploitation of women by men is
worthy of sociological attention, then also worth studying is
the exploitation of students by teachers, of workers by management or union bureaucrats, of Negroes by whites, as well as
of patients by doctors.[25] If the analysis of sexual relations in
terms of the notion of exploitation is valuable, then it can be
of similar value in analysing many other kinds of social relations.

As cybernation and technology develop, it may be that the
term 'exploitation' becomes less relevant for a critique of the
economy. The important consideration, however, is certainly
not to rescue that word but, rather, the concept that it names
and the social reality to which it makes reference. The crucial
thing is to restore the problem of unequal exchange as a focus
of sociological analysis and research.

In any event, the present analysis of reciprocity opens up
long-neglected questions, yielding a new perspective on the
relation between functional theory and the concepts of 'survival'
and 'exploitation'. In the latter case, moreover, intimations
emerge of some of the ways in which two diverse theoretical

traditions contain surprising convergences.

These two traditions are, first, that which is commonly if questionably[26] held to begin with Comte, was developed by Durkheim, and reaches its fullest current expression in the work of Parsons. The second tradition, while often ideologically distorted, nevertheless retains significant sociological substance, derives from Marx and Engels, was developed by Kautsky, Bukharin and others. The latent convergence between these two schools involves the implicit stress that each gives to reciprocity, albeit to polar ends of its continuum.

The 'Comteian' tradition, of course, approached reciprocity through its emphasis on the division of labour, viewed as a major source of social cohesion. Characteristically focusing on the problem of social instability and change, rather than stability and cohesion, the 'Marxian' tradition emphasized the opposite end of reciprocity, namely, exploitation. This, I suspect, is one of the major but overlooked convergences in the history of sociological theory.

This latent convergence becomes most evident in Durkheim's lectures on 'Professional Ethics and Civic Morals'.[27] Durkheim contends that the existence of social classes, characterized by significant inequalities, in principle makes it impossible for 'just' contracts to be negotiated. This system of stratification, Durkheim argues, constrains to an unequal exchange of goods and services, thereby offending the moral expectations of people in industrial societies. The exploitation rendered possible by notable disparities of power among the contracting parties encourages a sense of injustice which has socially unstabilizing consequences. Thus both Durkheim and Marx use a concept of 'exploitation' for analysing social instabilities. Durkheim, however, adds an important element that was systematically neglected by Marx, namely, that unequal exchanges of goods and services are socially disruptive because they violate certain pervasive *values*. But the specific nature of this value element is never fully confronted and explored by Durkheim; we must here take as problematic what Durkheim took as given.

Complementarity and Reciprocity

First, however, the question of the meaning of the concept of reciprocity should be re-examined. Consideration of some of the ways in which the reciprocity problem is treated by Parsons helps to distinguish reciprocity from other cognate concepts. 'It is inherent in the nature of social interaction,' writes Parsons, 'that the gratification of ego's need-dispositions is contingent on alter's reaction and vice versa.'[28] Presumably, therefore, if the gratification of either party's needs is not contingent upon the other's reactions, the stability of their relation is undermined. This, in turn, implies that if a social system is to be stable there must always be some 'mutuality of gratification'.[29] Social system stability, then, presumably depends in part on the mutually contingent exchange of gratifications, that is, on reciprocity as exchange.

This, however, remains an insight the implications of which are never systematically explored. For example, the implications of differences in the *degree* of mutuality or in the symmetry of reciprocity are neglected. Again, while the concept of 'exploitation' assumes *central* importance in Parsons' commentary on the patient–doctor relation, it is never precisely defined, examined, and located in his *general* theory.

One reason for Parsons' neglect of reciprocity is that he, like some other sociologists, does not distinguish it from the concept of complementarity. Parsons uses the two concepts as if they are synonymous[30] and, for the most part, centres his analysis on complementarity to the systematic neglect of reciprocity rigorously construed. The term complementarity, however, is itself an ambiguous one and is not, in all of its meaning, synonymous with reciprocity. Complementarity has at least four distinct meanings:[31]

Complementarity 1 may mean that a right (x) of Ego against Alter implies a duty ($-x$) of Alter to Ego. Given the often vague use of the term 'right', it is quite possible that this proposition, in one aspect, is only an expansion of some definition of the concept 'right'. To that degree, of course, this is simply an analytic proposition. The interesting sociological questions, however, arise only when issues of empirical substance rather than logical implication are raised. For example, where a group shares a belief that some status occupant has a certain right, say the right of a wife to receive support from her husband, does the group in fact also share a belief that the husband has an obligation to support the wife? Furthermore, even though rights may logically or empirically imply duties, it need not follow that the reverse is true. In other words, it does not follow that rights and duties are always transitive. This can be seen in a second meaning of complementarity.

Complementarity 2 may mean that what is a duty (—x) of Alter to Ego implies a right (x) of Ego against Alter. On the *empirical* level, while this is often true, of course, it is also sometimes false. For example, what may be regarded as a duty of charity or forbearance, say a duty to 'turn the other cheek', need not be *socially* defined as the *right* of the recipient. While a man may be regarded as having an unconditional obligation to tell the truth to everyone, even to a confirmed liar, people in his group might not claim that the liar has a *right* to have the truth told him.

The other two meanings of complementarity differ substantially. Complementarity 3 may mean that a right (x) of Alter against Ego implies a duty (—y) of Alter to Ego. Similarly, complementarity 4 may mean that a duty (—x) of Ego to Alter implies a right (y) of Ego against Alter.

In these four implications of complementarity – sometimes called reciprocal rights and obligations – there are two distinctive types of cases. Properly speaking, *complementarity* refers only to the first two meanings sketched above, where what is a right of Ego implies an obligation of Alter, or where a duty of Alter to Ego implies a right of Ego against Alter. Only the other two meanings, however, involve true instances of *reciprocity*, for only in these does what one party receives from the other require some return, so that giving and receiving are mutually contingent.

In short, complementarity connotes that one's rights are another's obligations, and *vice versa*. Reciprocity, however, connotes that *each* party has rights *and* duties. This is more than an analytic distinction: it is an *empirical* generalization concerning role systems the importance of which as a datum is so elemental that it is commonly neglected and rarely made problematic. The English philosopher MacBeath suggests that this empirical generalization may be accounted for by the principle of reciprocity.[32] This would seem possible in several senses, one of which is that, were there only rights on the one side and duties on the other, there need be no exchange whatsoever. Stated differently, it would seem that there can be stable patterns of reciprocity *qua* exchange only insofar as *each* party has both rights and duties. In effect, then, reciprocity has its significance for *role systems* in that it tends to structure *each* role so as to include both rights and duties. It is now clear, at any rate, that reciprocity is by no means identical with complementarity and that the two are confused only at theoretical peril.

Malinowski on Reciprocity

Renewing the effort to clarify the diverse meanings of reciprocity, we turn to Malinowski's seminal contribution. This is most fully elaborated in his *Crime and Custom*,[33] which opens with the following question: Why is it that rules of conduct in a primitive society are obeyed, even though they are hard and irksome? Even under normal conditions, the savage's compliance with his moral code is at best partial, conditional, and evasive. These, says Malinowski, are the elementary facts of ethnography, and consequently we cannot assume that the savage's conformity is due only to his awe and reverence for traditional custom, or that he slavishly and spontaneously complies with its dictates.

Above all, Malinowski rejects the assumption that it is the sacred authority of the moral code, or the 'collective conscience', which accounts for the conformity given it. It is to this anti-Durkheimian point that he directs the brunt of his polemic. Conformity, says Malinowski, is not sanctioned 'by a mere psychological force, but by a definite social machinery. . . .'[34] Thus Malinowski expressly rejects a psychological account of conformity and seeks instead a distinctively sociological explanation.[35] This he finds in the 'principle of reciprocity'.

One of Malinowski's central theses holds that people *owe obligations to each other* and that, therefore, conformity with norms is something they give *to each other*. He notes, for example, that almost every religious or ceremonial act is regarded as an obligation between groups and living individuals, and not only to the immortal gods. For Malinowski, therefore, one meaning of reciprocity refers to the interlocking status duties which people owe one another. Thus he speaks of reciprocity as taking place 'within a standing partnership, or as associated with definite social ties or coupled with mutuality in non-economic matters'.[36]

Reciprocity also entails a 'mutual dependence and [is] realized in the equivalent arrangement of reciprocal services. . . .'[37] Here reciprocity is conceived as the complement to the fulfilment of the division of labour. It is the pattern of exchange through which the mutual dependence of people, brought about by the division of labour, is realized. Reciprocity, therefore, is a mutually gratifying pattern of exchanging goods and services.

As noted above, Malinowski speaks of reciprocity as involving an exchange of *equivalent* services; he further stresses this by insisting that 'most if not all economic acts are found to belong to some chain of reciprocal gifts and counter-gifts, which in the long run balance, benefiting both sides equally'.[38] For Malinowski, then, the exchange of goods and services is not only mutually gratifying but is equally so, 'in the long run'.

Speaking of the reciprocal exchange of vegetables and fish between inland communities and fishing villages, Malinowski remarks that there is a 'system of mutual obligations which forces the fisherman to repay whenever he has received a gift from his inland partner, and *vice versa*. Neither partner can refuse, neither may stint, neither should delay.'[39] This is seen to be related to the group's existential beliefs about reciprocity. That is, men are not regarded as blindly involving themselves in reciprocal transactions; they are viewed as having some presentiment of the consequences of reciprocity and of its breakdown. In this vein, Malinowski writes: 'Though no native, however intelligent, can formulate this state of affairs in a general abstract manner, or present it as a sociological theory, yet everyone is well aware of its existence and in each concrete case he can foresee the consequences.'[40] More specifically, it seems to be implied that people believe that (a) in the long run the mutual exchange of goods and services will balance out; or (b) if people do not aid those who helped them certain penalties will be imposed upon them; or (c) those whom they have helped *can* be expected to help them; or (d) some or all of these.

It is clear that two basically different elements were caught up in Malinowski's 'principle of reciprocity'. One of these is a set of sentiments or existential folk beliefs about reciprocity. The other is a mutually contingent exchange of benefits or gratifications. (The latter conception converges, though it is not completely identical, with the ecological concept of symbiosis.) There is, however, a third analytically distinct element which, if implicit in Malinowski, remained murky. This is a *value* element, the same value that Durkheim, as mentioned earlier, invoked but did not clarify. Like Durkheim, Malinowski never fully disentangles it from the other elements.

In the exchanges between the fishing and the inland villages, cited above, we may suggest that each side lives up to its obligations, not simply because of constraints imposed by the division of labour with its attendant mutual dependency, but also because the partners share the higher level *moral norm*: 'You *should* give benefits to those who give you benefits.' Note that this norm does not simply make it unconditionally imperative, say, for the fisherman to give the inland gardeners fish. I refer here not to the *specific* obligation to give fish but rather to a *general* obligation to repay benefits.

In sum, beyond reciprocity as a pattern of exchange and beyond folk beliefs about reciprocity as a fact of life, there is another element: a generalized moral norm of reciprocity which defines certain actions and *obligations* as repayments for benefits received.

Malinowski frequently seems to confuse this general norm with the existence of complementary and concrete status rights and duties. It is theoretically necessary, however, to distinguish specific status duties from the general norm. Specific and complementary duties are owed by role partners to one another by virtue of the socially standardized roles they play. These may require an almost unconditional compliance in the sense that they are incumbent on all those in a given status simply by virtue of its occupancy. In contrast, the generalized norm of reciprocity evokes obligations toward others on the basis of their past behaviour. In the first case, Ego's obligations to Alter depend upon Ego's status *vis-à-vis* Alter; in the second case, Ego's obligations toward Alter depend upon what Alter has done for Ego. There are certain duties that people owe one another, not as human beings, or as fellow members of a group, or even as occupants of social statuses within the group but, rather, because of their prior actions. We owe others certain things because of what they have previously done for us, because of the history of previous interaction we have had with them. It is this kind of obligation which is entailed by the generalized norm of reciprocity.

The Norm of Reciprocity

Contrary to some cultural relativists, it can be hypothesized that a norm of reciprocity is universal. As Westermarck stated, 'To requite a benefit, or to be grateful to him who bestows it, is probably everywhere, at least under certain circumstances, regarded as a duty.'[41] A norm of reciprocity is, I suspect, no less universal and important an element of culture than the incest taboo, although, similarly, its concrete formulations may vary with time and place.

Specifically, I suggest that a norm of reciprocity, in its universal form, makes two interrelated, minimal demands: (1) people should help those who have helped them, and (2) people should not injure those who have helped them. Generically, the norm of reciprocity may be conceived of as a dimension to be found in all value systems and, in particular, as one among a *number* of 'Principal Components' universally present in moral codes. (The task of the sociologist, in this regard, parallels that of the physicist who seeks to identify the basic particles of matter, the conditions under which they vary, and their relations to one another.)

To suggest that a norm of reciprocity is universal is not, of course, to assert that it is unconditional. Unconditionality would, indeed, be at variance with the basic character of the reciprocity norm which imposes obligations only contingently, that is, in response to the benefits conferred by others. Moreover, such obligations of repayment are contingent upon the imputed *value* of the benefit received. The value of the benefit and hence the debt is in proportion to and varies with – among other things – the intensity of the recipient's need at the time the benefit was bestowed ('a friend in need . . .'), the resources of the donor ('he gave although he could ill afford it'), the motives imputed to the donor ('without thought of gain') and the nature of the constraints which are perceived to exist or to be absent ('he gave of his own free will . . .'). Thus the obligations imposed by the norm of reciprocity may vary with the *status* of the participants within a society.

Similarly, this norm functions differently in some degree in different *cultures*. In the Philippines, for example, the *compadre* system cuts across and pervades the political, economic, and other institutional spheres. *Compadres* are bound by a norm of reciprocity. If one man pays his *compadre*'s doctor's bill in time of need, for example, the latter may be obligated to help the former's son to get a government job. Here the tendency to govern all relations by the norm of reciprocity, thereby undermining bureaucratic impersonality, is relatively legitimate, hence overt and powerful. In the United States, however, such tendencies are weaker, in part because friendship relations are less institutionalized. Nonetheless, even in bureaucracies in this country such tendencies are endemic, albeit less legitimate and overt. Except in friendship, kinship, and neighbourly relations, a norm of reciprocity is not imposed on Americans by the 'dominant cultural profile', although it is commonly found in the latent or 'substitute' culture structure in all institutional sectors, even the most rationalized, in the United States.

In otherwise contrasting discussions of the norm of reciprocity one emphasis is notable. Some scholars, especially Homans, Thurwald, Simmel, and Malinowski, assert or imply that the reciprocity norm stipulates that the amount of the return to be made is 'roughly equivalent' to what had been received. The problem of equivalence is a difficult but important one. Whether in fact there is a reciprocity norm specifically requiring that returns for benefits received be *equivalent* is an empirical question. So, too, is the problem of whether such a norm is part of or distinct from a more general norm which simply requires that one return some (unspecified) benefits to benefactors. Logically prior to such empirical problems, however, is the question of what the meaning of equivalence would be in the former norm of equivalent reciprocity.

Equivalence may have at least two forms, the sociological and psychodynamic significance of which are apt to be quite distinct. In the first case, heteromorphic reciprocity, equivalence may mean that the things exchanged may be concretely different but should be equal in *value*, as defined by the actors in the situation. In the second case, homeomorphic reciprocity, equivalence may mean that exchanges should be concretely alike, or identical in form, either with respect to the things exchanged or to the circumstances under which they are exchanged. In the former, equivalence calls for 'tit for tat'; in the latter, equivalence calls for 'tat for tat'. Historically, the most important expression of homeomorphic reciprocity is found in the *negative* norms of reciprocity, that is, in sentiments of retaliation where the emphasis is placed not on the return of benefits but on the return of injuries, and is best exemplified by the *lex talionis*.[42]

Finally, it should be stressed that equivalence in the above cases refers to a definition of the exchangeables made by actors in the situation. This differs, of course, from holding that the things exchanged by people, in the long run, will be *objectively* equal in value, as measured by economists or other social scientists. Here, again, the adequacy of these conceptual distinctions will be determined ultimately by empirical test. For example, can we find reciprocity norms which, in fact, require that returns be equivalent in value and are these empirically distinguishable from norms requiring that returns be concretely alike? Are these uni-dimensional or multi-dimensional? Similarly, only research can resolve the question whether a norm of retaliation exists in any given group, is the polar side of the norm of reciprocity, or is a distinctive norm which may vary independently of the reciprocity norm. These conceptual distinctions only suggest a set of research possibilities and have value primarily as guides to investigation.[43]

Reciprocity and Social Systems

As mentioned above, sociologists have sometimes confused the notion of complementarity with that of reciprocity and have recently tended to focus on the former. Presumably, the reason for this is because of the importance of complementarity in maintaining the stability of social systems. Clearly, if what one party deems his right is accepted by the other as his obligation, their relation will be more stable than if the latter fails to so define it. But if the group stabilizing consequences of complementarity are the basis of its theoretical significance, then the same consideration underwrites with equal potency the significance of reciprocity. For reciprocity has no less a role in maintaining the stability of social systems.

Note that there are at least two ways, not merely one, in which complementarity as such can break down. In the one case, Alter can refuse to acknowledge Ego's rights as his own duties. In the other case, however, Ego may not regard as rights that which Alter acknowledges as duties. The former is commonly viewed as the empirically more frequent and as the theoretically more significant case. That this often seems to be taken as a matter of course suggests the presence of certain tacit assumptions about basic human dispositions. It seems to assume, as Aristotle put it, that people are more ready to receive than to give benefits. In short, it premises a common tendency toward what used to be called 'egoism', a salient (but not exclusive) concern with the satisfaction of one's own needs.

This or some cognate assumption appears to be eminently reasonable and empirically justified. There can be no adequate systematic sociological theory which boggles at the issue; indeed, it is one of the many virtues of Parsons' work that it confronts the egoism problem. His solution seems to be sidetracked, however, because his overwhelming focus on the problem of complementarity leads to the neglect of reciprocity. If assumptions about egoistic dispositions are valid, however, a complementarity of rights and obligations should be exposed to a persistent strain, in which each party is somewhat more actively concerned to defend or extend his own rights than those of others. There is nothing in complementarity as such which would seem able to control egoism.

One way out may be obtained by premising that socialization internalizes complementary rights and obligations in persons, before they fully assume responsible participation in a social system. Even if socialization were to work perfectly and so internalize such rights and obligations, there still remains the question as to what mechanism can sustain and reinforce these during full participation in the social system. The concept of complementarity takes mutually compatible expectations as given; it does not and cannot explain how they are maintained once established. For this we need to turn to the reciprocities processes because these, unlike pure complementarity, actually mobilize egoistic motivations and channel them into the maintenance of the social system. Benthamite utilitarianism has long understood that egoism can motivate one party to satisfy the expectations of the other, since by doing so he induces the latter to reciprocate and to satisfy his own. As Max Gluckman might put it with his penchant for Hegelian paradox, there is an altruism in egoism, made possible through reciprocity.

Furthermore, the existential belief in reciprocity says something like this, 'People will usually help those who help them.' Similarly, the *norm* of reciprocity holds that people should help those who help them and, therefore, those whom you have helped have an obligation to help you. The conclusion is clear: if you want to be helped by others you must help them; hence it is not only proper but also expedient to conform with the specific status rights of others and with the general norm. Both the existential belief in and the norm of reciprocity enlist egoistic motivations in the service of social system stability.[44]

A full analysis of the ways in which the whole reciprocities complex is involved in the maintenance of social systems would require consideration of the linkages between each of its various elements, and their relation to other general properties of social systems. There is no space for such consideration here. Instead, I examine only one part of the complex, namely, the generalized *norm* of reciprocity, and suggest some of the ways in which it contributes to social system stability.

If, following Parsons, we suppose that social systems are stable to the extent that Ego and Alter conform with one another's expectations, we are confronted with the problem of why men *reciprocate* gratifications. Parsons holds that once a stable relation of mutual gratification has been established the system is self-perpetuating; presumably, no special mechanisms are necessary to maintain it. Insofar as this is not simply postulated in analogy with the principle of inertia in physics, apparently reciprocity is accounted for by Parsons, and also by Homans, as a result of the development of a beneficent cycle of mutual reinforcement. That is, Ego's conformity with Alter's expectations reinforces Alter's conformity with Ego's expectations, and so on.

This explanation of reciprocity *qua* transaction is particularly strange in Parsons' case since he often stresses, but here neglects, the significance of shared values as a source of stability in social systems. So far as the question here is not simply the general one of why men conform with the expectations of others but, rather, the more specific problem of why they *reciprocate* benefits, part of the answer would seem to be that they have commonly internalized some general *moral norm*. In short, the suggestion is that the motivation of reciprocity stems not only from the sheer gratification which Alter receives from Ego but also from Alter's internalization of a specific norm of reciprocity which morally obliges him to give benefits to those from whom he has received them. In this respect, the *norm* of reciprocity is a concrete and special mechanism involved in the maintenance of any stable social system.

Why should such a norm be necessary? Why is it that expedient considerations do not suffice to mobilize motivations to comply with others' expectations, thereby inducing them to provide reciprocal compliances? One major line of analysis here would certainly indicate the disruptive potentialities of power differences. Given significant power differences, egoistic motivations may seek to get benefits without returning them. (It is notable that Parsons fails to define the power situation in his basic model of Ego–Alter equilibrium.) The situation is then ripe for the breakdown of reciprocity and for the development of system-disrupting exploitation. The norm of reciprocity, however, engenders motives for returning benefits even when power differences might invite exploitation. The norm thus safeguards powerful people against the temptations of their own status; it motivates and regulates reciprocity as an exchange pattern, serving to inhibit the emergence of exploitative relations which would undermine the social system and the very power arrangements which had made exploitation possible.[45]

As we have seen, Parsons stresses that the stability of social systems largely derives from the *conformity* of role partners to each other's expectations, particularly when they do their duty to one another. This formulation induces a focus on conformity and deviance, and the degrees and types of each. Presumably, the more that people pay their social debts the more stable the social system. But much more than conformity and deviance are involved here.

The idea of the reciprocities complex leads us to the historical or genetic dimension of social interaction. For example, Malinowski, in his discussion of the Kula Ring, carefully notes that the gifts given are not immediately returned and repayment may take as long as a year. What is the significance of this intervening time period? It is a period governed by the norm of reciprocity in a double sense. First, the actor is accumulating, mobilizing, liquidating, or earmarking resources so that he can make a suitable repayment. Second, it is a period governed by the rule that you should not do harm to those who have done you a benefit. This is a time, then, when men are morally constrained to manifest their gratitude toward, or at least to maintain peace with, their benefactors.

Insofar as men live under such a rule of reciprocity, when one party benefits another, an obligation is generated. The recipient is now *indebted* to the donor, and he remains so until he repays. Once interaction is seen as taking place over time, we may note that the norm of reciprocity so structures social relations that, between the time of Ego's provision of a gratification and the time of Alter's repayment, falls the shadow of indebtedness. An adequate analysis of the dynamics of social interaction is thus required to go beyond the question of deviance from or conformity with the parties' obligations to one another. A second basic dimension needs to be examined systematically, namely, the time period when there is an obligation still to be performed, when commitments which have been made are yet to be fulfilled.

These outstanding obligations, no less than those already

given compliance, contribute substantially to the stability of social systems. It is obviously inexpedient for creditors to break off relationships with those who have outstanding obligations to them. It may also be inexpedient for *debtors* to do so because their creditors may not again allow them to run up a bill of social indebtedness. In addition, it is *morally* improper, under the norm of reciprocity, to break off relations or to launch hostilities against those to whom you are still indebted.

If this conclusion is correct, then we should not only look for mechanisms which constrain or motivate men to do their duty and to pay off their debts. We should also expect to find mechanisms which induce people to *remain* socially indebted to each other and which *inhibit* their complete repayment. This suggests another function performed by the requirement of only *rough* equivalence of repayment that may be involved in one of the norms of reciprocity. For it induces a certain amount of ambiguity as to whether indebtedness has been repaid and, over time, generates uncertainty about who is in whose debt.[46] This all hinges, however, on a shared conception of the moral propriety of repayment, engendered by the norm of reciprocity.

Still another way in which the general norm of reciprocity is implicated in the maintenance of social system stability is related to an important attribute of the norm, namely, its comparative indeterminancy. Unlike specific status duties and like other general norms, this norm does not require highly specific and uniform performances from people whose behaviour it regulates. For example, unlike the status duties of American wives, it does not call upon them to cook and to take care of the children. Instead, the concrete demands it makes change substantially from situation to situation and vary with the benefits which one party receives from another.

This indeterminancy enables the norm of reciprocity to perform some of its most important system-stabilizing functions. Being indeterminate, the norm can be applied to countless *ad hoc* transactions, thus providing a flexible moral sanction for transactions which might not otherwise be regulated by specific status obligations. The norm, in this respect, is a kind of plastic filler, capable of being poured into the shifting crevices of social structures, and serving as a kind of all-purpose moral cement.

Not only does the norm of reciprocity play a stabilizing role in human relations in the *absence* of a well-developed system of specific status duties, but it contributes to social stability even when these are *present* and well established. Status duties shape behaviour because the status occupant believes them binding in their own right; they possess a kind of *prima facie* legitimacy for properly socialized group members. The general norm of reciprocity, however, is a second-order defence of stability; it provides a further source of motivation and an additional moral sanction for conforming with specific status obligations. For example, the employer may pay his workers not merely because he has contracted to do so; he may also feel that the workman has earned his wages. The housewife may take pains with her husband's meals not merely because cooking may be incumbent on her as a wife; she may also have a particularly considerate husband. In each case, the specific status duties are complied with not only because they are inherent in the status and are believed to be right in themselves, but also because each is further defined as a *'repayment'*. In sum, the norm of reciprocity requires that if others have been fulfilling their status duties to you, you in turn have an additional or second-order obligation (repayment) to fulfil your status duties to them. In this manner, the sentiment of gratitude joins forces with the sentiment of rectitude and adds a safety-margin in the motivation to conformity.

The matter can be put differently from the standpoint of potential deviance or non-conformity. All status obligations are vulnerable to challenge and, at times, may have to be justified. If, for any reason, people refuse to do their duty, those demanding compliance may be required to justify their claims. Obviously, there are many standardized ways in which this might be done. Invoking the general norm of reciprocity is one way of justifying the more concrete demands of status obligations. Forced to the wall, the man demanding his 'rights' may say, in effect, 'Very well, if you won't do this simply because it is your duty, then remember all that I have done for you in the past and do it to repay your debt to me.' The norm of reciprocity thus provides a second-order defence of the stability of social systems in that it can be used to overcome incipient deviance and to mobilize auxiliary motivations for conformity with existent status demands.[47]

Starting Mechanisms

Two distinct points have been made about the social functions of the norm of reciprocity. One is that this norm serves a group *stabilizing* function and thus is quite familiar in functional theory. The second point, however, is the view that the norm is not only in some sense a defence or stabilizing mechanism but is also what may be called a 'starting mechanism'. That is, it helps to initiate social interaction and is functional in the early phases of certain groups before they have developed a differentiated and customary set of status duties.

In speaking of the norm of reciprocity as a 'starting mechanism', indeed in conceiving of starting mechanisms, we find ourselves outside the usual perspective of functional theory. Functional theory commonly focuses on already-established, ongoing systems, and on the mechanisms by means of which an established social system is enabled to maintain itself. Although functional theory is concerned with the problems of how individual actors are prepared by socialization to play a role in social systems, its general theoretical models rarely, if ever, include systematic treatment of the beginnings of a social system as such and, consequently, do not formally raise the question of the nature of the mechanisms needed to start such a system.[48]

Every social system of course has a history, which means that it has had its beginnings even if these are shrouded in antiquity. Granted that the question of origins can readily bog down in a metaphysical morass, the fact is that many concrete social systems do have determinate beginnings. Marriages are not made in heaven, and whether they end in divorce or continue in bliss, they have some identifiable origins. Similarly, corporations, political parties, and all manner of groups have their beginnings. (Recent studies of friendship and other interpersonal relations in housing projects have begun to explore this problem.)

People are continually brought together in new juxta-positions and combinations, bringing with them the possibilities of new social systems. How are these possibilities realized? Is such realization entirely a random matter? There are the kinds of questions that were familiar to the earlier students of 'collective behaviour', who, in focusing on crowds, riots, and rumours, were often primarily concerned with investigating the development of groups in *statu nascendi*.[49] Although this perspective may at first seem somewhat alien to the functionalist, once it is put to him, he may suspect that certain kinds of mechanisms, conducive to the crystallization of social systems out of ephemeral contacts, will in some measure be institutionalized or otherwise patterned in any society. At this point he would be considering 'starting mechanisms'. In this way, I suggest, the norm of reciprocity provides one among many starting mechanisms.

From the standpoint of a purely economic or utilitarian model,[50] there are certain difficulties in accounting for the manner in which social interaction begins. Let us suppose two people or groups, Ego and Alter, each possesses valuables sought by the other. Suppose further that each feels that the only motive the other has to conduct an exchange is the anticipated gratification it will bring. Each may then feel that it would be advantageous to lay hold of the other's valuables without relinquishing his own. Furthermore, suppose that each party suspects the other of precisely such an intention, perhaps because of the operation of projective or empathic mechanisms. At least since Hobbes, it has been recognized that under such circumstances, each is likely to regard the impending exchange as dangerous and to view the other with some suspicion.[51] Each may then hesitate to part with his valuables before the other has first turned his over. Like participants in a disarmament conference, each may say to other, 'You first!' Thus the exchange may be delayed or altogether flounder and the relationship may be prevented from developing.

The norm of reciprocity may serve as a starting mechanism in such circumstances by preventing or enabling the parties to break out of this impasse. When internalized in both parties, the norm *obliges* the one who has first received a benefit to repay it at some time; it thus provides some realistic grounds for confidence, in the one who first parts with his valuables, that he will be repaid. Consequently, there may be less hesitancy in being the first and a greater facility with which the exchange and the social relation can get underway.

Conclusion

I have limited this discussion of the norm of reciprocity to its functions and its contribution to the stability of social systems, omitting examination of its dysfunctions and of the manner in which it induces tensions and changes in social systems. That the norm commonly imposes obligations of reciprocity only 'when the individual is able' to reciprocate does not guarantee agreement concerning the individual's 'ability'. Furthermore there may be occasions when questions as to whether the individual's return is appropriate or sufficient (apart from whether it is equivalent) arise by virtue of the absence of common yardsticks in terms of which giving and returning may be compared. Moreover, the norm may lead individuals to establish relations only or primarily with those who can reciprocate, thus inducing neglect of the needs of those unable to do so. Clearly, the norm of reciprocity cannot apply with full force in relations with children, old people, or with those who are mentally or physically handicapped, and it is theoretically inferable that other, fundamentally different kinds of normative orientations will develop in moral codes. I hope to explore these and related problems in subsequent discussions.

NOTES

1. Sections of this paper were read at the annual meeting of the American Sociological Association, September 1959. The author is indebted to Robert K. Merton, Howard S. Becker, John W. Bennett, Louis Schneider, and Gregory Stone for reading an earlier draft but knows of no adequate 'reciprocity' for their many valuable suggestions.

2. Howard Becker, *Man in Reciprocity*, New York, Praeger, 1956, p. 1.

3. L. T. Hobhouse, *Morals in Evolution: A Study in Comparative Ethics*, Chapman & Hall, 1951 (first edition, 1906), p. 12.

4. Richard Thurnwald, *Economics in Primitive Communities*, Oxford University Press, 1932, p. 106.

5. ibid., p. 137. See also, Richard Thurnwald, 'Banaro Society: Social Organization and Kinship System of a Tribe in the Interior of New Guinea', *Memoirs of the American Anthropological Association*, 8, 1916; among other matters of relevance to the analysis of reciprocity, Thurnwald's discussion here (p. 275) opens the issue of the 'exchange of women', which Lévi-Strauss later developed.

6. Georg Simmel, *The Sociology of Georg Simmel*, translated and edited by Kurt H. Wolff, Glencoe, Ill., Free Press, 1950, p. 387.

7. See, respectively, George Homans, 'Social Behavior as Exchange', *American Journal of Sociology*, 63 (May, 1958), pp. 597–606; C. Lévi-Strauss, *Les Structures élémentaires de la parenté*, Paris, Presses Universitaires, 1949; and Raymond Firth, *Primitive Polynesian Economy*, New York, Humanities Press, 1950.

8. R. K. Merton, *Social Theory and Social Structure*, Glencoe, Ill., Free Press, 1957, pp. 46–7.

9. ibid., p. 33.

10. ibid., p. 34.

11. ibid.

12. ibid., p. 73. Among the functions of the political machine to which Merton refers are: the organization and centralization of power so that it can be mobilized to satisfy the needs of different groups, provision of personalized forms of assistance for lower-class groups, giving political privileges and aid to business groups, and granting protection for illicit rackets.

13. An initial statement of this point is to be found in Chapter 7 of the present volume, 'Reciprocity and Autonomy in Functional Theory'.

14. For fuller discussion of this concept, see Chapter 7.

15. Use of terms such as 'pattern' or 'unit' is intended to indicate that the present discussion deliberately collapses distinctions between institutional, interpersonal, group, or role reciprocities, treating them here under a single rubric for reasons of space.

16. Raymond Firth, ed., *Man and Culture: An Evaluation of the Work of Bronislaw Malinowski*, New York, The Humanities Press, 1957, p. 19.

17. The views of these and other analysts of exploitation are ably summarized in C. Gide and C. Rist, *A History of Economic Doctrines*, translated by R. Richards, Boston, Heath, revised edition, 1918.

18. See, e.g., E. A. Ross, *New-Age Sociology*, New York, Appleton-Century, 1940, esp. Chapter 9.

19. Note von Wiese and Becker's comment: 'The Marxians trace the social process of exploitation to the "capitalistic" economic order; their thesis is that capitalism creates exploitation. We, on the other hand, do not deny the existence of capitalistic exploitation, but it is for us only one of the forms which are found among the phenomena of exploitation. The destruction of capitalism will not signalize the end of exploitation, but will merely prevent the appearance of some of its forms and will open up new opportunities for others.' L. von Wiese and Howard Becker, *Systematic Sociology*, New York, Wiley, 1932, p. 700.

20. E. Kanin and D. H. Howard, 'Postmarital Consequences of Premarital Sex Adjustments', *American Sociological Review*, 23 (October, 1958), p. 558. (My italics.)

21. Kingsley Davis, *Human Society*, New York, Macmillan, 1949, p. 403.

22. ibid., p. 404.

23. Note Davis' tendency to assume that legitimate sexual relations entail an exchange of *equal* values even though his previous sentence indicates that there may be no more than 'a *certain amount* of reciprocity' involved. The latter is a way of talking about *un*equal exchanges and thus implies that these occur in institutionalized and not only in illicit relations. This is an important problem that cannot be developed here.

24. Willard Waller, *The Family: A Dynamic Interpretation*, revised by Reuben Hill, New York, Dryden, 1951, p. 163.

25. The point is not to stress, as Parsons does, the unique exploitability of the patient or the peculiar power of the physician, but to see this relationship as but one dramatic case of a larger class of phenomena of basic theoretic significance which should be explicitly dealt with in systematic theory rather than given only *ad hoc* treatment in specific empirical contexts. See Talcott Parsons, *The Social System*, Glencoe, Ill., Free Press, 1951, p. 445.

26. The thesis that this is more mythological than real is developed in my introduction to Émile Durkheim, *Socialism and Saint-Simon*, translated by C. Sattler and edited by A. W. Gouldner, Yellow Springs, Antioch Press, 1958, esp. p. ix.

27. Émile Durkheim, *Professional Ethics and Civic Morals*, translated by C. Brookfield, Glencoe, Ill., Free Press, 1958; see esp. pp. 209–14.

28. Parsons, op. cit., p. 21.

29. Talcott Parsons and Edward A. Shils, eds., *Toward a General Theory of Action*, Cambridge, Harvard University Press, 1951, p. 107.

30. Parsons' tendency to equate complementarity and reciprocity may be illustrated by his comment that 'Role expectations organize . . . the reciprocities, expectations, and responses to these expectations in the specific interaction systems of ego and one or more alters. This reciprocal aspect must be borne in mind since the expectations of an ego *always* imply the expectations of one or more alters. It is in this *reciprocity* or *complementarity* that sanctions enter. . . .' ibid., pp. 190–91 (my italics); see also p. 105. The burden of Parsons' analysis attends to the conditions and consequences of complementarity, by which he means that a role player requires of himself what his role partner requires of him. It is precisely for this reason that Parsons emphasizes that values must be held in common by the actors if their expectations are to be compatible. The equation of reciprocity with complementarity is not peculiar to Parsons. It is evident in the work of other sociologists who sometimes speak of the rights and obligations in a pair of roles as 'reciprocal' and other times as 'complementary'. And, like Parsons, others state that rights and duties, or role expectations, are always complementary.

31. The analysis here closely follows W. D. Ross, *The Right and the Good*, Oxford, Clarendon Press, 1950.

32. Alexander MacBeath, *Experiments in Living*, Macmillan, 1952; see esp. pp. 127 ff.

33. Bronislaw Malinowski, *Crime and Custom in Savage Society*, Paul, Trench, Trubner, 1932.

34. ibid., p. 55.

35. This, by the way, is why I cannot concur in Parsons' judgement that Malinowski never disentangled a social system level of analysis from an encyclopedic concept of culture. See Talcott Parsons, 'Malinowski and the Theory of Social Systems', in *Man and Culture . . .*, op. cit., pp. 53–70. Malinowski's *Crime and Custom* transcends a clinical case analysis of specific primitive societies and presents a generalized and basic contribution to the theory of social systems when it addresses itself to the problem of *reciprocity*. Parsons, however, does not mention the significance of reciprocity in Malinowski's work and is able to support his claim that it ignores social system analysis only by this noteworthy omission. Parsons' neglect of the principle of reciprocity in Malinowski's work, it would seem, is consistent with his own neglect of the distinction between reciprocity and complementarity.

36. Malinowski, op. cit., p. 39.

37. ibid., p. 55.

38. ibid., p. 39.

39. ibid., p. 22.

40. ibid., p. 40. This is not to say, however, that Malinowski regards reciprocity *qua* transaction as *always* intended by all the actors or as something of which they are always aware. In brief – and I agree – there are both latent and manifest reciprocities.

41. Edward Westermarck, *The Origin and Development of the Moral Ideas*, Macmillan, 1908, vol. 2, p. 154.

42. It is further indicative of our terminological difficulties in this area that this is often what Piaget spoke of as 'reciprocity'. For example, '. . . reciprocity stands so high in the eyes of the child that he will apply it even where to us it seems to border on crude vengeance.' J. Piaget, *The Moral Judgment of the Child*, New York, Harcourt, Brace, 1932, p. 216.

43. A further point that fuller discussion should develop concerns the terms 'roughly' equivalent. Use of the term 'roughly', in one part, indicates that a certain range of concrete behaviour will be viewed by the actors as compliance with this reciprocity norm and that more than one specific return will be acceptable and defined as equivalent. The norm of reciprocity *qua* equivalence is thus like most other norms which also tolerate a range of variability. The demand for *exact* equality would place an impossible burden even on actors highly motivated to comply with the reciprocity norm and would yield endemic tensions. Conversely, a notion of 'rough' equivalence held by the actors allows for easier compliance with the norm and can be regarded as one of the mechanisms sustaining it. Recognition that the requirement is for 'rough' equivalence, however, should not be allowed to obscure the fact that there may be a specific reciprocity norm which does in fact call for equivalence. This would be a distinguishing feature of the hypothesized norm and should no more be concealed by reference to a 'rough' equivalent than should the distinctive content of any other norm be obscured by the fact that a variable range of behaviours will be acceptable to those holding it.

44. I suppose that one can take two different attitudes toward this transmutation of the base metal of egoism. One can deplore the situation and say with Eliot:

> The last temptation is the greatest treason;
> To do the right thing for the wrong reason.

Or one can adopt the older and perhaps sociologically wiser view that here, once more, 'private vices make public benefits', and provide an indispensable basis for the *spontaneous self-regulation* of social systems.

45. This line of analysis is further strengthened if we consider the possibility that Ego's continued conformity with Alter's expectations may eventually lead Alter to take Ego's conformity for 'granted' and thus lead Alter to reciprocate less for later acts of conformity by Ego. In short, the value of Ego's conformity may undergo an inflationary spiral in which his later conforming action are worth less than earlier ones, in terms of the

reciprocities they yield. As reciprocities tend to decline, the social system may experience mounting strain, either collapsing in apathy or being disrupted by conflict. In this connection, the general norm of reciprocity may serve as a brake, slowing the rate at which reciprocities decline or preventing them from declining beyond a certain (unknown) level, and thus contributing to the stability of the system. This is more fully developed in A. W. Gouldner, 'Organizational Analysis', in R. K. Merton *et al.*, eds., *Sociology Today*, New York, Basic Books, 1959, esp. pp. 423 ff.

46. An interesting case of a mechanism serving to create and maintain outstanding obligations is part of the Vartan Bhanji, a form of ritual gift exchange in Pakistan and other parts of India. Eglar's study of this pattern makes it clear that a fundamental rule of Vartan Bhanji is reciprocity, that a gift should be returned for a gift, and a favour for a favour. It is also notable that the system painstakingly prevents the total elimination of outstanding obligations. Thus, on the occasion of a marriage, departing guests are given gifts of sweets. In weighing them out, the hostess may say, 'These five are yours', meaning 'these are a repayment for what you formerly gave me', and she then adds an extra measure, saying, 'These are mine.' On the next occasion, she will receive these back along with an additional measure which she later returns, and so on. See Z. E. Eglar, *Vartan Bhanji: Institutionalized Reciprocity in a Changing Punjab Village*, Ph.D. thesis, Columbia University, 1958.

Other mechanisms for maintaining outstanding obligations may be found in cultural prescriptions which require men not to be overly eager to repay their social obligations. It still seems to be understood that there is a certain impropriety in this, even if we do not go as far as Seneca in holding that 'a person who wants to repay a gift too quickly with a gift in return is an unwilling debtor and an ungrateful person'.

47. A cogent illustration of this is provided by William F. Whyte: 'When life in the group runs smoothly, the obligations binding members are not explicitly recognized. . . . It is only when the relationship breaks down that the underlying obligations are brought to light. While Alec and Frank were friends I never heard either one of them discuss the services he was performing for the other, but when they had a falling out . . . each man complained to Doc that the other was not acting as he should in view of the services which had been done for him.' *Street Corner Society*, Chicago: University of Chicago Press, 1945, p. 256.

48. Modern functionalism emerged in a world in which Newtonian mechanics was the overshadowing scientific achievement and a basic model for the development of social science. The Newtonian standpoint was not, of course, a cosmology concerned with the question of planetary origins but took the existent relations among planets as given. Today, however, two developments of global significance encourage and perhaps require a shift in social perspectives. In one, rocket engineering, the question is raised as to how new, man-made, planets may be 'shot' into stable

orbits. Secondly, international politics require us to help 'underdeveloped' countries to *begin* a beneficent cycle of capital accumulation which will be self-sustaining. In both instances, practical 'engineering' problems forcefully direct attention to the question of 'starting mechanisms' and would seem likely to heighten dissatisfaction with general sociological models that largely confine themselves to already established systems.

49. I am indebted to Howard S. Becker for this and many other insights into what seemed to be the guiding impulses of the 'Chicago School' of collective behaviour.

50. Some indications of the utilitarian approach to this problem may be derived from the stimulating paper by T. C. Schelling, 'An Essay on Bargaining', *American Economic Review*, 46 (June 1956), pp. 281–306.

51. cf. M. Deutsch, 'A Study of Conditions Affecting Cooperation', New York, Research Center for Human Relations, 1955, p. 25, dittoed.

9

The Importance of Something for Nothing

In the previous paper, I had proposed that *one* basic dimension of morality, cross-cutting all specific moral codes, was the norm of *reciprocity*. In its trans-cultural form (the previous paper indicated) this norm made two interrelated minimal demands: (1) people should help those who help them, and (2) people should not injure those who have helped them. It was also suggested that the norm of reciprocity was a no less universal and no less important element of culture than the incest taboo, although similarly, its concrete versions will vary with time and place.

The Weaknesses of Reciprocity

My paper on reciprocity ended by noting the functional *limitations* of the norm of reciprocity:

> Clearly, the norm . . . cannot apply with full force in relations with children, old people, or with those who are mentally or physically handicapped, and it is theoretically inferable that other, fundamentally different kinds of normative orientations will develop in moral codes.

I then concluded by promising to 'explore these and related problems in subsequent discussions'. What follows is an effort to keep this promise, at least in some part.

If men were guided solely by the norm of reciprocity many who needed help might never receive it and would be destroyed or deeply discontent. At any given time there are some persons who cannot reciprocate benefits they once received. Some, such as those stricken with serious illness, are manifestly unable to do so within any foreseeable future time. Some, such as children, are unable to do so within the time that the donor may have need of such reciprocation. And some, such as the mentally handicapped, are clearly unable to reciprocate at all and ever.

Moreover, to the extent that men can empathize with the weak and poor, or to the degree that they can imagine themselves as some day weak and in need of aid, their exclusive operation in terms of a norm of reciprocity may create a foreboding awareness of the precariousness of their own future position, however secure they may be at the moment. Men at all times and places have observed how others like themselves may come upon hard times, ill fortune, illness, ingratitude, and how all in time inevitably grow old, tired, infirm, unbeautiful, weaker – diminished in some way. In anticipating and in experiencing such circumstances men are reminded that there may come a time when they, too, need help from others which they will be unable to reciprocate. They may thus grow aware of the hazards of a singular reliance upon the norm of reciprocity.

There are still other difficulties in an exclusive reliance upon the norm of reciprocity. One of these stems from the uncertainty that often exists concerning the net balance of indebtedness that occurs in any longstanding relationship. After a while it may become difficult for the parties to determine who is in who's debt. This can have contradictory consequences. On the one hand, it makes it difficult for one of the parties easily to reject a claim made by the other and, to this extent, it stabilizes their relations. On the other hand, however, it also makes it difficult clearly to authenticate and justify a claim. As a result, there may always be a measure of uncertainty as to which claims are legitimate and should be satisfied, and which not.

Moreover, to the extent that past reciprocities have been 'heteromorphic', that is, have involved exchanges of different kinds of objects, the relationship may be strained when one party proffers or claims an object that the other may regard as unequal in value with what he has given or claimed. A wide latitude of permissible performances in conformity with the norm of reciprocity may, in some circumstances, facilitate mutual compliance and thus stabilize the relationship; in other circumstances, however, it may induce uncertainty as to what constitutes appropriate compliance: one party may be unsure about what to give, the other about what to accept.

Persons who have over time engaged in a series of transactions governed by the norm of reciprocity may also come to develop a personalized attachment to those who have aided them in the past. The norm of reciprocity is conducive to a concern with the past. Given an experience of compliance with the norm's requirements, persons develop *past*-oriented sentiments, such as loyalty and gratitude, to those who have kept the faith with them. Conversely, however, the norm of reciprocity also sensitizes the person to the *future*. It implies that those whom you have helped in the past have, in turn, an obligation to help you in the future. If the *past* orientations of the norm generate personalized and non-rational sentiments that foster a readiness to help others, the *future* orientations may generate an impersonal and rational calculus of the other's ability to repay.

When the net judgement is that the other can and will repay, an established relation continues without strain; but where one has doubts about the future willingness and ability to repay there may be a reluctance and refusal to help. Such reluctance is likely to be stronger to the extent that benefits received in the past come to be viewed as small and unreal, while the present costs or future dangers of repaying this aid loom large and tangible. In this circumstance, the person on whom a claim for repayment has been made may become ambivalent: he wishes to be thought neither an ingrate nor a fool. By itself, the norm of reciprocity often does not resolve these recurrent ambiguities and fails to provide clear-cut directives for action. For this and other reasons the norm of reciprocity, however necessary for the stability of social systems, does not produce moral requirements sufficient for that purpose.[1]

One conception of social system stability common to many sociologists assumes that a stable social system may be organized around a single principal component of moral codes, the norm of reciprocity, supplemented by the ambiguity-resolving specificities of concrete social statuses. It suggests that system stability depends upon the degree to which actors comply with the obligations of their own, and conform to the rights of others' culturally prescribed social statuses; that is, system stability is seen as a function of mutual compliance with one another's rights.

Beyond Justice and Reciprocity

Far from being the hard won prize of modern sociological analysis, this formula is of course nothing less than the most ancient wisdom. As Plato long since observed, the survival of the city requires that there be 'justice' and that justice exists when each man seeks no more than his due and when he is given what is due him. Many of the ancients substantially agreed: Aristotle, Cicero, as well as Ambrose and Augustine. Augustine, however, seems to have understood very well that it would not suffice for social system stability if men were concerned *solely* with complying with the rights of others and gave them *only* their due.

Which brings us to our central point: justice may be a *necessary* condition for social system stability but it is *not sufficient*. For even when a man is given what is deemed rightfully his he may still have woefully less than he either needs or wants. A man's rights, on the one side, and his needs or wants, on the other, will hardly ever be identical, unless we suppose all of the following: a perfect system of socialization in which men can be reared never to want more than is rightfully theirs; a perfect system of social statuses whose culturally prescribed rights will satisfy all men's needs; and a perfect system for allocating these statuses among men, so that the different needs and wants of different men will invariably coincide with the different rights and obligations of the statuses they come to occupy.

Unless we are willing to postulate such a utopia, we must suppose that in all social systems there is *some* disparity between the wants or needs of different persons and their culturally prescribed status rights. We must, in consequence, conclude that, by itself, conformity with the status rights of men cannot *suffice* to maintain the stability of social systems. If a system is to be stable (and there is no reason why it 'must'), it needs to be so arranged that rights and duties of interacting status incumbents are *not*, in many instances, complementary. It must be arranged so that men have some duties to others which are *not* the rights of these others, and that satisfaction of the needs and wants of others is *not* always contingent upon their ability to repay. Certain aspects of social relationships must be exempt from both the requirements of complementarity and from the norm of reciprocity.

It is perhaps not too much to say that there are few societies which have been more single-mindedly devoted than our own to the proposition that all a man is entitled to is his due. In one sense, the market is one of the most rational institutions historically developed for the arrangement of reciprocities, removing from individual hands the question of how much a man is entitled to for his contribution, and placing it under the control of an impersonal mechanism. That this has not sufficed to bring industrial peace is a matter of historical record, and, in part, testifies to the insufficiencies of the norm of reciprocity or of conformity to concrete status rights to maintain social system stability.

Not even the modern industrial system can be stable in the absence of traditional, non-contractually stipulated, patterns in which men are given *more than their rights*. Close inspection of the factory system provides a critical case in point. Factory studies usually reveal some pattern of allocating goods other than those stipulated either by the norm of reciprocity or by the concrete rights of factory statuses. During the course of my early factory studies, I had occasion to characterize this pattern as the 'indulgency pattern'.

I noticed that many of the workers in the plant being studied liked it and, in expressing this, approvingly called the plant and management 'lenient'. When broken down into its component elements, 'leniency' in this case constituted compliance with the following concrete expectations, widely shared by the plant's workers: (1) there should be no close supervision, no constant 'check-up' on the worker; (2) workers should be given a 'second chance', in the event that they make a mistake; (3) plant rules should be flexibly applied, so that, for example, if a worker's family responsibilities demanded, he could leave work earlier than usual; (4) workers should be allowed various forms of mobility, horizontal no less than vertical; (5) if a worker was injured on the job he should be permitted to take another and easier one in the plant until he recovered; (6) workers should have preferential access to the company's raw materials, tools, and finished products, so that they could use, borrow, or consume these for their own private purposes, at less than usual cost.

These various expectations, though concretely different, nonetheless have certain common underlying properties, and it is these that are most relevant. As I noted in my original study:

> . . . the expectations incorporated in the indulgency pattern differed from others held by workers. It may be observed that workers did not define management as 'lenient' when the latter gave 'tit for tat'. Specifically, workers did not tend to speak of 'leniency' when they were given something that they already felt to be rightfully theirs. Instead, this approving judgement was reserved for management behaviour which complied with expectations of tenuous legitimacy, and when management gave up something for which workers could make no compelling claim.
>
> For example, workers never commended management, or spoke of its 'leniency', when they were paid their proper wages; it is, in part, for this reason that wage satisfactions are not an element in the indulgency pattern. On the other hand, management would be within its *legal rights* if it kept workers busy for every minute of the time for which they were being paid. . . . It is clear, then, that workers did not define 'leniency' as a managerial *obligation*. Instead, 'leniency' seems to refer to managerial compliances with workers' role preferences, rather than role prescriptions. Furthermore, 'leniency' also involves managerial behaviour which is tempered by taking into account the worker's obligations in his other roles, for example, his obligations as a family member to maintain the family's income, to fix broken things around the house, to leave work early to 'take the wife' on a special outing. . . . These expectations, however, were of dubious validity in a business and industrial context, and it is in part for this reason that management's compliance with them was especially noted and commended. (*Wildcat Strike*: pp. 21–2.)

There seems little question but that what I had called the 'indulgency pattern' is *not* a form of *reciprocity* but, rather, is a contemporary expression of a different norm – a norm of *beneficence*. It contributes to the stability of factory social systems precisely insofar as it allows workers to receive *more* than they are legally owed under their union contract or is customarily due them in their worker-status: it is stabilizing precisely insofar as it goes beyond the norm of reciprocity and does not merely give 'tit for tat'.

That justice – in the sense of giving men their due – does not suffice for social system stability is a most unoriginal thought. Nonetheless, it is an idea whose full theoretical ramifications remain to be explored. For it insists that social system stability requires that people must sometimes be given *more* than they can clearly claim as legitimately theirs, and hence have no manifest 'right' to, and that others must give them this – if the system is to be stable – despite the fact that their claim cannot be legitimated either by their concrete social status or the norm of reciprocity.

The Norm of Beneficence

If this inference is correct it may be expected that the moral code of any relatively stable social system will contain a principal component that requires men to do more than conform with the norm of reciprocity and, also, to do more than is required of them by the specific obligations of their concrete social statuses. We propose to term this (hypothetically) universal component the norm of *beneficence* or 'goodness'.

This norm requires men to give others such help as they *need*. Rather than making help contingent upon past benefits received or future benefits expected, the norm of beneficence calls upon men to aid others without thought of what they have done or can do for them, and solely in terms of a need imputed to the potential recipient. As we view it here, the norm of beneficence is a diffuse one encompassing a number of somewhat more concrete normative orientations such as 'altruism', 'charity', or 'hospitality'. In short, the norm calls on men to give something for nothing. Such norms are apparently found in the most diverse of primitive or non-literate societies, no less than in 'Christian' cultures where we once heard of the duty of 'charity'.

In a society such as our own – with a market economy and a strongly utilitarian culture – those who want something for nothing are commonly viewed as flawed, distorted, or incomplete people. It is assumed that they are either avaricious or naïve. Thus there is sometimes a radical ambiguity in our perception of those who want something for nothing. They may be thought to be among the very good, perhaps even the saintly, as well as the very bad. Those who want something for nothing may, in other words, be seen as either the vicious, worldly exploiters, or the pure, unworldly idealists.

Part of the negative response to those who want something for nothing may stem from an accusing Puritan conscience that 'knows' that men must always pay for their pleasures or sins – if the two are not the same. But suspicion of the desire for something for nothing goes far deeper than either Protestant culture or commercialism. The ascetic streak in Western civilization is far older than Protestantism and even Christianity itself. The ancient Greek concept of retribution, for example, predicated the bleak belief that there was a cycle in the affairs of men, such that life exacts a price for the victories and joys that it allows. (So far as I am aware, however, there was and is no optimistic counter-concept which promises us victories to compensate for the catastrophes we have suffered. Retribution is a one-way street, promising only that every good has its cost, but not that every cost brings us a good.)

If the rejection of something for nothing is ancient, the hidden, and, sometimes, the not-so-hidden yearning for it, is equally old and profound. To want one's cake and to eat it too; to be forgiven our sins; to be given a 'second chance' when we have made a mistake – these and other hopes and fantasies give expression to a wish for something for nothing, a wish commonly repressed. Repressed, because it violates the usual law of the social world, the law of reciprocity. Repressed, because to want something for nothing is to expose oneself to criticism as being either naïve or vicious.

So something for nothing becomes the stuff of which dreams and fantasies are made. It is the fuel that is burned by Aladdin's Lamp; it is the unwritten Law of Utopias or of the lost gardens of Paradise. The wish for something for nothing is – and must be – as ancient and deep as its prohibition. In effect, and in one of its sides, the very law of reciprocity itself, the norm that insists that men *must* give something in return for what they have received, is in some part a criticism of, a reply to, and an effort to control men's readiness to seek and to take, something for nothing.

In its institutionalized forms, the wish for something for nothing is acknowledged only as an *obligation* to *give*, never as a *right* to *receive*. 'Charity' may be the obligation of the donor, but it is not the *right* of the recipient. An obligation must be institutionalized precisely because the impulse to *give* something for nothing is not as powerful as that to *receive* it and, moreover, it is at variance with the norm of reciprocity that only acknowledges men's right to receive something in return for what they have given. In short, the institutionalization of the obligation to give something for nothing premises that such donors are relatively few and unwilling; the corresponding *failure* to institutionalize an obligation to *accept* something for nothing premises that such recipients are relatively many and willing to do so. It premises that men are far more likely to want, and far less likely to give, something for nothing.

In some part because of this, it is indeed improbable that men will get something for nothing; therefore, those who seek it are truly 'unrealistic', while those who deny its possibility are, by a self-fulfilling prophecy, indeed 'realistic'. Reciprocity is the defensive and minimal demand of the world-chastened adult who can and is willing to give – or, at least, to *settle for* – 'something for *some*thing'. 'Something for nothing' is the yearning of the 'unrealistic' young – of the child and adolescent – who desire something better than the adult world has to offer and who, in any event, have little to give in return for what they want. It should be expected that the two orientations, then, are distributed differentially among people of different ages and generations.

Reciprocity is the norm of the 'realistic' world of work. Something for nothing is the ideal of the world beyond work, the world of fantasy and imagination. Something for nothing is the surrealism of the world of *art*. For aesthetic gratification keeps no books and does not measure out returns against investments. Aesthetic gratification is possible even without an investment of any effort, without work, or even without education; aesthetic gratification may come merely from seeing, hearing, or touching things we never made: from the sound of an ocean or the sight of a cloud.

Beneficence, Reciprocity and the Self

Why isn't reciprocity enough to maintain the social world? Why must there also be a norm of beneficence that provides for something for nothing? In some part the answer has to do with the nature of the self and, in some part, with the nature of social worlds. The self constituted out of conformity with the norm of reciprocity is a subjectively contingent self: its right to exist is dependent upon and must be continually renewed by its demonstrated utility. In short, the self that grows out of reciprocity depends for its existence upon being useful to someone else. Here it is not what the self *is*, but what the self *does*, its *function*, upon which the security and survival of the self is made to depend and which certifies its value. Here, then, the self lives for others; it is a 'mature' self having surrendered childish narcissism; it is the self seemingly required for the maintenance of social cooperation and the sustenance of social systems.

The appearance, then, is this: the self born of reciprocity is 'adult' not childish, social not egoistic. The self of reciprocity has, in short, made the appropriate sacrifices to be admitted to the world of adults. Yet the performances of such a self have an element of the precarious: for such a self has relinquished narcissism out of necessity; much of what it gives to and thinks of others grows out of necessity. To that extent the adultness and the social responsibility of such a self is precarious because its ultimate aim is to secure satisfaction of egoistic, individualistic needs. That we define and regard such a self as 'grown up' is due to assumptions – and social conventions about – the 'reality principle'. Only when a self has sacrificed its own impulses and compromised with 'reality' can we trust it and bequeath it the medal of 'maturity'. But although it has compromised with reality, its egoistic impulses have not been obliterated: part of it remains in love with itself and open to the demands of its own impelling needs.

The self that seeks something for nothing, however, does so, in some part, because it seeks a *non*-contingent existence, a *non*-dependent existence, an existence whose security, not resting on its usefulness to others, is presumably unconditional. Here, too, reality is at odds with appearances. For if the self rooted in reciprocity has a contingent existence, it is still able *by its own efforts* to affect the conditions and security of its existence by what it itself does for others. Its very dependence upon others is a condition for its own autonomy. Correspondingly, the self rooted in the quest for 'something for nothing' is no less dependent upon the reaction of others, but here, in this case, the donor's reactions cannot be influenced by the *behaviour* of the potential recipient but only by his *'condition'*. The donor gives because of what the recipient *is*, not because of what he *does*. *The recipient self that seeks something for nothing is therefore powerless to modify the conditions of his existence.* Indeed, he often advocates and seeks something for nothing *because* he has nothing to give for what he wants. If he is to get something it is often only on the principle: something for nothing. The absolute non-contingency of this self, then, premises its powerlessness; it is a self that cannot influence its own environment and hence its own destiny. It must perforce throw itself on the mercy of others and it must not have the *pride* of an adult in its own autonomy.

The functional self rooted in reciprocity achieves its maturity and influences its own destiny on the condition that it performs and produces for others – on the condition that it does *not* live for, and is not for, itself alone. 'Maturity' as we know it thus means transforming the self into a usable thing – into objects or performances useful to others. In our culture, maturity is the *willing* thingafication of the self; maturity is the recognition of the necessity of the thingafication of the self.

The self centred on reciprocity attains maturity only by *not* doing what *it* wants, but what *others* want. This self becomes mature by denying itself; by producing things that it may *not* want or value in order that it may get, from others, things that it *does*. It thus protects itself by doing things alien to itself.

'Maturity' thus premises (in Hegel's sense) a divided, 'unhappy consciousness', in which alienation seems to be the price of growing up.

The self that wants something for *nothing*, however, seeks an existence without such alienation. It seeks an uncompromised and undivided existence; it would do only what it *wants* to do. It does not want to be loved or accepted because it is useful; it wants to be loved 'for itself'. But in the nature of the case it is powerless to bring this about – except when, seeking to appear good or desirable, it accentuates its desirability, conceals its undesirability, and thus must be something that it is not.

Refusing to compromise with the world, this self is unable to affect the response the world makes to it and such acceptance as it wins is given only when and how the world wishes. The price for such acceptance is precisely the lack of autonomy. For unconditional love is bought only at the cost of a basic dependence upon another. In other words, the price of unconditional help is the helplessness and unconditional dependence of the recipient on the donor, the paradigm of which is the parent–child relation.

Beneficence and Everyday Life in Society

In Christian Europe, the relation between reciprocity and beneficence has been the contradictory relation between reality and appearance, between operative everyday morality and the ethical ideal, between practice and preachment. In short, while Christian Europe preached beneficence, it institutionalized this only in a limited social sector as 'charity', but the everyday life of its class societies was dominated by reciprocity. In some part, the tension between these two moralities was controlled by institutionalizing distinctions between an everyday morality suitable for ordinary men and a high morality appropriate to those with a religious calling, and by exempting the high morality from application in everyday life. The Church made its peace with the world – it 'gave unto Caesar' – by allowing the laity to forgo the Golden Rule of beneficence and to live by the lesser morality of reciprocity.

This distinction between the higher morality of beneficence

and the lesser morality of reciprocity was based on certain pervasive conditions embedded in and tacitly assumed by everyday life, that is, the condition of relative scarcity, of life lived under a zero-sum game, where people are frequently tempted to extort something from one another. The experience of everyday life was the experience of the *rarity* of people voluntarily *giving* something for nothing in a situation where a zero-sum game prevailed. Under these conditions of scarcity, the possibilities of actually receiving something for nothing are indeed remote and unrealistic and must be exiled to a special extra-mundane, higher sphere.

Élites often give something for nothing and, in a way, élites are defined – or define themselves – by reason of their giving something for nothing. Charity and *noblesse oblige*, forms of something for nothing, are only given to those who are 'lesser beings'. The paradox of élites is this: like all dominating social strata, they exploit and take something for nothing. But what transforms them from merely powerful strata into a legitimate élite, in short, what transforms their domination into hegemony, is that they can and sometimes do give something for nothing. Indeed, insofar as they give something for nothing, then they may be seen as remarkable, higher, extra-mundane – as beyond the ordinary run of mankind.

But there is an ultimate selfishness in their selflessness: a reciprocity lurks in their beneficence. For no upper class is ever secure unless it is an *élite* whose dominance is a hegemony, whose power is an authority willingly accepted. The merely dominant seek to transform themselves by giving something for nothing. The security of an upper class, then, is fortified when it repays the exploitation it practises, the taking of something for nothing, by the giving of something for nothing. The contradictions between mundane reciprocity and extra-mundane beneficence serve, then, to enhance the *mystique* of élites. It is precisely because beneficence is precarious and rare in everyday life that those who practise it may receive a high price in return for their beneficence.

What happens, however, when technology develops productivity and when scarcity is alleviated drastically and may, for some, even be replaced by abundance? For one thing, many people then come by their gratifications a good deal earlier or sooner, and a good deal easier and more readily, and often *without having to give something in return*. Most specifically, as children they receive and enjoy the now larger gifts of their parents through a now longer period of time – through college and through marriage – than has ever been known to middle-class families before.

Affluence and the Decline of Reciprocity

Put otherwise, generous parental support and provision in the child-rearing situation in an industrial society that ideologically approves of 'permissiveness' toward children means that there is great latitude and diversity in what will be expected from children. As a result, the connection between what middle-class children are given, and what they are expected to do becomes so attenuated that this 'return' loses its salience and clarity; *it almost seems as if nothing were given or expected in return*. Such reciprocities as undoubtedly remain have become harder to see, so that on the one hand a norm of reciprocity comes to be seen as 'harsh' and a norm of beneficence is easier to demand and defend.

It is in this context of the aggressive de-institutionalization of reciprocity that one may understand the practice of begging or 'panhandling' that prevailed for a while in some hippie communities. For panhandling was a public ritual having the rhetoric appeal of an exemplary act that was subversive of the norm of reciprocity. Substantial numbers of the middle class, then, have learned out of their own experience, and are aggressively attempting to teach others, that beneficence – giving and receiving something for nothing – *is* possible and *does* happen. For they know it is truly possible and not 'unrealistic' because it has happened to them. A world of increasing plenitude and radically reduced scarcity undermines the norm of reciprocity and strengthens the norm of beneficence.

Beneficence thus comes slowly to change its historical character. From a spiritual compensation for the experience of material scarcity, it becomes an endorsement of material abundance for all. Parental beneficence toward children becomes the tacit, unlabelled paradigm for proper human relationships in general.

The sociological or 'worldly' significance of norms of beneficence can, in part, be interpreted from the standpoint of the norm of reciprocity. As suggested in my previous paper, social systems are in part held together not merely by the *fulfilment* of obligations, but by the existence of certain 'outstanding obligations', by social debts yet to be discharged. Although compliance with the norm of reciprocity may foster complex, long-linked social interactions over time, each act inducing another and each return requiring a new return, it is nonetheless sometimes possible for people in a relationship governed solely by the norm of reciprocity to be 'even' with one another at some point – or, at least, to view their relationship in this way – and to call it 'quits'. This is a dangerous moment in the life of social systems. Indeed, when we hear men talk about 'balancing' or 'squaring' accounts with one another we commonly suspect an aggressive intent, and rightly expect that there is trouble ahead.

Social systems may thus develop mechanisms that foster the continued existence of undischarged, outstanding obligations. One way this can be done is to develop and internalize norms of beneficence in group members which sanction the giving of aid even to those who cannot reciprocate it. By requiring men to aid others, regardless of what they have already received from them or expect to receive in the future, norms of beneficence serve as 'credit' mechanisms which enlarge the store of outstanding obligations in a social system, and generate assistance even for those seen as unable to reciprocate.

In exploring the system-maintaining function of the norms of beneficence, one other function of this norm deserves special mention; it serves as a mechanism for *stopping vicious cycles* of social interaction. It is characteristic of social systems, when they operate under the norm of reciprocity, that a failure to give aid in return for aid given is resented and, indeed, is commonly taken as a hostile act. It often induces the disappointed party to retaliate, and this, in turn, induces the other to behave in a hostile manner, and so on until their interaction is caught up in an unmanageable web of conflict, mutual antagonism, and progressive mutual alienation. It is extremely difficult to stop such a vicious cycle or to extricate oneself from it. Of the few things that may be done to stop it, among the most necessary is that one of the parties must manifest *forbearance*: he must 'turn the other cheek', 'go the second mile'. It is precisely such forbearance that the norm of beneficence encourages; for, to the extent that it exists as an explicit and recognized norm in which he believes, a person may then forbear without defining himself as fearful or weak; he may, indeed, view and present himself as in some way superior and (at least morally) stronger.

What then appears to be the 'creative' act of forbearance, which presumably derives from the idiosyncratic motives of an individual, is thus grounded in a cultural norm. When a man is seen as able to tear himself out of the field of tightly con-straining social forces comprised by a developing vicious cycle, when he restrains himself from returning hurt for hurt, insult for insult, he is often, and in a way rightly, viewed as possessing certain special individual qualities of almost heroic cast – he appears as a Hero of Social Interaction. Without in the least intending to deprecate the *individual* significance and value of such an act – for not all individuals will utilize the same opportunity with the same readiness and courage – the fact still remains that the moral code with its principal component of beneficence does provide an individual, who is otherwise prepared to use it, with leverage to wrest himself free of an entangling vicious cycle of social interaction.

Norms of beneficence also serve as a 'starting mechanism' helping to initiate social interaction. In my previous article, I had suggested that the norm of reciprocity itself can serve as a 'starting mechanism', for it can reduce an actor's hesitancy to be the first to part with his valuables and thus enable exchange to get under way. In a similar and indeed more powerful manner, norms of beneficence also serve as system-starting mechanisms, since they call upon the individual to give without making his aid contingent upon a reciprocal gratification. To use a crude analogy: the norm of beneficence is an ignition key that activates the starting engine (the norm of reciprocity) which, in turn, gets the motor – the ongoing cycle of mutual exchanges – to turn over. The analogy, however, is a crude one because there is continuing interaction between the norms of beneficence and reciprocity.

Interaction of Beneficence and Reciprocity

Indeed, it is precisely because of the various ways that the norm of beneficence is interwoven with the norm of reciprocity that it can serve as an effective starting mechanism. To begin, we must note that while a specific action may be *motivated* by the norm of beneficence, the *consequences* of this benign action ramify far beyond its link to the starting norm. Even if a *donor* defines his act solely in terms of the norm of beneficence, and entirely without reference to past aid received or future aid expected, this does not mean that an action is interpreted by the *recipient* as the donor conceives it. The recipient may well interpret a beneficently motivated action in terms of the norm of reciprocity and he may feel himself obliged to repay. The same action can, in short, be posted to different accounts in the ledgers kept by different people; the donor can place it in his beneficence account, the recipient in his reciprocity account.

Even if a beneficently motivated donor does not feel that the recipient is *obliged* to make a return he will, nonetheless, *appreciate* such a return and may reward an actor for making it. Both donor and recipient may also feel that some expression of gratitude is due the donor and that, at the very least, the recipient has an obligation of forbearance. That is, even if a recipient is not viewed as obliged to return the benefits given him, he may be viewed as obliged to forgo injuring those who have aided him. As the 'cliché' puts it: 'You should not bite the hand that feeds you.' The duty of beneficence may, therefore, entail reciprocal rights of forbearance and gratitude and here, again, there is a reciprocity even in charity.

There is still another way in which norms of beneficence and reciprocity are conjoined: at any one moment in time, and *time* is the crucial consideration here, Ego's aid to Alter may in truth be motivated primarily by a norm of beneficence; no return may be expected because, at the *time*, it may be plain that Ego cannot provide one. Yet, at a *later* time, Alter may be in a position to reciprocate and Ego may then need this help and may, indeed, demand it. The same action, then, may be referred to and interpreted by the donor in terms of the norm of beneficence at *one* time and the norm of reciprocity at a *later* time. An investment that was originally placed in account marked 'gifts', and was written off as a loss, may with the changed fortunes of each party, be reactivated and transferred to the 'accounts payable' ledger. In these ways, then, through its interconnections with the norm of reciprocity, the norm of beneficence may serve as a starting mechanism and launch a new and ongoing series of reciprocal exchanges. As Marcel Mauss noted, the beginnings of new social systems are often attended by the giving of gifts.

To note that an exchange of reciprocities may be the *consequence* of a given action is, of course, no basis for interpreting that act as having been *motivated* by the norm of reciprocity. The 'earthy' consequences of mutual exchange may be activated by the 'heavenly' motive of an altruistic beneficence.[2]

Perhaps we can conclude this section with a positive statement concerning beneficence. It is this: there is no surer way to stop a vicious cycle of social interaction than for one party to give the other something for nothing. There is no gift more certain to command attention than the gift that need not have been given because of our past indebtedness, our future ambitions, or our present sense of obligation. The paradox is this: there is no gift that brings a higher return than the free gift, the gift given with no strings attached. For that which is truly given freely moves men deeply and makes them most indebted to their benefactors. In the end, if it is reciprocity that holds the mundane world together, it is beneficence that transcends this world and can make men weep the tears of reconciliation. If such prodigies of social interaction are rare, it is not for want of knowing how to produce them.

The Beneficence of Élites

There are two empirical patterns with which norms of beneficence and reciprocity are commonly associated. An examination of these may enable us better to understand differences in the functioning of these norms, and the different conditions under which each develops. The first empirical pattern is that duties of beneficence (charity, indulgence, or hospitality) are not applied with equal force to *all* members of a social system. In the most widely differing cultures, *obligations* of beneficence are commonly held to apply with special force to those in the *higher* reaches of the system of stratification, *to the more wealthy and more powerful*. The Roman notion of clemency and the feudal norm of *noblesse oblige* are cases in point.

Why should the duty of beneficence be held to be particularly incumbent on the high and mighty? For one thing, it is obvious to other members of their group that they have more to give, and that giving without a required return entails less personal sacrifice and, generally, less cost to them. This aspect of the situation, however, often cuts in two opposing directions. For while those who have more can more readily give to others without a return, at less cost to themselves, yet, at the same time, and precisely in so far as their gift is seen as costing them little, it may win little in return, even in the way of symbolic rewards in the form of gratitude. But another and opposing consideration here, however, is that while such *giving* may win them little gratitude, the *failure* to give – niggardliness – may well evoke considerable censure, or may leave them vulnerable to the envy that commonly focuses on the rich and powerful.

There are still other functions that conformity with norms of beneficence perform for the rich and powerful. As implied earlier, the 'charity' of those in the upper reaches of a system of stratification is a symbolic token of their *responsibility* and, hence, of their basic credentials for power and leadership in the group. The universal and basic legitimation for leadership in all collectivities, regardless of the historically specific and varying standards in terms of which group leadership is legitimated in different times and cultures, is that the leadership must always be *defined* as acting in conformity with the needs or interests of the group as a *whole*, rather than on behalf of the *special* interests of some segment of the group or on behalf of *the leader's own partisan* interests alone. Conversely, the attack on a group leadership that most effectively subverts its legitimacy is (successfully) to impute partisan or selfish motives to them.

Conformity with norms of beneficence by the rich and

powerful dramatizes that they are *not* operating in terms of the norm of reciprocity, that they give with no thought of the common return. It thus symbolizes that their high position is not being used for selfish gratification alone but, rather, be tokens a kind of 'altruistic' concern with and even empathy for those beneath them. Charity is, at once, a token of the collective *responsibility* and of the individual *superiority* (or success) of those who give it. Conformity with norms of beneficence projects an image of the rich and powerful as an *élite* who do not play the political game by vulgar tradesmen's rules. If charity expresses the rich and powerful's benign interest in and concern for the common mass, it thus, also, raises them *above* the mass and contributes to the *mystique* of power.

Even charity, then, has its earthly rewards: for charity legitimates the leadership positions of those who give and, by creating an 'outstanding obligation' of the lowly toward the high, it fortifies the position of those who are dominant. By enhancing the prestige of the advantaged, and by fostering the respect, gratitude and deference – in short, a readiness to obey – that the lowly feel toward them, it endows the advantaged with legitimacy.

In addition to deference or gratitude of the *lowly*, the charitable also receive – depending on the measure of their charity – respect from their *peers* and fellow donors. Charity, in short, often becomes an instrument by means of which members of an élite jockey with one another for social position and prestige. Such competitive inducements toward charity may serve in effect to protect advantaged groups from themselves. For the rich and powerful can easily spoil the game – either of beneficence or of reciprocity. It is they who, if they wish, can *take* without giving or without giving back in proper measure; it is they who can refuse to give without receiving repayment.

Their very wealth and power means that they are not constrained to give in order to receive, or to give in return for what they are given. Should they succumb to the temptations of their own power, they can impair the stability of the entire system and, with this, their own advantaged position in it. In this sense, then, the various norms of beneficence, and the competitive inducements among the élite for conformity to them, serve not only to aid the disadvantaged but, also, to protect the *advantaged* from their own special temptations by counterposing against their special opportunities certain special *duties* of beneficence. When given compliance, these duties serve to reduce the danger that the advantaged will come to be defined as 'exploiters', i.e., as those lacking in legitimate authority because they violate the norm of reciprocity.

If this analysis is correct, then norms of beneficence should not only be imposed especially *upon* the rich and powerful, but should, also, require that the latter *give to* certain categories of people, to the less powerful or the particularly vulnerable: to children, to the mentally and physically handicapped, to the poor, to the infirm aged. And if norms of beneficence are especially incumbent on the high, in their relations with the lowly, the above analysis correspondingly implies that they are *less* incumbent on the high in their relations with *one another*. It would appear, then, that *peer* relationships are less likely to be governed by norms of beneficence and more likely to be governed by reciprocity. This hypothesized tendency for peer relations to be governed by the norm of reciprocity is reinforced by the fact that peers cannot, by reason of their equality, *constrain* one another to give without a return and that each is, therefore, more dependent upon the willing compliance of the other to get what he wants.

A second empirical pattern with which the norm of beneficence is commonly and cross-culturally associated and which is *not* associated with the norm of reciprocity, is one of *supernatural* sanctioning. In contrast to the norm of reciprocity, the duty of beneficence is far more often viewed as sanctioned by *supernatural* forces. Why should this be so?

This difference seems to be related to the fact that the norm of reciprocity has its own *built-in* inducements to conformity. That is, under its provisions we are obliged to give benefits to those from whom we receive or expect them, or we forfeit our rights to assistance from them. The association of norms of beneficence with supernatural sanctions, however, serves in effect as a functional substitute for such earthy reciprocities and, conversely, the threat of supernaturally induced punishment (for failure to comply with duties of beneficence) serves as a constraint which is a functional equivalent for the actual with-holding of earthy aid.

In short, conformity to the norm of reciprocity is reinforced by the very exchange of gratifications it fosters, and which the conforming person might not otherwise receive from his equals. Conformity with the norms of beneficence, however, commonly requires the provision of gratification by a superior to a subordinate, and there is little (or less) a subordinate can do to reinforce a superior's conformity to the norm.

The Supernatural Sanctioning of Beneficence

It is for this reason that conformity with beneficence is not left entirely in the laps of the gods, and that a supernatural sanction is often 'delegated' to subordinates. What we frequently find is that the disadvantaged, who cannot give 'tit for tat' in the usual mundane coin of the realm, are often culturally endowed with a special instrument of requital: i.e., they may be culturally defined as possessing divinely endowed powers of 'blessing' and 'cursing'. This capacity to bless or curse is not randomly distributed in a population but – in addition to being invested in specialized priesthoods or groups of magicians whose business this is – it is especially the poor and handicapped who are often culturally defined as repositories of the charismatic power to bless and to curse. Indeed, such charismatic powers are frequently viewed as correlated with the degree of disability suffered by the person – the more fearsome or exceptional his handicap, the greater the imputed charismatic power. The poor, the weak, the wretched are thus provided special instruments of requital with which they may now, therefore, reward or constrain conformity with the duties of beneficence.

At this point, however, it may well be asked in what way does the resultant social interaction differ from that governed by the norm of reciprocity? Isn't the imputed supernatural power to bless or curse one way in which a culture, in effect, stakes the disadvantaged player, providing him with something to give or withhold from those who can aid him, so that he can participate in the game of reciprocity? Hasn't a pattern of beneficence been thus transformed into a pattern of reciprocity?

Doesn't a belief that conformity with (or deviance from) a norm of beneficence will result in supernaturally originated gains or losses mean that the donor will expect some return or seek to avoid some loss by aiding another, and does this not contradict our conception that a norm of beneficence requires one to give without expectation of a return?

This anomalous situation does not so much contradict our conception of the norm of beneficence as it requires and enables us further to clarify its character. In particular, it directs attention to and requires us to examine the agency *to* and *from* whom a return is expected under the norms discussed, and whether these differ in the case of reciprocity and beneficence. Provisionally, we may suggest – and this is no more than a development of the implications of the above analysis – that the norm of reciprocity institutes obligations to and from *individuals* (or groups) – the donors and recipients of help. In contrast, under the norms of beneficence a donor's *obligation* is not primarily to the potential *recipient* of his beneficence, nor is the recipient indebted primarily to the *donor*. Where there is a supernatural sanction for the norm of beneficence, both parties are obligated to some imputed supernatural power or diety; they are obligated to something other than one another, to some kind of entity conceived as superorganic. At any rate, the norm of beneficence is not given compliance merely because the 'needy' expect or have a 'right' to it – and certainly not because of what they have done or might do in return. It is a 'duty', either deemed right in and of itself or as something that supernatural powers expect, and it is to *them* that conformity with the norm of beneficence is an obligation.

When a culture endows the poor or handicapped with the power to bless or curse it is, tacitly, using this as a compensation for the deprivations he has been made to suffer: 'God' has taken something from the person, and God has given something in return. In aiding the poor and needy, the charitable are in this view fulfilling an obligation that God has imposed upon them toward one another; in giving aid to the needy, one gives *conformity* to a divine mandate. In return, God *may elect* to reward men for the beneficence they manifest toward one another; God *may* reciprocate, but not for the beneficence shown to *him* but for the *obedience* shown his commandments.

Not only is there a complex and ongoing interconnection between the norms of beneficence and reciprocity here but there is also some suggestion that the norm of beneficence crystallizes and develops historically in polemical reaction against the norm of reciprocity. The vestigial gills of reciprocity can be detected in the birth of beneficence, and there may be a sense in which the norm of reciprocity is more sociologically 'primitive' than the norm of beneficence. Something of this dialectical evolution may be noted in the development of Confucian ethics. When Confucius was asked, 'Is there any single word that can serve as a principle of conduct for life', he replied 'Perhaps the word "reciprocity" (*shu*) will do. Do not do unto others what you would not want them to do to you.' To this stipulation of the virtue of reciprocity, Lao-Tze countered, 'To those who are good to me, I am good; and to those who are not good to me, I am also good; and thus all get to be good . . . Recompense injury with kindness.' Here there is not only an indication of the ongoing tensions between the norms of reciprocity and beneficence but some direct indication of the *historical* polemic between them.

In a similar manner, the Platonic dialogues also bear the trace marks of a polemic between the norms of reciprocity and beneficence, and suggest that Socrates formulated his affirmation and quest for the good in the course of his opposition to those who thought of justice as a form of reciprocity or retaliation. The Christian 'Golden Rule' – 'Do unto others as you would have them do unto you' – is also interesting here because it seems to have taken the rule of reciprocity as a linguistic paradigm, while at the same time being formulated in polemical opposition to it. The rule of reciprocity is not, however, expelled from Christian ethics, for 'Whatsoever a man soweth, that shall he also reap'. And again in the Gospel of Luke, it is said,

And judge not and ye shall not be judged; and condemn not, and ye shall not be condemned; release and ye shall be released; give, and it shall be given unto you: good measure, pressed down, shaken together, running over, they shall give into your bosom. For what measure ye mete, it shall be measured to you again. (Luke 6:37–8.)

It is evident to a person that his relation to a supernatural power is an hierarchical one; it is not a relation between peers but between those whose powers are imputed to be vastly unequal. Thus, in terms of our previous assumptions about the differing nature of the hierarchical relations within which each of the different norms is more likely to operate, we cannot expect that the norm of reciprocity will be defined as properly governing a relation with the supernatural. However much men may *hope* that the gods will favour them for worshipping them properly – whatever that entails in different cultures – they will not expect that the gods have an *obligation* to reciprocate. The aid that the gods give men must be seen either as their free gift, as an act of friendly caprice, or as an act of love or mercy – in short, as some form of divine *beneficence*. A stress upon the proper performance of ritual is not so much viewed as a way of imposing an obligation upon the gods for reciprocal aid as it is an effort to avoid a ritual laxity which could bring divine punishment and retaliation. Thus in some societies, such as classical Greece, ritual respect is not viewed as obliging the gods to aid men; it shows men to be worthy of aid should the gods *wish* to do so, and it minimizes the dangers of godly displeasure.

It is, of course, precisely because the gods are imputed to have *power* over men that a supernatural sanctioning of the norm of beneficence generates motives for conforming with it, and this, in turn, facilitates the system-stabilizing consequences attributed to it above. This chain of consequences, however, depends upon the existence of certain religious beliefs and convictions – upon a genuine belief in gods, in their powers, and in curses and blessings. It entails a belief that a man may incur supernaturally imposed consequences. It implies that the gods are seen as judging men, that a man may be acceptable or unacceptable to his gods, and that this depends upon his *actions*.

What happens to these mechanisms, however, and how are the defects of operating under the norm of reciprocity dealt with, when men believe in a Protestant God of Predestination who has decided men's fates before their birth, and who will not be moved to mercy by charitable or 'good works'? Again, and in a similar vein, what happens when men come to demand their rewards here on earth, when they lose belief in an after-world with its terrors or rewards, and when proletarian poets compose ironical rhymes about workers getting their 'pie in the sky, by and by'?

This problem was clearly perceived by the eighteenth-century *philosophes*, and discussion raged among them as to whether men would do their duty without a belief in the gods and in the punishments or rewards of an afterlife. Perhaps, some thought, it would be desirable to at least keep a god for the uncouth 'footmen' of the world. When men become sceptical, agnostic, or atheistic, the bases for the supernatural sanctioning of the norms of beneficence have been undermined. Conformity with this norm may be impaired, then, unless other, functionally equivalent supports for the norm exist or are developed. If, as the norm of beneficence prescribes, one must aid the needy without expectation of reciprocal aid, and if men also relinquish belief in the supernatural sanctioning of the norm, what reasons can men give themselves for conforming to its dictates? This suggests that our analysis of the principal components of moral codes thus far is insufficient, and that these must involve something more than either beneficence or reciprocity. Without such other, functionally equivalent supports we must expect that: men are less likely to believe in or conform with norms of beneficence the less religious they are, and the less they believe that the norm of beneficence is supernaturally sanctioned.

Moral Absolutism – Beyond Beneficence

Each of the two principal components discussed so far – reciprocity and beneficence – can be seen as fostering the provision of gratifications to others, and each contains an (at least) implicit justification for the provision of such gratifications. The norm of reciprocity *justifies* an obligation to help another on the grounds that he has or will help you; the norm of bene-ficence justifies the obligation to help on the grounds of the other's *need*. Under these norms it is right to help others either because they have helped you, or may do so in the future, and because they are needy.

Yet each of these justifications is, in itself, open to challenge even when the condition required is present. That is, it may be asked: *why* should I help people who have helped me, and *why* should I help the needy? From this perspective, also, there is a further indication that still another principal component of moral codes must be postulated. There has to be some basis in terms of which the norms of beneficence and reciprocity are *themselves* justified. In particular, there must be a moral component which removes the need of still further justification and which short-circuits the danger of an infinite regress of justifications. There must, in short, be a principal component of moral codes in which the performance of certain services and actions for others is not defined as depending on what they have done or will do for you, or upon their need. Such a principal component we will call 'moral absolutism'.

Moral absolutism as a principal component of moral codes does not embody specific status obligations – such as parental duties to support a family or to nurture children – but, rather, refers to the way in which such concrete status duties or other general norms are viewed and defined. Moral absolutism is, in short, a basic dimension of morality that concerns the ways in which specific status duties and the other principal components are to be regarded.

Moral absolutism is the 'prime injunction' of every moral code, stipulating a general rule that regulates the manner in which other moral rules are to be applied. As a general rule, it states in effect only that: 'The code must be obeyed.' In so far as every moral code consists of a set of prescriptions for action, it would seem that there must also be a higher-order, more general normative orientation – a prescription of 'moral absolutism' – which states that these prescriptions or rules must be obeyed.

Moral absolutism is a *dimension* of moral codes in the sense that (1) it is a continuum which varies in degree and (2) it is distinctive and independent of the other principal components of moral codes. It is 'independent' of the other principal components not in the sense that it is *un*correlated with them, but that the correlation which it has with them should be less than 'one'. Indeed, in the light of the above discussion of the other basic norms and, especially, of the built-in reinforcements for conformity with the norm of reciprocity as distinguished from the vulnerability of the norm of beneficence, it would seem that *beneficence should be positively correlated with the norm of moral absolutism* and, further, that these should be *more highly* correlated than should reciprocity and moral absolutism. In effect, *a generalized moral absolutism is a substitute for* (if not a sublimation of) *a supernatural sanctioning*.

As a *dimension*, the norm of moral absolutism varies in the conditionality of the obedience felt to be due the other norms. At one polar extreme, which is of special interest here, is that zone in the dimension of moral absolutism which requires complete and unconditional obedience to specific status duties and to other moral norms. This is the zone of moral absolutism *per se*. At the opposite pole of the dimension would be a zone of moral *relativism*, where the demand for compliance with moral prescriptions is regarded as completely contingent upon the concrete times, places, people involved, and their unique and changing circumstances. This implies, then, that every moral code requires some measure of moral absolutism, although the degree required may differ from culture to culture, and that there are always some – even if only a few – concrete expectations and general rules to which such an *unconditional* compliance is demanded.

By reason of the norm of moral absolutism there are always some demands which can be legitimately placed on persons simply by virtue of the fact that they are members of the same group, or by virtue of the social positions which they occupy in the group. Moral absolutism requires that one do his 'duty', *even if others do not do theirs and even if they have not helped or are not needy*: it therefore unavoidably generates certain 'outstanding obligations', and it thus contributes to social system maintenance in the various ways performed by such outstanding obligations.[3]

So far we have focused on the *functions* of moral absolutism and we are now in imminent danger of neglecting its *dys*functions, which are of vital importance, both theoretically and practically. We have a long-standing and theoretically dubious tradition in sociology, perhaps stemming largely from that aberrant disciple of Saint-Simon, namely, Auguste Comte, which tends to over-state the functional contributions which shared systems of morality make to the cohesion and stability of social systems. This tradition reached a culmination in Émile Durkheim's concept of *anomie*, which stresses that social disorganization follows upon *normlessness*. Here it is the absence of moral norms that is seen as a crucial source of social system instability. This conception of the matter is still central to Talcott Parsons' sociology, which overstresses the significance of conformity with moral norms, and the need for shared systems of values, as requirements of social-system stability. Similarly, Durkheim and other functionalists commonly failed to indicate that it is not the sharing of *all* or *any* moral norms that contributed to social cohesion equally, but that some shared norms do so *more* than others.

Like many subsequent functionalists, Durkheim tended to focus on the functions of shared norms, neglecting their dys-functions. He centred his attention on the ways in which a deficiency of shared moral norms might generate social *dis*-organization and, although he did not ignore it, this tended to overshadow analysis of the ways an *excess* of morality (or of certain of its dimensions) might have *disruptive* consequences. There is a disruptive potential in each of the three dimensions of morality – reciprocity, beneficence, and moral absolutism – which will be explored below.

1 *Reciprocity.* The norm of reciprocity entails a flexible set of instructions to the actor, saying, or implying, 'help helpers', 'do not hurt helpers', and 'do not help hurters'. Ego is educated to inspect his own past actions to determine whether they have made him a debtor or creditor, *vis-à-vis* Alter, and thus also to classify Alter as creditor or debtor. Ego must then examine his impending action to see that it is consistent with the comple-mentary roles involved. The crux of action under the norm of reciprocity is that it is seen to depend not simply on the application of concrete, culturally standardized status prescrip-tions, but on the prior classification of self and others into latent *debtor–creditor* roles. There is, in short, a consultation of the 'memory bank' which tells Ego of his present balance of in-

debtedness, whether he must help a creditor or can be helped by a debtor.

In this framework, a certain distribution of disruptive consequences seems particularly possible. These are:

(a) possible violation of other moral rules; that is, in so far as helping or hurting others is seen as contingent on what they have done for us or will do in the future, under the norm of reciprocity the individual may feel obliged to help even social 'deviants', that is, those who fail to comply with certain moral rules, because of their past help or his expectation of future help from them. Thus Ego may lend support to the deviance of others. Or, again, he may feel justified in not helping those who have hurt him, despite the fact that there are norms of beneficence or concrete status duties that prescribe that he be of help. In either case, conformity with the norm of reciprocity may undermine the other two principal components of a group's moral code.

(b) The norm of reciprocity, in so far as it implies retaliation – 'hurt hurters' – may also dispose the individual to injure others who have hurt him, lending a moral justification to aggressive behaviour and conducing to the development of vicious cycles of widening conflict and increasing tension.

(c) The norm of reciprocity may further lead Ego to reinspect the history of his past interaction with Alter and to focus on the implications of his prospective behaviour toward Alter, to consider whether it helps him or not. It may thus induce a kind of *dyad-centrism* (as distinct from ego-centrism) in that Ego may be led to ignore the *ramifying* consequences for the *larger* collectivity of his aiding Alter or refusing to do so. That is, Ego may fail to consider the ramifying consequences that helping or hurting Alter may have for Ego's relations with others (perhaps Alter's enemies or friends), or for Alter's relations to others.

(d) Finally, the norm of reciprocity contains certain tendencies toward the calculation of a *quid pro quo*, toward the assessment of who owes what to whom. In short, the norm of reciprocity probably has certain tendencies to break down in the direction of utilitarian expedience, with all the tensions to which this is so vulnerable.

2 *Beneficence*. The *key* injunction here seems to be to help needy others or to give to others. Specific moral prescriptions, or their application, may be appraised in terms of the consequences they have for the needs of the other. Like reciprocity, beneficence may also induce people to disregard certain concrete status duties or the requirements of moral absolutism, should they be judged *hurtful* to others.

Of all the three principles of morality, however, consistent conformity with the dictates of beneficence is probably *least socially disruptive*. This, however, does not mean that it is equally functional for all types of historical societies. One can well imagine that, in its early stages, consistent and high conformity with norms of beneficence could well have impaired or prevented – through inhibiting capital accumulation and the expansion of trade – the development and functioning of modern industrial societies.

3 *Moral Absolutism*. The model of absolute morality implies a complex set of rules governing behaviour; the principal demand of absolute morality is the injunction not to do 'good' but to 'do *right*'. That is, one must inspect a problematic case to see which rule applies to it and, having determined this, one must apply it. If it is a case of Z, then the rule governing Z must be applied. The main focus here is on producing conformity between action and moral prescriptions. It is this that is problematic to those oriented by moral absolutism. How a prospective action relates to a history of prior interaction, or how it may generate consequences harmful or hurtful to Alter, is irrelevant. One *must* at all times do the right thing – and these 'right things' are prescribed by specific norms in various situations. Sometimes absolutism may be supportive of reciprocity. In many situations it may be *right* to reciprocate on the basis of past action, particularly if there are no specific status obligations that conflict. Moreover, moral absolutism may also constrain one to perform one's status duties to others who are viewed as having refused to help us or who cannot now repay the aid they need from us.

Moral absolutism, however, also has evident potentialities for the *violation* of the reciprocity norm. It may lead one to withhold assistance from someone who has helped us, if this entails violation of a moral prescription held to be relevant to the situation. Conversely, it may induce us, out of a desire to conform with an appropriate moral prescription, to hurt someone who has helped us. This is likely to be seriously disruptive of social systems, giving rise to particularly bitter accusations of 'ingratitude'. This is especially conducive to conflict because Alter now has two reasons for hostility: first, the sheer *injury* that Ego's morally motivated behaviour happens to have inflicted and, second, Alter's sense of *moral indignation* at this injury if he feels that Ego has violated the norm of reciprocity, upon which Alter believes action should have been predicted.

Conformity with the dictates of moral absolutism is also sometimes at variance with those of beneficence. We are here again dealing with a very ancient wisdom. Moral absolutism conduces to doing *right*, and the 'right' thing is often far from identical with the 'good' thing. Indeed, the merest perusal of history suggests that men motivated by moral absolutism and bent on doing the right thing have sometimes perpetrated (what others have considered to be) monstrosities of evil.

It is not those who have turned their backs on moral absolutism who are invariably the 'bad' or the most hurtful men. It is not, for example, the grafting politician – the corrupt mayor who plays fast and loose with the city treasury – who build crematoria and concentration camps. It takes a righteous man of moral indignation to do so: an Adolf Hitler who was characteristically concerned with minute conformity with certain moral prescriptions, and indeed, who was for a while nicknamed 'legality Adolf'.

There is more explosive fury in moral absolutism than in either reciprocity or beneficence. There can be more freeflowing sadism in moral absolutism at high tide and, hence, a greater potential for social-system cataclysm, than even in the *lex talionis* version of reciprocity. It is when man is at his most purely moral that he may be most dangerous to the interests, and most callously indifferent to the needs, of others. Social systems know no fury like the man of moral absolutism aroused. For he cares neither for the good that others have once done him, for the past when their histories intertwined, nor for the hurt or help which now ramify from his actions. He can become the impersonal, avenging sword of the law – or of the Lord – a Calvin, Zwingli, or Luther. Surely the 'right' of moral absolutism must be tempered with reciprocity and beneficence if social systems are not to be torn apart.

In his analysis of *anomie*, Durkheim notes that insatiability is one of the symptoms of social disorganization. Durkheim assumes that, unless men have some internalized norms which limit their egoistic appetites, they will press on ceaselessly for gratifications that never come and that they will, therefore, be perpetually restless and dissatisfied. It seems not to have occurred to Durkheim that there could be some whose hunger after righteousness was also insatiable and that this insatiability is no less disruptive of social systems. While Durkheim recognized that certain particular norms might expose men and groups to strain, what he failed to see was that there are certain strains, inherent in any moral code, between its various principal components: reciprocity, beneficence, and moral absolutism. Each is in some ways disruptive of the other, even if in other ways each is supportive of the other.

A stable social system without all three basic dimensions in the moral code seems impossible, precisely because of the tensions that each by itself generates and which the other two help relieve. Nonetheless, each also exerts strains on the other two dimensions. If it is evident that the righteousness of moral absolutism must be tempered with reciprocity and beneficence if there is to be social stability, it is equally clear that reciprocity norms may undermine beneficence and lead to action at variance with moral absolutism or, in its turn, be undermined by moral absolutism. Our view of any moral code, then, is far from one that sees it as harmonious and homeostatic. In its most fundamental organization a moral code is a tensionful system of precarious values and fragile adjustments, in which conflict is not merely residual but nuclear.

Conditions Conducive to Different Moral Dimensions

Under what conditions is there a development or an inhibition, an extension or a retrenchment, of the different principal components of moral codes – reciprocity, beneficence, and moral absolutism? The norm of reciprocity, to anticipate, is a hedge against tensions that proliferate in social relationships when the parties involved are engaged in a 'zero-sum' game. By definition, a zero-sum game is one in which it is possible for an actor to accumulate resources *only* by taking them from another. If any one player is to increase his assets, in a zero-sum game, he must defeat another. Each increase in a player's assets means that the loser is going down the ladder both relatively and absolutely.

For this reason, zero-sum games are particularly conducive to aggressive sentiments, to competitiveness, envy, and resentment. To the loser, at least, the winner's rejoicing is indistinguishable from an expression of pleasure in the loser's defeat. A zero-sum game, therefore, undermines the social solidarity of the players. It generates a kind of bitterness that motivates players to win at any cost. The zero-sum game also means that there is an endemic tension between the interests of the individual and those of the collectivity, for a man may not wish even his own team to win if the resultant team winnings are internally divided among the team members in a way that improves his competitors' position at cost to his own.

If the zero-sum game predicates that the relationship among the players is in the nature of a *contest*, the norm of reciprocity, however, by demanding that there be a rough equivalence in what is given and taken, defines the relationship among players as an *exchange*; no one is seen as winning at the expense of another, and no one loses to the gain of another on his own team. The norm of reciprocity thus protects the solidarity of the group from the strain-inducing contest of the zero-sum game.

Under what conditions are players more likely to engage in a zero-sum game or, conversely, under what conditions will they more likely play a *non*-zero-sum game? One of the most basic considerations here is whether players can increase their assets *without* taking them from one another. Are there, in short, workable alternatives for increasing one's assets? The only way in which a *non*-zero-sum game can be established – and men can increase their own assets without depriving other players of theirs – is when someone *outside* the game provides the stakes or puts up the prize. Such a non-zero-sum condition is fostered in a society with an increasing development of science and technology applied to productive purposes, and when routine productive activity is viewed as honourable. Correspondingly, a zero-sum game is more likely to be played when technology is *not* developing productivity and/or when such productive activity is not viewed as honourable or legitimate.

It may be expected that *a group will operate more extensively under the norm of beneficence where science, technology, and production are developing and legitimate, while a norm of reciprocity will more likely operate where they are not.* This is also consistent with our earlier suggestion that a lessening scarcity undermines conformity with the norm of reciprocity.

It is also possible for the stakes to be supplied from some source outside of economic development, such as a set of religious beliefs. When a religion places a stress upon the 'goods of the soul', what it is doing – in the above terms – is, first, to *devalue* the stakes of everyday life and thus to reduce the importance of winning or losing these, while, secondly, it mints and distributes a new coinage of which there is no *scarcity*, thus eliminating the need for players to take it from one another. In short, economic development and religion, particularly where religion holds out promise of a gratifying after-life, may serve as functional equivalents; each in its own way serves to withdraw the players from a sole reliance on increasing their assets by winning them from one another. The pay-off is now made by someone outside of the system of players and, in the case of a pay-off in an after-life, occurs after the game is over. Again, religions or philosophies may, by encouraging certain forms of other-worldly asceticism, induce players to *forgo* the desire to increase their assets, thus leading them to withdraw from the zero-sum game.

It also makes a difference whether players aim to increase their holdings of certain *particular* and unique assets, or whether they are seeking to increase holdings of a certain *class* of assets. To the extent that players want the particular things held by the others they can only get them by winning, or otherwise taking, these from them; but, to the extent that a player is interested in acquiring a *class* of objects – but not necessarily the particular ones held by others – the pressure to play according to zero-sum rules is diminished.

Of the various sources from which a player can increase his holdings without taking them from someone else, the most easily accessible and controllable is *himself*. The player may reward himself. In essence, the norm of moral absolutism permits a man to play a form of social *solitaire* in which he can reward *himself* – i.e., give himself approval – simply by following the rules.

From this standpoint, then, moral absolutism should be increased to the extent that actors are (or feel) less able reliably to control the behaviour of others, and to induce them to behave as desired. Moral absolutism, then, is a strategy of enhancing the personal autonomy of individuals: it is a way of making the actor less dependent upon others for his gratifications and to endure isolation; which is precisely why it has the system-*disruptive* potential discussed above.

Moral absolutism develops as a response to situations in which men feel that others may fail them – where the behaviour desired is viewed as precarious. Moral absolutism, however, does not develop only in situations where the self desires actions from *others* whose conformity it defines as precarious; it also arises when men are likely to feel *themselves* unwilling or unable to do as they otherwise desire or believe desirable. It arises, then, when there is an internal conflict of motives, a conflict between impulses and certain moral values, between impulses, or between values. Moral absolutism then serves to cut the Gordian knot of indecision; it enables decisions to be made and action to be taken despite ambivalence and uncertainty concerning the course to be taken.

It is not only, however, that moral absolutism enables men to overcome *moral* conflicts or indecision about competing lines of gratification. Men may simply be unable to act because they are unable to *know* or *predict* the consequences of given courses of action. Moral absolutism, like magical ritual, serves to enable men to carry on in the face of sheer ignorance – and its resultant anxieties – concerning the personally significant consequences of their actions. That men should find the net consequences of a line of action difficult to predict is not the rare but the

common human estate, for net consequences are usually obscured in a tangle of long-range ramifications.

Meaninglessness and Moral Absolutism

Moral absolutism is the essence of the morality that has developed
historically in Western civilization where it stands behind both
reciprocity and beneficence. Essentially, moral absolutism is a
way of answering the questions: why should I help those who
have helped me, why should I do good, and why should I do
any of the many things traditionally incumbent upon me as a
person in a given social position? The answer that moral absolutism gives comes down to this: do this because it is 'right'.
But what kind of an answer is *that*, and what does it *mean*?

I have suggested above that the meaning of this answer is in
part to be understood in terms of moral absolutism's functions:
in some part it helps the person to survive a world in which he
is unable to rely upon others; it helps him to endure social
isolation; it enables him to reward himself; and it enables him
to control his anxieties in the face of internal conflict and
ignorance of the consequences of his decisions. In other words,
moral absolutism is a whip constraining the person to carry on,
to perform his role, to help others who have helped him and to
help the needy, even when he is reluctant to do so because these
entail dangers and costs that are not at all clearly counterbalanced by the convenience and rewards of doing so.

Conformity with rules for their own sake, the righteous
enactments of the moral absolutist, provide him with a compensatory satisfaction for the pleasures he is forced to forgo
and the deprivations he is forced to endure. It gives him a sense
of superiority to those whose lives have greater worldly gratifications. In short, it enables him to bear the costs of his existence
by defining himself as a member of a moral élite.

Moral absolutism girds the individual to conform despite the
costs. And precisely because it premises costs – deprivation,
suffering, and pain – moral absolutism invariably manifests an
edge of punitiveness, a readiness to make others suffer. There is,
in short, an edge of sadism in moral absolutism.

Fundamentally, this sadism and indeed moral absolutism itself, derive from the failure of gratifications. Which is to say, moral absolutism enjoins the person to do things for their own sake alone precisely when doing things for *their* own sake is *not* gratifying enough, when there is an attenuation or failure of *intrinsic* gratification. If doing these things was *intrinsically* gratifying, the person would not need to be whipped into doing them for 'duty's sake', but would do them because of the satisfaction that they themselves provided.

In some part, then, the sheer development of science, technology, and productivity is the development of a reservoir of alternative rewards, of gratifications that men may enjoy in addition to those which may derive from (a) the sense of rectitude and self-approval coming from sheer conformity with certain concrete rules, or (b) from the pleasure intrinsically provided by certain kinds of activities.

Herewith is a basic source of the meaninglessness so pervasively experienced in our time. With the increase of technological affluence, men increasingly do all manner of things, not for the joy or sense of rectitude that these *intrinsically* provide, but for the *extrinsic* rewards that doing them may achieve. Now, with the increase in productivity, men may do things not because they believe them to be right, nor because doing them provides an intrinsic satisfaction, but simply because doing these things may be rewarded extrinsically from the growing cornucopia of a technologically provided abundance. To the extent that modern technology keeps men 'at it', conscientiously plying daily routines from which they derive neither a sense of righteousness nor a feeling of joy, the possibilities of an absurd and meaningless existence, devoid of either pleasure or rectitude, expand out into the social universe.

NOTES

1. These ambiguities, derived from operating in terms of the norm of reciprocity, can be resolved in various ways: (1) to the extent that 'deviance credits' are accorded to the other, a doubtfully compliant performance or claim will more likely be accepted. (2) The amount of deviance credits extended is probably a function of the extent to which previous transactions with the other have fostered diffuse sentiments of affection, trust, loyalty, or liking; a performance is more likely to be regarded as compliant,

and a claim is more likely to be defined as legitimate, the more the performer or claimant is likely to be trusted by the other. Yet it is precisely this variance in response to the same performance of claim – so that it is sometimes suitable, sometimes not, or suitable for one person but not for another – that may make people uneasy and uncertain about the nature of their indebtedness to others, about what may be offered or what must be accepted as a legitimate return. (3) Finally, the ambiguities of the rights and duties incumbent upon persons operating under the norm of reciprocity may be reduced or removed to the extent that each person is assigned some culturally standardized identity or status, to which attaches a set of relatively explicit rights and duties. However diffusely organized, such concrete statuses usually provide clearer stipulations of rights and duties in a given situation than does the generalized norm of reciprocity alone, and they establish a more accurate basis for predicting what is required and what will be acceptable. But see what follows in the main text.

2. This difference between the norms of beneficence and reciprocity, and their resultant obligations, may be examined if we exhume the old controversy between Mauss and Malinowski.

Bronislaw Malinowski had, in his earlier work, spoken of the gifts given by a husband to his wife as 'free' or 'pure' gifts. Mauss, however, in re-examining Malinowski's own data, had noticed that, in due time, some return was in fact given the husband: women returned their husbands' gifts with sexual favours. Consequently, said Mauss, the husband's gift could not be called 'free' or pure because it did bring a return.

In his own *Essay on the Gift*, Mauss stressed that there is a culturally pervasive rule which requires that those who accept a gift must later return it. He therefore concluded that what had appeared to Malinowski to be a case of beneficence was, in reality, a case of reciprocity. Interestingly enough (in light of the usual defensive reaction to criticism), Malinowski accepted Mauss's criticism, doing so perhaps in part because Mauss's case rested upon and acknowledged the accuracy of Malinowski's own field notes. Thus in the end the two of them agreed; the only party that might have suffered from this *entente cordiale* was social theory. For we have here the unusual case of a scientist agreeing to criticisms of his work which are deeply dubious, and rest upon certain ambiguities that obscure important theoretical issues. How had this happened?

Basically, Mauss had correctly sensed the functional interconnection between beneficence and reciprocity; but he had failed to see and to work out the conceptual *distinctions* between the two. In some measure, he was trapped by his own diffuse notion of 'total' social phenomena and his self-imposed demand to study things as 'wholes'. In particular, Mauss failed to clarify the distinction between two types of *norms* in the gift exchange situation. Because they were both involved in the same total system of *action*, he did not separate norms calling upon people to be beneficent and to give gifts freely under certain circumstances, from norms of reciprocity which make giving contingent upon returns.

Simply because beneficence and reciprocity are both normative orientations and require some transference of valuables does not mean that they are otherwise alike. In particular, Mauss had failed to distinguish the *motivation* for beneficent actions from their unanticipated *consequences*. He had missed the fact that action *initiated* in accordance with a norm of beneficence may lead to continued interaction in accordance with the different norm of reciprocity. While Mauss makes it clear that the giving of a gift commonly eventuates in a pattern of reciprocal exchange, he fails to note that this is *not* always the *intention* of the donor. If the donor happens to be oriented to the norm of reciprocity when giving, then the intentions and consequences of his action will more closely coincide. If, however, the donor is oriented to norms of beneficence, this may indeed motivate him to give a gift without any consideration or expectation of a return from the recipient.

3. More specifically, moral absolutism generates outstanding obligations in the following ways: (1) They create a *presumption* in favour of the legitimacy of certain demands made upon status incumbents in that these usually involve some expectations taken by normally socialized members of the group, to have a *prima facie* legitimacy. Consequently, it is not the claimant who must justify his demands but the recalcitrant who must justify his refusal. (2) Moral absolutism requires that certain things must be done under every and all circumstances – for example, one must always keep his promises or must always tell the truth. Since such demands are unconditional they come to bear continually upon the flow of social interaction and they can never be given full and final compliance, once and for all. The very unconditional character of moral absolutism enlarges the number of situations in which obligations will be activated and it thus increases the number of outstanding obligations. (3) Since the number of failures to comply with an obligation is probably a function of the number of circumstances in which it must be performed – on the assumption that the more frequently a thing is to be done the greater the absolute number of failures experienced – then operation under a prescription of unconditional compliance means that the number of 'moral failures' will increase. The number of moral failures is also likely to be increased by the norm of moral absolutism for it has no escape clauses and allows no legitimate exemptions by very reason of its unconditionality. The occurrence of moral failures, in turn, exposes those who fail to what may be called the principle of 'compensatory conformity'; this generates a second-order obligation designed to 'make up' for their default. (4) Finally, in so far as he conforms to the demands of moral absolutism, the person is making 'deposits' to his account which, should circumstances subsequently require, he can later transform into 'accounts payable' then due him – that is, he can redefine them as 'outstanding obligations' that others owe him. In effect, then, moral absolutism provides for a system of 'deficit financing' that generates obligations to others despite their inability to repay at the time

10

Personal Reality, Social Theory and the Tragic Dimension in Science

Gunnar Boalt's work on the *Sociology of Social Research* is a major contribution to a sociology of sociology and it provides substantial testimony to the seriousness with which many sociologists throughout the world today are probing toward a heightened self-awareness. It is not only in its social implications, however, but also in its scientific contribution that Professor Boalt's work is impressive. Indeed, I am tempted to suggest that his is perhaps the first systematic (if partial) theory of the sociology of sociology. Boalt's theory is enhanced by its ample discussion of the formal requirements for testing the theory systematically, by its provocative suggestions of a mathematical model that might further this testing, and, far from least, by its author's sensitivity to the problems and limits of his own theory as well as his full awareness of the way it ranges beyond a sociology of sociology to more general problems of sociological analysis. An appreciation of his work, moreover, cannot fail to be enlivened by its informal dimensions, by its casual, quiet thrusts of wry wit, and the civilized sensibility with which it firmly grasps the distinction between understanding something and having a theory about it.

Gunnar Boalt is a major Swedish sociologist who – with all this implies in a European university – occupies the Chair in Sociology at the University of Stockholm. This biographical remark is not, however, intended as an introductory nicety, or as a way of introducing him to American scholars unfamiliar with Swedish sociology; rather, and as will be seen shortly, it is mentioned because of its specific relevance to the work he presents here. In particular, it will soon be apparent that, in formulating his theory about the sociology of social research, Professor Boalt has drawn freely and extensively from his own experience, both as a working sociologist and as an academic administrator. His work is enriched by the fact that he knows whereof he speaks; his 'theoretical self' has remained in open communication with his other roles or selves. He has pursued his work here not simply as an intellectual puzzle conducted within the narrow framework of an insulated professional role but also, it seems to me, as an effort at personal orientation disciplined by scholarly requirements.

This observation is, I think, of pointed relevance for the sociology of sociology. For insofar as this continues to develop, it will inevitably be subjected to pressures that aim to transform it into just one other technical speciality, and to make it serve as just one other topic for specialized panels at professional congresses. To the extent that the emerging sociology of sociology succumbs to this pressure, it will probably be crippled in its capacity to further sociologists' understanding of their own personal situation, or of their profession as a personal situation. Boalt's work is a paradigm, in this respect as in others, of what a humanely conceived sociology of sociology should be. It is a technically disciplined effort at an understanding of a social role that has special (because personal) value to sociologists, namely, their roles as researchers and teachers.

The development of a sociology of sociology that would avoid a confrontation between the sociologist and himself would, I fear, be the development of a redundant specialization. It would fail to achieve and to fulfil the only distinctive function that can be performed by a sociology of sociology. The development of a sociology of sociology as just one other technical specialization would, in effect, be to use this intellectual innovation as a kind of sociological defence mechanism against the potential illuminations of self that such an enterprise inherently possesses.

While this connection between personal meaning and scholarly work is particularly visible in Boalt's work, it is a relationship that is germane to the sociology of sociology precisely because it is not peculiar to Boalt's work. For some appreciable part of any sociological enterprise is activated by the sociologist's effort to explore, to objectify, and to universalize some of his own most deeply personal experiences. Some part of the sociologist's effort to know the social world around him is an effort – more or less deliberate and disguised – to understand himself: his experiences in his social world and his relationship to it. While this has no bearing on the validity of the resultant knowledge or theory, it does bear on another interest legitimate to the sociology of sociology: the sources, the motives, and the aims of the sociological quest.

In the following, I want to suggest something of the larger significance of a concern about the relation between the personal and the scholarly. I shall begin with the commonplace that all sociologists, however theoretical their bent, seek to explain – tacitly or overtly – some part of the social world. Not all parts of the social world are of equal interest or importance to sociologists, and they focus their attention upon it selectively. Very much under the influence of Talcott Parsons, many American sociologists during the forties and fifties assumed that this selectivity of focus was largely a function of the theory to which the sociologist was committed. 'Facts' were seen as the products of an effort to pursue the inferences of theories and, indeed, as constituted in terms of the conceptual schemes embedded in the structure of theories. From the standpoint of a sociology of sociology, however, we are interested in the *extra*-theoretical sources of theory, and in developing a view that acknowledges social theories as the work product of certain individuals who are seen as having a specific location in a specific social and cultural matrix.

With this as background, I will add that sociologists like others impute 'reality' to certain things in their social world; which is to say, they believe, sometimes with focal and sometimes with only subsidiary awareness, that the world has a certain character, that certain things are truly attributable to it. In what follows, I will suggest that it is not only theories or facts but anything that the sociologist defines as 'real' that will shape his work importantly. For simplicity's sake, I will suggest there are two kinds of things that are imputed to have reality by any sociologist. One consists of 'facts' yielded by previous researches, whether conducted by themselves or others. The second, however, consists of what I will call the 'personally real'. These are aspects of the social world to which sociologists will, like those who are not sociologists, impute reality because of their personal experiences: because of what they have seen, heard, been told, or read, and which are distinct from 'facts' that have been systematically gathered and scientifically evaluated. Indeed, many elements in personal reality have been developed long before the sociologist was professionally trained or intellectually mature. The personal reality of the sociologist is every bit as real to him as the facts he has acquired through sociological research, although *his own* research – far more than that of others – becomes an especially important component of his personal reality.

Things to which the sociologist imputes reality, whether the factual or the personally real, may play a role in his sociological research in at least two ways, either as elements in his explanatory efforts or as foci around which these efforts develop. Here I want to concentrate in particular on the manner in which the imputedly real often becomes a focus around which certain (but not necessarily all) explanatory efforts converge, or as elements in the explanation. Most specifically, I want to suggest that the imputedly real enters into theory construction by being treated as possessed of a generalizable significance, by being regarded as examples of or cases of a larger set of realities. In other words, sociologists use what they impute to be real as paradigms or, in Stephan Pepper's terms, as a 'root metaphor'; they assume that things which they have researched or with which they have had some personal acquaintance are like other things with which they are unacquainted or have not yet researched.

Social theories or accounting schemes tend, therefore, to be generalized to a set of events that extend beyond the sociologist's facts or personal realities; yet, at the same time, such social theories tend to be influenced, limited or informed by the distinctive characteristics of the things to which the sociologist has imputed reality.

To put the matter in another way: for the purpose of theory construction, sociologists treat imputed realities as models of a more extensive set of as yet unobserved events. They tend to assume that sections of the world that they have not yet encountered are similar to the smaller section incorporated in their facts or personal realities. Theory-making thus proceeds in a manner similar to the fable of the blind men and the elephant, each man generalizing his theory from and anchoring it in a limited sector of the world to which he imputes reality and on the basis of which he generalizes about larger wholes. Theories, therefore, are influenced by the distinctive character of the limited things to which we impute reality and which we use as root metaphors or paradigms. Thus, for example, one reason why Malinowski's theory of magic differed from Radcliffe-Brown's was because the data that each had used differed from the other's, Malinowski focusing on cases of work magic and Radcliffe-Brown on childbirth magic, and because each regarded his limited data as paradigmatic, that is, as exemplary of or essentially akin to other kinds of magic.

Sociologists, of course, are familiar with these dangers, at least *en principe*, and they seek to use systematic sampling as a way of obviating them. Nonetheless, sampling techniques cannot fully avoid the problem, for these only provide a basis for testing a theory subsequent to its formulation. If systematic research entails the use of a systematic sample in order to test inferences from a theory, then, in the nature of the case, the theory must be formulated prior to acquiring a systematic sample. Indeed, the more the sociologist stresses the importance of articulate theory the more this is likely to be the case. The theory will therefore tend to revolve around, and will consequently be skewed or shaped by, the limited facts and personal realities available to the theorist, and in particular by those imputed realities that he treats as paradigms.

Moreover, systematic sampling only constitutes a restraint on unjustified generalizations from 'facts', but does not similarly restrain the influence of 'personal realities'. Since the latter are deemed scientifically irrelevant, it is often assumed that they are scientifically inconsequential – which merely means that the sociologist has here confused the morality of science with its actual practice. In point of fact, the personally real and problematic often enough becomes the starting point for disciplined inquiry – and, indeed, there is no scientific reason why this should not be the case.

What is personally real to men is real, frequently enough though not always, precisely because it is not personal to them – in the sense of idiosyncratic to or uniquely different for them – but because it is social and collective. Collectively held imputations of reality are, of course, among the most firmly constituted components of personal reality. Yet the personally real does not entirely consist of, or depend upon, collective definitions of social reality but may also derive from recurrent personal experiences – unique to the person or shared by others – in a sector of the social world. What becomes personally real, then, is not such simply because it is also personally real to others, or because these others have communicated their conception of reality. But whether deriving from collective definitions or from recurrent personal experiences, imputed realities are of special importance to the kinds of theories that sociologists formulate: 'facts' are only a special case of imputed realities.

It may therefore be instructive to review some of the things that are a part of Professor Boalt's 'personal reality', and which have formed the foci around which his theory of social research was constructed. We will notice that the personal reality of a Swedish sociologist may differ from that of an American sociologist. It would be naïve in the extreme, however, were we to conclude that this difference explains only the lacunae in Boalt's theory and if we fail to see that it also infuses his theory with certain strengths. It would also be naïve in the extreme were we to use the occasion only to observe how Swedish society affects the personal reality of Swedish sociologists in intellectually consequential ways, but failed to recognize that American society does exactly the same thing to American sociologists, even if in somewhat different ways.

In mentioning some of the elements in Professor Boalt's personal reality, I do not mean to be comprehensive but only exemplary. In the main, I shall focus on those elements that Professor Boalt tacitly tends to assume may be universal, that is, which he tends to treat as paradigmatic, but which I – from my different American personal reality – may not regard as universal. Thus, for example:

'I suppose most researchers reach their apex with their doctor's thesis or shortly afterwards. Once they have finally got a permanent position one of the motives urging them on to a high scientific standard disappears.' It is relevant to note here that Professor Boalt speaks explicitly of 'most' researchers as manifesting this pattern, thereby exemplifying precisely what I mean when I say that personal reality often tends to be taken as paradigmatic, that is, as indicative of the character of a larger sector than one has information about. Professor Boalt's observation above also seems to imply, first, that departments that train professional sociologists set extremely demanding scientific standards for their students and, secondly, that this high standard is expressed and enforced most especially in the preparation of a doctoral dissertation. It is my somewhat different impression, however, that many departments of sociology in the United States, particularly since the rapid expansion of the academic market for doctorates, perhaps since the mid-1950s, have come to stress that a candidate should not take 'too long' to complete his degree and have, therefore, searched for ways of expediting the preparation of the dissertation. (In some part, it may be that the growing emphasis on the use of 'secondary analysis' as a way of writing dissertations may reflect this pressure to expedite the training of Ph.Ds.)

While this speed-up may not necessarily lead to a general decline in scientific standards – most endorsing an educational speed-up would deny that it does – nonetheless, it would seem to make the dissertation a less demanding task. Certainly, students are now less likely to be reminded that *The Division of Labor in Society* was Émile Durkheim's dissertation! In consequence of the tendency to 'relax' standards for the dissertation, one may at least wonder whether there is not a more general 'relaxation' of the scientific standards communicated to candidates. To teach students appropriate techniques and methodologies in seminars while, at the same time, telling them – as is now often done in the United States – that they must not dally over their dissertations, may be in effect to tell students that they can get by without applying and without internalizing high scientific standards.

Many American students that I have known in the last decade

take the attitude that their dissertation is a job of work that they must 'get out of the way'; presumably, after they graduate and take up positions elsewhere, they will then do work of importance and high standards. The relevant consideration here, however, is not the factuality but the personal reality of my statements about these patterns of training in some American universities, and my clear conviction that my 'personal reality' differs from Professor Boalt's – or that his differs from mine. Were I to take my own distinctive personal reality and treat it as paradigmatic and problematic, I might go on to propose a theoretical explanation along the following lines: namely, that the degree to which graduate-training centres emphasize scientific values may be a function of the market situation for those with new doctorate degrees. In other words, when there is a very limited and only slowly growing number of academic places for those with doctorates – as in Sweden and other European countries – an insistence on extremely high scientific standards serves to curtail the supply of doctorates and to accommodate to the smaller demand for them. Correspondingly, the reduction of scientific standards may be a way of increasing the supply of doctorates to fill a larger or growing demand for them. So much for our theoretical sketch. The important consideration here is that theory often tends to get constructed around a personal reality that is treated as paradigmatic and problematic. Yet Professor Boalt has been most unreasonable; he has constructed his theory around his personal reality rather than around mine!

Again: 'It is not hard to acquire the scientific values, but it is all the harder to satisfy them. Young research students have no idea of this, and it upsets them when they find that so many of the investigations they come across are full of shortcomings in so many respects.' Two points are worth developing here. First, there is a suggestion that an important part of Professor Boalt's personal reality entails a tacit focus on the researcher as a student. In other words, Swedish educators, like those in different cultures, seem to develop the conviction that an important part of their reality consists of students and of efforts to educate them. It may be, therefore, that of all the people an educator has an opportunity to observe doing research, a relatively large and salient group of them happen to be students.

Furthermore, the extent to which a sociologist takes his educational responsibilities seriously, rather than subordinating them to his own research, will shape the extent to which he defines students as part of his personal reality.

In any event, my own personal reality in this respect seems to differ somewhat from Professor Boalt's; for my part, I seem to find that some academic sociologists take their educational responsibilities to students rather more lightly than is implied by Professor Boalt's conception of the matter, and that some seem to treat their students as 'hired hands', or as paid subordinates. In short, they may treat students not as people to whom they have responsibility as educators, but as research clerks who have an obligation to do as they have been told. And while such academic sociologists may be few in number, since they so violate my own conception of the educational enterprise, even these few loom large in my own personal reality, thus anchoring it at some remove from Professor Boalt's.

That, so far as professors are concerned. Now, insofar as students are concerned, I should also confess that here, too, my personal reality appears different from Professor Boalt's. For my part, I simply would not have described the young research students whom I have known in quite the manner that Professor Boalt did, namely, as upset about the difficulty in realizing scientific values. I, instead, see some of them as all too willing to do any tacky piece of work, so long as it is acceptable to their faculty and enables them to acquire a doctorate (the 'union card', as they say), even though they *know* that their work is tacky. Such student expectations are the counterpart of those held by professors who urge them to do almost any kind of study, just so long as they can complete it in short order. Still other students whom I have known – perhaps the better ones – far from being upset when they encounter scientifically deficient work, seem to be delighted; they may see this as confirmation of their own sense of superiority, and as justifying the contempt that they feel for those whose scientific values differ from their own. In short, Professor Boalt's and my personal realities seem to be somewhat different concerning both students and professors.

Indeed, it may well be that Professor Boalt's personal

reality does not merely differ from mine with respect to students and professors but, further, that he thinks of men more generally somewhat differently than I do. He tends, I suspect, to think of them as being more highly conscientious, as being disposed to pursue fixed values with tenacious effort, as suffering deeply or as losing self-confidence when unable to achieve these values, and as persevering in the face of difficulty. Professor Boalt thus remarks that typically the researcher 'suffers setbacks [yet] we know that notwithstanding he usually perseveres'.

In other words, I suspect that Professor Boalt's personal reality contains an image of man broadly different from my own, and perhaps from that of many other Americans. I get the impression that Boalt tends to assume generally that men are more reluctant to surrender their high values, even in the face of difficulty, that they are more controlled by a punishing super-ego, that they are men of a Lutheran inwardness struggling within themselves to achieve conformity with high ideals, and who seek a kind of inner rectitude rather than success in the world and validation by others.

My point here, of course, is not that my personal reality is superior to Boalt's, nor that his is wrong and mine is right. I can well imagine that the opposite might be the case. Not only do I suspect that our personal realities differ, but I further suspect that this has a great deal to do with the fact that he is, in some large part, a product of Swedish culture and that I, in contrast, am a product of a more pragmatic, more gratification-seeking, and more exchange-oriented American culture. My point, then, is not at all – indeed, most definitely not – that a personal reality acquired in American culture provides a sounder basis for theory construction than one acquired in Swedish culture. My point simply is that these two cultures do generate somewhat different personal realities for those who have lived in them and that these provide different (not superior or inferior) bases for theory construction. In short, my point is that these culturally patterned differences in personal reality are theoretically consequential. In sum, I have the impression – and I know this will come as no surprise to Professor Boalt – that his theory about the sociology of social research was formed around his experiences in Swedish culture and society, just as mine would be informed and limited by my experiences in American culture and society, and that, to some extent, both the penetration and the limitations of his theory are related to the personal reality he has acquired in Swedish society more generally, and in the Swedish university more particularly.

Let me develop this by elaborating a bit on my own impressions – in other words, by presenting my personal reality, not the 'facts' – concerning certain relevant aspects of Swedish culture and Swedish sociology derived in part from my reading, and in part from a brief visit in the summer of 1965 which provided me with an opportunity to talk with some Swedish sociologists, including Professor Boalt. Let me reiterate: these are impressions and are very far indeed from being the product of systematic observation.

As I poked about it, I somehow acquired a sense of the Platonic and, more particularly, the Apollonian, character of Swedish culture: the attitude towards sex was, it seemed to me, a far cry from frenzied promiscuity; I saw it, rather, as a disciplined effort to do the 'right' and 'rational' thing – to manage sex intelligently, to control the irrational rationally. I saw a similar Apollonianism in the widespread concern about excess drinking and the fear of drunkenness which, incidentally, was also one of Plato's pet anxieties. Above all, there was the Apollonian sense of Stockholm's public architecture and squares, each building well boundaried, sitting firmly in its own space and well demarcated from others, balanced and orderly. I had the impression that many of the men I met in various walks of life felt that Reason and Theory were powerful forces and could see and plan much. Indeed, I felt that nowhere in Europe do ordinary men, as well as men of affairs, give a truer or at least a more energetic expression to their belief in a life of reason. I came to feel that what was developing there was Plato's 'second best city', the city of the Laws, permeated (in the Swedish case) by a humane but pervasive superintendence of daily life, by a measured *gravitas* that settles invisibly upon spontaneity, transforming joy into education, movies into theatre, and conversation into discussion.

It seemed to me that Swedish sociology was of one piece with Swedish culture, most particularly with respect to the consensus that was given concerning the importance of using formalized, systematic, and external methodologies. It was my impression that there is no group of sociologists anywhere in the world today who, more than those in Sweden, have a clearer and more agreed-upon view of the standards and values to which good sociology should conform. Swedish sociologists seemed to me to be the people of, by, and for a formal methodology. This methodological drive of Swedish sociologists appears to be typically Apollonian; to express a quest for something firm, hard-edged, well-boundaried, and clearly structured.

The culturally shared emphasis, then, among Swedish sociologists, as I gleaned it, is on a self-conscious use of sophisticated methodologies, research designs, experimental techniques, measurement systems, questionnaire technologies, explicit norms of inference – on all of the devices of formalization. Aside from the indications of their research reports, one of the main linguistic clues that I would cite concerning the pervasiveness of this formal conception of research is the repetition of, and the accented reference to, the term 'model'. There is hardly a discussion with Swedish sociologists in which this sacred term is not presented in an invocatory mood, as a pathos-resonating statement on both the method and the objective of social research.

Before developing this point, allow me at once to qualify and to clarify it. In describing the Swedish style of sociology as formal and 'high science'-oriented, I am not saying that this describes the *behaviour* of all Swedish sociologists but, rather, their research culture, their ideology of procedure, their methodological morality.

What must be understood, of course, is that the rules of methodology are always a morality that can be more or less believed in and given more or less conformity. Such rules are often an ideology with which one group of sociologists seeks to influence, control, change, and dominate another group. In the United States, 'high science' methodology is the priestly ideology of a relatively small, somewhat embattled, group who identify themselves as 'methodologists'. Their self-appointed mission is not simply to better their own work, but actively to reform the behaviour of other sociologists whom they regard as misguidedly

employing informal, unjustified, and ultimately immoral procedures.

The methodological subculture of American sociologists
seems much more varied and differentiated than the Swedish.
There are many unregenerate sociological sinners among us
who do not heed the message. There are even some who
formulate counter-methodological ideologies. Perhaps worst of
all, there are those who can live such deviant intellectual lives
guiltlessly, without even experiencing a need for elaborating a
counter-ideology. In Sweden, however, the high-science model
has a commanding, almost unchallenged place; while many
Swedish sociologists, perhaps especially among the young, do
fail to practise what is preached to them – and this is a central
part of Boalt's argument – few do so with an easy conscience.
This is very much to the point in attempting to understand the
personal reality that has shaped the character of Professor
Boalt's theory about social research.

The world of social science is unavoidably a moral world –
and nowhere more than in its methodologies. But what needs
to be stressed here is that men can relate to their moralities, and
hence to their methodologies, in rather different ways. What I
am suggesting, then, is that many Swedish sociologists, it
seemed to me, related to their methodologies in ways that I felt
to be discernibly different from the manner in which Americans
do. Americans, it seems to me, are somewhat more prone to
temper their commitment to morality and methodology by a
greater concern for what 'other people think', how other people
will react, and by an estimate of what the consequences or
outcomes will be. In short, American orientation to methodology and morality seem to be tempered by American sociability
and pragmatism.

I am suggesting, then, that there is an interplay between
Swedish culture and Swedish sociology which expresses itself
most pointedly in Swedish methodological morality. I am suggesting that their apparently more formalistic approach to social
research must be seen within a broader set of conventions that
regulate the social intercourse of intellectual life more broadly.
Here I am especially reminded of certain patterns of conversation that seem to me to characterize Swedish academicians, at

least in contrast to Americans, and, most especially, the reluctance of the former to express personal views unless they
were very sure of what they were saying. For example, I often
found myself asking very broad and open-ended questions –
as much to move discussion along as to acquire information –
about subjects that I thought were well within the other's
personal experience, only to be told that he had no 'information' about the subject. Perhaps a relevant hunch here is that
Swedish sociologists may, more than Americans, suppress or
exclude their 'personal reality' from their intellectually responsible efforts and that this may be one way in which Boalt's work
is not characteristically Swedish. On one occasion, when a
person did reply to such an open-ended question, he did so only
with evident tension, with the tight clasping and unclasping of
hands, and with numerous qualifications. Swedish academicians, including many sociologists among them, seemed to be
engaged in an undeclared war against uncertainty, seemed to be
reluctant to play with ideas, and reluctant to reward those who
could and did. I wondered if this reluctance to play with ideas
did not also inhibit the development of new ideas; for if one is
morally opposed to talking about the uncertain, it seemed
possible that there might also be discomfort and unwillingness
even to think about uncertain things. In short, there was, it
seemed, a danger that the speculative and creative imagination
could become an unintended casualty of such an undeclared war
against uncertainty.

A few Swedish sociologists have themselves reacted critically
against the distinctively formal and high-science aspirations of
Swedish sociology, and I believe that one of the most astute of
these is Gunnar Boalt. Most particularly I believe that Boalt's
theory of social research is, in some part, a polemic against and
perhaps an 'unmasking' of the Swedish emphasis upon
formalization. What I am suggesting, then, is not only that
Boalt's theory of social research is a generalization from his
Swedish experience but that it is also a *critique* of it.

It is notable, however, that this last implication of his work
became clearly apparent to me only after I had spent time with
him in Stockholm and had talked rather extensively with him
about his own theories. Indeed, after that experience, I began to

suspect that every sustained theoretical analysis emerges out of a matrix of personal reality that is socially derived and socially relevant. It would be most instructive to have and to record personal discussions with all contemporary theorists and to compare their full, ranging, oral commentaries with their lean, antiseptic, published prose. There is, I believe, usually an important gap between the two, and the oral commentary commonly contains much additional information of value for interpreting the published work, and in particular gives us clues about the personal reality in which it is grounded. If this is correct, then we are surely training our graduate students badly. For, in effect, we are training them to conceal and to obfuscate their deepest intentions and meanings when we teach them to write reports in the usual 'professional' style, an understanding of which requires special training in a kind of intellectual archaeology.

As Boalt and I discovered our common passion for the sociology of sociology, and as we talked at great and animated length about his work, it became clear to me that his sociology of social research focused precisely on (and against) Swedish sociology's penchant for high-science models; it was a polemic against the 'hell' – as he put it – that this inflicts upon their students, and the manner in which this makes them into 'mashed potatoes'.

While the deepest structure of Boalt's work here rests on his tacit critique of Swedish sociology, his is nonetheless a very characteristically Swedish work. In some part, this may be seen in its own thrust toward formal explication and the development of a systematic model. Yet there may be another way in which it manifests kinship with and expresses a personal reality derived from Swedish culture and Swedish sociology. To clarify this, however, it now becomes necessary to say a few words about Boalt's theory itself. The theory goes something like this.

Sociologists have a special, scientific subculture into which they train and socialize their students. Boalt conceives of this culture as a set of regulative ideals concerning research, and indeed much of the discussion in his monograph entails an effort to explicate them systematically: these comprise, for instance, the formulation of the intellectual problem and hypotheses concerning it, securing an appropriate sample, measurement techniques, etc. The decisive consideration for Boalt, however, is that no one can fulfil all of these values in his own research. In some ways and in some degree, even the most talented and most mature of scientists – let alone their students – will always fail. All social scientists, therefore, must learn to cope with failure. The problem of adapting to failure is the pivotal problem in Boalt's entire theory, while the centrality of failure is, perhaps, the pivotal 'personal reality'. The point that Boalt stresses, the point around which all his thinking revolves, is not simply the occasional and idiosyncratic occurrence of failure but, rather, failure seen as a universal experience of all science and indeed (one clearly feels) of all human enterprise. It is the inescapability and universality of failure, not failure as an aberration or as an accident, not failure as marginal to the human enterprise, to which Boalt is drawn with humane fascination. Boalt's sociology of social research is therefore directly expressive of a tragic vision and, indeed, it is, in my view, the only sociology of science that centres on this tragic dimension.

Men make some adaptation to and seek some compensation for these inevitable failures, says Boalt. They may, within their scientific role, shift from an emphasis on scientific values that are difficult or impossible to fulfil, to an emphasis upon values that they are able to achieve. In short, they may balance their scientific deficiencies and failures with their successes in achieving other scientific values, on which they come to place enhanced importance. This is an intra-role compensation or strategy for adapting to failure. There is, however, another strategy, namely, an inter-role form of compensation. Here, for instance, men who fail as scientists may adapt by increasing their investment in their other roles, in their domestic or familial roles or in their roles as teachers.

In his personal discussion of his theory with me, Boalt also emphasized that there were two kinds of students. There were, first, those who recognized that they must deviate from the high-science rules taught them and there were, secondly, those who could not and did not do so. The latter, suggested Boalt, may be particularly represented among those who fail to complete their dissertations and never get their degree. In other words, scientific success may be contingent on *deviance* from scientific values, as well as conformity to them. The former, or 'deviant', students are those who have greater talent and flexibility in departing from the high-science model and in learning how to get this departure accepted by their professors. To use an analogy, it may be that the student faces a problem similar to that of an unmarried girl still living at home who has become pregnant: she must somehow tell her parents that she is pregnant, without a breakdown in their relationship.

To revert to the suggestion concerning the Swedish 'nature' of Boalt's work, it can be seen how Boalt believes, as part of his personal reality, that there is a set of scientific values that are treated as givens and hypostasized; that is, he postulates that social scientists do in fact commonly use an externalized methodological model which they view as a set of moral imperatives rather than only as heuristic benchmarks.

This conception of professors having and demanding conformity to a single, externalized, morally tinged, high-science model seems to me much more distinctly Swedish than American. American sociologists, it appears to me in terms of my own different personal reality, hold a number of different methodological models; they use a variety of different methodological moralities that they claim to be scientifically legitimate. Such variety may, as Boalt himself suggests, be a function of the greater number of professors in American departments. The more 'informal' styles of work in the United States are not simply felt to be compromise adaptations to difficulties in conforming with a single high-science model but are, rather, often deemed legitimate in their own right. Moreover, and this is a distinct point, major American methodologists – such as Paul F. Lazarsfeld – have developed an entirely different conception of what methodology is. In this conception, methodology is not conceived of simply as the formal explication of logically defensible and *a priori* models but, rather, as the inductive codification of successful patterns of work – whatever they may be – which are in fact used by working sociologists.

To put the matter otherwise, it appears as if American sociologists are somewhat less likely to use externalized models and are more likely to use 'paradigms' (in Thomas Kuhn's sense) to guide their work. That is, they identify certain specific and concrete pieces of research as good or outstanding and then use these specific works as guides for their own efforts. It may be that this is an informal style of evaluation relatively more characteristic of Americans. It may also be that an American readiness to utilize specific and concrete researches, as paradigms to guide and evaluate their own work, is not radically different from what Swedish sociologists do. Rather, Americans may have a relatively greater readiness to allow their paradigms to surface into focal awareness while, correspondingly, Swedish sociologists may differ only in their tendency to suppress their orientations to such paradigms and to retain them only in subsidiary awareness. Furthermore, I would hypothesize that one of the functions of such concrete paradigms is precisely to provide a mechanism for accommodating to the difficulty in achieving the high science models or formal methodologies. I would not wish to be understood, however, as suggesting that the only relationship of paradigms to formal methodological models is simply one in which the paradigms reduce tensions that derive from departing from the model. Without elaborating here, I would suggest, rather, that this relationship is a much more complex one in which the paradigm may serve not only to enable men to adjust to failure in achieving high scientific values, but also subverts and undermines them. At the same time, however, commitment to the model correspondingly undermines a commitment to the paradigm. Each, in short, constitutes a solution to the problems of the other and, moreover, each 'subverts' the other. A paradigm permits the researcher to do somewhat less than a formal model requires, while a model always requires that the researcher do somewhat more than the paradigm indicates.

It is clear that Boalt's theory is not simply a limited theory about social research but has far broader implications; tacitly but importantly, it links up with a more generalized theory of role behaviour and of anomie. Boalt assumes – indeed he emphasizes – that (1) men have multiple, culturally sanctioned values even in one role and, (2) with the failure to achieve one or some of these values, they may then switch their involvements to other values – which are no less culturally sanctioned. In short, in this aspect of his theory Boalt presents what I would call a theory of 'selective conformity' with, no less than of deviance from, role requirements.

Boalt's theory, then, stresses that a failure to achieve certain legitimate norms may elicit conforming behaviour. Unlike certain American theories, which stress that when men fail they become deviant, this Swedish theorist says that failure may simply lead men to try, try again, to conform; that is, to conform with some other, more readily achievable, socially sanctioned value. Men are seen as loath to violate their values.

Responses to failure, then, are not held to be confined to withdrawing belief in or activity on behalf of a legitimate value; nor as continuing to behave in conformity with the value but without genuine belief in its ultimate achievement; nor, again, as claiming legitimacy for new patterns of behaviour that are not as yet widely accepted. Boalt's theory makes salient a distinctive addition to the various possible strategies of adapting to failure, namely, selective conformity – i.e., an increasing effort to achieve certain already established values, and an attribution of increased importance to them, with resultant reorganization of role behaviour.

Boalt's theory thus contributes toward a generalizable model for explaining role change, or variations in role behaviour, within which one may account for both deviant and conforming changes. Stated in other terms, Boalt's work makes it very clear that a theory of deviant behaviour is just a special case of role change; it provides a parsimonious framework within which deviant changes may be linked with conforming role changes. And it not only includes within its purview changes that occur within one role but, also, systematically focuses on the ways in which different roles may be interconnected, and shows how changes in any one of these may induce changes in an altogether different role-set. It thus contributes to a deepening of our understanding concerning inter-role dynamics.

One of the central aspects of Boalt's work, then, is its focus upon the consequences of failure; we might say Boalt's theory rests upon an unshakeable belief in the reality of failure. One wonders whether corresponding American theories may not differ fundamentally precisely because they are not permeated by such a conviction in the reality of failure but, to the contrary, tend to think of failure as peripheral, marginal, accidental to the human enterprise and, instead, dwell in a world whose 'reality' centres upon success. It may be that European cultures are somewhat ahead of American culture in their understanding of the profound and permeating significance of failure, and that Americans are only in the process of catching up with them. In contrast, it may be that Americans are somewhat more sensitive than Europeans to the 'failure of success', and that we recognize the manner in which continued success, no less than failure, may also induce tensions that promote role and value changes.

Be that as it may, I suspect that Boalt's theory is of particular value to American social scientists because it dwells in a personal reality that makes failure central, that sees the tragic component in science as well as elsewhere, that accepts the necessity of paying for one's achievements and successes with deficiencies and failures elsewhere, that sees scientific values not as a harmoniously integrated system but as heteronomous and, indeed, as conflicting. For instance, Boalt notes that what he calls the 'news value', in other words the originality of a scientific research, is a central value in the culture of science. He notes, therefore, the possibility that scientists seeking to establish their originality and priority may press their work forward rapidly, to publish before others do, even at the sacrifice of certain other scientific values. Boalt notes, however, that it is not only originality but replication also that is a value of science and he observes that these two values conflict; since a replication cannot be original, there is a tendency not to use one's scarce time in producing replications. Indeed, he observes with characteristic paradox that replications are so rare that they might actually be regarded as a form of originality!

Because of his sensitivity to these conflicts and to the tragic dimension more generally, Boalt provides a welcome contrast to those sociologists of science who tend to focus on the manner in which the various components of science are harmoniously integrated, who assume that there is an identity between the fate of science and the fate of individual scientists, and who miss the manner in which the milestones of science are the tombstones of individual scientists.

To what is this tragic component in science due? Is it the inevitable outcome of an insurmountable gap between science's great eternal demands and the inevitably limited, smaller talents of individual men? I think not. It is, I believe, only insofar as men cleave compulsively to a culturally prescribed and historically transient definition of what they should be doing scientifically, and only where conformity to these demands is viewed as an absolute moral requirement apart from their own varying individual impulses and talents, that they develop the sense of tragic incompleteness. It is only when men fall spellbound to the demands of cultural prescription, but fail to heed their own inner impulses, to know their own special bents or aptitudes, and fail to grasp that there are many valuable ways they can live and contribute as scientists – and not only one culture-prescribed way – that their lives must be tragic. Men may escape tragedy when they recognize that they need not allow themselves to be assimilated to their cultural masks; when they insist on the difference between themselves and their roles; when they insist that it is they who are the measure, and they who do the measuring – one man with and one against the others – and not one man against the standards of culture and the requirements of roles.

To do this, men must accept their own unique talents and varying ambitions as authentic. If they find these are distant from the requirements of their culture and role, they should, at least, face up if not surrender to the difference; they must consider the possibility that their personal impulses and special talents have as much right to be heard as the cultural norms, while all the while accepting the possibility that they may simply be in the wrong business. When ordinary men can do this they need not be inescapably burdened by a sense of their own failure and inadequacy. When great men can do this they will no longer need tacitly to project an inflated image of themselves as gods. When either ordinary or great men can do this, both will recognize the value of their human contribution as sufficient to justify their lives.

Men surmount tragedy, then, when they use themselves up

fully; when they use what they have and what they are, whatever they are, and wherever they find themselves, whether this requires them to ignore certain cultural prescriptions or to behave in innovating ways that are uninvited by their roles. The tragic sense does not derive from men's feeling that they must always be less than history and culture demand; it derives, rather, from the sense that they have been less than they needed to be, that they have needlessly betrayed themselves, needlessly forgone fulfilments that would have injured no one – needlessly wasted the possibilities of their lives.

The sociological enterprise, like others, becomes edged with a tragic sense, I suspect, precisely because in confining work to the requirements of a demanding and unfulfillable paradigm, sociologists are not using themselves up in their work but are, indeed, sacrificing unexpressed parts of themselves – their playful impulses, their unverified hunches, and speculative imagination – in a wager that this sacrifice is 'best for science'. Whether this is really so, they cannot confirm; but they often need no further confirmation of the pain that this self-confinement causes them.

The more that sociologists commit themselves to a high-science model the more they flirt with this most untestable of metaphysics. My point, of course, is not that there can be a sociology without such a metaphysical wager but, rather, that various wagers are possible. The question is not whether the sociologist must make a bet, but on what. He can bet that the paradigm or model of science presently prescribed is right and trustworthy, and that his own errant impulses are not. In short, he can bet against himself. He can also bet on himself; that is, he can trust his own individuating impulses, unique aptitudes, and all the fainter powers of apprehension – as Gilbert Murray called them – with which these endow him. To say that the sociologist need not make only one kind of bet is not, of course, to say that the number of bets he can make is unlimited. If the basic problem is how to link himself as a person with the requirements of his role as a sociologist there would seem to be, for the sociologists as others, a limited number of solutions.

The culturally standardized role of the sociologist, like any other social role, can be thought of as a 'bridge' – both facilitating and limiting certain tasks, enabling men to 'overcome' certain obstacles, and to get to the 'other side'. But social roles are always unfinished bridges and invariably incomplete; they reach out only part way across the void. It is their incompleteness that is the eternal problem, and thus even those who love and respect the bridge cannot entirely rely upon it to get them safely across.

There are a limited number of attitudes one can adopt toward this situation. For example, some men say: So be it; if this is the way of bridges then we must learn to live with them as they are. They will parade back and forth along the completed section of the bridge, sometimes dangling their feet over the unfinished edge, looking down. Other men say: We must be grateful for whatever we have and, repaying those who built it, we must continue working, each adding his own little plank to the unfinished end; occasionally resting at the edge, they may dangle their feet over it. In both cases, one is bound to have something of a tragic sense, a sad whimsical wish that things were not like that.

But there is another possibility. One thing is certain, a man might feel: the building of this bridge will never be completed, but my life will surely have its end. A man might therefore risk a running leap from the unfinished edge to the shore that he thinks he sees ahead. Perhaps he has seen right and has estimated his own powers correctly. In which event, applause. Perhaps he has badly miscalculated on both counts. In which event, a certain dampness sets in. Maybe he can swim back to safety, even if somewhat less than applauded. In any event, he has found out how far he can see and how well he can jump. Even if he is never heard from again, perhaps those who are still dawdling at the edge will learn something useful.

Romanticism and Classicism:
Deep Structures in Social Science

The industrialization of nineteenth-century Europe was uneven, and this meant that the eastward parts of Europe, which underwent industrialization somewhat later, had to cope with two tasks simultaneously: on the one hand, they had all the problems intrinsic to their own emerging industrialization; on the other, they also had to formulate a position about the industrialization and the rise of the middle class that had appeared earlier in the West. The Germans, therefore, were influenced not only by their own local situation, but were also affected by the earlier experience of the middle classes in *France*. The French experience was widely watched and intensively analysed by the Germans, and it became a pivot around which the Germans developed a reaction to their own cultural situation.

Following the French Revolution, the still nascent middle classes in Germany thus faced two problems at once. First, they sought to modify the social reality of German society and to create a new conception of the emerging social order more fully consistent with their own distinctive interests and assumptions. Secondly, however, many were also disposed to reject the new order that revolutionary France had offered Europe. Germany, then, faced the problem of being unable to live with the old feudal order and of being unable to accept the most visible alternative presented by the French.[1] The subsequent development of German modernization was to be shaped profoundly by its effort to cope with this quandary.

Romanticism as a Movement for Cultural Revitalization

Caught within this dilemma, German intellectuals were restive but uncertain of their direction. In the first quarter of the nineteenth century, and perhaps particularly before the War of Liberation, they were therefore unable to mount an offensive against their own 'old régime', or to give full support to the emerging new order. Thus, even though change was felt to be necessary, politics and a political solution were then widely experienced as impossible. Many educated Germans of that period turned therefore to the sphere of culture, to the achievements of intellect and art that were more individually controllable: they fostered a movement for cultural revitalization instead of a political revolution. Unable to revolutionize society, German intellectuals sought to revolutionize culture. As Madame de Staël remarked,[2] it was not difficult to find Germans who composed the most comprehensive philosophical systems, but it was almost impossible to find Germans who wrote on politics.

Seeking to respond to the German problem while rejecting the French solution, living in a society where feudalism was still relatively strong although visibly decaying, *and* where the middle classes were still weak although manifestly emerging, certain German intellectuals developed an especially uninhibited expression of the powerful movement for cultural revitalization which they called Romanticism.[3] This social movement had three main cultural expressions: first, the philosophical idealism of Kant, Hegel, Schelling and Fichte; secondly, *historismus* and the new historiography; and third and finally, there was a revolution in art, aesthetics and literary criticism. Each of these parameters conditioned the others and all were institutionally consolidated within the German university; together they became the core culture of the German Mandarins.

Dissatisfied with the condition of Germany, yet unable to accept the future offered by the French, the German Romantics sought to devise an alternative image of the social order that would be neither bourgeois nor feudal, or would at least combine elements of the two. Unable to move forward to the future or to accept the present, the German Romantic image of an alternative social order could be located only in the past, in myth and history. They immersed themselves in the past, however, and to a great extent they *knew* they did so, in order that they might more clearly distinguish the characteristics of the new *present* within which they lived and to gain perspective on it.

The time orientations of the early nineteenth century and, in particular, of the 'systematic' (i.e., post-*Sturm und Drang*) German Romanticists, the Berlin–Jena School, are implicit in the new concepts with which they characterized historical European cultures. Specifically, toward the end of the eighteenth and the beginning of the nineteenth centuries, and in *an effort to clarify the nature of the 'modern'*, August and Friedrich Schlegel[4] advanced a distinction between 'Classical' and 'Romantic' cultures, and came to eulogize the latter as the truly modern. Since, however, the Schlegels regarded Romantic culture as distinctively Christian in character, they therefore conceived themselves as living with an encompassing time-unit that included the Middle Ages, and thus also the literature of the Renaissance and of the Elizabethan periods.

In the Romantic view, therefore, the 'modern' was not marked by the eruption of science and of rationalism but, rather, by certain innovations in the arts and especially in literary culture. This distinction between the Romantic and the Classical, with its focus on artistic and religious components, thus had the effect of redefining the place of science in modern life, and therefore it also redefined the nature of the modern itself. Specifically, it *diminished* the significance that the French had attributed to science as the characterizing innovation of the modern epoch. Conversely, we might say that it was out of an anterior impulse to diminish the value attributed to a reifying science that the 'modern' and the 'Romantic' came to be defined in this particular manner. Nineteenth-century Romanticism thus rejected the specifically French Enlightenment conception of the modern as centred on reason/science/technology. Moreover, for them the modern was not therefore critical of or in opposition to religion. In effect, the Romantics were searching for a way to be modern without having to reject religion and the values they associated with religion.[5]

While the distinction between the Classical and the Romantic initially aimed at discerning the differences between the modern and the ancient, it ended by fusing the then contemporaneous present with the Middle Ages, and by bidding the modern to seek a similar glory. Through their idealization of the Middle Ages, the Romantics could establish a standpoint for criticism of the new German present and, at the same time, they could crystallize an image of a social order that was obviously critical of the French alternative. The distinction between the Romantic and the Classical thereby enabled German Romantics simultaneously to reject both the political backwardness of the German present and the 'irreligion' of the French future.

The German Romantics could now have the best of both possible worlds: linking the modern to the past, they could extol the achievements of German culture, while at the same time calling for its improvement. They could now reject the French alternative and still acknowledge that the German present needed to be transcended. They could pursue 'development' without endorsing 'progress'. They could look forward to renewed greatness without neglecting the past or holding it in contempt.

Moreover, they could also maintain that the mechanism of this development was already in hand. That is, they did not need to wait for a political re-ordering of the social world, for the necessary mechanism was already in existence. This mechanism was a kind of puissant spirituality; it was the *Geist* that was also *Macht*. The Romantics, then, were the intellectual shamans that sought to summon the German *Geist* to find a distinctive path to the revitalization of German culture.

Romanticism, then, was not only a philosophical and aesthetic doctrine; it was also a social movement.[6] It was a movement for the revitalization of German, and indeed of all, culture in post-revolutionary Europe. In the German case, with its special concern for autonomy from French culture, this movement for cultural revitalization took strongly 'nativistic' or nationalistic forms; and in its emphasis upon the value and depth of the German historical past, it also took strongly 'revivalistic' forms.

Despite this, the Romantic movement cannot be understood simply as an expression of traditionalism and, on the contrary, it had certain strongly *anti*-traditionalistic emphases. For Romanticism was, in another of its aspects, a revolt of intellectual and artistic élites against their own cultural establishments, and against the standards that had been conventionally used to govern their own specialized spheres of cultural activity. Thus, if the *Enlightenment* was the intellectual's critique of society, of religion and of politics, Romanticism was the revolt of an intellectual and an artistic élite against its own internal subculture. In this degree, then, Romanticism was the substitution of aesthetics for politics, of cultural criticism for social criticism; and it was a demand for artistic freedom in place of political freedom.

Romantic Perspectives and Doctrines

Perhaps the most general aspect of Romantic anti-traditionalism was its revolt against the conception that art should be governed by reason, i.e., by a disciplined conformity to certain received and impersonal rules. Romanticism was thus free enterprise in art and literature. It was the artistic equivalent of the bourgeois doctrine of *laissez faire*.

At the spearhead of the Romantics' attack there was a doctrine of unfettered aesthetic individualism that took the form of a polemic against the dominant aesthetic doctrines of Classicism: the unities of time and place; the universality and permanence of the truly beautiful; the objectivity of taste; conformity to the semblances of probability, and to the requirements of decorum; and the avoidance of mixed genres, styles or tones and moods.

The Romantics rebelled on every front against the once-honoured conventions of the artistic community and its classical tradition: they welcomed a *mélange* of times, tones, moods and places in one artistic product, counterposing it to the classical doctrine of the unities; they affirmed the value of the contingent, the changing and the local, counterposing this to the doctrines of universality and permanence; they prized inward conviction, counterposing it to judgements oriented to externalized and objectified standards; they delighted in the exotic, deviant or special case, counterposing these to the probable or average case; they portrayed the indecorous as a way of conferring reality on an individuality that was to be defined by its departure from, rather than its conformity with, social convention.

As against the established tradition of conveying meaning as some kind of unity, the Romantics countered by affirming the reality of plurality. The world was seen as a mosaic, each tile of which had some unique reality or value in itself. The whole itself was often seen, however, not as a harmonious and integrated entity, but as an incongruous assemblage and as a tensionful conjunction of parts. The Romantic concern with the 'grotesque'[7] was a concern with a conjunction of parts perceived as incongruous and ominous. Romanticism rejected received artistic rules and conventional aesthetic doctrines, and, instead, sought a liberation of the imagination and a mobilization of sentiment to provide the vision and the energy to carry artistic work forward.

The Romantics lived in a twilight world of transition, between an unsatisfactory present and an unworkable past, between decaying feudal tradition and emerging bourgeois reform. Living in a world in which the conventional social maps had lost their effectiveness, but in which acceptable new ones had not yet been formulated, it was to the individual self as the maker of meanings that they turned rather than to the traditional rules. Living in a world where received cultural categories and conventional social identities no longer made social reality meaningful, they came to see reality as possessed of intrinsic vagueness. They saw objects as blending into one another, rather than as well demarcated by clear-cut boundaries. They therefore felt that those who sought to conquer truth by the careful dissections of analytic reason were engaged in a vivisection that could only destroy living reality.

The Romantics experienced the object world as no longer isomorphic with the neat categories wrought by the classical mind. It was therefore characteristic of Romantic poetry that it commonly loved the imagery of twilight, of a boundary-dissolving moonlight, or of the fleeting moments before dawn, rather than the imagery of the clear, boundary-sharpening light of the classical mind. It was thus that the casual and the irregular, or the wild and the disorderly in nature, was prized by the Romantic aesthetic – particularly if it could be viewed from some safe distance. In this, the Romantics were not above mixing feudal heroics with a dash of bourgeois prudence.

In this twilight social world, a new structure of sentiments was being activated to which the Classical–Aristotelian logic – in which an object was either 'A' or 'not-A' – was no longer felt to correspond. In this breach between the new sentiments and the inadequate old languages provided by classical logic and convention, the Romanticists – and perhaps especially those of the earlier *Sturm und Drang* period – could, at first, only *affirm* dogmatically the truth of their new vision. They could only polemically insist on the vitality and reality of their own inner sentiments – the 'reasons of the heart' – since they at first lacked the rationale of a new language or a new logic.

In the prefigurings of Romanticism, as in the *Sturm und Drang* school, the gap between the new sentiments and a way to talk about them was greatest. The next generation of Romanticists may be called the 'systematic Romantics', however, precisely because they did create new languages, new conceptual schema and a new set of theories to express and communicate their sentiments. The Schlegel brothers' very distinction between the Classical and Romantic signified an emerging new language and contributed to a growing self-awareness.

The Romantic breakthrough to a new language of the sentiments and of the imagination took several discernible forms. Among its earliest intellectual achievements were important new aesthetic doctrines, particularly doctrines stressing the importance of symbolism, irony and the grotesque. Another major language breakthrough occurred with the development of a non-Aristotelian logic. This first developed from a more diffuse notion of a 'logic of polarities' into the systematic Hegelian dialectic of the self or *Geist*, which was then 'stood upon its feet' and was developed in turn by Marx into a materialist dialectic of society.

In the twentieth century there emerged, with Freudianism, a systematic psychology of the irrational sentiments. The importance attributed by the Freudians to the unconscious, as well as the assumption that a 'cure' requires an awareness of the hitherto unconscious and its reintegration into the consciousness, are rooted in the Romantic paradigm fundamental to German idealism. The latter's basic problematic revolves on the relationship between a knowing 'Subject' and a known

'Object', and it regarded this very distinction as a false consciousness of the Subject, since the Object, rather than being that which was *not* the Subject, was actually unconsciously created by it. Idealism premised that human Emancipation entailed the Subject's achievement of awareness about its own hitherto unconscious role in shaping the Object, its discovery of *itself* in the Object-other. In short, German idealism clearly foreshadowed Freudianism's concept of the unconsciousness as well as its conception of a therapy.

In contrast to the French revolutionaries, who had largely defeated the old régime with its own cognitive weapons, it remained for the Romantics to begin the serious and systematic reconstruction of the language and images used for talking about man and society. It remained for them to take as central the language of sentiment; although the language of the sentiments was already emerging in France, the *philosophes* had largely continued to employ the rhetoric of Reason during the Enlightenment epoch. Even later, it is perfectly plain from the National Assembly's 'Declaration of the Rights of Man and Citizen' that the public discourse of the Revolution remained far closer, in its images of man and society, to the classical tradition with its conception of eternal natural reason and of unchanging natural law, than it was to the emerging Romantic Age.

The 'modern' only begins to manifest itself when, in answer to the question, 'What is distinctively human?', Romanticism replies not by referring to man's eternal capacity for reason and universal rationality, but, instead, to his creative originality, to his individuated capacity to feel and to dream uniquely. The modern begins to emerge when man is seen, not merely as a creature that can *discover* the world, but also as one who can *create* new meanings and values, and can thus change himself and fundamentally transform his world, rather than unearth, recover or 'mirror' an essentially unchanging world order.

The thing to see is that Romanticism was not only an aesthetic, but that it was a many-faceted and enduring social movement. It was a movement for the revitalization of European culture in all of its manifestations – artistic, literary, philosophical, religious and even scientific.

Faced with a changing social reality, in which the social structure to be understood as well as the traditional ways of understanding it were both dissolving simultaneously, and faced with the collapse of the conventional hierarchies of value, the Romantics sought to rescue a world of meaning by 'romanticizing'. Which means: by endowing the ordinary, everyday world with the pathos of the extraordinary – by 'idealizing' mundane reality. The 'ordinary', the everyday, the lowly, the fleshly and the deviant were to be rescued by viewing them from a perspective that endowed them with new and enhanced value, rather than being routinized, ignored or thingafied. As Novalis said, to romanticize was to see the infinite in the finite – the universe in the grain of sand, in Blake's terms. It was to gaze deeply into the 'blue flower' and to see eternity in it.

There were no longer things that were inherently lowly but only pedestrian *perspectives* on the world. The 'Classical' view of the world had generated excluded enclaves of underprivileged reality, whose neglect it had no hesitation in justifying. The Romantic view believed that the insignificance of things was born of a failure of imagination: reality was now democratized.

Above all, Romanticism rejected bourgeois, vulgar materialism's tendency to 'deaden' the universe and men with it. In the words of Georg Lukács, Romanticism was a rejection of 'reification'[8] and, we might add, it expressed a refusal to equate modernity with reification. Romanticism sought a path to a *non*-reifying modernism. If bourgeois reification transformed men into inanimate objects, no different from other passive 'things', Romanticism resonated with an animism or Pantheism that sought to transform even inanimate objects by a de-thingafying 'spiritualization'. To 'romanticize' was thus to endow those parts of the world that had been exposed to a deadening reification with a new enlivening by insisting that *all* things were *loci* of *self*-movement, of potency, and of value. To this extent, Romanticism was profoundly anti-mechanical and *anti*-bourgeois; it was thus by no means exclusively 'reactionary', despite its sponsorship by aristocratic and other Old Régime élites and even though at first expressive of their defensive manoeuvres against the emerging bourgeoisie.

It is clear, then, that our interpretation of Romanticism

differs from that of Karl Mannheim, who tended (as did the *later* Lukács) to over-emphasize Romanticism's backward-looking conservatism.[9] Insofar as Romanticism rejects a reification of men and provides a basis for a critique of reification, insofar as it expresses a resistance to historically obsolescent and unnecessary rules or limits, then Romanticism is indeed an *emancipatory* standpoint. It provides leverage for the great breakthrough into a *Subject*-sensitive modernism, as distinct from the *Objectivistic* modernism of the Enlightenment which sought to free reason from superstition that it might better 'mirror' the world. However, insofar as Romanticism seeks to *replace* (rather than complement) Enlightenment objectivism with subject-sensitive modernism, then the latter becomes a *subjectivism* vulnerable to irrationalism and to anti-intellectualism.

All this, by way only of the faintest outline of Romanticism. It is all that space will permit here. This preface completed, we now turn to the relationship between Romanticism and the social sciences.

Positivism and Romanticism in France

Both sociology in France and anthropology in Germany and England, emerged as elements in a Romantically-tinged, European-wide movement for cultural revitalization.

F. M. H. Markham observes that 'in 1830 there was the first performance of Victor Hugo's *Hernani*: in 1831, that of Hector Berlioz' *Symphonie Fantastique*. Paris experienced an orgy of grandiose and romantic ideas.' Leaving aside Markham's Goethian inclination to see Romanticism as a pathology, he is quite correct in noting that the Saint-Simonians, 'like the rest of their generation . . . were intoxicated by the . . . romantic movement . . .'[10] Henri Lefebvre is also correct in characterizing Saint-Simon as belonging to the 'left wing of romanticism'.[11] In a similar vein, we might distinguish Comte from Saint-Simon by conceiving of the former as belonging to the 'right wing' of Romanticism. In what follows, however, I want to focus not on their differential politics but on certain common elements in their Romanticism.

Like the German Romantics, French positivism – particularly in its Comtian version – held constitution-making in contempt. It stressed the weakness of reason and the power of sentiment, and, parenthetically, it thus agreed with the Schlegels and other Romantics on the heightened significance to be accorded women as the alleged bearers and guardians of sentiment. In the modern era, 'Women's Liberation' begins with the Romantics. In their conceptions of man and society, both German Romantics and French positivists thus agreed on the unique value of sentiment, as well as on the vulnerability and limitations of reason.

Both also looked to the past for their models of a hierarchical and coherent society. The French positivists, however, were more ambivalent in their attitudes toward the past, since, after all, they, unlike the Germans, lived in a society in which the middle classes had succeeded in making a revolution, even if this was stalemated and threatened during the Restoration. The French positivists thus created a *new* religion of humanity rather than returning, as did some of the German Romanticists, to the venerable Mother Church.

Still, France under the Restoration was a stalemate society in which the middle classes could not go forward, while the returned Royalists could not go back. Saint-Simon and Comte responded to this by creating positivism as a fusion of religion and of science. They wanted to be modern without rejecting religion. The positivists' new 'religion of humanity' was patently such a patchwork compromise; its new priests would be scientists, but its scientists would also be priests. And it aimed at progress, no less than order and love. French positivism was, thus, in the beginning a characteristically Romantic compromise between older images of hierarchical order and the new bourgeois order, spurred on by the conflicts of the Restoration, but subject to the more powerful modernizing influences of a French middle class that was far stronger than the German.

It would be utterly wrong, then, to think of positivism and Romanticism as two entirely separate and altogether opposing responses to the crisis of their time. Both, for example, sought to find new bases for social norms and authority, to replace those of their discredited old régimes. The positivists sought to find this new authority in science; for all their critique of the Enlightenment, they carried forward the Enlightenment's effort to emancipate men from reason-shackling superstitions, and it is this which lurked behind their rejection of the non-empirical and metaphysical. The Romanticists also sought a new basis for crumbling authority, but they sought it in the certitudes of inner feeling and artistic imagination.

Both the positivists and Romanticists wanted to be modern without relinquishing religion. The positivists identified the modern with the scientific and they sought to accommodate religion to science by creating a new religion of humanity. The Romanticists identified the modern with the emancipation of the sentiments or feeling, not of reason or science, and defined sentiment as near the core of religion. That Romanticism and positivism were not altogether exclusive may be seen even on the grossest level. Recall that the father of positivism, Saint-Simon himself, made the 'grand' gesture of offering to marry Madame de Staël, the propagandist and interpreter of German Romanticism. Nor would it be amiss to remember Saint-Simon's less illustrious followers, Enfantin and Bazard, whose epistemology stressed the importance of intuition, hypothesis and of the genius that produces these; or Saint-Simonism's search for *la femme libre*, and its agonizing over the question of 'free love'. Initially, French positivism was a *blend* of science and of Romanticism; it was an intellectual marriage that Saint-Simon consummated without the benefit of de Staël's consent. It was a blend, however, in which the scientific element was the more focal and dominant. In short, what positivism was in the beginning, and the colourless enterprise that it later evolved into, are two different things.

In its initial structure, French positivism was a social movement based upon and attractive to the *new* professions – engineering, medicine and science – while German Romanticism was at first largely created by artists and by humanistic scholars of an *older* vintage. Positivism was from the very beginning intricately linked to the emerging new *infra*structure – to the new industrial society whose prophet Saint-Simon was. Romanticism, however, was from the very beginning the vocalized *ressentiment* of those in a newly devalued *super*structure.

Positivism, in short, was a social movement led by a new technological élite whom the new industrialism had almost immediately advantaged, who had better prospects in bourgeois society, and who could, therefore, be more easily integrated into it. Romanticism, however, was the product of older, culture-creating élites – artists, dramatists, poets, musicians – who at first were squeezed aside and had no place in the new world of business, industry, and science, and who would not be needed widely in this new world until the media of mass communication developed.

But if positivism was a compromise between science and Romanticism, it was a compromise in which its *methodology* was developed under the hegemony of a natural science model, and in which natural science methods became in time progressively dominant. So far as the later development of Western sociology is concerned, the positivists' 'religion of humanity' was defrocked and was gradually secularized as a tool of the Welfare State. The most Romantic and religious components of positivism were thus increasingly subordinated. This is not to say, however, that they disappeared altogether, but only that they were ultimately suppressed or repressed. In other words, the Romantic and religious components in academic sociology lost out as elements in the *focal* awareness of its practitioners; but they did not disappear, as the work of Robert Friedrichs makes clear.[12]

German Social Sciences and Romanticism

In Germany, however, something more nearly like the opposite process occurred. That is, the German social sciences also developed out of a dialectic between Romanticism and science; but here, in Germany, the Romantic component was far more influential than in Western Europe, even if not unchallenged. The power of the Romantic component in Germany may be appraised if it is remembered that the German social sciences matured in the shadow of the triumphant natural sciences in Germany, with their very great public and university prestige. Yet, despite this, the German social sciences were not dominated by a natural science model.

The Romantic influence on German social science was both manifested in and preserved by the German development of a systematic distinction between the human or cultural sciences, on the one hand, and the natural sciences, on the other hand. This distinction was consonant with another that had been persistently produced by German social scientists, that between 'culture' a nd'civilization'. And this, in *its* turn, also resonated a still deeper distinction in German culture between *Geist* and *Natur*.

The distinction between *Geisteswissenschaften* and *Naturwissenschaften* remains important to the contemporary School of Critical Theory at Frankfurt. In *one* of its basic dimensions, Critical Theory is surely rooted in a hermeneutics that seeks to formulate 'interpretations' that enhance 'understanding' of social worlds, rather than to develop 'laws' that 'explain' phenomena. And there is little question but that hermeneutics' roots in the modern era are traceable to Romanticism. Indeed, we have it on the authority of the leading modern philosopher of hermeneutics, Hans Georg Gadamer, that 'hermeneutics came to flower in the Romantic era . . .'[13] It did so, it might be added, most specifically in the work of the theologian Friedrich Schleiermacher,[14] who was associated with the Schlegels and the Berlin–Jena Romanticists.

In discussing recent developments in the Critical School, it is quite obvious that many Europeans, whether positivists or hermeneuticists, share an understanding of Critical Theory's relation to Romanticism. Thus Gadamer says of Jürgen Habermas' position: 'I believe this is pure romanticism, and such romanticism creates an artistic abyss between tradition and the reflection which is grounded in historical consciousness.'[15] (It is characteristic that Gadamer uses 'romantic' as a dyslogism, despite his own indebtedness to it; ever since Hegel, romantics have expressed their sense of distance from others by condemning them as 'romantics'.) This judgement on Critical Theory is shared by Ernst Topitsch, although his own neo-positivism is far removed from Gadamer's Heidegerrian phenomenology. Topitsch holds (according to Paul Lorenzen) that 'All Marxists and neo-Hegelians, including the dialectical philosophers and sociologists of the Frankfurt School . . . belong to this group of left Romantics.'[16]

If Critical Theory and hermeneutics are in part rooted in Romanticism, they are only the most recent expression of the continuing *creativity* of that infrastructure for social theory. Earlier, the continuing efforts of German social science to work out the relationship between Romanticism and science had manifested itself in the sociology of Max Weber and, still earlier, had found a powerful expression in the work of Karl Marx.

Karl Marx

In this connection, we may be reminded of Marx's aphorism that 'philosophy is the head of emancipation, and the proletariat is the heart'. Certainly, for Marx, reason alone could not liberate the world or the proletariat; reason had to be embodied in and liberated by a theory-correcting *praxis*. For Marx, praxis was not simply a scientific experiment to be conducted in the laboratory. It was a commitment of the whole man, to be expressed in the world and in the course of his everyday life. It was a commitment of his passions as well as of his cognitive faculties, to change the world and, through this, to change himself.

Marx's abiding aim to transcend 'alienation' is a characteristically Romantic effort to mend the split *between* and *within* men, and to reunite sensuous man with rational man. In the end, Marx wanted a society in which *all* men's faculties and senses – and not only his intellect – would find a home. Marx, therefore, counterposed to the Socratic rule – one man, one task – and to medieval organicism, the new vision of a society in which one man could play *many* parts, not simply during his lifetime, but even during a single day, uniting manual and intellectual, aesthetic and cognitive activities.

Like the Romantics, Marx also stressed a pluralism of perspectives. *Un*like them, however, he situated this pluralism not in the will or imagination of the individual, but rather in the social location of the individual's group or class. At the same time, however, Marx also sought a universalistic transcendence of pluralism by conceiving of certain social perspectives as entailing a 'false consciousness'. In short, Marx's pluralism of perspectives was counterbalanced by the universalism of human reason.

The very concept of a 'capitalist society', that we owe to Marx, bears witness to his abiding effort to transcend the conflict between Romantic and Classical perspectives. For, in insisting that capitalism was only one *type* of society, Marx is here attempting to combine the Romantics' concern with concrete *uniqueness* and historical individuality with the Classical concern for abstracted universals. Marx's emphasis on *types* of societies is in the nature of a half-way house between the Classical abstraction and the Romantic concrete.

Again, for Marx like the Romantics, the future remains to some degree an emergent: its full character cannot be seen or predicted except insofar as one approaches it. It is therefore useless to attempt to predict it in blueprinted detail. Thus, Marx polemicizes against the French socialists, whom he terms 'utopians', and rejects the idea of blueprinting the future. This is consonant with the Romantic component in Marx's politics which insists that political outcomes depend on struggle, on individual commitment and effort, as well as on class solidarity and revolutionary will.

On the other hand, there is also the Classical component in Marx's theory and politics that calls for patient waiting until there is a maturation of the appropriate *objective* conditions for social change. From *this* perspective, then, the revolution for Marx is not waiting in the wings of history, ready to be ushered in at any time through a merely wilful *coup d'état*. Here, then, there is a *rejection* of political Romanticism. Since Marx's time, the history of Marxism has been a cyclical oscillation between these two versions of politics, but this oscillation occurs around a long-range *trend* toward an increasingly Romantic politics. This Romantic upsurge in Marxism begins with the Leninist breakthrough in Russia,[17] and continues today in the still more Romantic strategies of Mao and Ché Guevara. Our discussion of 'The Two Marxisms' and of 'The Red Guard' will develop this further.

When Marx spoke of the 'contradictions of capitalism', he was giving voice to an essentially Romantic sense of the grotesqueness of modern life, in which incongruous cultural elements cohabit, in which things give birth to their very opposites, in which death comes with life, and things bear the 'seeds of their own destruction'. Here we might note the remark by that authentic fountainhead of Romanticism, Friedrich Schlegel, who observed that 'States disappear; the most powerful often bear within themselves, from their very origin, the germ of their own decay.'[18] In this vein, Marx's critique of modern science and technology sees their development as leading to increased misery, suffering, unemployment, and to the reserve army of the unemployed. Under the conditions of a capitalist society, science and technology do not liberate man, says Marx, but rather enslave him, and at the height of these technological triumphs man becomes a tool of his machines. Man becomes a marionette, while the marionettes take on life. Here, Marx is in the tradition of the Romantic enjoyment of the grotesque. Yet something more is involved, for he also sees this grotesque condition from a Hegelian perspective, as something that will give rise to its own negation, and whose own tensions guarantee an ultimate transcendence by a more harmonious order.

In discussing Marx's relation to Romanticism, I have not intended to say and I have not said that he was 'a Romantic'. I have, however, intended to show that there were important *components* of Romanticism in his thought[19] and to suggest that if Marxism is to be understood as a whole, then these components must be firmly grasped. It is not amiss to notice that Marx was actually a student of August Schlegel at the University of Bonn, although one should not make too much of this in understanding the *sources* of Marx's Romanticism. Marx is a crucial episode in the effort to accommodate Romanticism and science within the framework of a *social* theory. Essentially similar effort had been earlier made within the framework of German philosophy, where the culminating formulation had been Hegel's. It was Marx's historical task to formulate the Hegelian synthesis in the idiom of a political economy rather than that of academic philosophy.

On those few occasions that Marx mentions Romanticism directly, there is no doubt that his comments are negative. (This also seems to be true of Nietzsche!) But such negative remarks usually focus on Romanticism as the ideology of the German monarchy, as something reactionary and ineffectual.

Marx's critique of 'true' socialism, of its stress on the role of sentiment as a source of social change, converges with his critique of Romanticism as ineffectual. Here Marx's rejection of the sentimentality and political ineffectuality of Romanticism is, in one way, a critique of Romanticism's *feminine* component. (There is little question but that Romanticism placed a particularly *high* value on what were *then* culturally defined as feminine qualities – sentimentality, affective expressivity – and, indeed, was associated with earliest efforts at the liberation of women from male-dominated sexual standards, in the family and in private life generally.) In viewing the Romanticism of his period as lacking in resoluteness and 'hardness', Marx is in effect rejecting a feminized Romanticism. Conversely, Marx's mission, we might say, was not to reject but to 'masculinize' Romanticism; he adopts much the same masculinizing mission toward historical Romanticism as Max Weber and Nietzsche later did, and Hegel earlier had.

Hegel's relation to Romanticism has much in common with Marx's. Hegel, like Marx, took the Romantics to task, criticizing their effusive expressivity, their lack of a hard-edged clarity and rigorous system, and sought to make philosophy more scientifically serious. Like the Romantics, however, Hegel held that men never achieve anything great without passion, that history develops through struggle and conflict, and, as epitomized by his master-bondsman paradigm, is characterized by ironic reversals. The most fundamentally Romantic aspect of Hegelianism is that what the Hegelian Subject at last discovers in the Object-other is *himself*.

Max Weber

The effort of German social science to accommodate Romanticism and science to one another is renewed and brought to a new development in the sociology of Max Weber.[20] As Weber conceived it, social science was far from the generalizing, universalizing and externalizing social science formulated in the tradition of Comteian Positivism. Rather than stressing its cultural autonomy, Weber's social science conceived of social science as changing, both in fact and with propriety, as historical problems themselves changed. Its starting point was the cultural-value interest of the social scientist and not necessarily a purely technical hypothesis. Weber's social science was thus conceived as responsive to changing cultural perspectives, and thus as a science to which 'eternal youth was granted', rather than as one that grew progressively and continuously with age.

Weber's social science focused on understanding individual events and historically located entities, conceived in their uniquely given individuality, rather than searching for universal generalizations about classes of units or events. For all its comparative method, Weber's concern was primarily with the unique development and destiny of Europe. And it was a comparative method that was to proceed with the use of 'ideal types' that focused on extreme cases rather than on the *average* case, and which were formulated intuitively, rather than through statistical induction.

Such a manifestly Romantic conception of social science also stressed the significance of *verstehen*, of intuition and insight, through which the 'inwardness' of other men would be apprehended, and the importance of the 'mental experiment', through which the consequences of changes in values, ideas, and meanings would be gauged. In other words, Weber's focus was typically Romantic both in its ultimate objective as well as in its methodology.

Here, then, there was no image of the social scientist as a bloodless intellect, isolated from his culture and operating primarily with well-codified procedural rules. Here there was no conception of the social scientist painstakingly moulding his little brick, and modestly adding it to the growing wall of science. Instead of conceiving of the social scientist as a kind of bricklayer, the Weberian image is much more heroic. There is an image of the dedicated scholar who must find his lonely way without well-charted rules; who must rely on his own inner and very personal resources of empathy and intuition; there is an image of a man whose own unrelenting self-discipline sacrifices his other, science-irrelevant passions or political ambitions to his calling and to his culture. This, then, is the protean and recurrent image of the German scholar, where scholarly work is conceived as a form of suffering and entails the 'tormented surmounting of self'.

The creation of a social science is, in Weber's view, seen as contingent ultimately on the exertion of essentially *personal* powers rather than professional skills. Its focal concern is on the quality of a man's inwardness, his sense of responsibility, individual intuition and empathy, rather than on the cumulative resources of the scientific community outside of himself. The Weberian conception of social science thus entailed a systematic application of Romantic premises.

Weber's theory of plural perspectives, of plural values and plural ideal types, comes down to the Romantic assumption that each man makes his own world and fights for it, rather than searching for a more universal map. The unity of the world is, in characteristically Romantic style, not vouchsafed by anything external to the individual but is created, rather, by his own personal and passionate commitment.

Here there is no one overarching order or *logos* in the world that awaits discovery or in which the sociologist, like others, participates. On the contrary, the world is one of cosmic conflict among divergent, heteronomous values. It is a grotesque world, therefore, in which the highest values may and do compete with the lowest, and live alongside of them without being able to command distinction. It is a cosmos in which good and evil are intertwined, and often mutually productive of one another; in which, for example, *Geist* is defenceless without *Macht*, but is, at the same time, perpetually corrupted and threatened by it. It is a grotesque world in which there is no way to choose one's path, except to feel an inner certainty that the path is one's own.

There is nothing more deeply Nietzschean in Weber's perspective than his injunction to fight only for what is one's own. Yet, while Nietzsche was contemptuous of the German state and of German *Kultur*, Weber, in contrast, seems to have been sure that only these were his very own. He thus gave his commitment to the German nation-state as his highest value. And at this point, the tragic is grotesquely mixed with the comic. The story ends in a kind of black humour. Weber's exaltation of the local and the contingent as the very highest value is characteristically Romantic; but it is a Romanticism through which the winds of an invisible grotesqueness had begun to blow.

Toward a Sociology of Anthropological Romanticism

An analysis of the historical development of anthropology in the nineteenth century would similarly reveal the profound impress of the Romantic movement. This will be particularly clear to those familiar with the German development of the concept of 'culture' which, early in the nineteenth century, began to replace the classical doctrine of a 'uniformitarian' human nature with a view that stressed the reality and value of a cultural variability that was seen as something more than changes in external stage props or customs that overlay a constant human nature, pursuing essentially similar motives in merely different garb. Similarly, so far as nineteenth-century evolutionary theory in England is concerned, J. W. Burrow stresses that it was 'very largely . . . the outcome of a tension between English positivistic attitudes to science on the one hand and, on the other, a more profound reading of history, coming to a large extent from German romanticism . . .'[21] There is no doubt that the history of anthropology has been and can be further illuminated by exploring its connections with Romanticism.

Rather than pursuing such historical concerns here, however, I should like to change course. Having spoken about the relationship between Romanticism and the social sciences in the past century, I now want to explore briefly some of their present connections. In particular, I want to shift over to a concern with the sociology (rather than the history) of Romanticism in its bearing on the contemporary social sciences. To suggest just a few of the possibilities here, it may be useful to attempt a brief, impressionistic sketch of some of the current differences between American cultural anthropology and sociology today.

Looking at American anthropology and sociology today, not only as theoretical and research activities, but as modally differentiated occupational subcultures, it seems reasonable to suggest that anthropology, even today, still remains the more

Romantic, and sociology the more Classical, discipline. In suggesting this, let me reiterate that I mean to refer not only to differences in their articulated theories and focalized methodologies, but, also, to differences in their infrastructures: in their more inarticulate background assumptions and in their occupational subcultures. It is in this sense that I believe it may be said that anthropology is a much more Romantic discipline than sociology. For example, anthropology is based upon and also prizes a much more diffuse (less role-segmented) involvement in 'field work'. The anthropologist's is a more personal method, both in the intensity of involvement it permits and in the diversity of personal attributes that it requires the anthropologist to use.

The sociologist, however, is commonly seeking to extricate his person from his research, to deny or to reduce their connection, and to depend upon more impersonal and codified rules of work – that is, on a more formalized and externalized methodology. Anthropologists, however, are *less* likely to deny the significance *or the value* of the anthropologist's *person* for the results he produces. One way in which this is often expressed is to say that anthropology retains a greater linkage with the humanities than does sociology, and that it entails a form of creativity more nearly akin to the humanities, while sociology, in its turn, is more usually bent upon the use of a natural science model.

The very activities of the anthropologist require him to go to more exotic and romantic locales; sociology, however, remains, for the most part, a study of the familiar, the everyday, and the commonplace. The anthropologist himself is more likely to surface to public attention as a more highly individuated person, in his dress and in his manner, and he is more readily conceived there, as John Bennett puts it,[22] as a romantic hero. In contrast to the anthropologist, who is still felt to be rather more of a glamorous, adventuresome, and colourful person, the sociologist blends increasingly into the apparatus of the Welfare State and becomes one more species of staff expert and bureaucrat.

The writings of the anthropologist frequently take a less generalized form than those of the sociologist. The anthropologist is more concerned to present concrete ethnographic detail than the sociologist who, instead, is more inclined to elaborate on his abstractions. The anthropologist writes about extraordinary locales that have colour and vividness, in contrast to the sociologist's greater proclivity for the matter-of-fact and the prosaic. The anthropologist persuades and convinces his reader through his presentation of an interlocking set of mosaic details, which establish his intellectual authority because they imply his personal presence in the locale under discussion. To the anthropologist, the concrete details are often regarded as valuable in their own right; but to the sociologist the concrete details are often stage props subordinated to a more general problem, or to the development of generalizations.

In contrast to anthropology, sociology is a much more Classical discipline which remains based, tacitly if not nominally, on a uniformitarian doctrine of human nature, of a human nature which, being everywhere alike, may therefore be legitimately studied in the convenience of the sociologist's nearby laboratory or by observing his own easily accessible students. Cross-cultural study by sociologists, although increasingly regarded as an ideal, still remains relatively rare.

G. H. Mead and Chicago School Romanticism

In characterizing American cultural anthropology as relatively more Romantic than American sociology, I am well aware that anthropology has important Classical and Enlightenment aspects, and, also, that its heightened 'Structuralism' now manifests increasing tendencies to converge with sociology. Conversely, I am also aware that there are certain schools of thought within American *sociology* that are relatively more Romantic and, in fact, sometimes emphatically so. The purest vein of Romanticism in American sociology is, I believe, to be found in the 'Chicago School', which had the most concentrated exposure to the German tradition and was, in fact, established by many (A. W. Small, W. Y. Thomas and R. E. Park) who were directly trained in it. Currently, its leading exponents are Anselm Strauss, Erving Goffman and Howard S. Becker.

I think it notable that much of the focus of their work is not simply on the study of occupations and deviant behaviour, but that these Chicagoans' studies often produce a blending of the two. From this Chicago standpoint, the prostitute is just as much an *occupational* role as it is a manifestation of *deviant* behaviour. More generally, the style of these Chicago sociologists seems to have a greater tolerance of conceptual ambiguity; its conceptual distinctions are usually also deeply embedded in a rich texture of ethnographic detail; in fact, they commonly prefer an anthropologically informed style of field work. In this methodological vein Becker has been an advocate of participant observation and has sought to entrench the method by codifying it, while Strauss (together with B. Glaser)[23] has spoken for the merits of 'data-grounded theory', which is primarily a polemic against deductive, formal styles of sociological theorizing and an argument for inductive theorizing – once again revealing the paradoxical but abiding affinity of certain forms of Positivism and Romanticism.

To many of these Chicagoans, the *demi-monde* is not only a fact of life, to be treated like any other, but also provides a *standpoint* for pronouncing a judgement upon respectable society. Indeed, they seem to speak on behalf of the *demi-monde*, and to affirm the authenticity of 'disreputable' life styles. This Chicago standpoint embodies a species of naturalistic Romanticism: it prefers the offbeat, i.e., the extreme case, to the familiar or average case; the evocative ethnographic detail to the dispassionate and dull taxonomy; the sensuously expressive to dry, formal analysis; informal, naturalistic observation to formal questionnaires and rigorous laboratory experiments; the standpoint of the hip outsider to that of the square insider. In short, and as the nineteenth-century Romantics might have said, they prefer the standpoint of Bohemians to that of Philistines.

Crucial to this Chicago approach to deviance in particular, and to the social world in general, is the influence of Kenneth Burke's device of 'perspective by incongruity', which is to say, of seeing and understanding some part of the social world by looking at it from an unusual or incongruous perspective. Thus, respectable occupations are seen as kin to deviant occupations; correspondingly, the pimp is viewed as just another type of salesman. In effect, 'perspective by incongruity' is Kenneth

Burke's pragmatic routinization of the Romantics' concept of the grotesque – that is, it is the Americanization of the grotesque.

The strategy of perspective by incongruity has, of course, been most fully applied by Erving Goffman. In Goffman's work, for example, the relationship between psychiatrists and patients, or between priests and parishioners, are held to be akin to the relationship between 'con men' and their 'marks'; the behaviour of children on a carousel becomes a device for understanding the 'serious' world of adults; the stage becomes a model which is not merely casually but systematically exploited for understanding social life in all its complexities. Here, in Goffman's work, perspective by incongruity becomes a central method and as a result, the world as unified hierarchy is shattered and abandoned.

The linkage of this Chicago School of sociology to Romanticism is a complex and authentic one, and indeed it is the closest by far of any important American school of sociology. The major transmission belt for the saturation of the Chicago perspective by Romanticism was the social psychology of George Herbert Mead as developed by Herbert Blumer.

More than any other major figure in modern sociological theory, and more than any of the other founders of the Chicago School, Mead was the most thoroughly in command of the technical details of Romanticism;[24] he was the most deeply appreciative of its originality and viability, as well as being most knowingly sympathetic with its animating spirit – and this despite the fact that he did not receive his formal training in Germany. As Anselm Strauss says, 'The Romantic writers had a profound influence upon Mead . . .'[25]

The convergences between Mead and the Romantics, to outline them simply and briefly, consist in the following:

(1) They commonly feel that there is some tensionful *difference* between at least a private component of the self and some other more socially oriented part of the self, which is expressed by Mead's distinction between the 'I' and the 'me'.

(2) They also commonly believe (with the Idealists) that the self and the not-self are bound up together in and constituted by one single process; so that the objects of the experienced

world cannot stand apart from 'subjects' who constitute them as objects.

(3) Mead and the Romantics also agree that a crucial aspect in the development of self depends upon its capacity to look back upon the *past*, and to claim certain events in it as its own.

(4) Again, both agree that the forms, no less than the concrete contents of awareness, of self and others, are continually evolving rather than being statically given.

(5) Both, therefore, stress that the self is an evolving and changing process.

(6) Again, both Mead and the Romantics agree that the 'past' has no one fixed significance but varies instead in its relationship to ongoing or contemplated action; one therefore does not discover but rather one reconstructs and creates pasts, seeing them differently at different points in the action process.

(7) Furthermore, both believe that the self is not a passive recipient of outside forms but is, rather, an active and selective agent, changing itself as it acts upon and toward others.

(8) So far as both Mead and the Romantics are concerned, moreover, at the end of an action, the self is always somewhat changed, as is the object world it deals with, and hence,

(9) the future is always somewhat unpredictably emergent from action that is continually seeking to surmount the ambiguities that it confronts.

Mead, then, like the Romantics, rejects an image of the social world as a given, neatly arranged static order; both view it instead as a tensionful, changing, open-ended, loosely stranded, somewhat indeterminate and fluid process. Mead's emphasis that a plurality or multiplicity of selves is a *normal* and creative phenomenon may be regarded as an effort to transcend the fragmentation of the self and to deny that this fragmentation constitutes *grotesqueness*. In this respect, Mead's social psychology of the self is akin to the Hegelian dialectic which, too, seeks to transcend the grotesque, and invest it with meaning.

For all his convergences with Romanticism, however, Mead was not – and we should not expect him to be – a nineteenth-century German Romantic. He is, of course, a post-Darwinian American, who understood Romanticism in an optimistic mood and conceived it as a philosophy of evolution. As

Anselm Strauss says, 'The Romantic treatment becomes in Mead's hands divested of its mysticism and is given biological and scientific traits.' Strauss is also substantially correct in interpreting Mead as seeking to provide an 'empirical under-pinning for the revolutionary but inadequate notions of evolution' that the Romanticists had inaugurated, on the one side, while, on the other, as using Romanticism as a lever to pry open the deterministic framework of modern science and to 'restate problems of autonomy, freedom and innovation'.

It was largely through Mead's influence, I believe, that systematic Romanticism permeated one wing of the Chicago School of sociology, gave it its coherence and its unique character and marked it off as a school apart from – and, in-deed, often in conflict with – the scientistic orientations more characteristic of American sociology. The coherence and the vitality of this wing of the Chicago School of sociology derived as much from the unmistakable imprint of Romanticism, as from its own creative adaptation of Romanticism to distinctive American traditions and ideologies.

Methodology and Romanticism

In much that I have said so far, I have directed attention to the manner in which *conceptual* schemes and substantive *theories* in social science contain, on the level of their deep structures, certain distinguishably Romantic and Classical syndromes. In the remaining parts of this discussion, however, I want to change the focus somewhat. Here, in what follows, I want to concentrate, not upon conceptual schemas and substantive theories, but, rather, on what sociologists commonly call 'methodology'. In particular, I want to suggest that not only may substantive theories of social science differ when implicated in the different infrastructures of Romanticism or Classicism but so, too, may its 'methodologies'. Romanticism, for example, is not I believe manifested only by a rejection of all formal methods. Within almost all fields of methodology there are some standpoints that are more Romantic and others more Classical. In saying this, however, I would not wish to deny that there is a Romantic standpoint that may take a radically *anti*-methodological standpoint. The most talented expression of this position is of course that of the philosopher Paul Feyerabend (especially in his *Against Method: Outline of an Anarchistic Theory of Knowledge.*)

Within sociology, the fullest expression of a Romantic methodology was Max Weber's with his concern for *verstehen*, for projected, imaginatively constructed ideal types as opposed to inductively established average types, and with his conception of the 'mental experiment' through which one might move toward causal inference. It is interesting to note that the specifically Romantic antecedents of the 'mental experiment' may be seen in Schlegel's remark, '. . . it is no idle speculation in history to inquire what, under different circumstances, might have occurred. . . . What would have been the consequence, what form would have Europe have assumed, if the Catholic powers had completely triumphed . . .'[26]

The Nature of Data

While the effect of Romanticism on the methodology of the social sciences finds its culmination in the sociology of Max Weber, this is scarcely the earliest indication of Romanticism's importance for the methodology of the social sciences. One of the earliest of these was the encouragement that Romanticism gave to the direct and first-hand research – in short, to 'field work' methods – as a way of studying peasant and other pre-industrial cultures. As Anthony Oberschall remarks,

The incentive for field work originated in the Romantics' discovery of the notion of the *Volk*, which brought with it a positive evaluation [*sic*] of the beliefs and customs of the German peasantry. Since the time of the Grimm brothers, a number of researchers were criss-crossing the land, noting down dialects and fairy tales as well as observing dress, customs, and inscriptions in the village houses and churches. . . . Growing out of the romantic tradition but directed more to immediate social and political problems was the work of Wilhelm Heinrich von Riehl [and] his notion of *Volkskunde* as an empirical science. The purpose of the study of the *Volk* was to discover the laws of *Volk*life. . . . The way to discover these laws was through direct observation of the people: 'Especially the research directed at contemporary *Volk*life is inadequate when performed on secondary sources. Whoever wants to represent the individuality [*sic*] of the *Volk* only through data that are in the libraries, archives or statistical bureaus will put together but a rattling skeleton and not a picture that breathes life. For that purpose first hand sources are necessary, and they can only be gotten by walking through the country on one's own feet.'[27]

The most profound expression of the methodological influence of early Romanticism, however, was not its polemic against secondary sources nor its call for first-hand observation and field work. Rather, it was its conception of what was *valuable* and worthy of study, on the one hand, and, correspondingly, of *who* provided legitimate and *valuable* sources of data, on the other hand.

Romanticists contributed to shaping modern social science's core conception of the very nature of data itself. Despite the common view of Romanticism as politically conservative (if not reactionary), Romantic pluralism actually contributed importantly to the 'democratization' of the concept of data. Specifically, Romantic pluralism undermined the Classical metaphysics which had ordered reality hierarchically and which in consequence had, overtly or tacitly, conceived of some portions of reality as being 'high' and worthy of emulation and attention, and of others as 'low', indecorously deviant, and worthy only either of contempt or neglect. To the Romanticists, every object was a world in itself, every grain of sand a cosmos. Each object being uniquely individual was therefore worthy of attention in itself; it was valuable in itself not simply as a paradigm to be emulated or decried. It was seen as worth knowing quite apart from its *moral* implications, and not because it needed to be reformed and improved. Romanticism thus contributed to a concern with the lowly or deviant parts of the social world.

The nineteenth-century Romantic attitude toward objects was akin to that of the collector's aesthetic. Thus Oberschall notes that 'a man like Mannhardt in the [eighteen] sixties was conscious of a race against time in collecting this material for genuine rural life was disappearing all around him'.[28] Such a 'collector's' orientation toward objects was quite distinct from the attitude of many nineteenth-century reformers who wanted to study and know under-privileged social worlds in order to uplift, reform, or protect them legislatively. The Romantic attitude toward social worlds – its collector's posture – was thus much more nearly akin to that of certain modern social science conceptions of 'pure' science 'objectivity' than it was to instrumental conceptions of a 'policy-oriented' or applied sociology. But even that is not entirely correct, for the Romantics' aesthetic relation to the object seeks to possess or protect it, to 'appreciate' and understand it, and not to use it as grist even for generalizations or laws. The Romantic wants and appreciates the object in its concrete totality, in its uniqueness and individuality.

The Romantic conception of pluralistic worlds, each unique and each valuable, invited attention to hitherto lowly or neglected social worlds and people, thereby influencing conceptions of *what* was worth studying. It also encouraged direct contact and immersal in these worlds as ways of studying them, thus influencing notions of *how* to study them, and from whom one could derive 'data'. Romanticism thus transformed the ontology and epistemology of the social sciences. Most specifically, it moved beyond either aristocratic conceptions of 'taking evidence' or bureaucratic conceptions of writing to notables – to gentry, ministers, or schoolteachers – and asking them to describe the conditions of life of *others* in the 'lower orders'. Each order might now give testimony concerning its own condition. Romanticism created new conceptions of the 'sources' of data. Stressing the importance of the intuitive in the knowing process, and of the ineffable in the object to be known, Romanticism encouraged a research process that entailed a communion-generating direct contact between the inquiring subject and the object inquired about. In an extreme expression it might foster a radical relativism that held that 'you had to be one to know one' – e.g., that only Blacks could know Blacks, the epistemology of the 'Insider', as Robert Merton refers to it.

Romanticism also encouraged resistance to the quantitative study of what were taken to be unique and ineffable entities. By reason of the importance it attributed to the subjective and inward, of the significance it attributed to ideas, values, and

world-views, it was a basic source of concern with the subjective and phenomenological standpoints, and of resistance to
the application of the mechanistic models of physical science
and to 'external' conceptions of causation to the study of social
worlds. In American sociology this crystallized, during the
Classical period of the 'Chicago School', in the insistence of
W. I. Thomas and Florian Znaniecki that whatever is *defined* as
real is real, in its consequences. Thus, while the later growth of
attitude surveys and public opinion polls represents an extension of an essentially positivistic methodology, it was paradoxically based upon a prior triumph of Romanticism and of a
Romantic conception of what was sociologically important
data.

Analytic Induction

Still another expression of a relatively Romantic methodology
may be found in the concept of 'analytic induction' as developed
by Florian Znaniecki and Alfred Lindesmith. In this technique,
one arrives at general conclusions concerning a set of phenomena from the successive and intensive study of individual
cases, treated one at a time, rather than from inferences drawn
from a sample of cases that are simultaneously and statistically
examined. Analytic induction is therefore a case-by-case technique and, in its emphasis upon the value of the individual
event, is characteristically Romantic. In the light of my previous
remarks about the distinctive importance of Romanticism for a
wing of the Chicago School of sociology, it is worth noting the
special connection that the development of analytic induction
had with the history of the University of Chicago, through
Znaniecki who taught there and Alfred Lindesmith who was
trained there.

To reiterate, my emphasis here is not that a Romantic social
science rejects methodology but that it tends to have a distinctive orientation to methodology. Still, as my earlier remarks
imply, if one were to compare two samples of modern social
scientists, one of relatively pure Classicists and the other of
relatively pure Romanticists, that we would find that Romanticists are, on the average, somewhat more hostile to highly

codified and formalized methodologies. Perhaps the prototype of such a Romantic rejection of formalization in the social sciences may be found in the work of C. Wright Mills.

C. Wright Mills as Romanticist

I am aware, of course, that in various works, Mills was at pains to exhibit his competence in handling a 'modern' research technology. This is especially notable in those works that he did when associated with the Bureau of Applied Social Research. I am also aware that, at one point, Mills even issued forth with the formulaic slogan that I.B.M. + humanism = sociology. But even in his statistically grounded researches, it is clear that Mills' major intellectual gratifications derived from *qualitative* analysis, for which his statistical materials primarily served as a springboard. Mills, however, was in many ways character-istically American in his enjoyment of various kinds of tools and machines. But perhaps it is neither unfair nor untrue to suggest that Mills loved especially those tools and machines that enhanced men's sense of individual control and personal mastery. He loved machines or tools which would either strengthen individual independence or enable men to move freely and easily among different places. Perhaps this is in some part why Mills loved the motorcycle. But Romanticism need not entail a radical rejection of the machine, and perhaps Mills' love of the motorcycle was akin to Gabriel D'Annunzio's equally romantic love of the airplane. In short, twentieth-century Romantics need not be Luddites.

Far more revealing of Mills' central methodological position, however, are the main themes of his *Sociological Imagination*. I believe these represent an essentially Romantic perspective, most particularly with regard to his rejection of any kind of autonomous and *im*personal methodology. In his *Sociological Imagination*, it will be remembered that Mills' critique was a twofold one: on the one hand, it was a rejection of mindless statistical empiricism and, on the other hand, it was a rejection of what he called abstracted grand theorizing. Here Mills rejected formalizations that were used as substitutes for personalized thought and, in particular, insofar as they were emptied of data possessing concrete richness. He, too, wanted a picture of social worlds that 'breathed life'.

Mills' own conception of his methodology is revealed primarily in his metaphor of 'intellectual craftsmanship', and nothing could be more characteristically Romantic than Mills' remarks in his essay on 'Intellectual Craftsmanship'. Here he held that the 'social science tradition of the last hundred years amounts to this: . . . in the *mind* that has hold of it, in the *mind* that has been formed by it, there sometimes comes about a kind of sociological *imagination*'.[29]

Mills' emphasis is clearly upon the value of the sociological *imagination*, and not on methodological *discipline*. As if the Romanticism of this perspective was not plain enough, Mills adds immediately thereafter that the sociological imagination resides 'in the capacity to shift from one perspective to another, and in the process to build up an adequate view of a total society . . .' It is, he insists, 'this *imagination* that sets off the social scientist from the mere technician'. A sociological imagination, adds Mills, contains 'an *unexpected quality* about it, perhaps because its essence is the combination of *ideas that no one expected were combinable*'. In short, the essence of the sociological imagination to Mills is a Romantic *pluralism of perspectives* blended with Kenneth Burke's version of the grotesque, namely, perspective by incongruity. For Mills, the collation of systematic data was above all 'one way to invite imagination'. In short, he suggested that it was not the formal machinery of research that produced results, but, rather, its stimulus to the imagination – a personal and inward quality. One may further stir the imagination, Mills adds in a bland aside, by a glass of Irish whisky.[30]

It is in these remarks, I believe, that we have the essence of Mills' conception of a pluralistic, a personal, and an imaginative style of research that was plainly Romantic. Nor is it irrelevant to note, in passing, that an effort to trace the intellectual sources of Mills' outlook would surely lead to the seminal influence that was exerted upon him both by George Herbert Mead and Max Weber, two important viaducts of Romanticism in sociology.

It may seem that, while I have promised to discuss the

influences of Romanticism on sociological methodology, the
examples given thus far do not really represent the methodological concerns truly characteristic of the social sciences today.
In other words, there may be some who agree that, once upon
a time, there was such a thing as a Romantic methodology of
the social sciences, but that this time is long since past, and that
it is now useless to attempt to understand current developments
in modern social science methodology in terms of the Romantic–
Classical distinction.

P. F. Lazarsfeld's Romantic Premises

With that in mind, let me briefly refer to the work of Paul
Felix Larzasfeld, who is surely the dean of social science
methodologists in the United States today. The essence of
Lazarsfeld's methodological position is that the social scientist
ought to be guided, first and above all, not so much by the
formal canons of science, as these are articulated and codified
by logicians, but rather, Lazarsfeld emphasizes, by the *implicit*
rules and procedures which successful social scientists *tacitly*
employ and embody in their researches. In other words,
Lazarsfeld's methodological position rejects a view of social
science methodologies that sees them as a set of eternal and
externalized rules of procedure or of proof. It is thus a distinctly
anti-Classical conception of methodology, in its derivation if not
in its application.

That Lazarsfeld's methodological posture *ensues* in a Classical
emphasis on the importance of codifying and formalizing rules
of research should not be allowed to conceal that it *derives* from
quite different, Romantic premises. In other words, while
Lazarsfeld is a Classicist as a methodological *moralist*, he is a
Romantic who assumes that in the beginning was the creative
deed.

What Lazarsfeld stresses is the search for the guiding pro-
prieties, for the paradigms and the models that lie *implicitly* in the
research of working social scientists. It is implied, by his view,
that great social science proceeds on the basis of (at first) inarticulate operational rules and often ineffable information or
experience. Here, then, in characteristically Romantic manner,

Lazarsfeld's emphasis is on the inwardness of an effective social science methodology, on the inarticulateness of the creative, which needs, however, to be rendered articulate. In his unstated but evident premise, it is not the rulebook that is the measure, but, rather, the social scientist and his concrete work.

I might add here that this Romantic aspect of Lazarsfeld's methodological orientation seems to be of one piece with the style of the Bureau of Applied Research's statistics, at least insofar as it has treated tests of statistical significance[31] in a relatively more 'flexible' way than some sociological statisticians elsewhere. Some, it has seemed to me, have objected to the neglect of tests of significance partly because this allowed too much variability in the interpretation of statistical tables, and placed undue reliance upon individual choice and personal judgement. In short, they objected to the intrusion of the subjective. While sociological *theorists* at Chicago University were more Romantic than those at Columbia University, it may be that statistical *methodologists* at Columbia University were more Romantic than those elsewhere.

Computer-Using Romanticism

This brief example may suffice to *suggest* that not all emphases upon methodology are intrinsically Classical in character, and that there are *Romantic* methodologists no less than Classical methodologists. This is true even with respect to the so-called 'hard' or computer-emphasizing social sciences. For example, if one compares 'systems analysis' with, say, operations research, programme budgeting, or cost–benefit analysis, it seems to me that systems analysis is by far the most Romantic. This conjecture appears to be borne out by the work of Aaron Wildavsky. Thus Wildavsky characterizes the good systems analyst as a man whose 'forte is creativity'. And he also stresses that the good systems analyst strives to relate various elements 'imaginatively into new systems . . .'.[32]

Wildavsky also notes that E. S. Quade speaks of systems analysis as constituting a 'form of art' in which it is not possible to assert 'fast rules' that can be followed with exactness. 'In systems analysis,' says Quade, 'there is more judgement and intuition and less reliance on quantitative methods than in operations research.' Systems analysis is also very much concerned with the development of techniques – such as contingency analysis – for dealing with situations that contain a high degree of uncertainty.

Similar Romantic orientations to computer simulation may be inferred from the work of Robert Boguslaw.[33] In an effort to develop computer programs for playing chess, Boguslaw did with chess players essentially the same thing that Lazarsfeld had done with sociologists. That is, Boguslaw studied the work of good chess players, attempted to render explicit the 'heuristics' or working rules that they *tacitly* employed, and then proceeded to program the computer in terms of these heuristics.

Résumé

In brief summary, the central assumptions I have made in the discussion above are:

(1) Serious historical studies of both sociology and anthropology – and these, I believe, are only now emerging – will find it illuminating to trace their connections with nineteenth-century Romanticism. This constitutes *one* of the keys to the modern effort at the reconstruction of the history (and therefore of the consciousness) of the social sciences. It is this that will enable us to go beyond a concern for the narrowly political implications of various sociologies to their other and more complex social sources, particularly as they bear upon styles of sociological work as well as patterns of problem formulation.

(2) Romantic and Classical syndromes refer to enduring deep structures that underlie the theories of sociology even today. They are embedded in and help to differentiate various schools of thought and, also, various professional subcultures. In short, Romantic and Classical syndromes are in my view promising intellectual tools for the empirical study of the ongoing social sciences today – i.e., they are as valuable for a *sociology* of sociology as for a *history* of sociology.

(3) It is not only the substantive theories but the 'methodologies'

of the social sciences themselves that bear the differentiating impress of Romantic and Classical deep structures.

(4) From both a developmental, historical standpoint and from a synchronic sociological standpoint, a core conflict within and among schools of thought centres on the tensions between Romantic and Classical (or other) deep structures.

We can, then, think of Romanticism and Classicism as syndromes or latent dimensions that underpin sociology and the other social sciences. We can think of them as different genotypes underlying certain phenotypes.

A 'Classical Sociology', then, would be one which – ideal typically – stresses the *universality* of the governing standards, norms, or values, or of the functional requisites of a society. A 'Romantic Sociology', however, stresses – again, ideal typically – the relativity, the uniqueness, or historical character of the standards or needs of any society or group. If Classicism tends toward *structuralism* in social science, Romanticism tends toward *historicism*.

A Classical sociology is concerned with more careful statistical analysis of the 'average' case and with the fuller statistical distribution of cases, in its concern for 'the normal'. A Romantic sociology, by contrast, focuses on the reality of the deviant case and tolerates deviance from normative or role requirements; a Classical sociology places greater emphasis upon the indispensability of some measure of conformity to them. Classical sociology, then, focuses on the value of assimilating self and person to culture and role, while Romantic sociology, however, focuses on the value of distance from roles and values, and of those occasions when men have failed to be controlled by or assimilated to their roles and values.

The methodology of a Classical sociology stresses the importance of 'formal' reason, of codifications, and of self-conscious conformity to known rules. The methodology of a Romantic sociology places greater emphasis on the *extra*-technical or social sources of theory and knowledge, such as the sociology of knowledge. A Classical sociology places greater stress on the situation-transcending potency of human reason. A Classical sociology therefore implies that there is one best model for work, and that it is the researcher's obligation to determine what this is and to attempt to conform to it at all times. A Romantic sociology, however, stresses that different intellectual problems and different research sites each have their own differing properties or paradigms. A Romantic sociology tends to attribute greater significance to informal procedures that are tailored to individual cases. That is, there is more than one best way, and appropriate techniques and methodologies are expected to change over time and with shifting value perspectives. (Compare page 317.)

Classical sociology searches for the more enduring structures and seeks laws that are more universal in application. Romantic sociology seeks *historical* laws or may work only with ethnography, or with hermeneutic interpretations or descriptions of unique events, or concrete totalities. Classical sociology places its emphasis on order and order-inducing mechanisms in society; Romantic sociology, on the sources of change, process, of negotiations and becomings. To the Classical sociologist, 'objectivity' means conformity with the requirements of reason or the logic of science, and entails a kind of selflessness. To the Romanticist, however, objectivity means the consensus of scholars achieved through debate, and is grounded in a certain kind of subjectivity.

The Classical sociologist sees society's requirements for coherence and order; the Romantic sociologist stresses society's needs for conflicts and friction. A Romantic sociology believes that there are all manner of tensions and conflicts within society – among ideas, classes, institutions, types of men – and it expects that there is an inherent conflict between man and society. The Classicist sees the dependence of men upon some society for the realization of their humanness. The Romanticist believes that men's humanness is limited by the established society. The Classical sociologist therefore sees the value of harmony, consensus, and decorum, while the Romantic sees the value of the grotesque, the dissonant, and the indecorous in society.

Clearly, then, I do not believe that Romanticism or Classicism is, by itself, a sufficient infrastructure for a valid social theory. Both, I believe, are necessary. But this needs qualification in at least two important ways:

First, if the theorist has access to both Romantic and Classical infrastructures, but if he *isolates* each from the other, then each will fail to provide a liberating perspective on the other. There may then develop a kind of theoretical schizophrenia, where one perspective is used for one purpose and the other for a different purpose. The most liberating relationship of the two exists, however, when neither is insulated from the other; when neither is repressed; when each can therefore provide a perspective on the other; and when each can be brought into a theory-energizing tension with the other.

The above implications lean in a 'structuralist' direction. The following implications, however, lean in an 'historicist' direction: given the above implications (that is, invoking the same and not different assumptions), it follows that there can be specific historical conditions when one of the infrastructures is suppressed by the larger society, or by the professionally dominant technical tradition, and when, therefore, it may be intellectually valuable to place a compensatory *stress* on what has been culturally excluded. I believe that our own epoch, however shrill its 'counter-culture', is precisely such an historical period. The Classical infrastructure has been the dominant force in the development of the academic social sciences; developments of the late sixties have manifested what is only a counter-cyclical *trend* of *secondary* significance. In such an epoch, in which social theory has been exposed to an establishment-sponsored Classicism, it is especially necessary to protect theoretical creativity and the tensionful 'balance' of infrastructures by a compensatory emphasis on the special value of the *Romantic* infrastructure. In an epoch such as our own, where the Romantic largely remains underground, marginal to the dominant culture, there are also very grave dangers of its own equally one-sided development, particularly in irrational and anti-intellectual directions.

NOTES

1. Why the Germans rejected the French mapping of the new social order is a separate and distinct question. In briefest outline, they rejected it because it was borne to them on the points of Napoleonic bayonets. These had added injury to insult. They saw this as the military culmination of a

French cultural dominance, that had earlier expressed itself in the popularity of French language and manners among the courts and élites of the German provinces. The German middle classes were ambivalent about the French solution because they had much the same anxieties about their property, and about the urban mob, that the French middle classes themselves had developed, and which had brought their own Revolution to its Thermidorian halt. Naturally, the German aristocracy had less ambivalence than the middle classes in rejecting the French model.

2. De Staël's important discussion of German Romanticism, *On Germany*, is to be found in M. Berger (ed. and trans.), *Mme. de Staël on Politics, Literature and National Character*, New York, Doubleday, 1964.

3. One may gauge just how large the literature on Romanticism is by remembering how huge the Rousseau-literature alone is. Then there is the literature about each of the Romantic poets; then the philosophers, Hegel, Fichte, Schelling, etc. The literature on 'Romanticism' is appallingly huge, and I cannot here do more than intimate, allude to, or suggest some of its dimensions and a very few of its contents. The problem of Romanticism has been studied more or less systematically at the very least since Alfred de Musset's *Lettres de Dupuis et Cotonet* in 1836. It has since been the preserve of academicians studying comparative literature, specialists in each of the Euro-American languages, including English, so that whole academic disciplines have, with fully institutionalized continuity, spent many decades writing about Romanticism, Romanticism in their own country's literature, and in its relations to the Romanticism of many other countries' literatures. Moreover, there is an extensive analysis of Romanticism not only in literature but in the other arts: music, of course, but also in painting. The literature on Romanticism is so vast that the categories in terms of which bibliographies are divided are more or less standardized: e.g., the history of Romanticism, on a European-wide basis and country by country; critiques of Romanticism; definitions of Romanticism; anthologies of Romantic writing; biographies of Romantic authors; and bibliographies of Romantic literature and analysis, etc.

What follows, then, makes no pretence to being in the least complete or systematic but must be viewed only as a sampler of some of the things that happen to have shaped my own thinking about the problem. First, for any American, there is of course Arthur O. Lovejoy. Without in the least meaning to deprecate his scholarly contribution, it might not be amiss to regard certain of his writings as brilliant, annotated bibliographies. While by no means for this reason alone, still this reason alone would make his *Essays in the History of Ideas* (Baltimore, Johns Hopkins, and O.U.P., 1960) a masterful contribution to the analytic bibliographies about Romanticism. Much the same might be said about Rene Wellek's *Concepts of Criticism* (New Haven and London, Yale U.P., 1963) and Volume II of his *A History of Modern Criticism* (New Haven, Yale U.P., and London, Cape, 1955). I would add, however, that Wellek's conceptualizing courage, perhaps nerve, seem stronger than Lovejoy's; perhaps overwhelmed by his own massive scholarship, it sometimes seems as if Lovejoy surrenders too easily in the difficult task of conceptualizing the nature of Romanticism. *The Cambridge Bibliography of English Literature*, F. W. Bateson (ed.) (Cambridge, 1940–57), is of course always a major source. See also the Publications of the Modern Language Association, Volume LV (New York, 1940), *Romanticism: A Symposium*. Among the many books that outsiders might consult with profit for some *initial* orientation are: Georg Brandes, *Main Currents in Nineteenth Century Literature* (Heinemann, 1901–5); Arthur O. Lovejoy, *The Great Chain of Being* (Baltimore, Harvard U.P., and O.U.P., 1936); Irving Babbitt, *Rousseau and Romanticism* (Boston, Houghton Mifflin, 1919) and the review of this by Lovejoy in *Modern Language Notes*, XXXV (New York, May 1920).

See also:

M. H. Abrams, *The Mirror and the Lamp*, O.U.P., 1953.

J. Barzun, *Classic, Romantic, and Modern*, Boston, Little, Brown, 1961.

H. A. Beers, *A History of English Romanticism in the Eighteenth Century*, New York, 1898; paperback, Dover, 1969.

G. Bianquis, *La Vie quotidienne en Allemagne à l'époque romantique*, Paris, 1959.

C. Bouglé, *Le Romanticisme social*, Paris, 1938.

C. M. Bowra, *The Romantic Imagination*, O.U.P., 1961.

Crane Brinton, *The Political Ideals of the English Romanticists*, O.U.P., 1926.

Christopher Caudwell, *Illusion and Reality*, Macmillan, 1937.

Alec Comfort, *Art and Social Responsibility*, Falcon Press, 1946.

Northrup Frye (ed.), *Romanticism Reconsidered*, New York, Columbia U.P., 1963.

Northrup Frye (ed.), *A Study of English Romanticism*, New York, Random House, 1968.

R. W. Harris, *Romanticism and the Social Order, 1780–1830*, Blandford, 1969.

R. Haym, *Die Romantische Schule*, Berlin, 1870.

R. Huch, *Die Blutezeit der Romantik*, Leipzig, 1913.

W. T. Jones, *The Romantic Syndrome*, The Hague, Nijhoff, 1961.

Frank Kermode, *Romantic Image*, Routledge, 1957.

Robert Langbaum, *The Poetry of Experience*, New York, Random House and London, Chatto & Windus, 1957.

F. L. Lucas, *The Decline and Fall of the Romantic Ideal*, Cambridge U.P., 1936; 2nd ed., 1948.

R. B. Mowat, *The Romantic Age: Europe in the Early Nineteenth Century*, Harrap, 1937.

Morse Peckham, *Beyond the Tragic Vision*, New York, Braziller, 1962.

Morse Peckham, *Romanticism: The Culture of the 19th Century*, New York, Braziller, 1965.

T. M. Raysor (ed.), *The English Romantic Poets: A Review of Research*, New York, Modern Language Association, 1956, and O.U.P., 1957.

Paul Roubiczek, *The Misinterpretation of Man*, New York, Scribner, 1947.

I. Siciliano, *Il Romanticismo francese*, Florence, 1964.

Leslie Stephens, *History of English Thought in the 18th Century*, 2 vols., Murray, 1876.

J. L. Talmon, *Romanticism and Revolt: Europe 1815-1848*, Thames and Hudson, and New York, Harcourt Brace, 1967.

Oskar Walzel, *German Romanticism*, New York, Ungar, 1966.

Raymond Williams, *Culture and Society, 1780-1950*, Chatto & Windus, and New York, Columbia U.P., 1958.

L. A. Willoughby, *Romantic Movement in Germany*, London and New York, Oxford U.P., 1930.

4. A. W. Schlegel, *Vorlesungen über dramatische Kunst und Literatur*, Heidelberg, 1817.

F. Schlegel, *Kritische Schriften* (W. Rasch (ed.)), Munich, 1956.

F. Schlegel, *Geschichte der alten und neuen Literatur*, Munich, 1961.

5. '. . . At the close of the century, the religious crisis was acute. Either a medieval man and a Christian, or a modern man and a sceptic – this seemed the sole alternative. . . . That the effort should be made to transcend them was inevitable. The efforts were many.' A. C. McGiffert, *Protestant Thought Before Kant*, New York, Harper & Row, 1962.

Our point, of course, is that Romanticism is in part to be interpreted as one of the many efforts made to transcend this choice, seeking a way to include the medieval and the modern.

6. cf. A. F. Wallace, 'Revitalization Movements', in S. M. Lipset and N. J. Smelser (eds.), *Sociology: The Progress of a Decade*, New York, Prentice-Hall, 1961, pp. 206–20.

7. See the suggestive discussion by Wolfgang Kayser, *The Grotesque in Art and Literature*, Bloomington, Indiana U.P., and O.U.P., 1963.

8. Georg Lukács, *History and Class Consciousness*, London, Merlin Press, and Cambridge (Mass.), M.I.T. Press, 1971, p. 214. Lukács suggests (and it is no more than that here) that 'the concept of "organic growth" was converted from a protest against reification into an increasingly reactionary slogan'. Lukács would later stress the reactionary outcome of Romanticism. But this creates grave difficulties for him as a Marxist, particularly an Hegelianizing Marxist, for he sees that both Solger's and Friedrich Schlegel's work on 'irony' make them pioneers of the 'dialectical method between Schelling and Hegel . . .', ibid., p. 215.

9. Mannheim's main analysis of Romanticism, convergent with the later Lukács', deals with it in the framework of an analysis of conservative thought. See chapter V of K. A. Wolff (ed.), *From Karl Mannheim*, Oxford U.P., 1971.

10. Henri Saint-Simon, *Social Organization, The Science of Man and Other Writings*, trans. and ed. F. Markham, New York, Harper & Row, 1964, p. 42; see also pp. xxx–xxxi.

11. Henri Lefebvre, *The Sociology of Marx*, Allen Lane, The Penguin Press, and New York, Pantheon Books, 1968, p. 22.

12. R. W. Friedrichs, *A Sociology of Sociology*, New York, Free Press, 1970; see especially his discussions of the 'prophetic' and 'priestly' modes of sociology. See also A. W. Gouldner, *The Coming Crisis of Western Sociology*, New York, Basic Books, 1970, and Heinemann, 1971, p. 254, etc.

13. Hans-Georg Gadamer, 'On the Scope and Function of Hermeneutical Reflection', *Continuum*, Vol. 8, No. 1, Spring-Summer, 1970, p. 80.

14. Richard E. Palmer, *Hermeneutics*, Evanston, Northwestern U.P., 1969. See esp. ch. 6–7.

15. Gadamer, op. cit., p. 90.

16. Paul Lorenzen, 'Enlightenment and Reason', *Continuum*, ibid., p. 5.

17. George Lichtheim, *From Marx to Hegel*, New York, and London, Orbach & Chambers, 1971. Lichtheim speaks of 'the introduction by Lenin of a species of voluntarism which had more in common with Bergson and Nietzsche than with Engels' own rather deterministic manner of treating historical types' (p. 67).

18. F. Schlegel, *A Course of Lectures on Modern History*, London, 1849, p. 298.

19. Which is precisely why Gareth Stedman Jones may have been a bit unkind to Lukács in recently speaking of him as the 'first' irruption of romanticism in Marxism.

20. cf. George Lichtheim, ibid., 'Max Weber's sociology was taking shape as part of an attempt to overcome the cleavages between scientific rationalism and romantic intuitionism' (p. 201). Of all those currently concerned with such matters, Lichtheim has by far the best insight into the importance of Romanticism for modern social theory, academic and Marxist, although he has not yet consolidated his understanding of Romanticism and is far too ready to reduce it to Nazism.

21. J. W. Burrow, *Evolution and Society*, Cambridge U.P., 1966, p. xv.

22. J. W. Bennett, 'Myth, Theory, and Value in Cultural Anthropology', in Count and Bowles (eds.), *Fact and Theory in Social Science*, Syracuse, 1964.

23. B. G. Glaser and A. L. Strauss, *The Discovery of Grounded Theory*, Chicago, Aldine Publications, 1967, and London, Weidenfeld & Nicolson, 1968.

24. Mead's fullest confrontation with Romanticism and his most systematic expression of his understanding of it is to be found in his much neglected *Movements of Thought in the Nineteenth Century* (ed. M. H. Moore), Chicago, University of Chicago Press, 1936.

25. A Strauss (ed.), *The Social Psychology of George Herbert Mead*, Chicago, 1959, p. vii.

26. F. Schlegel, op. cit., p. 258.

27. Anthony Oberschall, *Empirical Social Research in Germany, 1849–1914*, New York, Humanities Press, 1965, pp. 64–5.

28. ibid.

29. C. W. Mills, 'The Sociological Imagination', in L. Z. Gross (ed.), *Symposium on Sociological Theory*, Evanston, Harper & Row, 1959, p. 40.

30. ibid.

31. See, for example, H. C. Selvin, 'A Critique of Tests of Significance in Survey Research', *American Sociological Review*, Oct. 1957, pp. 519–27; R. McGinnis, 'Randomization and Inference in Sociological Research', *American Sociological Review*, Aug. 1958, pp. 408–14.

32. A. Wildavsky, 'The Political Economy of Efficiency: Cost-Benefit Analysis, Systems Analysis and Program Budgeting', *Public Administration Review*, Dec. 1966, pp. 292–309.

33. R. Boguslaw, 'Situation Analysis and the Problem of Action', *Social Problems*, Vol. VIII, No. 3, Winter 1961.

Part Three

Marxisms and Sociology

12

Émile Durkheim and the Critique of Socialism

Durkheim's study of socialism is a document of exceptional intellectual interest for several reasons. Not least of these is that it presents us with the now somewhat unusual case of a truly first-rate thinker who had the inclination to contribute to the history of sociological theory and to comment extensively on the work of a key figure in that history, Henri Saint-Simon. The core of this volume contains Durkheim's presentation of Saint-Simon's ideas, their sources and their development.

Indeed, Durkheim so subordinates himself in these pages that we might well wish that he had developed his own critical reactions to Saint-Simon at greater length. This is somewhat unusual in the annals of current sociological scholarship in America, which has tended to leave 'mere' exegesis and historical commentary to text-book writers, and which sometimes unwittingly fosters the barbaric assumption that books and ideas more than twenty years old are beyond scientific salvation. In contrast to such current preoccupations with the modern, it is noteworthy that at the time Durkheim (1858–1917) wrote these lectures on socialism and Saint-Simon (1760–1825), the latter was dead some seventy years.

In some quarters a concern for the history of sociological theory is now regarded as misguided. Of course, it is easy to understand how the usual trite chronicle of thinkers and ideas could foster such a disillusioned appraisal. Yet this dim view of the history of sociological theory may be prematurely pessimistic about earlier theory and unduly optimistic about the state of current theory.

Though current theoretical accomplishments in sociology are frequently substantial and occasionally brilliant, nothing is to be gained by short-circuiting this discipline's sense of historical continuity. We may, of course, burnish our generation's attainments by neglecting the earlier sources from which they derive. But such a rupture of historical continuity may well undermine even our own generation's accomplishments. For it may set a precedent, disposing later scholars to turn their back on our work.

There is, it would seem, some inconsistency between the sociologist's growing recognition of the importance of deliberately cultivated theoretical continuity – as a methodological imperative – and a growing tendency to neglect the earlier contributors to sociological theory. An awareness of the historical development of sociology, of its past as well as its present state, is the only firm basis for evaluating whether we have 'progressed', and, if so, how much and in what ways. Alfred North Whitehead has said that 'a science which hesitates to forget its founders is lost'. But to forget something, one must have known it in the first place. A science *ignorant* of its founders does not know how far it has travelled nor in what direction; it, too, is lost.

There is one basic justification for a social scientist's neglect of the history of his discipline: he must demonstrate that current theory and research have substantially assimilated the problems and perspectives formulated by the earlier thinkers. Failing in this, he must demonstrate that these earlier problems and perspectives are no longer to be regarded as a proper concern of his discipline.[1]

Since Durkheim's time, however, academic sociologists have increasingly neglected some of the central social problems of our time. (Your editor is no exception to this statement.) For example, there are few sociological researches into the sources, growth, and diffusion of modern socialism, however numerous studies of the Soviet Union have become. While there have been careful studies of various marginal sects and cults, there are few detailed sociological analyses of a socialist or communist party.

Related to this lacuna is the common neglect of property

institutions by sociologists, apparently on the assumption that this is the economist's job alone. If this is reasonable, however, one wonders why sociologists have not also left studies of industrial relations to economists, and studies of political parties and elections to political scientists. Furthermore, since the decline of the 'culture lag' school, which for a period flourished at the University of Chicago, there has been little systematic analysis of the role of modern science and technology,[2] and these institutions now find only a peripheral place in the sociological theories current today. Finally, although there are numerous sociological studies of family discord and even some of industrial tensions, there are few sociological studies of international relations, of war and peace.[3]

Durkheim's study of socialism and Saint-Simon assumes importance today precisely because, at various points, it considers all of these major questions and, in some measure, does so in their interrelationship to each other. Because it has something to say about these problems, it may be expected that educated laymen as well as professional sociologists will find much of interest in the pages.

One way in which this study is of special value to sociologists, and others interested in the development of sociological theory, is that it provides us with a basis for a fuller understanding of Durkheim's own contribution as a sociologist, producing greater clarity concerning some of the intellectual forces which shaped it, and, in particular, of its links to Saint-Simon, to the latter's disciple, Auguste Comte, and to Karl Marx. Some recent analyses of Durkheim's work have viewed it too much in terms of what it presumably became, and too little in terms of what it came from. There has also been a tendency to over-emphasize Durkheim's Comteian heritage and the influence which this had upon him,[4] to the neglect of other influences.

Without doubt Durkheim's theory and research was much influenced by Comte's. But if Durkheim's work comes out of Comte's, it does not come *only* from this source; if there was continuity between Durkheim and Comte, there was also discontinuity. In Durkheim, we see a man who sometimes found himself constrained to oppose his own intellectual mentor. Durkheim, we may say, was an uneasy Comteian.

One striking demonstration that Durkheim was not simply the devoted disciple of Comte can be seen in this study of socialism. Here, Durkheim firmly denies to Comte, and bestows on Saint-Simon, the 'honour' of having founded both positivist philosophy and sociology.[5] It should be clear from this alone that references to Comte as Durkheim's 'acknowledged master' are misleadingly simple; they do not portray their relationship in anything like its true complexity. Above all, the usual formula fails to indicate that, in certain pivotal ways, Durkheim's work constituted a deep-going polemic against Comte. Durkheim's study of *The Division of Labor* has been interpreted as an expression of his opposition to the utilitarian individualists, and particularly Herbert Spencer.[6] In actuality, this volume has another polemical target, namely, Comte himself, a fact which comes out forcefully in its culminating chapter.

The Polemic Against Comte

In Comte's view, the increasing division of labour in modern society threatened its social cohesion. For it brought with it 'a fatal disposition towards a fundamental dispersion of ideas, sentiments, and interests. . . .'[7] The increasing division of labour was, in this analysis, subversive of social stability because it undermined the fundamental requisite of order, namely, the consensus of moral beliefs. It was one of the basic aims of Durkheim's *Division of Labor* to refute this Comteian view. Durkheim flatly rejected Comte's analysis, holding that it was not the division of labour as such which 'normally' induced social disorder.

Durkheim's argument, in effect, hinges on a Saint-Simonian assumption: namely, that with the emergence of the new industrial order new social needs arose and new ways of satisfying old needs were required. Like Saint-Simon's, Durkheim's position was relativistic. The growing division of labour is 'natural' in modern society, Durkheim maintains; it normally produces social solidarity. Indeed it produces what he seems to have regarded as a 'higher' type of solidarity, an 'organic' solidarity. This he contrasted with the 'mechanical' solidarity of earlier societies which had rested upon shared moral beliefs, or on uniformity in their 'collective conscience'. Comte, he says, failed to see that the social solidarity produced by the division of labour with its web of interdependence, was gradually being substituted for the earlier solidarity which had rested mainly on shared moral beliefs.

Of course, says Durkheim, modern society requires consensus in moral beliefs. Shared moral beliefs as well as the division of labour both contribute to the maintenance of social solidarity. But modern society no longer requires the *same degree* of moral consensus, nor does this consensus entail the same items of belief, necessary for earlier periods. In Durkheim's view, the respective roles of mechanical and organic solidarity were changing. 'What is necessary is to give each, at each moment in history, the place that is fitting to it. . . .'[8] The division of labour 'more and more tends to become the essential condition of social solidarity'.[9] Indeed, 'the ideal of human fraternity can be realized only in proportion to the progress of division of labour'.[10] We cannot look to the past as a guide, says Durkheim. In a manner reminiscent of Saint-Simon, who has also held that the division of labour must become the basis of a new morality, Durkheim indicates[11] that contemporary society must develop a new moral code corresponding to changed modern conditions.

It is sometimes suggested that there was an important change in focus in Durkheim's later work, and that he gradually re-emphasized and saw new importance in the role of shared beliefs.[12] Whatever the validity of this observation, here, in *The Division of Labor*, his first great work, Durkheim is unmistakeably conducting a polemic against Comte *for having overstressed the need for moral consensus in maintaining social stability*. It is certainly not the case that Durkheim neglects the role of shared beliefs in *The Division of Labor*; it is not that he is then unaware of their significance and only later works through to an understanding of them. From the beginning, he was fully aware of the significance which had long since been imputed to shared beliefs by Comte, but he deliberately chose to oppose Comte's estimate of their role in modern society.

Durkheim readily admits that the division of labour presently engenders social tensions. These arise, however, 'because all the conditions of organic solidarity [i.e., social solidarity deriving from increased occupational specialization] have not been realized'.[13] His position is again fundamentally Saint-Simonian. Saint-Simon had held that social patterns engendering tension do so, either because they are the archaic survivals of earlier conditions which no longer obtain, or are the first growths of a new social system which has not yet matured.[14] It is in both of these ways that Durkheim explains the tensions associated with the increasing division of labour.

He holds, for example, that the new moral rules appropriate to the new division of labour have not yet developed. Because of this, class war and crises of over-production result, for the relations between specialized functions are not yet properly integrated and regulated. Or, again, Durkheim states that the division of labour engenders tensions because people have been forced into occupations at variance with their natural talents. It is not the division of labour as such, but an archaic 'forced division of labour' that generates social tensions.

Occupational specializations must be assigned, says Durkheim, in keeping with the natural distribution of talents and not on the basis of hereditary wealth or birth. He does not, however, develop this into a critique of private property, as had the Saint-Simonians, Bazard and Enfantin, in which it was indicated that private ownership of industrial property can inhibit its rational administration and productivity, since those owning factories may not be those who can best administer them.

In his *Division of Labor*, at any rate, Durkheim was not gropingly moving toward an appreciation of shared moral norms; he was, in fact, moving away from Comte's emphasis on their significance in modern society. Durkheim was, also, much more self-consciously aware than Comte of the ways in which *commitment* to certain types of norms might yield forms of social disorganization. For example, in the *Division of Labor* he notes that it is because people in modern society *share* certain conceptions of 'justice' that they object to the 'forced' division of labour, and to the assignment of roles on the basis of inherited wealth or birth. In his later work on *Suicide*,[15] Durkheim stresses that Protestant norms actually induce a higher rate of suicide. He stresses that normlessness (or anomie) is not the only source of social disorganization or the only stimulant to a high suicide rate. A commitment to Protestant beliefs may also induce a disorganizing 'egoism', Durkheim argues. And he regards anomie and egoism as having a close connection, a 'peculiar affinity' for each other.

Durkheim makes an interesting point in his discussion of 'acute anomie'. This, he says, arises during periods of sudden prosperity or depression which rapidly change people's class position. People exposed to such sudden class shifts are prone to suicide, he says, because they are normless. But here 'normless' is used in a peculiar sense. It does not mean that people lack norms, but rather that the norms which they *do have* no longer correspond to the new class position in which they suddenly find themselves. It is this disparity between their old norms and their new circumstances which induces tension. Thus moral norms play a positive role in *generating* disorganization; they can disrupt social order rather than strengthen it, unless they are in keeping with the changing circumstances of life.[16] Social order does not rest on norms alone, Durkheim is saying here; it depends on the way in which norms are integrated with other conditions.

Similarly, Durkheim maintains that to the extent that people believe in 'progress' there will always be a strain toward anomie, involving a perpetually restless dissatisfaction with the *status quo*.[17] A certain amount of anomie is therefore a normal condition in modern society. The 'enfeeblement' of the 'collective conscience' is an inevitable and normal development in a modern industrial society with an increasing division of labour.

Comte had stressed the need for social consensus, regarding its decline as the principal peril to modern society. Durkheim, however, maintained that *too high* a degree of social cohesion could also induce disorganization. This is clearly expressed in his *Suicide* where he remarks,

> If, as we have seen, excessive individuation leads to suicide, insufficient individuation has the same results. When a man has become detached from society, he encounters less resistance to suicide in himself, and he does so likewise when social integration is too strong.[18]

Thus a collective conscience which was either too weak *or too strong* could induce social disorganization.

In contrast again with Comte, Durkheim held that a certain amount of social conflict was normal and natural in modern society. In part, he sees it as the price of modern freedom. In the *Division of Labor*, for example, he makes the point that conflict and competition among individuals was natural. It was the prevention of such conflicts, by the imposition of outmoded arrangements based on inherited wealth and position, that was abnormal. Let natural talents rather than artificial institutions decide the issue, he says.[19]

The contrast of Durkheim's position with Comte's also comes out forcefully in respect of their differing strategies for controlling the divisive effects of the increasing division of labour. Interestingly enough, Comte had held that the dispersing effects of occupational differentiation should be checked by government regulation. This is at variance with Comte's tendency to minimize the role of political intervention and his usual reliance on the 'spontaneous' sources of social solidarity. Durkheim takes issue with this proposal and is, in this respect, a more consistent Comteian than Comte himself. The central difficulty of modern society, Durkheim insists, is the lack of social structures mediating between the individual and the state. Comte's solution, he holds, would only compound the atomizing heritage of the French Revolution.

Project for a Corporative Society

In the *Division of Labor*, he never proposes a clear-cut alternative solution to the problem, although the direction which his solution is to take is already manifest there. It is only in the *Suicide* that he proposes a specific remedy for the dispersing effects of the division of labour which he later expands upon in the preface to the second edition of the *Division of Labor*. In this he takes a step beyond and against Comte in maintaining that not only was the state incompetent to control this problem, but so too were the family and religious organizations. None of these could supply the necessary connective tissue in modern society.

What is needed, holds Durkheim, are new kinds of inter-mediary groups which can regulate the specialized occupational life of modern men. He advances a plan for the development of communal or corporative organization among people working in the same occupations and industries. Men in the same seg-ment of the economy will understand each other's problems well enough to respond to them flexibly. They can establish a viable group life which can exercise effective moral control over all the participants on the basis of intimate knowledge.

These occupational corporations were to be represented in a national assembly, with employers and employees each having separate representation. The number of representatives for each was to be determined by the importance that public opinion assigns to their group. The corporations are to be organized on a national basis, coextensive with the national development of the modern economy. They are to maintain carefully their in-dependence of the state.

Ultimately, however, they will become the basis of political organization and the fundamental political entity. This is notably convergent with Saint-Simon's conception of govern-ment in the new positivist-industrial order. In a formula later adopted by Marx, Saint-Simon had expected that government would cease being political in any special sense, and would not involve the coercion of men but the rational administration of things. Territorial and geographic bases of social and political organization will not disappear, claims Durkheim, but will play a less important role in the corporatively organized society. This, too, converges with Saint-Simon's prediction that in modern industrial society loyalties will be less localistic and more cosmopolitan.

Durkheim's rationale for introducing this plan is noteworthy. In a manner at variance with Saint-Simon's, Comte's and Marx's evolutionism, Durkheim does not claim that the corpora-tive organization of society is already embedded in the evolution-ary drift, or that it is inevitably predestined by evolutionary design. Nor does he merely justify his proposal on the grounds that it conforms with certain values which he takes for granted. His position is that historical analysis shows that such corpora-tive organization has been functional in the past and that there are current social needs for which such groups could again be useful. In short, he does not simply describe what it is, nor does he hold that corporative organization 'must be'; he maintains that it *can be* instituted, and that if it were it would prove useful in reducing current social disorganization.

The plan is an interesting synthesis of diverse intellectual streams. It is a blend of the Comteian concern for small groups, with their complex and spontaneous bonds of social interaction, together with the Saint-Simonian emphasis on planned associations. It is a 'utopian' plan in the sense that no plausible mechanisms are suggested for instituting it. Significantly enough, however, it is presented in a deliberately anti-utopian framework, in that it explicitly eschews any effort to specify particulars. Durkheim's formulations here bear the impress of the Marxian polemic against utopianism; indeed, it seems that Durkheim knew Marx well enough to quote the latter's metaphors freely.[20]

What Durkheim seems to have been attempting was a synthesis of Marxist and Comteian views, a compromise which leads him back to Saint-Simonian formulations which had influenced both Marx and Comte. Above all, Durkheim was here seeking to combine the Comteian focus on regulating moral norms with the Marxian focus on economic institutions. The decisive need today, suggests Durkheim, is to provide a moral regulation not merely of society in general but of the economy in particular. What is needed is a regulation that will correspond to the characteristics of the new *industrialism* which, as Saint-Simon had also forcefully emphasized, Durkheim holds to be the distinctive feature of modern society.

What brings about the exceptional gravity of this state [of anomic normlessness] is the heretofore unknown development that economic functions have experienced for about two centuries. Whereas formerly they played only a secondary role, they are now of the first importance. We are far from the time when they were disdainfully abandoned to the inferior classes. In the face of the economic, administrative, military, and religious functions become steadily less important. Only the scientific functions seem to dispute their place, and even science has scarcely any prestige save to the extent that it can serve practical occupations, which are largely economic. That is why it can be said, with some justice, that society is or tends to be essentially industrial.[21]

Durkheim also seems to have regarded his proposal for occupational corporations as consistent with socialist proposals. For even a socialist society, he insists, will require means of morally regulating interpersonal relations and adjusting the activities of different groups to each other. If socialist society is to be stable, it will have to do more than increase productivity and living standards; even elimination of the 'forced division of labour' will not suffice; socialism, too, requires a set of regulating moral norms, capable of daily implementation.

To reiterate the main line of Durkheim's argument in *The Division of Labor*: the increasing division of labour is a normal development in modern industrial society. It does not naturally produce social disorganization, but does so only under certain conditions. The two most important of these are, first, where anomie prevails in the economy, that is, where there is a lack of moral norms governing industrial activities or relations. The second is where there is a 'forced division of labour', that is, where people are constrained to take up positions in the division of labour at variance with their natural talents.

At this point, Durkheim could have pursued two different directions: he could have focused either on the problem of anomie or on the study of the forced division of labour. If he had pursued the latter he could, for example, have examined the reasons why the hereditary transmission of wealth or position does not disappear and give way to new social arrangements more in keeping with the modern division of labour.

He does not take this direction at all. This cannot be explained by stating that Durkheim believed that the forced division of labour would naturally wither away in the course of time, and that it therefore required no planned remedy. For he clearly rejects this tack with respect to normlessness or anomie in the economic sphere. In the latter case, he does not count on the 'natural' or spontaneous development of new ethical beliefs to provide the required regulation of economic activities; he deliberately proposes a planned solution to the problem, the occupational corporation.

Attention is focused on the problem of anomie, rather than the forced division of labour, because Durkheim was still deeply committed to Comteian assumptions. He still believes that *some* degree of moral consensus is indispensable to social solidarity, either in a capitalist or a socialist society. If, however, he had further developed the problem of the forced division of labour this could only have obscured his differences with the socialists (as well as the utilitarian individualists) whose basic weakness, he maintained, was their neglect of the role of moral norms.

This tack would also, at some point, have constrained Durkheim into a concern with systems of stratification and power relations, in short into a greater convergence with Marxism. This would have made it difficult, if not impossible, for him to continue using the Comteian model of modern society which saw it as basically tending toward order and stability. Unlike Saint-Simon, who had stressed the role of social classes and of class conflict in providing an impetus or resistance to change, Comte had minimized the role of internal class conflicts.

To Durkheim, as to Comte, the basic features of the new society were already in existence – that is, modern industrialism with its rational methods and its increasing division of labour. Consequently, their problem was to develop a new moral order consistent with it, so that it might remain stable and develop in an orderly manner. Their central task was not defined as producing social change so much as facilitating a natural tendency toward social order. Their problem was, in short, that of 'fine-tuning' the new industrial régime rather than basically re-organizing it. They saw modern society as young and immature, as an insufficiently developed industrialism. One merely needed to stimulate and gently guide the natural processes of its maturation. In contrast, of course, Marx – who had retained the Saint-Simonian emphasis on social classes and class conflict – did not regard modern society as an adolescent *industrialism* but as a senile *capitalism* which, containing the ripe 'seeds of its own destruction', needed to be readied for burial. Expecting that the capitalist would resist his own dismissal, Marx believed that change would not be smooth and orderly, and that therefore modern society possessed deep instabilities.

It is in part because he views modern society in the Comteian manner, as requiring moral rearmament rather than economic reconstruction, that Durkheim focuses on the problem of anomie and proposes the development of occupational corporations to control it. This is partly a supplement to and partly a polemic against the socialist's neglect of the role of moral norms.[22] But even in this, Durkheim's attitude is no longer that of Comte's; he does not seem to view moral reform as necessarily prior to political or economic reform, as Comte had, but rather as corollary or coincident with it.

The question for Durkheim was *how* the needed moral reform was to be obtained. How could the new morality be developed? Saint-Simon and Comte had in part supposed that the new morality would not be developed but would be (indeed, had been) discovered by positive science and sociology. Durkheim, however, is not sanguine about this solution on several grounds. While he continues to believe that social science can ultimately provide a basis for values, and that a scientific ethics will someday be possible, he nonetheless argues that, at this time, science is not sufficiently advanced to do so. Science could not yet discern the content or the particulars of the new morality. '. . . it is vain to delay by seeking precisely what this law must be, for in the present state of knowledge, our approximation will be clumsy and always open to doubt.'[23] The problem is too pressing to wait for the development of a positive or scientific ethic.

The Development of Moral Beliefs

How then could a new morality appropriate to modern circumstances be secured? It would have to be naturally or spontaneously developed, if it could not now be scientifically discovered. But this raises the question as to how, in general, systems of moral beliefs normally and spontaneously arise. For there is no reason to suppose that the spontaneous development of a new morality will differ from the spontaneous development of earlier moralities. The question of values then becomes a thoroughly empirical one. In short, Durkheim is led to a consistently positivistic position about moral beliefs, becoming concerned with the study of the ways in which they actually evolve and develop. This knowledge about the *spontaneous* development of values could then be used to further the *planned* development of a morality suitable for modern times.

It is in some part because he becomes growingly interested in the spontaneous development of social norms, the ways in which they emerge and become internalized in the individual, that he comes to focus on the role of educational institutions and of the family. This is also one of the reasons for his study of religion, which is essentially a study of the development of moral beliefs in their most dramatic expression. A central point in most of these studies is his concern with the factors that shape and sustain moral beliefs, and not merely in what *they* sustain. In this, again, Durkheim differs importantly from Comte who was basically concerned about the *consequences* of moral beliefs for social consensus and who had contributed little to an empirical understanding of the social forces fostering their development.

The problem was far from definitively resolved in Durkheim's work. Nonetheless, there is one theme which recurs in his studies. It is, above all, that moral norms grow up around sustained patterns of social interaction. It is clear, even in *The Division of Labor*, that he was beginning to focus on patterns of social interaction, as providing the focus around which moral beliefs emerge and develop.

The trouble was that Durkheim never clearly worked out an explicit analytic distinction between patterns of social interaction, or social structures, and patterns of moral beliefs or sentiments, the 'collective conscience'. This confusion is especially discernible in his *Suicide*, and particularly in his discussion of types of suicide. For example, the 'anomic suicide' is characterized as being both normless and socially detached, that is, he is described in terms of both his moral beliefs (or absence of them) and his social relations. The 'egoistic suicide' is held to be burdened by norms calling upon him to take individual responsibility for his own decisions and, also, by being socially isolated from others. Despite this theoretical failure to clearly distinguish between patterns of moral belief and social interaction, Durkheim does break through to a clear solution in his *practical* proposals.

In the final chapter of *Suicide*, for example, he says that the problem of suicide 'bears witness . . . to an alarming poverty of morality'.[24] We cannot simply 'will' the problem out of existence in a utopian way. A people's morality 'depends on the grouping and organization of social elements', on the social arrangements which exist. Ways of thinking and acting cannot be changed without

changing the collective existence itself and this cannot be done without modifying its anatomical constitution. By calling the evil of which the abnormal increase in suicide is symptomatic a moral evil, we are far from thinking to reduce it to some superficial ill which may be conjured away by soft words. On the contrary, the change in moral temperament thus betrayed bears witness to a profound change in our social structure. To cure one, therefore, the other must be reformed.[25]

Since the older forms of social organization, the family, the guild, the church, have been weakened or eliminated, new forms of social organization must be erected in their place to stem the tide of anomie. What Durkheim seems to have been assuming is that patterns of social interaction form the basis upon which moral beliefs spontaneously develop. It is precisely for this reason that he advances as his remedy for moral anarchy in industry the establishment of new modes of social interaction, the occupational corporation. If science cannot yet invent or discover a new morality, then we must use what we know about the spontaneous development of moral beliefs to planfully foster their natural emergence.

Convergences with Marx

In many ways this is a significant convergence with Marx, at least on the level of the working assumptions which they used in their roles as applied social scientists.[26] For Durkheim was here saying something quite consistent with the Marxian formula that 'social being determines social consciousness'.[27] What Durkheim did, however, was to generalize the Marxian formula. Instead of focusing mainly, as Marx usually did, on the manner in which class or economic relations shape patterns of belief, Durkheim holds that social (not merely economic) relations influence the development of beliefs.

Durkheim's analysis of religion and religious beliefs[28] also has important convergences with Marx's, although it is much more acute and sophisticated than the latter's, particularly in its analysis of symbolism. For example, Durkheim notes that in certain primitive societies the totem is the symbol of the god or godhead; but it is also a symbol or flag of the particular clan which worships it. The godhead and the clan are thus symbolically equal to each other. Consequently, concludes Durkheim, religious ideas emerge out of society.

In contrast with Marx, Durkheim does not deal solely with the relation between religion and class or work relations in a society. When Durkheim holds society to be the basis from which religion emerges, he conceives of society as containing a richer variety of relevant elements: power relations and economic conditions are included to be sure, but so, too, are kin and clan groupings as well as ecological factors. Here, too, he can be regarded as having relativized Marx's approach to the development of moral beliefs. Durkheim, then, was beginning to bridge the gap between Marxism and Comteianism.

What Durkheim began to see was that moral beliefs had to be treated in a systematically scientific manner, that their emergence and development as well as their contribution to society needed empirical study. He began to see that the problem of values could not be handled in the manner of radical positivism, that is, by postulating that science could, or would ultimately, formulate and validate moral beliefs. Nor could values be coped with in a theological way, by regarding them as divinely given and thus without a developmental history. Both of these positions had placed values beyond scientific study.

But once existent moral beliefs are no longer taken as given, and once they come to be viewed as problems for empirical investigation, then they must inevitably be seen as interconnected with many other elements of social life. Not only are many things contingent upon them, but they are reciprocally contingent upon many other things. Values then come to be regarded as one constituent of society, an important one to be sure, but still only one. Values and moral beliefs are no longer viewed as the sole or key constituent of society.

As Durkheim puts it, in the *Division of Labor*, society is the necessary condition of the moral world. This is almost a complete reversal of the Comteian position that moral consensus is *the* necessary condition of social order. Moreover, Durkheim adds, 'society cannot exist if its parts are not solidary, but solidarity is only *one* of the conditions of its existence. There are many others which are no less necessary and *which are not moral.*'²⁹ (Our emphases.)

The systematic exploitation of these early insights could have only been fatal to the Comteian position. For Comte had assumed that social solidarity was the prime condition for social survival, and he had further assumed that moral consensus was the basis of social solidarity. Durkheim's critique of Comte's stress on moral norms is inhibited, in part, by his simultaneous polemic against the socialists and individualist utilitarians for their neglect of moral norms. But though the critique of Comte is inhibited, it is, nonetheless, present and important to understand for a proper perspective on Durkheim.

To understand Durkheim's critical orientation to Comte, what needs to be remembered is that, unlike Comte, Durkheim was exposed to the full force of Marxism and to the growing challenge of European socialism. By 1870, the first French labour party had been formed. There was increasing class and industrial conflict in France, culminating in the great Décazeville strike of 1886, the year that Durkheim was drafting *The Division of Labor.* (One year later Durkheim gave the first French university course in sociology.) Durkheim's concern with 'solidarity' is probably related in part to the growing cleavages in French society which are reflected in the growth of socialism.

As a matter of fact, Durkheim began his sociological studies by focusing on the question of the relationship between individualism and *socialism.* These studies were interrupted and it was not until 1895, a decade later, that he returns to the study of socialism. Marcel Mauss, one of the intimate group of collaborators that Durkheim gathered around himself, relates in the introduction to this volume that some of Durkheim's students had been converted to socialism. There also seems to have been some mutual esteem between Durkheim and some of the leading socialists of the time, particularly Guesde and Jaures. Mauss further indicates that, although Durkheim always remained uncommitted to socialism, 'he "sympathized" (as it is now called) with the socialists, with Jaures, with socialism'. The picture that emerges of Durkheim, supported in part by Mauss' introduction, is that Durkheim was under pressure to adjust Comteianism to Marxism. That there was somewhere a bridge between these two traditions was suggested by their possession of a common ancestor, Saint-Simon. Durkheim's sympathetic re-visitation of Saint-Simon, the man most detested by Comte, may be understandable as an incompleted effort to find a passage and to mend the rift between two of the major theoretical systems of his time, Marxism and Comteianism.

This perspective on Durkheim's work finds further confirmation in his little known lectures on *Professional Ethics and Civic Morals*.[30] In these, many of which consist of an examination of the evolution of certain Western values, Durkheim stresses the following points of relevance to our own analysis:

1. He holds that it is the existence of social classes, characterized by significant economic inequalities, that makes it in principle impossible for 'just' contracts to be negotiated. It is this system of stratification which, he argues here, offends the moral expectations of people in contemporary cultures, because it constrains to an unequal exchange of goods and services. The exploitation thus rendered possible by notable power disparities among the contracting parties conduces to a sense of injustice which has socially unstabilizing consequences. Thus, almost surprisingly, both Durkheim and Marx converge on a concept of 'exploitation' as a contributant to current social instabilities.[31]

2. These power disparities derive largely, says Durkheim, from retention of the institution of inheritance. Inheritance *ab intestato*, Durkheim firmly insists, 'is today an archaic survival and without justification';[32] it is in conflict with modern contractual ethics and practices. Testamentary dispositions, in his view, are also likely to be outmoded. Durkheim anticipates their ultimate elimination in modern society and looks forward to a time when property will no longer be transmitted through the family.

3. But if inheritance is eliminated, asks Durkheim, what institution would become the repository of private wealth, upon the death of its original owner? In his answer, we see a totally

different and neglected aspect of Durkheim's project for the corporative reorganization of modern society. The corporative organization of people in the same industry or profession was not seen by Durkheim as having only a morality-building function. The occupational corporation was also expected to have important *economic* functions, inheriting and managing private property following the demise of its original owners. The occupational corporations were Durkheim's 'moral equivalent' for the Marxian nationalization of industry by the state, and were expected to 'satisfy all the conditions for becoming . . . in the economic sphere, the heirs of the family'.[33]

That Durkheim never succeeded in integrating the Marxian and Comteian traditions is evident; but he approached the foothills to an intellectual confrontation which challenges theorists to this very day.

NOTES

1. To obviate possible misunderstandings, let me stress that I am in no way suggesting that a distinction between the history of sociological theory and current theory be obliterated. I concur entirely in Robert Merton's judgement that 'although the history and the systematics of sociological theory should both be of concern in training sociologists, this is no reason for merging and confusing the two'. R. K. Merton, *Social Theory and Social Structure*, Free Press, rev. ed., 1957, p. 5. I believe, too, that I am also cognizant of the extent to which earlier theories are larded with false starts, archaic doctrines, and fruitless errors. I more than doubt, however, that present systematic sociological theory has come anywhere near assimilating the still viable parts of early theory. Moreover, I am not confident that *current* theory has a smaller proportion of false starts, archaic doctrines, and fruitless errors. If this is true, then these same deficiencies in earlier theories cannot justify their neglect. The decisive question is, of course, whether there is reason to believe that there is still something scientifically promising in the early work. By far the best indication that there is, can be found in the work of two of the most creative of contemporary sociological theorists, Robert Merton and Talcott Parsons. In the case of Parsons there can be little doubt that his immersal in the earlier theorists, as evidenced by his *Structure of Social Action*, provided an indispensable basis for his own systematic theory. More specifically, as Parsons himself has explicitly acknowledged, his 'pattern variables' schema is a direct outgrowth of his work on Ferdinand Tonnies' theory of *Gemeinschaft* and *Gesellschaft*. See T. Parsons and N. J. Smelser, *Economy and Society*, Free Press, 1956, p. 33. One may similarly note the extremely fruitful uses to

which Robert K. Merton has put such classic theorists as C. H. Cooley, H. Spencer, W. G. Sumner, and, above all, G. Simmel, in his recent essay on 'Continuities in the Theory of Reference Groups and Social Structure', ibid., pp. 281–386.

2. That the exceptions to be found in the work of Bernard Barber, W. F. Cottrell, Gerard de Gré, and Robert Merton are notable does not make them any the less exceptions. Note the similar discussion by Robert Merton concerning current deficiencies in the sociological study of science in his 'Priorities in Scientific Discovery', *American Sociological Review*, Dec. 1957, p. 635.

3. I have, previously, had occasion to examine a set of twenty-five text books in introductory sociology, published between 1945–54, to determine what they had to say about the causes and effects of war. I found that in the 17,000 pages which these volumes contained, there were only some 275 pages which dealt with war in any of its manifestations. More than half of the texts dealt with this single most important problem of the modern world in less than 10 pages.

4. Such an over-emphasis is to be found, I believe, in Parsons' interpretation of Durkheim. For example, 'Insofar as any influence is needed to account for his [Durkheim's] ideas, the most important one is certainly to be found in a source which is both authentically French and authentically positivistic – Auguste Comte, who was Durkheim's acknowledged master. Durkheim is the spiritual heir of Comte and all the principal elements of his earlier thought are to be found foreshadowed in Comte's writings. . . . Every element in his thinking is rooted deeply in the problems immanent in the system of thought of which Comte was so eminent an exponent.' Talcott Parsons, *The Structure of Social Action*, McGraw-Hill, 1937, p. 307. One might say exactly the same thing about the relationship between Durkheim's and Saint-Simon's thought, and, quite understandably so, since Comte derived practically all of his main ideas from Saint-Simon. (But more on this later.) It is therefore extremely difficult to distinguish between the Saint-Simonian and the Comteian influence on Durkheim.

5. Despite Durkheim's yeoman-like efforts to dispel the conception that Comte was the 'father' of sociology, the belief in 'Comte the father' persists, even among sociologists, as an almost indestructible myth. Contemporary sociologists, of course, no longer lend credence to such ebullient fantasies as Chugerman's, who held that '. . . shutting himself in his room for a day and a night, he [Comte] evolved the general conception of social science and the project of the positive philosophy . . .' S. Chugerman, *Lester F. Ward*, Duke University Press, 1939, p. 174. Nonetheless, one still finds fundamentally erroneous statements concerning Comte's significance in relation to Saint-Simon's. N. S. Timasheff, for example, has recently reaffirmed this myth in maintaining that 'Auguste Comte . . . was the first major figure to assert and then prove by deed that a science of society, both empiric and theoretical, was possible and desirable' (N.S. Timasheff,

Sociological Theory: Its Nature and Growth, Doubleday and Co., 1955, p. 15). Similarly erroneous judgements are to be found in Jacques Barzun and Henry Graff, *The Modern Researcher*, Harcourt, Brace, 1957, p. 203. Such judgements might have been understandable had they been made prior to 1859, when Saint-Simon's *Mémoire sur la science de l'homme*, originally written in 1813, was first published. This essay definitely establishes that Saint-Simon's formulation of positivist philosophy, and of sociology, clearly preceded his association with Comte. This is also borne out by Durkheim, Halévy, Bury, and Saint-Simon's recent biographers, Frank Manuel, Mathurin Dondo, and F. M. H. Markham. If the myth of 'Comte the founder of sociology' still persists in American sociology, despite long-standing evidence to the contrary, this suggests that it performs certain on-going social functions for those holding it. There is an interesting problem here for a study in the sociology of knowledge. One hypothesis for such a study might be that acknowledgement of Comte as the putative father of sociology is less professionally damaging than acknowledgement of Saint-Simon who, as Durkheim points out, was also one of the founders of modern socialism. If sociologists acknowledge descent from Saint-Simon rather than Comte they are not only acquiring a father, but a black-sheep brother, socialism, thus reinforcing lay opinions to the effect that socialism and sociology must be similar because they have the same prefix. Needless to say, such an hypothesis would not premise that there is a 'plot' afoot to do Saint-Simon out of his rightful heritage! While it may make no difference to the substance of a science concerning who, in fact, its 'founding father' was, nonetheless, shared professional *beliefs* concerning this may be significant for a discipline's professional organization and its practioners' self-images. A 'founding father' is a professional symbol which can be treated as a trivial detail by no one who wishes to understand the profession as a social organization. Where there are conflicts, by later generations, concerning who their 'founding father' was, we suspect that this may be a serious question essentially reflecting a dispute over the character of the profession.

6. Parsons notes that Durkheim 'directs attention immediately to the moral elements in social life', and that this is indicative of his polemic against Herbert Spencer, the utilitarian individualists, and the Manchester school of economists. Parsons, ibid., p. 310. Not only does this neglect consideration of the implications of Durkheim's polemic against Comte, but it also omits consideration of the manner in which Durkheim's stress on the 'moral' elements in society is related to his polemic against the socialists. In a review of Durkheim's study of *Suicide*, one of Durkheim's contemporaries, Gaston Richard, makes this clear. See *L'Année sociologique*, 1897, p. 404. Durkheim was engaged on several fronts simultaneously: on the one hand, opposing the socialists and the utilitarian individualist's neglect of moral elements and, on the other, opposing Comte's overstatement of the contemporary significance of moral norms in a society with an advanced division of labour.

7. As quoted in Durkheim's *The Division of Labor in Society*, tr. G. Simpson, Free Press, 1947, p. 358.

8. ibid., p. 398, see also pp. 364 *et seq.*

9. ibid., p. 400.

10. ibid., p. 406.

11. ibid., p. 401. The role of both the division of labour and of shared moral beliefs as bases of social solidarity are also to be found in Saint-Simon. With respect to the latter, note, as one of many instances cited by Durkheim in the following volume, Saint-Simon's comment in a letter to Chateaubriand: 'The similarity of positive moral ideas is the single bond which can unite men into society.'

12. cf. Parsons' comment that '. . . reversion to mechanical solidarity represents the authentic line of Durkheim's development'. ibid., p. 321.

13. Durkheim, ibid., p. 365.

14. cf. Frank E. Manuel, *The New World of Henri Saint-Simon*, Harvard University Press, 1956, p. 232.

15. Émile Durkheim, *Suicide*, tr. J. A. Spaulding and G. Simpson, Free Press, 1951, esp. ch. 2.

16. Comte's bitter polemic against the 'dogma of unlimited Liberty of Conscience' because it 'tends to hinder the uniform establishment of any system of social ideas', apparently misses the point that this 'dogma' was, in fact, a *shared moral belief*. Auguste Comte, *System of Positive Polity*, Vol. 4, tr. Richard Congreve, Longmans, Green, 1877, p. 531.

17. 'The entire morality of progress and perfection is thus inseparable from a certain amount of anomy.' *Suicide*, ibid., p. 364.

18. ibid., p. 217.

19. *Division of Labor*, see especially pp. 374, *et seq.*

20. ibid., p. 393.

21. ibid., p. 3.

22. cf. especially Durkheim, *Socialism and Saint-Simon*, Antioch Press, 1958, chapter X. Here the nub of Durkheim's critique of Saint-Simon and socialism is that it provides for no moral restraints on economic aspirations. Durkheim, however, is hard put to cope with Saint-Simon's final work on the 'New Christianity' in which a morality transcending economic interests is proposed. While Saint-Simon's approach to morality occasionally bears vestiges of Voltaire's 'Footman's God', it is clear in this final work that Saint-Simon had emphasized a need for a morality transcending economic objectives. Durkheim's subsequent effort to maintain his original

position concerning Saint-Simon's neglect of moral factors is, to my mind, not entirely successful, though it remains a telling criticism of contemporary communism. In the end, it seems as if Durkheim's criticism is not so much directed against Saint-Simon's neglect of moral elements, but, rather, at the latter's failure to spell out the mechanisms by means of which these were to be built into modern group life. In effect, then, his criticism of Saint-Simon is that he was a 'utopian', precisely in the Marxist sense, in that he had not worked out mechanisms adequate to the realization of his moral objectives. Marx had held that Saint-Simon was a utopian in that he had not conceived mechanisms to implement socialism's economic objectives. For Durkheim, the problem in part became one of the mechanics of producing a moral change.

23. *Division of Labor*, p. 31.

24. *Suicide*, p. 387.

25. ibid.

26. With reference to Durkheim and Marx as applied social scientists, see Alvin W. Gouldner, 'Theoretical Requirements of Applied Social Science', *American Sociological Review*, Vol. 22, No. 1, Feb. 1957, pp. 92–102.

27. For a classically Marxian statement of this, see K. Marx and F. Engels, *The German Ideology*, International Publishers, n.d.

28. É. Durkheim, *The Elementary Forms of the Religious Life*, tr. J. W. Swain, Free Press, 1941.

29. *Division of Labor*, p. 399.

30. These have recently been translated and published in the United States and Great Britain. See Émile Durkheim, *Professional Ethics and Civic Morals*, tr. C. Brookfield, Free Press, 1958.

31. ibid., p. 213 *et seq.* I have discussed this convergence, and its implications, somewhat more fully in 'Reciprocity and Autonomy in Functional Theory', Chapter 7 of the present volume.

32. ibid., p. 216.

33. ibid., p. 218.

13

Sociology and Marxism

The verve of Martin Shaw's critique in N.L.R. 70 of my book *The Coming Crisis of Western Sociology* derives largely from his effort to safeguard something he calls 'Marxism' from subversion by something called 'Radical Sociology'. It is on this issue, a matter of some substance, that I believe his analysis loses its way, and it is concerning this that some brief comment is in order.

Shaw's analysis falters here, I would suggest, for two reasons: first, because it *over*-ideologizes academic sociology and, secondly, because it *under*-ideologizes Marxism. Let me clarify. Shaw totally rejects the possibility that academic sociology has any enduring rational and liberative kernel that deserves rescue. He adopts the manifestly unconvincing position that sociology's decades of labour have been in vain, totally. He argues that academic sociology is completely reactionary, indeed, hopelessly so, and that there is nothing at all in its more than fifty years of research and theory-making that retains any serious value for the human race. In my view, this judgement is in error on both logical and empirical grounds.

Shaw's standpoint on the hopelessness of sociology is strangely in contradiction with the Hegelianizing, Lukácsian Marxism, from whose standpoint he more generally views matters. As he makes quite clear, at the very start of his review, Shaw adopts an Hegelian view of ideology critique; from this standpoint, of course, ideologists are not merely apologists, as he tells us, and ideologies have some rational dimension. From the standpoint of an Hegelian 'ideology-critique' ideologies are not totally false and, therefore, not simply to be unmasked. Rather, their national dimension is to be separated out from their false consciousness and is to be transmitted into and sublated by the next, higher theoretical synthesis. Yet, after acknowledging essentially this conception of 'ideology-critique' in the beginning of his review, Shaw then proceeds to argue exactly the opposite way, so far as sociology is concerned, in the central part of his review. That is, he holds it to be wrong (illegitimate, in his words) to compare present-day sociology with Hegelianism (before Marx 'stood it on its feet'), maintaining that Hegelianism once had a revolutionary kernel that sociology never possessed. From the standpoint of an Hegelian ideology critique, however, it is not incumbent on sociology to have a 'revolutionary' component, it is rather incumbent on Shaw to clarify sociology's rational kernel (which need not be revolutionary to be rational). It would seem rather remarkable, from this standpoint, that every other major ideological standpoint should have some rational kernel that deserves rescuing, but not sociology. Perhaps, therefore, the failure is not in sociology but in Shaw. For his flat rejection of this as a possibility is, at the very least, a contradiction of his own premises.

Quite apart from the logic, Shaw's judgement on this matter – that is, the totally reactionary character of sociology – is also unsatisfactory on empirical and historical grounds. For even classical sociological positivism, at its crassest, was not a totally reactionary standpoint. In its opposition to the proliferation of metaphysical invisibles, positivism placed itself in abrasive opposition to conventional established religions and, in this, even positivism had its own rational kernel. We might also remember that, at least in their beginnings, positivists were commonly suspect, frequently despised, and occasionally prosecuted and jailed. The early-nineteenth-century positivists were, after all, the preachers of a humanitarian socialism – they were Saint-Simonians! And as such they were one of the main sources of Marx's own socialism. Here one would detail the roles of Ludwig Gall, the Baron von Westphalen, and possibly Eduard Gans. No Marxist can conceivably regard (at least) classical positivism as unambivalently reactionary and totally devoid of rational substance.

But the matter does not end with early positivism. There is a liberative tendency in positivism, even today, manifested by its attraction for many radicals and even Marxists. For example, it is evident that radicals such as Maurice Zeitlin or Richard Flacks have a manifest attraction toward positivism, Zeitlin having gone off to study the Cuban revolution, questionnaires in hand, and Flacks studying the student revolt with essentially the same methodological assumptions. French radicals, too, have long been attracted to positivism; one may regard Louis Althusser as simply the most current in a long line of this sort. Bear in mind, though it is hard to credit, that Althusser actually regards Auguste Comte as 'the only mind worthy of interest' produced by French philosophy 'in the 130 years following the Revolution of 1789 . . .'![1] If even a positivistic sociology had some rational, conceivably revolutionary but, in any event, emancipatory, dimension, it would seem that matters were even more hopeful for other, more reflective, sociologies.

In dealing with Talcott Parsons, of course, we are by no means faced with a positivist. Far from it. The 'young' Parsons rejects positivism, tends to prefer Weber rather than Durkheim as his model; and stresses the importance of a 'voluntaristic' sociology in which human striving, energy, and values can make a difference. The young Parsons' theoretical position thus actually had much in common with the theoretical standpoint from which Georg Lukács mounted his critique of the Second International's mechanical evolutionism. Part of the reason for this convergence, of course, is that both Parsons and Lukács were alike influenced by the great classical German sociologists. It deserves to be stressed that, at precisely the time that the German social democrats were developing a 'scientific' and wooden Marxist determinism, German academic sociologists of that period, perhaps especially Max Weber, were developing a critique of *that* Marxism.

It is often said, and I have been one who has stressed it, that much of academic sociology's character was shaped by its polemic against Marxism. But it is rarely asked, Against *which* version of Marxism were these sociologists polemicizing? I would suggest that much of their polemic was against the Engels–Kautsky–Plekhanov version of Marxism. That is precisely what brings them into some convergence with Hegelian Marxism's critique of Second International Marxism. Once again this suggests that sociology possesses some *liberative* dimension, rather than being hopelessly reactionary, as Shaw holds. It is because of this that Lukács was able to learn much, methodologically and substantively, from Max Weber, as seems clear from the former's analysis of class consciousness and of reification. Shaw, however, explores nothing of this in his broadside references to Max Weber. The fact, of course, is that Lukács was a pupil of Georg Simmel, an associate and student of Weber, to say nothing of his association with Karl Mannheim. Lukács' own development makes it evident that both academic sociology and Marxism had considerable potentiality for a mutually fruitful interaction.

The liberative potential of an academic sociology, its rational kernel, is perfectly plain in the importance that it has long given to a critique of bureaucracy. At a time when Kautsky was congratulating Social Democrats that they had avoided the danger of bureaucracy, Weber's far more profound critique warned that the era of bureaucracy was just coming into its own, and that 'socialism' – the kind of socialism, of course, that he saw around him in Germany – did not mean the dictatorship of the proletariat, but the dictatorship of the official. Certainly, the subsequent development of Stalinism would seem fully to justify Weber's critique. And if this is so, then how can sociology be regarded as an intellectually bankrupt and totally reactionary discipline?

One might say a great deal in criticism of academic sociology's failure to foresee the rise of Black militancy in the United States during the late sixties. But if one does, then one should also simultaneously ask: *Which* Marxists saw this any more deeply and clearly than the sociologists? All this aside, however, the fact remains that it was liberal sociologists whose research helped to sharpen the sense of the 'American Dilemma'; who continued to expose the life conditions of Blacks in some concrete detail; who continued to criticize 'prejudice' and 'segregation' in countless undergraduate courses during the 'passive' fifties, and who may well have contributed in a modest way to the eruption of the activistic sixties. Moreover, as is well known, these social scientists – 'liberals' to be sure – played some small but useful role in helping to bring about the United States Supreme Court's decisive desegregation decision of 1954. Liberal reformism, of course; but it was also constructively emancipatory.

Again, not a little of what we know about the student rebellion, and about youth more generally, derives more from academic sociology, and even from Parsonian sociology which long since spotted the emerging importance of 'youth culture', rather than from Marxism, which has generally had little of systematic value to say about the social role of youth. Much the same may be said about our knowledge of the emerging 'drug culture', which is of growing importance for anyone wishing to understand modern culture. For these and other reasons that might be cited, it seems that academic sociology retains a substantial liberative potential. Shaw would be better advised to maintain a consistently Lukácsian position which sought to extricate sociology's rational kernel, rather than to condemn it wholesale.

The rational and liberative potential of sociology stems in part from its most fundamental *intellectual* commitments as a would-be social science, from the nature of its relationship to society and to the state, and, above all, from the contradictions involved in sociology's existence on these several levels. One of the central contradictions of academic sociology, as I discussed it in *The Coming Crisis*, derives from its role as market researcher for the Welfare–Warfare State. This induces two contradictory experiences: on one side, it limits the sociologist to the reformist solutions of the 'welfare state'; on the other, it also exposes the sociologist to the failures of this state and of the society with whose problems it seeks to cope. Their very work, then, makes sociologists intimately familiar with the human suffering engendered by such failures. While sociologists may be paid to help clean up the contemporary mess, they are often revolted by what their work necessitates them to see.

Secondly, the sociologist's conception of himself as a 'value-free' professional is, I have argued, a false consciousness. But it is a false consciousness which is real in its consequences. On the one hand, such a value-free self-conception allows one to take money from any source and to ignore the societal values that are bolstered by one's professional work. On the other hand, however, the same value-free doctrine sometimes *inhibits* a reflexive loyalty for conventional values and, indeed, sometimes conduces to a certain anomie among sociologists. In short, if the value-free doctrine means that some sociologists are mercenaries and accomplices, they are, nonetheless, sometimes quite cynical about or detached from the very cultural values that are in effect supported by their work. Indeed, their entire professional code, especially that of objectivity, serves as a 'higher value' that may justify withholding the very reflexive loyalty that men in power commonly want, while at the same time providing a kind of protective covering for sociologists' own critical and often resentful impulses.

Again, the central concepts of sociology – 'society', the 'group', or 'culture' – point in two directions: on the one side, they point toward the importance of the group or of culture in shaping and hence in understanding the beliefs and actions of men, and this often underwrites a plea for submission to the conventional; on the other side, the emphasis on society served at one point to liberate men from earlier notions that they faced unchangeable destiny as the puppets of biological or super-natural forces. Now, if sociology held men to be the products of a reified 'society' or 'culture', then at least *these* could be changed, a better world *was* possible, and men need not resign themselves to what was.

In conceiving itself as an *empirical* science devoid of meta-physical presuppositions, in this most dubious expression of sociology's false consciousness, there is nonetheless an important way in which sociology contributed to human emancipa-tion and continues to have a liberative potential. For now, with the emphasis on the empirical, the self-understanding of all societies (including their élites) was in principle made problem-atic; it could now be subject to systematic questioning, to examination, and to a demand for justification. There were now no social groups – neither priests, nor bourgeoisies, nor for that matter revolutionaries – whose pronouncements about them-selves or their worlds needed to be regarded as sacrosanct, simply by reason of their self-confident affirmation or the authoritative position of those making the affirmation. Opposing the most ancient traditionalism or the newest dogmatics, sociology's empiricism insisted that a man's social position or his political allegiance did not suffice to establish the truth of his declarations. Sociology's sheer empiricism, then, necessarily creates tension for all authoritative definitions of social reality, for the claims of the conventional, the sacred, the socially privileged. These claims must now be confirmed 'empirically', confirmed, in short, by 'science', before they could be regarded as true, or, if demonstrated to be beyond such confirmation, they must run the risk – as some later positivists would hold – of being defined as totally devoid of meaning.

A positivistic sociology's contradictions are complex. On the one side, as emphasized above, it stands ready in principle to compare the claims of society (and the self-understanding of its élites) with its own studies of 'what is'. To that extent it discomfits the present: any 'present', whether the 'bourgeois' present that now exists or the 'socialist' present that might exist at some future time. At the same time, however, faced with a choice between the present and some conceivable future, positivism always in effect affirms the reality and rationality of 'what is', of the *status quo*; its impulse is to sidestep issues and problems by avoiding conflicts over values, goals, or ends, and it believes that it can somehow do this by confining itself to a presumably neutral *description* of the social world.

The built-in ambivalence of a positivistic sociology, then, is also commonly resolved in favour of the *status quo* (whatever *status quo*, socialist or capitalist, in which it finds itself) and all the more so by reason of the practical and material support that it derives from that *status quo*. The problem of transcending this ambivalence without surrendering its liberative potential boils down to the problem of how, on the one hand, sociology can be made to surrender its objectivistic false consciousness as value-free and openly to adopt a commitment to the values of emancipation and human fulfilment – without, at the same time, becoming another appendage instrumental to the practical politics of socialism.

That sociological positivism possessed a liberative potential is easy enough to see if one contrasts it with the alternative epistemologies that were and, in some cases, remain its historical alternatives. Essentially, these came down to the claimed right of legitimate authority, in the secular and the 'spiritual' sectors of society, to define the nature of social reality, and to do so with central concern for consistency with the prior commitments of faith. Social reality, in short, was that which was consistent with the faith of the Church and the claims of nobility, taken as unexaminable givens. To this positivism, in effect, replied that if the question is, What is the case?, the answer is not derivable *solely* from determining, logically or morally, what *should* be the case, nor from affirming beliefs required to maintain oneself in good standing as a member of the community. That this emancipatory potential of positivism is not simply a matter of an archaic past but continues into the contemporary present is evident, as Jürgen Habermas reminds us, if we compare the objectivism of positivism with the party science of Stalinism or the racial doctrines of Nazism and their charismatic epistemologies that affirm the rightness of a single man's thought as a social standard.

On the deepest level, the rational core of academic sociology (in the tradition from Comte to Parsons) is in its concern with the self-maintenance of social systems. Much of this sociological tradition embodied a tacit generalization of a 'free market' economy; sociology sought a set of social relationships that were as homeostatically self-maintaining as were market relations in the economy, at least in that tradition's self-understanding. In short, the sociological focus on the 'equilibrium' problem transmitted a latent ideological commitment to a free market. But if ideological compulsiveness led to a one-sided over-emphasis on consensus and equilibrium, it is precisely in this focus that sociological concern had its most abiding rationality. For after a very long experience of the dangers of bureaucratization to the socialist movement and, especially, of a vast bureaucratized state apparatus that culminated in the overgrown and paranoid Stalinist state, socialists quite naturally concern themselves with the problem of how to avoid being crushed by a towering state apparatus.

This reduces itself to the question of how a socialist society may be maintained without – or with only minimal – development of the state apparatus and how it can avoid a totalitarian state superintendence of life. There is, as many socialists already know, only one answer to this vital problem: there must be a 'self-governance' by those involved in the economy and society. The relations between people in a socialist society must be spontaneously self-maintaining, which also means they must be mutually satisfactory. This is precisely what Parsons' system theory is all about. When he formulates the equilibrium problem, he asks, How can a social system be self-governing, self-adjusting, self-correcting, self-maintaining? *The Coming Crisis* argues that there is no way in which a capitalist system can any longer be that. At the same time, however, this failure of the capitalist system does not at all guarantee that a socialist solution of 'Workers' Councils' will itself necessarily solve the problem of self-maintenance. Without a thorough-going theoretical analysis of the problem of spontaneously self-maintaining social systems, 'workers' control' could remain an inoperable ideology that serves only as a new window dressing for a familiar élitism.

Seen in the context of Western capitalism, Parsonian equilibrium analysis is conservative, when not merely irrelevant; but in the context of certain Eastern European countries which are massively controlled from a separate political centre, this same equilibrium analysis has liberative potentialities. It provides certain theoretical clues as to how a socialist society may be organized with a minimum of bureaucracy and of state control. In effect, then, the rational core of sociology is that it suggests theoretical guidelines for the creation and maintenance of a free community of men under socialism.

Before leaving this point, however, let me stress that it has *not* been my aim here to argue that academic sociology as we know it is progressive or emancipatory, let alone revolutionary. In *The Coming Crisis* and elsewhere I repeatedly stressed that the ideological character of academic sociology is now *predominantly* conservative; but I have always added that I also believe that there is, underneath, an emancipatory potential that needs to be liberated from the domination of sociology's conservatism. My comments here have aimed to defend the latter judgement about this liberative potential; they are not to be understood, of course, as changing my overall judgement about the dominance of the conservative aspect of sociology.

There is a second basic reason why I believe Shaw's effort to protect 'Marxism' from subversion by radical sociology is misguided. This has to do with the contemporary condition of Marxism itself. If Shaw's treatment of academic sociology is mistaken because he sees it as all false consciousness and all ideology, then his view of Marxism is mistaken for the opposite reason, namely, that he sees it as in no way suffering from *any* false consciousness or ideologization. Which is to say that Shaw seems inconsistent in two ways: first, when he refuses to consider that academic sociology might have some rational kernel and fails to clarify what this might be; and, secondly, when he fails totally to consider that *Marxism itself* might also have its own false consciousness and when he fails to explore what this might be. Having thus arranged that academic sociology shall be deemed totally mired in false consciousness and ideology, while Marxism presumably floats serenely above any contaminating contact with them, Shaw has contrived a melodrama of an unblemished good versus an unredeemable evil that would warm the heart of any fundamentalist preacher. In doing so, he *exhibits* the false consciousness of his own Marxism, even if he does not admit its existence or talk about it analytically.

This corporealization of the false consciousness of Shaw's Marxism may indicate that the end is in sight not only for conventional academic sociologies but also for Marxism. Indeed, it would be surprising were that not the case. Both sociology and Marxism are essentially nineteenth-century theories which, however much engaged in mutual polemic, were also always joined together at the back like Siamese twins. The demise of one presages the demise of the other. They have a common destiny not *despite* the fact that they have developed in dialectical opposition but precisely *because* of it.

The most fundamental difficulty of Shaw's position, then, is that it premises a Marxism-in-being that can presumably be counterposed to the non-being of academic sociology. This conception of the matter is essentially a positivistic one, implying as it does that Marxism now exists as a 'thing' to which we may flee, as a kind of *place* to go, as a *space* already carved out and liberated and waiting for us as a haven. Those conceiving the situation in this reified manner manifest that they are simply going to substitute the crisis of Marxism for the crisis of academic sociology. If Marxism is already a constituted alternative to a radical sociology, *which* or *whose* Marxism is this to be? Do we rally around the Marxism of Lenin? Trotsky? Lukács? Korsch? Della Volpe? Althusser? Sartre? Do we rally around the Marxism of Engels or of Marx and, if Marx, the young or the older Marx? Certainly we cannot rally around them all, for they are often mutually contradictory and, are indeed in some cases, self-repudiated. So what, then, is the Marxism counterposed to the radical sociology that is to be repudiated?

NOTE
1. Louis Althusser, *For Marx*, Allen Lane The Penguin Press, 1969, and New York, Random House, 1970, p. 25.

14

The Red Guard

'Judging from this evening you seem to be in good condition,' I said. Mao Tse-tung smiled wryly and replied that there was perhaps some doubt about that. He said again that he was getting ready to see God very soon.
Interview with Mao Tse-tung, by Edgar Snow, *New Republic*, 27 February 1965.

In isolating ourselves from China, we have placed the West in a situation where every turn in the Chinese Revolution seems inexplicably mysterious and in which we are finally driven to explain mystery as due to madness. If the Russian Revolution seemed to be a 'mystery wrapped in an enigma', the Chinese Revolution seems increasingly – to certain Westerners – a mystery that enwraps and conceals a core of madness. When political fears are compounded by a confrontation with an alien culture the differences that become visible seem to be an expression of insanity. The explanation of political events as due to madness is a confession of intellectual impotence; it is another way of saying that we are incapable of offering rational explanations for events.

Nothing seems more insane, at first blush, than the recent reports of street skirmishing of the Red Guards with workers and detachments of the Red Army sent to curb them, attacks of Red Guards upon the home of Madame Sun Yat-sen, their damage to certain public properties, and above all their clashes with select local Communist Party cadres and headquarters.

Our job here is to seek and propose a sociological framework in which even the seeming madness of the Red Guard episode may be made intelligible.

First, we ought to be clear about what it is that needs explaining. What is it that seems so mysterious to us in the West about the behaviour of the Red Guards?

Surely we would not find it strange if it were some kind of *coup d'état* that had been perpetrated by a section of the army

This essay was co-authored with Irving L. Horowitz.

against the Communist Party or against the régime. We have seen that before in Latin America and in Indonesia. But despite its military designation, the Red Guard is not a wing of the army but basically is comprised of militant students, rural and urban youth – in some reports numbering as many as six million – who have remained more loyal to the ideals of the Revolution than to the organizational forms of the conventional Communist Party establishment. The Red Guard has put itself forward not as an opponent of Mao Tse-tung but, to the contrary, as his most vocal protector and truest follower. The avowed aim of the Red Guard is to protect Mao and his teachings and, indeed, to protect the entire Central Committee of the Communist Party. The Red Guards are a generation-cohort whose revolutionary fervour has not been blunted by *Realpolitik*.

What is strange, then, is that successful and established revolutionaries should incite and accept protection from student militants, even though the party hierarchy has created an enormous and far-ranging network of powerful institutions: the Communist Party, the Red Army, a newly emerging bureaucracy in almost all sectors of life, and upon whom – one might think – they might confidently rely for the perpetuation of the revolution and its régime.

The central question, then, is why has Mao turned to the students and allowed them – and quite probably, incited them – to speak on his behalf, on behalf of the Central Committee of the Chinese Communist Party? And why has he done so in this particular period in the history of the Chinese Revolution?

The question of its timing does not seem too difficult. Here, three considerations seem foremost. First, the succession problem grows increasingly critical with each passing year, and it must be seen as such by the old leaders of the Chinese Communist Party, who are already venerable even by Chinese standards. Unlike Western leaders such as Joseph Stalin and Charles de Gaulle whose public statements never intimated their mortality, Mao has for some time been publicly pondering his impending death. As his interviews with Edgar Snow and others indicate, he expects to die shortly. Whatever the publicity value of his recent swimming of the Yangtze river, it is clear that his private ratiocinations are sombre; he is thoroughly aware of his own mortality and of its political implications.

Second, this intensifying succession crisis has developed in an international context in which the old leaders of the Chinese Communist Party have become increasingly aware of the possibility that their own revolution, like any other, might be corrupted if not overthrown. The Chinese struggle against the Soviet Union (and in particular what they conceive to be its 'revisionism') has heightened their anxiety about the safety and future of the Chinese Revolution to which they have devoted their youth and their lives.

Third, the mobilization of the Red Guard can be considered as part of a general intensification of fervour as the international crisis deepens from the Chinese perspective. The Chinese have suffered diplomatic as well as political losses in such far-flung places as Cuba, where the Chinese régime was denounced by Castro; in Indonesia, where Sukarno has been replaced by Suharto as the actual leader of the régime and where the Chinese no less than the Communist Party have suffered intensive persecutions; in Africa, where Boumédienne's régime in Algeria replaced Ben Bellas', thus causing the collapse of a major 'third world' conference; and also, in Ghana, where Nkrumah was displaced as leader precisely when he was on a state visit to China. All of these genuine setbacks have occasioned intensification of the internal conflicts. In some part the phenomenon of the Red Guards is an answer to these recent defeats: they announce that the Revolution still lives. The Red Guards provide the form, if not always the substance, of the permanent revolution.

In this connection, it should be kept in mind that within the framework of Marxism there has always been a strong wing deeply troubled by national revolutions at the expense of the continuation of the revolution elsewhere. Whatever the basic differences between Maoism and Trotskyism on this point, there seems a common fear that stability can only bring about the conservatizing of the revolution. The Red Guards in such a context can symbolize the viability of the revolution, if not provide a guarantee against its natural ageing and decadence.

But where do Mao and his associates see the danger coming from? Here, it would be misleading if we sought to understand the Chinese Revolution on the model of the Russian. There is a continual temptation to misread Chinese history by seeing it as repeating the problems and the stages of the Russian Revolution. But this is misleading because the Chinese Revolution took place after, and developed in the context of, a prior and successful Soviet Revolution; the two can no more be expected to be the same than the second child in a family can be expected to be like the first.

One difference between the two revolutions is this: unlike the Chinese, the leaders of the Russian Revolution conceived of the danger to their revolution as coming, primarily and most powerfully, from the world outside. And with good reason. Immediately following upon the October Revolution the Bolsheviks found themselves beset by the armies of more than a dozen nations. The political trials of the old Bolsheviks and of others commonly sought to link their 'betrayal' to the direct and deliberate intervention and scheming of foreign powers. Thus, even where the enemy was seen as being within, he was essentially defined as an 'agent of a foreign power'. The Stalinist conception of the danger and of the enemy was thus very largely centred on the outside world.

But this does not seem to be the case for the Chinese Revolution. Certainly, the Chinese Communists believe that Chaing Kai-shek would like to invade their mainland and that, to do so successfully, he must and might receive the support of the United States. They were similarly aware of the possibilities of being militarily embroiled with the United States in any extension of the war in Vietnam. Yet these 'objective' dangers from without do not seem to be the dangers that weigh most heavily upon the minds of the aging Chinese Communist Party leaders, but, rather, the dangers that abide within their own culture.

The most essential point being made is not so much with respect to the location of the perceived dangers to the Revolution but, rather, with respect to the location of the perceived resources of and possible help to the Revolution. The Russian Bolsheviks, prior to the October Revolution, never believed in their own ability to bring the Russian Revolution to a successful culmination without international support. They expected that their seizure of power in Russia would be the signal for a European-wide, and especially a German, revolution from which they could receive aid for the own industrialization. They did not at first imagine they could overcome what they regarded as 'Russian backwardness' without outside assistance from industrially advanced nations. When the German and Hungarian revolutions failed, after the Bolshevik seizure of power in Russia, the Russian revolutionaries were despairing and disoriented.

The Russian Revolution was, from its earliest inception, a special sort of social movement: a movement for cultural revitalization which saw the solution to its problems as deriving from the *importation* of Western technologies. Its attention was from the first fastened upon its relation to and its dependence upon the West. After the failure of the revolution in the West, the Soviet leaders remained sensitive to the manner in which their security and their prospects were contingent upon the new society's relationship to the outside world. Even when their anxiety and pessimism were overcome and bound by the slogan of 'Socialism in One Country', the Soviet leaders never doubted that developments elsewhere – such as Fascism and Nazism – could (and were intended to) impair their new society. Russian intellectuals had long measured themselves by Western European standards and models and they continued to do so even when thrown back upon their own resources during the Stalinist 'anti-cosmopolitan' period.

The Chinese revolutionists have, to the contrary, long despised their subjection to outside influences of Western imperialism and to what they took to be its *alien* culture. Their basic impulse was not to import Western cultural models, nor to emulate and overtake the West. Their basic impulse was to liberate themselves from such outside influences. In short, China was a colonially dominated nation in a way that Russia had not been.

The Chinese did not expect help from their former foreign colonial overlords. During the process of their gathering revolutionary efforts, from 1927 onward, they also found that the needs of their own revolution were being subordinated to those of the Russians. They began to view the Soviet Union not as a paragon of international revolutionary solidarity but rather as a more sophisticated expression of the nationalist selfishness of Western nations. They began to see the Soviet Union not as an example of revolutionary vitality but as a sad case of revolutionary corruption and softness demonstrated by the collapse of fervour among its own younger generation, the bureaucratization of Communist Party workers, and the rise of party careerism. These sentiments finally expressed themselves in the Chinese attack on Khrushchev's 'revisionism', which was only one side of the coin. The other side entailed a demand that the revolution hew to its original purpose. They began to believe that the authenticity of the revolution depended more upon their internal spiritual purity than external material aid.

This internal preoccupation is evident in Mao's recurrent comments about the growing laxity of the Chinese youth, and of the possibility that they would not have the stomach to perpetuate the Chinese Revolution once he and his cohorts were gone. Again, it is just this sensitivity to the internal dangers that face the Chinese Revolution, and the willingness of the Chinese leaders to talk about them publicly – as they did, for example, on their recent visits to Eastern Europe – that makes their political diagnoses of their own situation *seem* to be surprisingly realistic, and quite different in character from those typically enunciated by the Russian leaders.

But there is not only a question of how they define and conceive the *location* of these dangers to the Chinese Revolution. There is also the further and equally important problem of how they conceive of the *character* of these dangers. To understand this properly, to see what the Chinese regard as the source of their present danger, it is also necessary to see what they regard as the source of their previous *success* and victory. Here the matter must be set in its historical context and viewed as part of the long-range evolution of Communist strategy, from Marx onward.

A central shift in political strategy has occurred in the Communist world since the time of Marx. It has been a shift from a view which at first emphasized the importance of objective economic conditions for a successful revolution, to a view that increasingly emphasized the importance of political initiative, party organization, and ideological commitment. This shift was first fully visible in Lenin's objections to Plekhanov's doctrine of 'spontaneity', which saw the revolution as a natural outgrowth of a mature working class. To this Lenin counterposed the need for a revolutionary élite that could seize and maintain the political initiative. The Chinese operated in an economy that was even less like that in which Marx had expected a socialist revolution than did the Russian Bolsheviks, and they developed an increasing emphasis upon the importance of ideology and the 'spiritual factor' as the mainspring and ultimate guarantor of the revolution. The Chinese emphasis on dialectics, on the power of self-criticism, can be interpreted as a further move away from the original focus on economics which Marx held in common with the classical economists. If Lenin added to the Marxist corpus the concept of party organization as fundamental to revolution-making, Mao added to Leninism the concept of personal will and military fortitude as the essence of nation-building. In Maoism, Marxism has thus turned full-circle toward an unembarrassed 'utopianism'. It is the wilful struggle – not the organizational machinery – that the ageing leadership trusts. Thus the Chinese leadership is even ready to risk the possibility of internal strife, not because it is oblivious to the possibilities of ramifying civil conflict, but rather because it is more concerned with the purifying value of conflict.

The older generation of Chinese Communists had, certainly from an orthodox Marxist viewpoint, achieved something of a miracle ever since their long march north to the Shensi province in 1927. By classical Marxist standards they could very well feel that they had achieved the impossible. For they had come to power in a country which was even more industrially backward and economically depressed than revolutionary Russia, and in which modern science, modern industry, and modern technology scarcely existed.

Indeed, it was only when the Chinese Communists abandoned orthodox Bolshevik tactics that victories were registered. In the early 1920s, they tried to capture large cities, such as Canton, where it was hoped the factory workers would rally to the revolutionary cause; but such strata were either too small or too intimidated to forge a revolutionary phalanx. But when the Communists were driven from the cities to the countryside, they changed not only their tactical emphasis from factory workers to peasants, but more significantly, their leadership – from the Moscow-trained cadres who had secret headquarters in Shanghai to indigenous Chinese elements (Chu Teh was a war lord, and Mao himself was of peasant origins) operating in the open. Thus, the victories of the Chinese Communists coincided with a turn from town to countryside, from Bolshevik to native party cadres, and from clandestine to military actions.

The 'miracle' of the Chinese Revolution was thus even greater than that of the Russian Revolution, not simply because of the industrial backwardness of Chiang's China in comparison to Czarist Russia, but because the Chinese Revolution succeeded in totally reorienting the temperament of the rural masses no less than the urban classes, whereas the Russian Revolution only reoriented a strata of the working classes. The Chinese Red Army smashed the Kuomin-tang in civil war. This experience also re-emphasized the role of 'will' in the making of the Chinese Revolution in contrast to the role of organization.

In short, their political and military experience leads the old Chinese leaders to conceive of themselves as having succeeded, not because of 'objective factors', but rather because of 'subjective factors' – because of correct theory, because of a steadfast commitment to ideology, because of a readiness for personal sacrifice. It is precisely this that leads them to emphasize the importance of the teachings of Mao Tse-tung. This emphasis on Mao's writings is not, as is sometimes suggested, to be understood simply as a part of the process of the deification of Mao. It is rather their conception of the meaning of Chinese experience: namely, that it was theory, indeed Mao's theory, that had made the primary difference for them and not objective conditions. In the hands of Mao, Marxism more than ever became a doctrine to live by rather than a dogma to abide by, and it is at this level that their exhortation to read and study Mao seems most intelligible.

In addition there has been a long-standing, if concealed, chasm between the struggling Communist movement of China and the established Bolshevik organization of the Soviet Union.

From the 1920s onward it was clear that Stalin was less concerned with fostering the Chinese revolution than with maintaining a legal correctness in his dealings with foreign nations that could provide a protective international framework for the Soviet Union. The Chinese were not merely disappointed with the withdrawal of Soviet aid once their own revolution succeeded, but were newly convinced of the parochial national character and bureaucratization of the Soviet revolution. The conversion of Chinese Marxism into a mass movement, such as that exhibited by the Red Guards, is an attempt to compensate for the loss of material foreign aid by strengthening their internal spiritual resources. For this reason the Chinese have ordered many slogans concerning the power of ideas to be put forward as a last gasp against the frustrations and inhibitions occasioned by the inexorable technological advance of Bolshevik Russia, no less than capitalist United States. Indeed, it might be said that Chinese Marxism-Maoism is the ultimate romanticization of Socialist doctrine; it is the elevation to a supreme level of the role of heart over that of head, of will over economic conditions, and people over weaponry.

The old Chinese leadership understand their past success as the product of their will and ideological commitment. At the same time, this is how they understand their failure, or at least the threat of possible failure that they see hanging over them with the passing of the older generation. Because their political experience has led the Chinese to assign so much significance to the importance of theoretical, ideological, and spiritual factors, they have come to define their present danger – no less than their former victory – as deriving from a decline in ideological commitment and from a loss of theoretical clarity. Correspondingly, if the danger is ideological and spiritual, then they must also see the solution and remedy as being ideological and spiritual. And that seems to be why the current turbulence in China has come to centre upon the problem of the completion of what is conceived to be a 'cultural' revolution, and thus on the need to complete the transformation of the values and beliefs of the Chinese people.

The aging Chinese political élite is a charismatic cohort: it not only stands above the institutions which it has created, but it also does not fully trust them – and indeed more than mildly distrusts them. It distrusts them, in some part, because it recognizes that some sectors and echelons in these new institutions, many composed of men immediately beneath them, have been trained in Moscow. They are thus not simply politically suspect on nationalistic grounds but also may be seen as ideologically contaminated by Russian revisionism. And in one way this is quite realistic. Some Russian intellectuals have not entirely despaired of reconciliation with the Chinese because when the old leaders die they will be replaced by young men who have been students of the Russians. But the aging Chinese leaders not only distrust these younger leaders; they also and more generally distrust all the institutions that they man, for they believe that the life of the revolution is in the *spirit* and not in its institutions.

What then are the Central Committee and the Chinese leadership attempting to do in unleashing the Red Guards? Fundamentally, they are seeking a revival of spirit and the purification of revolutionary ideology. The older generation is seeking to bypass part of the Moscow-tainted middle generation, and provide a check upon it, by allying itself with an ideologically reinvigorated younger generation. They are seeking to foster revolutionary fervour among a generation that has never known revolution, and thereby to commit this generation to a posture of ideological purity, thus providing a stable framework that will ensure the continuity of the revolution, as they conceive it.

In unleashing the Red Guards the Chinese Central Committee has also unlocked certain doors to social change. There were, indeed, middle-class styles and Western importations in Chinese urban regions. There were five per cent of men who lived off their previous commercial and land holdings. There were, indeed, bureaucrats unable or unwilling to perform everyday services in a competent manner. It would be a mistake to think that the enemy of the Red Guards is entirely a fiction. The enemy within was real, so much so that the Chinese leaders were willing to risk a paralysis of industrialization to combat it. It could well be that the Red Guards form the fighting wing of a twentieth-century Chinese puritanism, for their demand for purification has been made in the name of simplification of life styles, improving of work styles, and ordering of cultural styles. The fervour, the passion of such a movement may easily spill over into violence of an unbridled variety, but of a kind not unknown in the West and frequently found among those who are most fervently concerned with the purification of the spirit. The risks of the present course of action on the part of the Chinese leadership are indeed great. Undoubtedly they believe the possible consequences of its failure will be greater still.

One possible consequence of promoting the Red Guards may be to break the legitimation system of orthodox Communists. Instead of a system that operates through the organizational channels of the Communist Party system, the Red Guards symbolize a return to spontaneity and to the importance of ideological purity rather than party loyalty. The wheels for such an approach were already set in motion by the emphasis on 'national liberation' movements outside the orthodox Communist Party apparatus in many parts of the 'third world'. Khrushchev, in his critique of Maoism made just prior to his retirement, exhibited considerable fears lest such emphasis on liberation movements turn into 'anti-party' vehicles. It might well be that the Chinese leadership has taken the next logical step, and declared that the protection of the Chinese Revolution is no longer to be the exclusive duty of the 'vanguard party', but rather of the people as a whole. In short, neither charismatic nor bureaucratic routinization now obtains. Rather, China is witnessing a restructuring of both – made in a holy alliance between the militant antiquarians who have nothing to lose but their waning leadership and the militant youths who have nothing to lose but their reason for living.

If bypassing the middle generation – the transitional generation – can spare China the agonies of Stalinist totalitarianism, then the results of the 'cultural revolution' may well come to be judged as positive – even in the West. However, if this new generational coalition should tear Chinese culture apart in the name of ideological purity, it might well be that instead of sparing China the worst disruptions of the Soviet experience, it will make that seem a model of orderly evolution.

15

Comments on *History and Class Consciousness*

Georg Lukács' *History and Class Consciousness* is a truly extraordinary work, and its English translation,[1] after almost fifty years of neglect by English and American publishers, is a major event. Indeed, its sheer eventfulness is so fraught with implication that exploring this might overshadow the intellectual content of the book itself. Certainly this long overdue translation tells us something about the ineffectual state of the translation industry and in particular about the American segment of it; for if the book is now available to Americans, it is primarily thanks to the initiative of its original translator, the British publisher.

That it took almost half a century to make this exceptional book available to English readers is due partly to the character of the publishing industry, but rather more, I would add, to the book's own intellectual character as a Marxist heresy; upon its original publication in 1923, it was assaulted at once by Social Democrats and Bolsheviks alike and, indeed, was officially condemned by Zinoviev at the 1924 Congress of the Third International. Europe, in short, has long known this book and taken it very seriously indeed. After its condemnation by the Third International, it remained an underground sensation even, and perhaps especially, among Communist intellectuals and other Marxists. That it appears now, along with a growing convoy of commentaries, is a symptom of emerging developments in Anglo-American culture as well as of the continuing crisis of Marxist 'orthodoxy'.

The significant commentaries that will most deeply express

and shape the American understanding of Lukács are only now being readied by young American scholars such as Paul Breines, Andrew Feenberg, Andrew Arato and Paul Piccone. Most Americans who know of Georg Lukács think of him primarily as a literary critic or as a sociologist of literature. But the narrowing concentration of his efforts to these fields signifies his political defeat in the Marxist world and embodies, in some part, a strategy of survival. For these were in a way the expression of his less controversial talents, even if of his first love. The full quality of Lukács' brilliance is most powerfully manifested in this 'youthful' work (done when merely 38!), where he reveals himself as by far and away the most talented philosopher among twentieth-century Marxists, and as their most penetrating critic of contemporary culture. While Susan Sontag's critique of Lukács as an uninspired sociologist of literature has something to justify it, Lukács work as a critic of general culture is an altogether different matter. In this general critique he anticipates and profoundly develops the whole current discussion of 'adversary' culture, and its recent emendation in Daniel Bell's thesis of a contradiction between contemporary culture and social structure.

In a recent book, *Georg Lukács: The Man, His Work and His Ideas*, edited by G. H. R. Parkinson (Random House and Vintage), István Mészáros gives a brilliant discussion of Lukács' dialectics and other contributors summarize Lukács' intellectual and political career. This portrays him as a rich young Hungarian Jew who assimilated the great traditions of German philosophical idealism and of classical academic sociology, as a student of Georg Simmel and associate of Max Weber and Karl Mannheim. Lukács was Commissar for Public Education in the ill-starred Hungarian–Soviet Republic of 1919 and subsequently fled to Vienna, there to edit *Kommunismus* in 1920–22, with an ultra-Left group that resisted all efforts to inhibit revolutionary militancy, whether these came from the newly prudent Bolsheviks or from the long revisionist Social Democrats. As Lukács later remarked candidly, he was then an advocate of 'revolutionary Messianism'; indeed, his *History and Class Consciousness* was the high-water mark of Marxist political voluntarism in the Europe of that period. It was, on the one side, the legitimate heir of the voluntaristic turn marked by Lenin's *What Is To Be Done?* and, on the other, it was the great theoretical anticipation of the voluntaristic upsurge in Marxism that was later to culminate in Mao and Fidel.

After his work was condemned by the Third International, Lukács proceeded, as he says, to complete his 'apprenticeship' in Marxism, in the course of which he supported Stalin on the question of 'socialism in one country'; indeed, after 1924 Lukács was a Stalinist. In 1929, and in order to survive politically, he issued a self-criticism of his political line on the Hungarian Revolution. In 1933 and, strangely enough, for the first time, he issued a public repudiation of *History and Class Consciousness*, a recantation that he later indicated was primarily a matter of political prudence, although subsequently affirming that there were indeed many things in *History and Class Consciousness* that he no longer accepted, and which we must, I think, believe him to have meant.

After his 1929 defeat, Lukács says that he concluded that he was not very effective as a political figure, and so devoted himself increasingly to intellectual and literary work. Nonetheless, he was imprisoned briefly in 1941 and released after world protests. In 1944 he returned to Hungary after a long sojourn in Moscow, and in 1951 he once more came under political attack, once more recanted, and once more retired from political life, only to re-emerge as the aging phoenix of the Hungarian Revolution of 1956. After this was crushed, he was deported to Rumania but was later allowed to return to Hungary, where, in his last years, he was immensely fruitful and fortunate in his work with many talented and devoted students. He died on 4 June 1971.

The crux of Lukács' Marxism is that it does not one-sidedly stress the distinctiveness of the Marxian contribution but *also* emphasizes its continuity with its mother traditions in German philosophy and, most particularly, Hegelianism. It is in part because of his emphasis on this continuity that Lukács, whose work has a most contemporary ring, repeatedly stressed the value of the works of the 'young' Marx. The decisive difference between Marxism and bourgeois thought was not the primacy of economics and of economic motives but, rather, the fact that

Marxism takes the standpoint of the 'totality', refuses to study social objects in isolation, and refuses to submit to the existing division of intellectual labour and separation of the different disciplines. Thus, Lukács' Marxism does not acknowledge the validity of the autonomous sciences of economics, history or law.

In clarifying his notion of the social totality, Lukács spells out a conception of its *systemness* which, while superficially akin to Nikolai Bukharin's, is less deterministic and more dialectical. The social 'totality' is composed of an interaction of social elements that, unlike interacting billiard balls, do not remain the same; they change not only their positions but also their character. The social system must be seen as a historical product, as a thing made and fashioned by men as active 'subjects', as continually remade and daily enacted by the ongoing doings of men, and hence as capable of being undone or redone by their future actions.

The system, in short, depends upon men. The social system is not something given in history, but is a social object that is selectively interpreted and is actively conceptualized by men in the here and now; it is seen as the product of the interaction of 'subject' and 'object'. Lukács understood that men establish their social worlds by constituting them conceptually, as well as by their practical enactments. In Lukács' Hegelian Marxism, then, thought and existence are regarded as different sides of one and the same reality.

For Lukács, the liberation from capitalism means a liberation from the domination of the economy. It will be the elimination of a society in which economic life was not a *means* to social life, but had become its dominating *end*. It is this autonomy and domination by the economic that is one of the major sources of the corruption of contemporary culture. Lukács had no doubt that capitalist culture can and does, from the very first, mount a critique of capitalist society; thus capitalist culture is *limited* by the interests of capitalist society, but also gives voice to the contradictions of capitalism. In short, while a cultural expression can be an authentic outcome of capitalist society it may still be in opposition to its interests.

At this point, let me stress that my focus here is on the young

Lukács who wrote *History and Class Consciousness* from the standpoint of a Marxism that was heavily Hegelian. Lukács himself subsequently repudiated many of the 'excesses' of his early Hegelianism, and this auto-criticism is incorporated in the introduction to the volume. But the book has been published, and the book will be read not for this repudiation, but for what it repudiates. I am thus in the strange position of having to centre my critique on a text that Lukács himself criticized. But it is right, I believe, that *History and Class Consciousness* should be read primarily for its text and not its repudiating introduction. For it is this text that epitomizes one historical potentiality of Marxism. And it is this text which has had a liberating historical role, precisely because it was both politically militant, and, at the same time, philosophically creative, never echoing the increasingly empty Bolshevik rhetoric.

For Lukács, a socialist economy will be one which, unlike the capitalist, will no longer be characterized by the blind autonomy of its own economic laws but will, rather, be subject to control by human reason operating through the planning process and the State administration. Here we have a paradoxical 'opening on the Right' to the development of bureaucratization, even though Lukács' own view of the revolutionary process was often critical of such tendencies. One cannot but wonder: How is it that a romantic, revolutionary messianist such as the young Lukács could hold such a pre-bureaucratic vision of socialism? In some part, this may have been because, for the young Lukács, the focus was on the revolution and not on socialism as such; his concern was to make the revolutionary 'leap', rather than with the nature of the ground onto which the leap would be made.

The bureaucratic vulnerability of Lukács' tradition of socialism also links up with the importance attributed to the role of consciousness in revolution-making and, in particular, with the cognitive, rational, and shaping character of consciousness that derives ultimately from German idealism. If rational, deliberative consciousness is prized, then we must not be surprised to find that those prizing it will have created a social system in which rational planning is stressed and which, in turn, creates its organizational conditions in the form of a bureaucracy. For all his revolutionary Messianism, then, Lukács began with a rationalistic pre-bureaucratic conception of socialism, and it is this, and not only his political defeat, that created in him an inner vulnerability to Stalinism. There was a part of Lukács that was in tune with Stalinism, that welcomed it rather than simply capitulating to it. For 'Stalinism', the skeleton in the Marxist closet, is not to be understood only as Asiatic backwardness, nor merely as a corruption extrinsic to Western rationality, but as a vulnerability inherent in its overweening ambitions, activated when it encounters recalcitrance, opposition or backwardness.

Like Marx, Lukács understood the proletariat as the prime historical actor, as the agency through which the programme and ambitions of classical German philosophy would be fulfilled. A vital difference between the two, however, is that Marx was a 'materialist', while Lukács, certainly the Hegelianizing Lukács of 1923, was somewhat embarrassed by this and primarily defined himself as a *dialectician*. Insofar as this is true, Lukács' Marxism exalted consciousness and held, in George Lichtheim's terms, that the '. . . role of consciousness (and of conscience) is decisive. . . .'

While it was precisely this dominating position of consciousness that Marx originally sought to control with the bridle of materialism, nonetheless consciousness was at least half the conceptual universe for Marx, even if the subordinated half. And he, too, prized consciousness in the form of a stress upon deliberately established social relationships and planned organization. Marxism contains, and Lukács made it perfectly plain that it contains, a cryptic polarity between the 'natural' and the 'social'. Thus, to 'socialize the means of production', the very definition of socialism, meant on the one hand to *denaturalize* them and, on the other, to *rationalize* them. 'Our task,' says Lenin in *What Is To Be Done?* 'is to fight the natural run of things, to divert the labour movement from its natural drift towards trade unionism.' To socialize the means of production meant to remove them from the 'blind' governance of nature and to bring them under conscious planning and deliberate control.

A decisive question here, of course, is who is actually in

control of socialism. The claim that socialism means that the workers themselves will indeed control the means of production was once a humane hope; today it is only a vestigial archaism; but it was always, and it remains, the core ideological mystification of Marxism.

My point, then, is that there was always an élitist potentiality in Marxist socialism, and that this is not an accidental corruption arising from Russian 'backwardness'. The Bolshevik organizational plan, after all, was in part inspired by the German Social Democrats. The élitist potentiality is part of the indigenous character of Marxist theory. It is grounded in the importance attributed to consciousness, an emphasis controlled, repressed, yet active even in orthodox Marxism, but salient and unbridled in its Hegelian formulation. It is this exaltation of consciousness that tends to transform the proletariat into the political raw material of history, to be assembled and reprocessed by the Party organization, which justifies its leadership precisely in the name of its possession of theory and consciousness. Under the banner of consciousness, the most 'conscious' elements proclaim themselves an *avant-garde* and endow themselves with the right to rule.

Behind the Hegelianizers' stress on the importance of consciousness, on the subjection of the world to consciousness, that is to say, on the 'identity of the subject-object', there is an abiding suspicion of nature, distrust of alienness and of otherness, partly because it is an autonomous thing, *vis-à-vis* man. There is a desire to define even 'nature' as a product of man, an impulse to reduce it to a socially shaped concept, to see it only as part of 'social reality'. Anything autonomous, anything 'other', anything not a part of ourselves, anything not controllable by ourselves is, from this perspective, to be rejected. The impulse is to eliminate anything in the world that is not us, or not totally dependent on us. What the Hegelianizers want is a world in which men will control and indeed dominate the universe. They are, in short, the proponents of a humanistic imperialism; they must therefore be the foe of the natural even in man. For the 'natural' is intrinsically that which has its own laws, spontaneities, and autonomies; it is not us, but another.

A Hegelianized Marxism may emphasize different sides of 'consciousness' and is vulnerable to breakdown in different directions. On the one side, it may become a politically deactivated academic Marxism; on the other, it may slide into a revolutionary Messianism. For a Hegelian Marxism may stress either the importance of the *knowing* consciousness, of awareness, or it may stress the wilful consciousness, both commonly rooted in an assumption concerning the ultimately unlimited potency of men. If a Hegelian Marxism stresses the importance of knowing or awareness, however, this may be experienced as an unbearable constraint upon the revolutionary will.

Hegelian Marxism thus has a paradoxical vulnerability to an anti-intellectualism in which theory is seen as a subversion of revolutionary militancy, thereby transforming itself into revolutionary Messianism. Presenting itself as a philosophy of consciousness, it attempts to conceal its anti-intellectualism by calling ritualistically for the 'unity of theory and praxis'; Messianism really seeks to *subordinate* theory to praxis, to use it really to disguise the mindlessness of its political practice. This, at any rate, seems one important pathology that is a potential of a Hegelianizing Marxism, although not a necessary consequence of it.

The other outcome of this contradiction between the willing and knowing consciousness is the atrophy of the will, and its total subordination to the knowing consciousness. In short, another outcome of this contradiction may be to *academicize* Marxism, a critique which has been directed against the 'Critical School' at Frankfurt.

A Hegelian revolutionary Messianism such as Lukács' is a philosophy of the 'leap' which transports men and societies away from the jurisdiction of routine processes and the natural regularities of laws. It seeks the defiance of routine and an escape from the everyday world. It substitutes consciousness-raising and courage for knowledge and discipline. The paradox of Hegelian Marxism is this: in the beginning it is most attractive to those Marxists who have a respect for mind and freedom. In the end, however, it may be they who have the fewest inhibitions about revolutionary adventurism and adopting élitist measures to destroy the corrupt old order, precisely because it is they who most feel themselves in legitimating contact with the Absolute Consciousness.

The élitist potentialities of the Hegelianizers in Marxism are not to be underestimated, precisely because of the extent to which they exalt consciousness. For under what conditions is the need for consciousness invoked? Primarily, when there is a hiatus between the immediate and the long-term gratifications available to men; between their experiences and their expectations; between gratifications known and gratifications promised. Workers are said to need 'consciousness' precisely because consciousness is required to act against or to depart from their short-run, therefore visible, interests. One needs no 'theory', however, when one is acting only in accordance with one's own immediate and hence visible interests. One needs theory, that is to say, one needs a rationale, for diverging from the immediately apprehensible, from the 'natural', from the most obvious course of behaviour.

Consciousness always embodies a measure of 'idealism', because consciousness always entails the overcoming of one's natural, materially and situationally-rooted impulses. Men 'need' theory in order to defy the evidence of their senses and of their experience and to live, instead, by their ideas and their imaginations. Theory and consciousness, then, have an uprooting function. It is precisely because the socialist consciousness does *not* stem from the material conditions of the proletariat's existence but must rather, as Lenin clearly saw, be brought to the proletariat from the *outside*, that it becomes the mission of the Party to cultivate theory and to protect it from corrupting contact with the world. Which is to say, the Party appoints itself the guardian of the working class's long-range interests. As Lukács put it,

> The form taken by the class consciousness of the proletariat is the Party. . . . The Party is assigned the sublime role of bearer of the class consciousness of the proletariat. . . . The Party is the historical embodiment and the active incarnation of class consciousness. . . .

In his *History and Class Consciousness*, Lukács spoke on behalf of the 'methodology' and not of the substantive theories of Marxism. The essence of Marxism is not to be found in any of its doctrines about capitalism, in any of its predictions or analyses concerning the capitalist economy, but, rather, in its dialectical apprehension of the totality. Marxism is thus above all a method. We can therefore still commit ourselves to Marxism today, argues Lukács, even if all of Marx's predictions about capitalism were proved wrong. This then loosens the specific connection between Marxism and capitalism. It transforms Marxism into a dialectic of the generalized revolution, into a consciousness of the imminent revolution, of the revolution anywhere and at any time. And this is precisely why the Lukács of 1923 is the most modern of Marxists.

To reduce Marxism to a method is, in effect, to deprecate, if not to eliminate, questions of observation, statistics, data, fact; it is a surrender of the empirical, a willing surrender, because the empirical is after all the manifestation of concern for the 'other', for alienness, for nature in its own autonomy. The young Lukács' methodological Marxism tables empirical interests precisely because he was a consciousness-enthralled Hegelian and partly, also, because he wished to outflank revisionist views about the reformed character and possibly peaceful evolution of contemporary capitalism. Lukács' methodological Marxism, therefore, sees the question of the day not as one of the objective readiness of capitalism for revolution. What counts is the will to revolution, not the established, structured, socio-economic conditions. For such callers to the Revolutionary Leap, what matters is will and consciousness. For them, revolution is always on the order of the day.

Yet it is precisely as a methodologist that Lukács firmly distinguished between Marxism and Bolshevism, refusing to reduce the former to the latter. It is in this sense that the Lukács of 1923 was very much an occidental or Westernizing Marxist. The Russian Revolution was made by socialists in a relatively underdeveloped industrial society and was fundamentally at variance with the deepest expectations of Marx and Engels. It thereby established the historical foundation for a thorough-going transformation of Marxism, the gist of which was to loosen its connection with a specific social system, capitalism. Lenin already saw many of the world implications of this, but he saw these from the standpoint of someone immersed in the experience of the Russian revolutions. Lukács, however, saw these from the standpoint of Western Europe. He could thus begin to develop a Marxism in which the Russian Revolution, vital paradigm that it was, was still only a dominating but never the *culminating* event.

Lukács thus contributed to a new epic in Marxism, an epic in which it achieves a deeper level of self-awareness; it is a new level of Marxist self-reflection which is not confined intellectually by the Russian Revolution, even though it was subjugated politically by its subsequent diversion. The new level of Marxist self-awareness crystallized by Lukács then becomes the bridge between orthodox Marxism and the subsequent development in Frankfurt of 'the Critical School', as G. E. Rusconi makes plain in his *La Teoria Critica della società*. In short, Lukács' importance is also to be found in the fact that he is a major stimulus in the development of what is certainly the most creative school of social theorists in the twentieth century, and of whom Herbert Marcuse is only the best known member. For all this, then, we owe homage to Georg Lukács.

NOTE
1. *History and Class Consciousness: Studies in Marxist Dialectics*, translated by Rodney Livingstone, London, Merlin Press, and Cambridge (Mass.), M.I.T. Press, 1971.

16

The Two Marxisms

This is the project: to begin a Marxist critique of Marxism it-self.* But on what would such a Marxist critique of Marxism focus? What would its central assumptions be? I submit that, at the minimum, a Marxist critique of Marxism would do two things. One of these is to situate its analysis of Marxism itself in an *historical* way. It would see, and insist on seeing, Marxism as an historical and social product. There is absolutely no doubt that Marxism itself requires and constrains us to under-stand all social theories in their own historical context. Despite this, however, it is also true that all too little has been done to understand Marxism as an historical product. There has been a great reluctance by Marxists, no less than non-Marxists, to view Marxism historically, perhaps because they feel that to view it in such a manner serves to devalue or 'unmask' it. Yet a Marxist standpoint requires us, it insists, that we see Marxism historically; that we do *not* see it only as a source or cause of historical development but, also, as an historical product. From our own standpoint, and from a Marxist standpoint, no social theory can be properly understood by viewing it only within its technical tradition, and by seeing it simply as the outcome of a previous set of theories, philosophies, or even ideologies. (But there is certainly a problem here, for if we wish to understand Marxism in its historical setting we will also have to clarify what we understand by history, and what kinds of things will be included or excluded under that heading.)

* I wish to thank Paul Piccone and Dick Howard for reading this essay in May 1972 and for their helpful suggestions.

The second minimal requirement of a Marxist critique of Marxism itself is that it absolutely must see Marxism itself as possessing its own internal *contradictions*.[1] A Marxist critique is concerned with the understanding of the internal contradictions of *any* object it studies; thus a Marxist critique of Marxism must identify and concern itself with the contradictions of Marxism itself. This objective will of course be threatening to a certain kind of Marxist – specifically, to a vulgar Marxist. But a concern with the contradictions of Marxism will not only seem indispensable but commonplace, from the standpoint of the most realistic Marxism of our own time, the Marxism of Mao. This is clear from Mao's 1937 lecture *On Contradiction*. An auto-critique of Marxism, then, must insist that Marxism, too, has its own contradictions; it must insist that these contradictions be its own, not simply the vestigial remnants of Marxism's past – its bourgeois heritage or Victorian prejudices – and that these contradictions remain an ongoing and living part of Marxism today, and that they are an essential key to an understanding of its present condition and its future prospect.

This stress on the unrestricted universality of contradictions is clearly one of the central thrusts of Mao's paper *On Contradiction*. Here, this question of the contradictions of Marxism can be opened only very provisionally and partially. I shall begin with the problem of the contradictions of Marxism as a theoretical-cultural system.

Among the most ingrained *theoretical* contradictions of Marxism is its ambivalence with respect to science. As an intellectual system, Marxism vacillates concerning its most fundamental 'paradigm' – to use Thomas Kuhn's term. At times Marxism looks to science, indeed to positive science, as its paradigm. Thus Marx's introduction to the second edition of *Das Kapital* could applaud the Russian reviewer of the first edition, who had interpreted it as an effort to apply the method of *science* to political economy. Indeed, Marx quotes approvingly from that laudatory review at some length:

The one thing which is of moment to Marx is to find the laws of the phenomena with whose investigation he is concerned . . . This law once discovered, he investigates in detail the effects in which it manifests itself in social life . . . Marx only troubles himself about one thing: to show, by rigid scientific investigation, the necessity of successive determinate orders of social conditions . . . Marx treated the social movement as a process of natural history, governed by laws not only independent of human will, consciousness and intelligence, but, rather, on the contrary determining that will, consciousness, and intelligence.

In the same introduction, Marx also affirms that there are 'naturalistic laws of capitalist production . . . working with iron necessity towards inevitable results'.

If at times Marx thinks himself a scientist among scientists, and of his work-paradigm as 'science', there are, however, *other* times when he clearly thinks himself something different; when he regards himself as a *critic* and his work as '*critique*'. Thus *Das Kapital*'s sub-title is, of course, not 'A Scientific Analysis of the Laws of Capitalism', but, rather, *A Critique of Political Economy*.

It is no easier to clarify the meaning of 'critique' than of science. Certainly, the object of a critique is *not* simply to produce a new and more correct set of scientific laws. A critique takes a given belief system, a theory, ideology, or indeed science itself – or any cultural 'objectification' – as problematic. It seeks to de-reify it, to de-mystify, to remove its objectivistic false consciousness, to offer an interpretation of it in terms of the everyday life of men living in and constrained by a specific society.

The aim of a critique is not simply to show a theory to be in error, formally or empirically, for the problem is not only the reliability of the theory's assertions. The 'truth' of a theory does not boil down to its reliability but also involves the nature of its selective perspective on the world. A critique is concerned with the meaning of this selective understanding, examining it in terms of the social forces that led to the *focalization* of certain perspectives and to the *repression* or rejection of others. As the structuralists might say, a critique is as much concerned with the '*silences*' of a theory as with what it dramatically accentuates. A critique, then, is an hermeneutic. It seeks an interpretation of the meaning of a theory or belief-system by linking it to the society or culture in which it lives – to show that the theory was not born of mind alone – and thus to undermine its false consciousness. It seeks to establish the manner in which the theory relates to and serves the larger society, especially its leading élites, and to show how this relation has shaped the theory itself.

To clarify Marx's notion of critique one should remember that the very model of a critique at the root of his concrete experience was the critique of *religion* developed by the Left Hegelians. The fundamental question of this critique of religion was to account for what appeared to be, from one standpoint, a certain fantastic quality in religious beliefs and in their theological systematizations. In the critique of religion, the primary object was not to reject, deny, or even test the truth of religion, but, rather, to account for its attraction. This, in turn, was interpreted as implying that, however fantastic, religion had a certain rational dimension and human serviceability, and it is this that lent it persuasiveness. This critique of religion was the historically specific paradigm from which the more generalized Marxist notion of an ideology-critique developed into a critique of politics and political economy.

Marxism created itself as a distinctive socialism precisely by developing its own critique of other socialisms. The *Communist Manifesto* begins with a critique of bourgeois society, but it culminates in a critique of *socialism*: of so-called reactionary socialism, feudal socialism, petit-bourgeois socialism, German or 'true' socialism, and conservative socialism. Marxism begins, then, as a critique of both capitalism *and* socialism.[2]

Of special relevance here is the *Manifesto*'s critique of 'Utopian' socialism. This socialism was doomed to failure, says the *Manifesto*, 'owing to the then undeveloped state of the proletariat, as well as to the absence of the economic conditions for its emancipation'. Lacking 'the material conditions for the emancipation of the proletariat, they therefore search after a new social science, after new social laws, that are to create these conditions . . .' Utopian socialists endeavour to win converts by creating small Utopian communities and they develop a 'fanatical and superstitious belief in the miraculous effects of their social science'.

Here Marxism as a critique of socialism specifically rejects Utopian socialism's reliance upon *social science* and social '*laws*' as the vehicle of socialism. At the same time, however, the *Manifesto* tacitly supposes that certain socio-economic conditions are indeed necessary for proletarian revolution. It suggests that the relation between these conditions and the revolution has a certain kind of knowable *regularity* if not lawfulness, being productive of their consequences seemingly apart from the will of men. The *Manifesto*'s critique of 'Utopian' socialism thus actually premises a lawful social science not altogether different from the very positivistic socialism that it expressly criticized. Ironically, then, in the very act of exhibiting its 'critique', the *Communist Manifesto* manifests its *ambivalence* between *critique* and *science*.

For the purposes at hand, I think I need only indicate the existence of two different paradigms in Marxism which constitute models of intellectual analysis that are partly interdependent or complementary and partly divergent. They are divergent paradigms because, as the Russian reviewer of *Das Kapital* made plain, the object of science was to discover laws independent of human will and determinative of it, while a 'critique' aims at establishing the manner in which human history is an outcome of the hidden potency of men. The basic conclusion of the Left Hegelian critique of *religion* was to show that God's being was entirely a postulation of *man* and an expression of *man's* own alienated being. A critique, then, aims at making men's potency more fully manifest so that men might then make their own history consciously rather than blindly. A natural science, in contrast, will, by providing laws that presumably determine the human will, allow those having technical knowledge of these laws to apply their knowledge in a technological way and to formulate the problem of social change as a *technical* problem.

In a 'scientific' socialism, the technical conferences of bureaucratized 'vanguards' tend to be substituted for the political discussion and education of masses. A critique, however, aims to transform the political process by deepening the mass consciousness and liberating it from its false consciousness. Here the political process and outcome are seen as profoundly affected by the nature of men's consciousness. The politics and praxis of a socialism conceived as a critique will thus differ substantially from that conceived as science. There are, then, two tendencies in Marxism: one toward critique, which I shall call 'Critical Marxism', and another toward science, which has called itself 'Scientific Marxism'. The way forward for Marxism, as theory or practice, requires that it surmount this contradiction. Whether this way forward can be found remains to be seen. In the meanwhile, it continues to provide one of the main bases of structural differentiation among Marxists today.

It is well known that theorists of the Marxist world have for some time now been divided between those conceiving of Marxism as some kind of critical theory and others conceiving it to be science. Among the former, there are the early Karl Korsch and Georg Lukács, Antonio Gramsci, J. P. Sartre, Lucien Goldmann, the *Telos* circle, the 'News and Letters' group and such members, or one-time members, of the 'Frankfurt School' as Max Horkheimer, T. W. Adorno, Franz Neumann, Leo Lowenthal, Erich Fromm, Walter Benjamin, Herbert Marcuse, or its 'younger' men such as Albrecht Wellmer, Alfred Schmidt, and its eminence in self-exile, Jürgen Habermas. Opposed to this remarkably distinguished group, there are other Marxists who eschew critical theory as mere ideology, and who conceive Marxism as a true science. They include such men as Galvano della Volpe, José Artur Gianotti, and the Marxist mandarin of l'École Normale Supérieure, Louis Althusser, and those influenced by him, such as Nicos Poulantzas, Maurice Godelier, Andre Glucksmann, Charles Bettelheim, the intellectual leader of their Swedish outpost in Lund, Göran Therborn, and an editor of the British *New Left Review*, Robin Blackburn. The divergent membership of these two networks is the sociological counterpart of an intellectual skirmish that has manifested itself among Marxists for some fifty years now. That it still continues vigorously is evident from the November–December 1971 issue of *New Left Review*, where Gareth Stedman Jones develops a sharp Althusserian critique of Lukács as the 'first irruption of Romanticism within Marxism'.[3]

Much of this theoretical conflict among Marxist theory is most visibly organized as a conflict between those supporting and those rejecting Hegelianism, the importance of Hegel for

Marx and a more Hegelian conception of ideology critique. It is in one part, then, a theoretical conflict between those stressing Marx as the culmination of the tradition of German idealism, and those others emphasizing Marx's differences from and superiority to that tradition. It is therefore also a difference between those who accept the young, and consequently more Hegelian, Marx as authentically Marxist, and those others who regard the young Marx as still mired in ideology.

On each side of this division there is then a syndrome of correlated commitments that is the mirror image of the syndrome of correlated commitments on the other side. Thus the Critical Marxists or Hegelianizers conceive of Marxism as critique rather than science; they stress the continuity of Marx with Hegel, the importance of the young Marx, the significance of the young Marx's emphasis on 'alienation', and adopt a more historicist ontology. The Scientific Marxists or anti-Hegelianizers stress a radical break (a *coupure épistémologique*) with Hegel after 1845; Marxism is then science, not critique, entailing a 'structuralist' methodology whose key is the 'mature' political economics of *Capital* rather than the ideologized anthropology of the 1844 Manuscripts. In one part, the controversy about the young *versus* the old Marx is to be understood as a discussion on the *concrete* and metaphoric level of the contradictions between critical and scientific Marxisms, a more serious and analytic distinction.

Despite their historicist sensitivities it is the Critical Marxists who stress the *continuity* between the young and old Marx, for they wish to establish the abiding influence of the Hegelian concern with alienation even in the technical political economy of the mature Marx. Correspondingly, while one might suppose that the Scientific Marxists' structuralist proclivities would dispose them to stress the structural continuities in the work of the young and old Marx, it is they who tend to stress the quantum leap that Marx presumably made from ideology to science, as well as emphasizing qualitative differences between ideology and science.[4]

The Critical Marxists have at least won the battle against Althusser on the textual and biographical levels, but it is not all that clear what they have actually won on the analytical level.

That is, does their victory on the textual level mean that Marx's continued concern with (or use of the concept of) alienation *meant* the same thing to the young as to the older Marx? When embedded in his early philosophical anthropology as in his later technical, political economy? And when in his early, more 'Promethean' optimism for a total human emancipation as in his later more limited stress on liberating men from the specific constraints of capitalism? (In my view, there is no more valuable discussion of these issues than that of the independent Swedish Marxist-sociologist – in self-imposed exile in Copenhagen – Joachim Israel, who is fully sensitive to both the continuities and the important changes in Marx's concept of alienation. Even if inconclusive, Israel's analysis[5] is unblemished by any sectarian impulse, and he accomplishes something not done since Lukács, namely, the re-establishment of a productive liaison between modern academic sociology and Marxism.)

While there is little doubt that the older Marx remained committed to the concept of alienation, there is much doubt that his understanding of this underwent no serious change. Marx's *understanding* of alienation changed, substantially and inevitably, as his theories deepened and developed, for these theories were the concept's defining context, and especially as they shifted in focus from Man as a species to a concern with men as members of capitalist societies. As Marx situates his concept of alienation within an historical analysis of capitalism as a constraining social system, the prospects of human liberation implicit in the notion of alienation are shifted. Human liberation is now increasingly guaranteed by the contradictions of capitalism itself, rather than by any qualities of man that may transcend that society. Increasingly, it is the contradictions of this society that not only produce alienation itself but, also, guarantee that men will *revolt* against that alienation.

In the mature Marx there is a growing movement toward a 'sociologism' or 'economism' in which it is the *structures* of *society* and their contradictions that determine social outcomes. To stress that it is the contradiction between the 'forces' and the 'relations' of production that ensures the uprooting of capitalism, says Albrecht Wellmer[6] quite correctly, is substantially different from the *Manifesto*'s stress on the liberating potential of class *struggle*. Both Althusser and Wellmer agree on the presence of this objectivistic focus on structures in Marx. Althusser, however, values it and sees it as an ontology appropriate to a true social science, while Wellmer subjects this aspect of Marx to a profound critique.

It is precisely in this vein that Althusser and Étienne Balibar suggest, in *Reading Capital*[7] (a truncated version of the French edition), that Marx's view that 'men' make their own history is an unexamined and deceptive idea. Their view is that this is the standpoint of the immature Marx, the philosophical anthropologist who is still an ideologist rather than a true scientist. (Marx's aphorism – men make their own history, even if in circumstances imposed on them – dates from 1853, and is thus after his supposed break from ideology, the *coupure épistémologique* which according to Althusser occurred in 1845.) In effect, Althusser and Balibar claim that it is not men and men's actions, but the social structures, formations, and systems that invisibly move them, that really shape history, and that these, therefore, comprise the proper object of a scientific Marxism. The Althusserians apparently conceive an emphasis on 'man' as a manifestation of 'subjectivity', and on (the plural) 'men' as a mere 'intersubjectivity'. Quite apart from the intrinsic merits of this for a conception of a sociology, this correctly suggests the difference between the young Marx, where 'men' in all their 'vulgar', visible embodiment are manifestly the acting subjects who make history, and his *Capital*, where 'social formations' such as the mode and relations of production become the subjects of history, and where men's conformity to or revolt against that social system is essentially determined by its social structures and their contradictions.

The unsparing condemnation of Althusser by some Hegelian Marxists, or by Kolakowski ('commonsense banalities . . . vague and ambiguous . . . striking historical inexactitudes . . . self-contradictory . . . ideological') gives no impression of the power and complexity of Althusser's mind. For all the venom directed at it, Althusser's reading of Marx is one of the most methodologically instructive that we have, telling us not only much about Marx but also a great deal about how to read *any* theorist. Althusser's stress on the importance of a 'symptomatic reading' of Marx, as attentive to his omissions as to his emphases, is an intellectual milestone in the development of Marx interpretations. In my view, the most fundamental limitations on Althusser's reading of Marxism are not Althusser's personal shortcomings, nor even the limits imposed by his Communist affiliation. Rather, they are those inherent in the Marxism he reads, in Marx–Engels 'themselves', in *their* contradictions, and in the inability of anyone to resolve these contradictions and still remain a 'Marxist' in more than a sentimental sense. One might say that just as he argued that Marx was pregnant with a new methodology that he was not yet able to articulate so, too, Althusser has undertaken a task of which he could not allow himself to become fully aware. For what Althusser has attempted is not so much a new interpretation but a thoroughgoing reconstitution of Marxism. His failure, and I believe it is a failure, derives most basically from his inability to accept the fact that Marxism itself has its own internal contradictions, from an avoidance of their analysis, and hence from an inability to transcend them.

Most especially, Althusser seeks to resolve Marxism's ambivalence about itself as science, on the one side, and as critique, on the other, essentially by a process of denial and splitting. He denies that the young Marx is importantly continuous and consequential for the older one; he denies that the young Marx is Marxist. He denies that Marxism contains ideology and insists that 'true' Marxism is science and science alone, free from its Hegelian origins. But this is not the Marx that was. It is a purified, logically possible, but not historically evident Marx. Like Lukács' early work, it is one of the objective possibilities of development in Marxism, but it is not Marxism itself. The objective possibilities of Marxism are not the same as the historical Marxism that existed or exists. The trouble is that Althusser is working within a concrete intellectual and political tradition that has transformed the works of Marx into untouchable texts so that the inevitable need to leave them behind cannot be openly and matter-of-factly acknowledged, but must instead be concealed and obscured. This commitment to the *concrete* Marx is a basic source of the false consciousness of Marxists. Althusserianism is a social theory that is in the process of becoming something more nearly like a 'socialist socio-logy' or, more ecumenically, a 'radical social theory'. To put the matter in another way: Althusser is about as much of a Marxist as August Comte was a Saint-Simonian.

That Althusser may have set himself a kind of Comteian mission is suggested by his remarkable praise for Comte as the only mind worthy of interest produced by French philosophy in 130 years after the French Revolution! Just as Comte sought to remove the contradictions of his mentor, Henri Saint-Simon, to systematize the latter's sprawling genius and, above all, to scientize it, so Althusser attempts much the same for Marx. And as Comte sought to divorce his sociology from meta-physics, Althusser seeks to foster the 'end of ideology', de-claring that authentic Marxism is not ideology but science. If, however, Comte's false consciousness manifested itself by denying any indebtedness to his mentor (that 'depraved juggler' Saint-Simon) and by stressing his own originality, Althusser's false consciousness manifests itself by piously affirming that he is simply exhibiting the authentic Marx rather than inventing a new one.

The most basic structural polarity in Althusser's conceptual system is its dualism between 'science' and 'ideology'. Yet, fundamental as these are for him, they both remain profoundly unclarified. In the end, we come away with no clearer a picture of the 'science' that Althusser prizes than of the 'ideology' he despises. His conception of science is that of an intellectual discipline essentially definable in terms of its theoretic constitu-tion and problematic, rather than its empirical component. What one must do to justify any claim to knowledge, in Althusser's vision of Marxism as science, remains badly blurred. All the more so because Althusser renounces any pragmatic standard or even praxis as the criterion of truth, and holds that Marxism succeeds because it is true rather than being true because it succeeds. At most, Althusser's science requires the making of a reasonable argument within the framework of an articulated theory. But much the same might be said about scholasticism or astrology. Are the claims of science, then, to be justified in no manner different from those of theology? From the standpoint of the methodological 'anarchism' of a

Paul Feyerabend one might accept such an ecumenical conclusion with equanimity. But this is quite impossible for an Althusser who started with the central aim of differentiating sharply between science and ideology and establishing Marxism's credentials as a science.

Quite apart from the method of science, Althusser is also vague concerning the character of the scientific product. For example: Is Althusser's Marxism scientific because it produces warranted laws? If so, what are they? Or is it scientific because it produces careful ethnographies and discursive historical analyses of concrete events? In some part, Althusser is inhibited from clarifying his conception of science because he needs one broad enough to encompass the diversity of scholarly works actually produced by Marx and Engels in their 'mature' lifetimes. In short, it must include both the *Capital* and the *Eighteenth Brumaire*, which exemplify (but do not exhaust) the tension between science and critique in originary Marxism. Althusser's awkward commentaries on these crucial questions conceal the fact of his essential silence about them which, in turn, betrays the presence of contradictions fundamental to Marxism itself.

There is, I believe, still another reason for Althusser's failure here. It is apparent that Althusser does not always view Marxism as a science such as physics. This is implicit in his own theoretical borrowings, which are from psychoanalysis and structural linguistics. Althusser thus sometimes operates with a working (if inarticulate) distinction between the physical and the social sciences. 'Inarticulate', because to confront the issue fully would run the risk of pushing Althusser back to the distinction between the *Naturwissenschaften* and *Geisteswissenschaften*, and this is exactly where his old enemy, Georg Lukács, began more than fifty years ago. Such a distinction implies a profound difference between the nature of the objects studied by the natural and social sciences. If that is so, then what reason is there to believe that the methods adequate to the established natural sciences will suffice for the new social sciences? Althusser never tells us.

While vague about it, one nonetheless gets the impression that sometimes he tacitly assumes that the object studied by

Marxism as social science has essentially the *same* character as the objects of the natural or physical sciences, being objects whose unique *subjectivity* does not fundamentally alter them so that they may be treated and studied as 'things'. Thus, for all his recognition of the role of theory in science, Althusser converges with sociological positivism. In general, however, Althusser never tells us much about his method of studying society. All he really exhibits is his method of studying social *theory*. This is fundamentally a form of qualitative analysis, a kind of hermeneutic in which I, for my part, think he is greatly talented and profoundly informative, but scarcely 'scientific'.

Anti-Hegelian Marxism sank some of its deepest roots in the Bolshevik rejection – as early as 1924 – of Karl Korsch's and Georg Lukács' Hegelian Marxism.[8] This rejection was originally prompted by the Bolshevik effort to avert a challenge to the hegemony of Leninism, then crystallizing as the official ideology of the Third International. (Lenin's close study of Hegel had come rather late in his political and intellectual development.) This rejection of Hegelianism was further crystallized in the Soviet Union during the hegemony of Stalinism, while the Soviet attitude toward Hegel appeared to have softened after the Twentieth Congress of the C.P.S.U.

Robin Blackburn and Gareth Jones[9] warn us, and quite properly, that it is wrong to over-emphasize the Stalinist character of Althusser's politics. They remind us that Gauchists, Maoists and Trotskyists have found Althusser interesting. Blackburn and Jones tend to view Althusser's involvement with the Communist Party as a kind of sentimentality, a wish to retain solidarity with the French proletariat, as the expression of a kind of emotional need for a Marxist ecumenism. Yet it may not be wrong to suggest that one difference between the Scientific and Critical Marxists is that the former make heavier organizational commitments, and that they value the organization as such; this in contrast to the Critical Marxists, whose deepest commitment is to a set of values, to a conception, a consciousness, the 'spirit' or ends of the revolution. The first grouping of Scientific Marxists risks surrendering the ends sought by the revolution in order to protect the *means* – the organizational vanguard. The pathological potentiality of this tendency is thus toward a kind of political 'ritualism' in which what were initially regarded as means have come to be viewed as ends in themselves. In the language of Marxist diagnosis, this is 'revisionism'.

The Critical Marxists' outlook, however, is not, of course, immune to political pathologies, but merely has different susceptibilities. Their lunge toward the revolutionary end is so dominating that they have less commitment to any specific organizational instrument such as the vanguard party, or even to any specific 'historical agent' such as the working class. They are in general less insistent on the prior presence of certain 'objective' historical conditions as the requisite for the revolutionary leap. If the political pathology of the Scientific Marxists is ritualism and revisionism, that of the Critical Marxists is adventurism or (as Georg Lukács once termed his early position) 'revolutionary messianism'. In one part, then, the tension between the Critical and the Scientific Marxists is the theoretical counterpart of an underlying sociological dilemma – the classical pitfalls of revolutionary politics: sectarianism and opportunism. Perhaps another difference between the two outlooks is a difference in their mental 'horizons'. The Scientific Marxists are seemingly more circumscribed in their attachments, being 'locals' of a sort; the Critical Marxists, for their part, seem more likely to be 'cosmopolitans' continually striving to link Marxism with a larger tradition and world.

If each side has pathological political potentials, each also has its own characteristic political strength. For the Critical Marxists, this is in their refusal to submit to 'what is', their refusal to wait interminably, their belief that the time is always right to change the world, that there is always some way to exert pressure against the *status quo* – in short, that one can always find some path forward to the revolution. In effect, they are constantly on guard against the dangers of political exhaustion, apathy, and of undue reliance upon forces external to men's own commitments or outside of their own control. Theirs is a political position that insists that people count more than technology and weapons; that men can and should do something

without waiting interminably for other 'forces' to mature. They
see the importance of courage and commitment in politics; of
consciousness; of the here-and-now transformation of human
relationships. In its *strengths*, no less than its weaknesses,
Critical Marxism is, of course, the more Romantic.

The Scientific Marxists, however, have different political
talents: they stress the cultivation of political endurance and
patience; the husbanding and developing of their cadres until
the time is right; the careful appraisal of historical conditions
for what they are, and not confusing them with what they
would like them to be. Above all, the Scientific Marxists
seek to protect their ability to act when objective conditions
promise to maximize their chance of success. They place their
greatest reliance on the development of the forces of production, and on the opportunities and contradictions this will
create.

Critical and Scientific Marxists may each be committed to
the revolution, but each views the revolution's future as protected in different ways. The Critical Marxists see the future of
the revolution as depending on the clarity of awareness and
vigour of conscious commitment, on a consciousness that can
be imprinted on history like a kind of germ matter. The
Scientific Marxists, however, see the future of the revolution
as essentially vouchsafed not by the heroism of the revolutionary,
but by history itself; by the inexorable contradictions of each
society; by the scientific appraisal of these contradictions; and
by seizing the political opportunities created by the crises
brought about by these unfolding contradictions. The mission
of a Hegelian Critical Marxism is to safeguard revolutionary
purpose and élan; the mission of an anti-Hegelian Scientific
Marxism is to protect the organizational instrument and its
future options. It is thus easier for revolutionaries out of power
to be Hegelians, while those in power will find more congenial
the prudence of an anti-Hegelian Marxism.[10]

The stress on consciousness typical of Hegelian or Critical
Marxists crystallized in the work of Karl Korsch and Georg
Lukács in the early 1920s, after the defeat of the revolutions in
Hungary and Germany and, also, in the wake of the successful
revolution in Russia. The defeat of the revolution in nations

that were industrially *advanced*, and its success in one that was *backward*, was then the most important historical conjuncture undermining the authority of a 'scientific' and materialistic Marxism and supporting a critical and idealistic Marxism.

An Hegelian or Critical Marxism is one that compensates for the deficiency of economic and technological conditions (once deemed) requisite for socialism, and it is, therefore, a Marxism appropriate to revolutionary efforts in 'underdeveloped' or Third World nations. Such a Marxism is, in effect, an effort to counterbalance deficient material socio-economic conditions by stressing the significance and potency of the 'human' agency and of his awareness, consciousness, sacrifice and discipline. Underlying the 'consciousness' of the Hegelian revolutionary, then, is his inability to rely on material conditions to lend support to his efforts, and his sense that the 'natural' drift of things is inimical to the revolution. The call to consciousness, then, is the ideology of those who do not believe that time is on their side, or that 'history is on our side'.

To develop this point further: Scientific Marxism relies on history and on the unfolding of certain natural tendencies in history to fulfil its socialist expectations. It sees itself as allied with history and nature. Correspondingly, however, a Scientific Marxism also sees such objectified history and objectified social structures as that which it would rely upon *rather than* 'men', and their will and consciousness. In short, a scientific socialism is sedimented with a tacit judgement of *human* nature as having a kind of unworthiness, as somehow falling short of the requirements of history, so that it cannot be relied upon to solve the historical problem. This contrasts with the tendencies of a Critical Marxism that does not rely upon an objectified history, on social structures or on nature but, rather, on men and on their will and consciousness to overcome the deficiencies of nature, history and economic structures. The adventurism of a Critical Marxism derives in part from its embattled and desperate sense that it must overcome (and perhaps combat) nature and history themselves. The bureaucratism of Scientific Marxism derives from its distrust of man himself and the feeling that it may use men as things on behalf of the higher purposes of history with which it sees itself allied.

The subsequent *embourgeoisement* of the working class in the most industrially advanced nations and its accommodation to capitalist society, as material standards of living improved, further and profoundly undermined the claims of scientific socialism. For the latter had supposed that it would be the economic contradictions of advanced capitalism that would be most acute and that it would be these that would make their societies vulnerable to socialism. When it was the proletariat's militancy rather than the capitalist class's hegemony that succumbed, scientific socialism came into continuous contradiction with the experience of everyday life. All the more so as some of the most manifestly militant of social strata, such as college students, were not economically impoverished or exploited.

The experience of everyday life, then, lent new support to the importance that Hegelian Marxists attributed to consciousness and to the flawed quality of everyday life in modern society. In moving from a scientific to a critical socialism, the socialist critique of modern society correspondingly moved from a condemnation of capitalism's economic exploitation to a denunciation of its sociological dehumanization: alienation and reification. The new Marxist emphasis on alienation and reification is most fundamentally rooted in capitalism's increasing gross national product, in the Keynesian control of the business cycle, and in the improving standard of living among the working class. The movement toward a Hegelian Marxism, then, has in part resulted from an effort to reformulate Marxism so that it would be consistent with the experience of everyday life under advanced capitalism.

A major transition occurred in the history of world communism when the Bolsheviks rejected the standpoint of the Second International. The Bolshevik position, however, did not entail the embracing of a fully Hegelian Critical Marxism so much as a partial and limited rejection of the wooden evolutionism of the Second International. Plekhanov and Lenin had learned much from Kautsky and they still accepted certain aspects of his politics as well as of his economics. This reflected itself, on the one side, in Lenin's emphasis on the importance of the 'professional revolutionary' and the party vanguard that would bring a socialist consciousness to the proletariat from the outside and which would take revolutionary initiatives.

On the other side, moreover, practically all of the Old Bolsheviks were committed to the economic premises of a scientific socialism; they thus at first believed implicitly that Russia lacked the economic conditions requisite to establish socialism, and that it was these economic conditions that were decisive. The Old Bolsheviks therefore looked forward to the coming of the revolution in Central Europe as the guarantor of their own socialism. When they found that the revolutionary lunge there had failed, leaving behind their own revolution as an isolated beachhead, they then fell back on the tactic of 'socialism in one country'. But this was an improvisation aimed at accommodating to what was, from the standpoint of their 'scientific socialism', a totally unexpected and highly threatening situation.

The Leninists had effected the Soviet Revolution by shifting (but not completing the movement) toward a political voluntarism consistent with a consciousness-stressing Hegelian Marxism. In short, the first 'successful' revolution made by Marxists predicated Lenin's movement toward a critical Marxism and a kind of Romanticism of the organization. But the Bolsheviks had not made a corresponding change in their *economics* or in the primacy attributed to it. Indeed, the theoretical change they had made did not fully register in their self-understanding. They did not, for example, conceive of themselves as having *changed* Marxism but, rather, as having merely adapted it to new historical circumstances. Their self-understanding was that they had changed only the political superstructure or 'starting mechanisms' of Marxism, but not its fundamental political economy. With the development of 'socialism in one country' and, most especially of Stalinism, Soviet socialism was essentially guided by a kind of Second International 'scientific' socialism in which primary emphasis was placed on the building of the right industrial, technological and scientific requisites. If socialism had once been conceived by Lenin as a fusion of 'electrification' × Soviets, Stalinization meant a conception of socialism that totally destroyed the latter and dwelt exclusively on the former.

Soviet Marxists could never face the fact that the success of their revolution was based on assumptions deeply deviant from the very version of Marxism they employed in building 'socialism' in one country. From the standpoint of the consciousness subsequently fostered by the Soviet State, the Soviet Revolution itself was an anomaly. It was something that should not have happened. The different consciousness that had guided the revolutionary Bolsheviks – 'Leninism' itself – inevitably became an embarrassment and a threat to those who later succeeded to the Soviet power. Stalinism, we might say, was an effort to deny and to extirpate the revolutionary voluntarism that was the heretical heritage of Leninism, because it threatened Soviet power internationally and domestically; it was an effort to conceal the fact that the Soviet State diverged from the requirements of 'scientific' socialism, while attempting to enact these requisites by a forceful imposition from above. Whatever else it was, Stalinism was the product of a consciousness that assumed that it did not matter how men behaved toward one another, but that what mattered were the social structures they created, and the 'objective', technological, scientific, industrial and economic conditions they left behind. These, it was believed, would 'absolve' them.

The Soviet State and its leaders thus defined themselves increasingly as the product and the defender of a scientific socialism, and they developed a corresponding false consciousness concerning their historical relation to Hegelian Marxism. The Stalinist development, then, meant a regression from Lenin's halting movement toward a Hegelian Marxism back to the scientific socialism of the Second International. It was this model of Marxism with which the Soviet State then associated itself. After the Leninist seizure of power in Russia, the maintenance and protection of the new Soviet State (the 'bastion') and its conception of Marxism became the fulcrum of Communist politics wherever Soviet influence held sway. The break away from Soviet influence on world socialism, as in Cuba and China, to a policy that was at once more autonomous and more militant, could thus only take the direction of a return to the Hegelian model of Marxism, but this time it was an uninhibited embrace, involving the resurgence or reinvention of a full-scale Hegelian Marxism, even if not of a concrete commitment to Hegel himself or to his specific works.

Maoism and the Contradictions of Marxism

Cuban and Chinese Marxism both converge with a Hegelian Critical Marxism far more than with a 'scientific' socialism. In both cases the importance attributed to revolutionary will and voluntarism, so characteristic of Critical Marxism, is indicated by the crucial place each assigns to military initiative, to the guerrilla column, to its *foco* and tactics, and by their common conviction that power comes out of the barrel of a gun. Both believed that the revolution need not require the prior maturation of the objective conditions of an advanced industrial economy. If the limited Leninist tendency toward voluntarism was indicated by the emphasis Lenin placed on the initiative of the political instrument, the party vanguard, then the full-blown voluntarism of Cuban and Chinese Marxism is indicated by the importance each attributes to the military instrument, the army, and to its influence on (if not priority over) the vanguard party itself.

Maoism, says Robert Jay Lifton, assumes two things: first, it views

. . . the human mind as infinitely malleable, capable of being reformed, transformed, and rectified without limit. The second is a related vision of the will as all-powerful, even to the extent that (in his own words) 'The Subjective creates the Objective.'[11]

Much the same may be and has been said of Castroism.

In a converging analysis, Richard R. Fagen stresses that the style of Cuban revolutionary politics was crystallized by the guerrilla experience in the Sierra Maestra during 1958–9, whose enduring legacy was 'voluntarism, egalitarianism, and ruralism'.[12] Voluntarism, Fagen indicates, refers to

the expansive sense of efficacy, competence, and personal power generated during the guerrilla period . . . [and denotes] a philosophy which conceives human will to be the dominant factor in experience and thus history.

Whether Cuba's voluntarism *derives* from (was 'generated by') the guerrilla period or, as seems far more likely, whether it preceded it and was the underlying consciousness that allowed Castro to launch guerrilla warfare, is a secondary point. The essential consideration here is that this voluntarism is clearly a salient feature of Castroism and a central symptom of its convergence with an Hegelian model of Marxism.

For my part, and unlike Fagen, I regard this as a salient but *not* as a *distinctive* feature of Castroism. I would also say the same about the two other components Fagen deems distinctive of the Cuban style of revolutionary politics, ruralism and egalitarianism. They are distinctive only in that they set it apart from political models consistent with a 'scientific socialism', but they are certainly *not* peculiar to *Cuba*. Exactly this same triad of voluntarism, ruralism, and egalitarianism also characterizes Mao's Marxism.

Fagen's analysis may be taken to suggest that the egalitarianism of Cuban socialism was accentuated by the experience of shared danger and shared struggle characteristic of a military brotherhood and that this brotherhood became the guerrillas' tacit paradigm of a good social order, which they subsequently sought to reproduce in society at large. It may be that it is precisely this use of the military brotherhood as societal paradigm that helps explain how egalitarianism can be associated with concentrated decision-making at the top and with strict control over dissent. ('In Cuba, a radical economic, social, and cultural egalitarianism is married to an authoritarian and hierarchical decisional structure.'[13]) For the stress of men in combat frequently generates informalities, mutual reliance, and a sense of shared fate without, however, actually changing the formal hierarchical social structure of the military unit and the differential authority of officers and men. As battle and danger recede with victory, the informal egalitarianism gives way to the abiding formal hierarchy. This was precisely the experience of the Yugoslavian Partisan fighters and it may be a central source of the disillusionment of those, such as Djilas, who somehow retained a vivid image of the older military brotherhood and therefore keenly resented the emergence of new socio-economic distinctions – the 'New Class'.

Cuban (and, as we will indicate, Chinese) voluntarism was also associated, in the manner characteristic of Critical Marxism, with a stress on the importance of consciousness and awareness. In Castro's view, socialism or communism is not simply a socialization of the means of production but the *transformation of men*, the creation of a new revolutionary man, 'a man devoid of *egoismo*, guided by *conciencia*, who puts service to society above service to self'. 'A communist society,' in Castro's own words, 'is one in which man will have reached the highest degree of social awareness ever achieved. . . . To live in a Communist society is to live without selfishness . . .'[14] Certainly this is far more reminiscent of the young Marx's philosophical manuscripts than of his *Capital*.

Castro's model of development, like Mao's, does not give first place to the classical verities of scientific Marxism: resources, capital, technology, efficiency or growth. Instead, it stresses 'mass participation, determination, selflessness, enthusiasm, and faith . . .' Again: '. . . a profound general faith in achieving economic progress through the *formación* and utilization of revolutionary man certainly pervades the highest decisional circles.' The leadership's commitment to development rests less on technological factors than on the transformation of human relations and consciousness. It rests, in Castro's own Hegelian formulation, on 'factors of a moral order, factors having to do with awareness'.

Essentially the same portrait of Maoist development policies has been drawn by E. L. Wheelwright and B. MacFarlane. In their analysis they note that

a fundamental axiom of Maoist thought is that public ownership is only a technical condition for solving the problems of Chinese society . . . the goal of Chinese socialism involves vast changes in human nature, in the way people relate to each other. . . . Once the basic essentials of food, clothing, and shelter for all have been achieved, it is not necessary to wait for higher productivity levels to be reached before attempting socialist ways of life.[15]

In an unusually probing discussion of their analysis, Michael Kosok expressly counterposes the 'Moscow' view of development with the Chinese, adumbrating the economistic side of 'scientific' socialism with penetrating clarity. Kosok holds that the economism of Scientific Marxism (what I have elsewhere called its 'utilitarianism') implies that 'the structure of society is essentially the development of *productivity* and the "level of production" . . .' and regards man as an 'efficiency machine serving the dictates of technology . . . Communism and socialism are seen [by Scientific Marxism] as contingent upon the availability of a sufficient number of things . . .', quantification and reification being characteristic of it. Again, Scientific Marxism stresses the importance of rational planning rather than will or motivation, and in holding that expertise is more important than 'redness', ultimately surrenders the economy to the control of specialists.[16]

Kosok's insight into the development policy of Scientific Marxism is, I believe, essentially correct, and it was a policy basically accepted by Stalin also. Stalin defined the basic law of 'socialism' (i.e. of the Soviet economy under his régime) as

the securing of the maximum satisfaction of the constantly rising material and cultural requirements of the whole of society through the continuous expansion and perfection of socialist production on the basis of higher techniques.[17]

Some subsequent Soviet planners, it has been argued, have reduced the priority Stalin assigned to production and given greater emphasis to consumer satisfaction.[18] Actually, however, Stalin's development policy is not best characterized, as certain formulations seem to imply, in terms of its focus on efficiency or rationalization. Indeed, Stalin expressly rejected the view 'that it is only necessary to organize the productive forces rationally and the transition to communism will take place . . .'[19] Rather, Stalin tended to counterpose growth to efficiency and to assign priority to the former.

Rationality of economic organization and economic growth are somewhat independent considerations. There can be great economic growth with relatively little increase in rationality, and increased rationality without economic growth. Stalin opted for the primacy of growth: 'It is necessary to ensure not a mythical "rational organisation" of the productive forces, but a continuous expansion of production of the means of production.'[20] To that extent, the economic imperatives of capitalism and Scientific Marxism converge. The issue, then, is whether it is the growth imperative or the efficiency imperative that controls the economy of a scientific socialism. In my view Stalin is quite correct, if he is thought of as having described the imperative controlling the Soviet economy and thus the forces that shape the character of much of everyday life in the Soviet Union. Soviet leaders, in contrast to some of their planners, opted for growth over efficiency; in some part because they were concerned with the aggregate power of the Soviet Union in comparison with that of the United States; in some part because labour has been relatively cheaper there; in some part because the criterion of 'catching up' is more readily visible on the 'growth' than on the 'efficiency' level; and in some part, finally, because the decline of traditional living standards means that consumers are always seeking *more* than they formerly had.

The question is a practical one of much significance; Kosok's focus on rationality leads him to define scientific socialism as rooted in and corrupted by the division of labour. The alternate view suggested here would, rather, view the trouble as rooted in the cold war or the hot competition between Soviet and American societies, and in their common insistence – now ecologically critical – on a policy of indefinite growth. This, in turn, is rooted in their common failure to develop a stable conception of a proper standard of living which, not being ever expanded, could therefore be capable of being satisfied. Once the importance of some morally validated conception of a standard of living is recognized, we are then thrust back to the decisive problem Émile Durkheim saw some sixty years ago – the need for a socialist *morality* as a requisite for a fulfilling and stable socialism. In any event, there is little question that scientific socialism, sedimented with the nineteenth-century mythos of an all-conquering science, rests solidly on the assumption of indefinite and unlimited economic growth, which is in flat and fundamental contradiction of all we are now learning from modern ecologists.

I have previously suggested that any social theory, including Marxism, changes when it is no longer vindicated by or consistent with the experiences of everyday life. It changes when everyday life changes and gives rise to sentiments, to a personal vision of what is real, or fosters a new set of assumptions that are at variance with those premised by and built into the social theory. A social theory may change, however, not because the old everyday life is changing into a new one, but simply when the theory is *transported* to a different culture in which everyday life generates and rests upon a quite different set of assumptions, sentiments, and conceptions of what is real. Here the theory is under pressure not because a once-congenial everyday life has ceased to be compatible with it, but simply because this theory is now brought into a new contact with an everyday life that was never compatible with it.

Transformations in the everyday life of Western capitalism seem to underlie the decline of Scientific Marxism and the rise of Critical Marxism: successful revolutions in industrially backward countries; the accommodation of the proletariat in industrially advanced countries; the militancy of non-impoverished groups, etc. The emergence of Maoism, however, as a special case of a Critical Marxism distinct, in part, from that of Cuban socialism, illustrates the way in which a theory is changed by diffusion to a society which has an everyday life that is (and always was) different from the everyday life of the society in which it first originated.

As suggested earlier in the first part of this analysis (p. 426), Maoism seems distinguished by the emphasis it places upon the universality of contradiction. To that extent Maoism represents a new and distinct stage in the world development of Marxism because it has achieved a reflexivity superior to that of Western Marxisms; it can and has faced the 'bad news' about its own internal contradictions. (This clearly was one aspect in the struggle between Mao and Liu Shao-chi whom Mao saw as ignoring the contradictions of socialism itself.)

Western Marxism, unlike Maoism, was developed in a Christian culture whose everyday life has long been sedimented with millennarian religious fantasies that were often sublimated into the political vision of some final, climactic coming. Western Marxism's conception of socialism and Communism have rested tacitly upon such profoundly ingrained (but not always manifest) millenarian expectations. Maoism, however, is the first Marxism that matured in a non-Christian civilization. Nourished in a deteriorating Confucian culture that has no concepts of salvation or of an afterlife, and which is oriented to an immanent order rather than one that is transcendental, Maoism is the most secular of Marxisms. It regards those Marxists who think socialism devoid of contradictions as naïve if not as faintly uncivilized.

There are, of course, various other conditions under which a theory may undergo change. Another of these is when the social strata that had created and had fostered the theory itself changes or passes away. And so it is with Marxism. It is not only the change in the everyday life of industrially advanced societies, and not only its move from the everyday life of a Christian to that of a Confucian society, but, also, a change in the social strata with which Marxism has been associated, that promises a radical change in Marxism. Here I refer *not* to the passivity and accommodation of the *proletariat* and its failure thus far as the promised historical agency of socialism, but, also, to the changes and crisis of the academic *intelligentsia*, the social strata by which Marxism was created, that brings us to the deepest level in the crisis of Marxism.

The most profound indication of this development is to be found in the societal re-mapping sought by Maoism which is laying the groundwork for the elimination of the academic intelligentsia. As Robert Guillain remarks in *Le Monde*, 'It is no over-simplification of the massive series of reforms [of the 'Cultural Revolution'] . . . to say that their key objective – defined by Chairman Mao himself – is the elimination of the "academic intellectual".'[21] As the intensity of the Red Guard movement subsided, it became increasingly evident that the elimination of the academic intelligentsia was one of the most important items on the agenda of the Cultural Revolution. This effort is resonated in the West by the anti-intellectualism of the bureaucratized *lumpen* intelligentsia and in the self-hatred of certain *gauchiste* intellectuals.

Jean-Paul Sartre expresses an essentially Maoist view of the intellectual's future when he remarks: 'his privileged status is over . . . it is sheer bad faith, hence counter-revolutionary, for the intellectual to dwell on his own problems . . . he owes his knowledge to [the masses] and must be with them and in them: he must be dedicated to work for their problems . . .'[22] Asked whether the recent publication of his massive book on Flaubert was not in contradiction to this very position, Sartre humbly replies, 'My book on Flaubert may, indeed, be a form of petty-bourgeois escapism . . .'

Maoism is a Marxism that, according to its self-understanding, strives to live in the purer morality of ordinary people, rather than through the theoretical acumen of a privileged élite. In this view, Mao's closing of the Chinese universities was a kind of sociological surgery that sought to create a new social order devoid of an academic intelligentsia. From June 1966 until about September 1970, universities throughout China were closed down and many (some ten out of forty in Peking) still remain shut. And not only the universities but Chinese culture more broadly appears, even in Guillain's sympathetic account,

to be in a state of suspended animation. Literature has virtually disappeared. . . . Painters and sculptors produce endless versions of the Great Architect. The cinema has almost ground to a halt and the theater has a repertory of half a dozen plays which are presented time and again . . .[23]

According to B. Michael Frolic of York University, the latest foreign book on the shelves of Peking University's library dates from 1966; and many municipal libraries, museums, research institutes and bookstores still remain closed.[24]

Marxism, however, was in the beginning the creation of a library-haunting, bookstore-browsing, museum-loving – and hence leisure-possessing – academic intelligentsia of the very sort that Maoism now seeks to excise. It does not matter, of course, that Engels himself had no university training; and it does not matter that Marx never achieved the professorship that, when young, he had coveted; for both were mandarins at heart. They had both assimilated and embodied the culture of the Western university. Marx was the product and possessor of a high European culture who knew his Goethe by heart; who read his Aeschylus in the original; who had a boundless respect for Shakespeare, whom he had his daughters memorize; who took pleasure in reading two or three novels at one time, ranking Balzac and Cervantes before other novelists; who, when disturbed, might take refuge in algebra; and who actually wrote an infinitesimal calculus. In a letter to his daughter Laura in 1868 he describes himself as '. . . a machine condemned to devour books . . .'.[25] When Marx died, on 14 March 1883, he was where one might expect him – at his desk.

Whatever its ultimate destiny and destination, Marxism was originally a creation of the West. Born of European culture, Marxism is simply unthinkable without the complex of institutions that centre on the university, which trains and provides livings for a secular intelligentsia. Marx and Engels, and all the epigones of every nationality that follow after them, are unthinkable without the countless books, journals, newspapers, libraries, bookstores, publishing houses, and even Party schools, whose cadres and culture constitute a dense infrastructure at whose centre there is the Western university. No university, no intelligentsia, no Marxism.

The gulf between Maoism and Soviet Marxism derives largely from the fact that Soviet Marxism understands and respects this, while Maoism understands but rejects it. Soviet Marxism and Stalinism sought to control the university and to guarantee the loyalty of intellectuals and scientists to Party precepts and leadership; it never sought to stop the university and to eliminate the self-reproduction of the academic intelligentsia, as Maoism has.

Intellectuals are an historically recent social stratum, essentially emerging with the bourgeois revolution during the onset of modernization in the West. They have, however, been largely recruited from the secular professions of relatively older and more humanistic vintage. They have more likely been scholars, journalists, academicians, artists, writers or lawyers, rather than engineers or scientists. Characteristically, then, the intelligentsia have been associated with long-established (but no longer well-protected) occupations, and were linked to educational and socializing systems that possess and insist on some measure of autonomy.

Unlike the new engineers and scientists, who almost immediately had greater career opportunities and public prestige with the advent of the bourgeois economy, the occupations with which intellectuals were associated had an ambivalent relation to the modern bourgeois order. On the one hand, some were given increased support by the state, in order to win the allegiance of secular ideologists who might help it in controlling the Church, and, in general, they were increasingly released from the personalized controls of patrons or from personalized service as tutors. On the other hand, however, their livelihoods were now often subject to the insecurities of the impersonal marketplace and, except for a few 'stars', the new world of emerging industrialism did not hold this language-manipu-lating élite in great esteem.

Intellectuals, then, were a social stratum that were freed of corporate and patron controls, but were also limited in the enjoyment of their new freedom by poverty and neglect: bohemia with its deprivations was not only a preferred style of life but for many it was also a necessity. Intellectuals were an élite possessed of a privileged education, but usually lacking in any commensurate *power* – to which they felt their superior education entitled them – as well as lacking a commensurate *income*. They were, in short, characterized by the tensions typically generated by such status disparities. The very society that had created intellectuals allowed them only a marginal place, so that they were at once both beholden and hostile to the new society. They were the structurally alienated.

Despite the differences between Enlightenment and Romantic intellectuals, Western intellectuals – Marxist or bourgeois – nonetheless shared certain important values. They were committed to the importance of intellectual productivity and performance; whether courtly *philosophes* or bohemian Romantics, they were commonly hard workers. They usually believed in the value of advanced education and of universities, even if they did not always agree on what constituted a good education. They were rationalists even when promulgating an anti-intellectualism. Even the Romantics, despite their special interest in Oriental civilization and languages, undoubtedly viewed European and Western societies as their paradigms – willy-nilly, all were Westernizers. Intellectuals were, too, commonly 'universalistic' in their value commitments, believing that a man's rewards should be proportionate to his performances and achievements. Thus even Marx says that under socialism the slogan should be: from each according to his ability, to each according to his work! In this universalism, intellectuals were essentially sanctioning the requirements of the *educated sector* of the middle class while embarrassing the *propertied* sector of the middle class, which believed that its property entitled it to unearned incomes. They were also commonly critical of established, respectable religions; if intellectuals were by no means uniformly atheists, they were often modernizers who felt that religion needed to adapt to the requirements of modernity. They commonly resented and challenged authority based on lineage and ascription, affirming the rights of the talented, whether talent was seen as due to educated practice or to inborn genius. While Romantic intellectuals might nostalgically idealize rusticity, even they were not slow to seek their fortunes in salons, courts, marketplaces and other urbane environments, and they had the cosmopolitans' urge to keep in touch with the urban centres. If intellectuals did not always say (with Socrates) that the city was their teacher, they had no doubt that the people of the city were important audiences and markets.

In contrast, Maoist socialism does not regard either urbanization or 'Westernization' as the last word. It is *not* obvious, moreover, that Maoism even conceives itself as engaged in 'modernization'. It is not modernization but 'cultural revitalization' to which the Chinese Revolution seems committed; it seeks an historically unique kind of revitalization, since it does not look to the glories of the past, and in that sense is not 'nativistic', and does not aim to change itself by Westernization. It is this unique 'development' policy that undergirds the educational policies of the Cultural Revolution and its effort to alter the intelligentsia. In the self-understanding of Maoism, the aim is to de-bourgeoisify the intellectual; to eliminate the rift between intellectuals and masses; to change the class character of intellectuals by changing their class origins, so that in future they derive predominantly from workers or peasants, and themselves have an extensive personal experience of labouring as peasants or workers. This, to repeat, is Maoism's self-understanding of its policy toward the intelligentsia.

Yet if Maoism is a critique of the bourgeois intellectual in terms of egalitarian values, if it rejects the old intellectuals because they were an élite set above the masses, it remains difficult to understand why Maoism has allowed a great gap to persist in the income levels of workers and intellectuals. Top academicians may earn as much as seven to eight times more than the average worker, and the ratio of the top and bottom levels in the university itself is about 12 to 1, and has over the years been growing.[26] This inconsistency, however, would be reconciled if we did not accept the self-understanding of Maoism and, instead of conceiving it as an effort to overthrow *all* élitism, we would think of it, rather, as an effort to make a *new* élite, an élite which has broken radically with the traditions of the past, an élite which rejects Western models of development.

Maoism's policy toward the intelligentsia is, in part, grounded in the very special conditions of the Chinese economy and social structure. Michael Frolic quotes a Chinese official who makes the major point: 'The new Chinese educational system is designed to maximize the even development of a peasant society.' The crucial statistic is that China has 150,000,000 city dwellers but some 650,000,000 peasants. (Contrast this with the United States where the college population now exceeds the farm population, even when the latter includes women and children.) Maoist policies, Frolic also indicates, limit the priorities assigned to urban development and aims to curb urbanization as well as to decentralize industry.

Kosok formulates this development from the standpoint of a critical Marxism:

. . . the Chinese are attempting to destroy at its root the classical Western antagonism between city and country, industry and agriculture, culture and the hinter-lands, 'production-control-direction' centers and 'consumption-living' centers . . . to decentralize and ruralize the land instead of regimenting the countryside to the city and turning the whole land into a gigantic production unit.[27]

(The proletariat is therefore not just the *industrial* worker, but the entire working population which is alienated from its praxis and the control of its living process.)[28]

This is an historically unique policy of economic development that must be understood as the domestic counterpart to the *foreign* policy of a country whose technologically superior enemies threaten it with nuclear blackmail. In one part, Mao's slowdown of urbanization is an effort to arrange China's internal social order so that, if it must, it will be able to survive even nuclear warfare. China will therefore for a long while remain a predominantly peasant and rural society, and, given Maoism's unique conception of development, it has far less need of academic intellectuals. Indeed, Guillain claims that 'China's need for university-educated personnel is still relatively limited . . . [and] the country even had a glut of graduates before the Cultural Revolution'.[29]

Maoism's policies toward intellectuals have in part to be understood, then, in the light of China's limited need for them at this stage of its development. Mao's unique policy of economic development is the infrastructure of his policy concerning the intellectuals. Nonetheless, the central fact remains that Mao's policies were *militantly* anti-intellectual. They were inspired less by market considerations of supply and demand than by *political* considerations: they were inspired, specifically, by the intellectuals' tendency to suspect and to resist precisely Mao's fundamental policy of limiting urbanization and decentralizing industry. It is, I believe, the intellectuals' resistance to *this* unique conception of development that Mao regards as proof of their abiding bourgeois and anti-socialist character. It is, above all, intellectuals' resistance to a new and non-Western form of development – including a commitment to an anti-élitist egalitarianism – that led Mao to seek the radical transformation of intellectuals.

In the Chairman's view the intellectuals are suspect because . . . they have been a source of resistance or reaction to Communist ideas. . . . A characteristic Mao statement given wide publicity during the Cultural Revolution ran: 'I shall always believe that the vast majority of intellectuals, both within and outside the party, are basically bourgeois.'[30]

Mao's attack upon intellectuals is grounded in an impulse to make a great rupture with the past, to make a vast leap forward away from it. It is thus not simply that intellectuals had a different, more Westernizing conception of economic development but also that their link with the past is so profound, that led Mao to come down against them. Inevitably, intellectuals do embody the heritage of the past. However radical they are, intellectuals are, in the history-rootedness of their learning, inevitably if unwittingly engaged in the *preservation* of the past. Their very 'bookishness' marks them as the agents of cultural continuity. Mao, however, wanted to make a break with the history of China; more than that, he also wanted to make a break with the history of *socialism* itself and with the history of revolutions past. Mao's anti-intellectualism, then, is a way of destroying the links with the past and the limits of the past itself; it is not an expression of a contempt for mind.

Mao has proceeded from the profound understanding that the most fundamental limits on the revolution were not located outside, in the enemy. The diagnosis that the main danger to the revolution is to be found in the resistance and power of the enemy society *outside* was certainly compatible with the experience of the Soviet State. But a voluntaristic Marxism such as Mao's, which believes in the potency of consciousness and commitment, is especially sensitive to the dangers that derive from ambivalence and faintheartedness. From a voluntaristic standpoint, intellectuals have a very special importance and, for that reason, it becomes especially important that they be viewed as politically trustworthy.

Those whose ideological view has been sharpened by a kind of Hegelian consciousness look out on the world from a very special perspective. They have a firm insight into the way in which the 'Object' is the creation of the 'Subject' – even if the Object be the enemy and the Subject the revolutionary Self – and they therefore always know that the trouble is not only in the stars but also in themselves. They are not, in short, given to vulgar externalizing; their talent and weakness is instead for the subtle searching out of the enemy within, and for internecine vigilance and struggle against him.

Maoism has the deepest and most troubling understanding

that a Marxist can have: it understands that Marxism, too, has a false consciousness; it knows that the weakness of Marxism is not only a weakness of its *enemies* but also of Marxism's *friends*. Maoism understands *this*: that Marxism is the child of the very society that it seeks to overthrow and that, as such, there is a way in which Marxism not only has a critical knowledge of the Old Régimes but also a measure of affinity with them. Maoism understands that if the capitalist order gives birth to the 'seeds of its own destruction', then the new order is indeed the affinal product of the old order's seed, not only its enemy, and that there is a certain continuity between Marxism and the old order, not only a revolutionary rupture. Maoism's fear is this: that the old order *lives on* in the new one; that the old order conquers in the midst of its defeat; that the old order passes part of its seed-heritage on and lives *through* the very triumph of the new order. Maoism understands that this is how it is with Marxism, too, in its relation to the old order that it seeks to destroy.

The wistful wisdom of the Chairman, then, is this: there is no permanent revolution, no way forward for a revolution that seeks to live, except by eating its own children; for it is they who constitute the last bridge to the past, and it is they who set the sturdiest limits on the revolution's future. Sartre's Maoist consciousness understands all this very well:

. . . in the past, the winners have always thought about stopping. Historians claim revolutionaries never know where or when to stop. But it is the contrary. They always do stop, so that the next generation of revolutionaries has felt obliged to go after the previous generation. It happened four times during the French Revolution of 1789–94. Perhaps it would be better if for once a revolutionary movement was ready and willing to go all the way . . . of all the groups within the left today, the undogmatic Maoists . . . are most prepared to do that . . .[31]

Maoism is the Marxism that recognizes – or better still, senses without recognizing – that there is no way forward for the revolution except through the death of Marxism; that the final limits on the revolution are those imposed and built into Marxism itself; that these limits lay sedimented in the revolutionary intelligentsia, and in the university system that socially reproduces the intelligentsia. Maoism is the Marxism that was brought to the brink of understanding that one has to choose: either Marxism or the permanent revolution – but not both!

One pole from which the crisis of Marxism spreads is the wandering and floundering of the working class; of the proletariat that surrendered its initiative to self-anointed vanguard parties; which accommodated itself both to the great economic crises of capitalism as well as to the seductions of capitalist affluence. At the other pole from which the crisis of Marxism spreads is the decline of the academic intelligentsia.

The relationship between the intelligentsia and proletariat is a relationship between an author and his protagonist; between the cameraman and the actor; between latent structure and manifest structure. Or, as Marx once spoke of them, it is a relation between the head and the heart of the revolution. Together, the proletariat and intelligentsia once constituted the basic infrastructure of enacted Marxism. As both are in the process of being historically transformed, the sociological foundations of Marxism itself are crumbling.

The ultimate false consciousness of Marxism is that the historical role attributed by it to the proletariat was assigned by an invisible intelligentsia, by an intelligentsia that never made an appearance in its own theory, and whose existence and nature are therefore never systematically known even to itself. It is precisely because Maoism has seen through to this ultimately concealed level in Marxism itself that Maoism marks the highest and final stage in the historical development of Marxism. It is precisely because of this that Maoism cannot allow itself to recognize what it gives every evidence of so clearly understanding, namely, that the way forward for the revolution requires an end to the contradictions of Marxism – which is to say, an end to 'Marxism'.

NOTES

1. I use the term 'contradiction' in the Hegelian and not in the Aristotelian sense. In this tradition it refers *not* to a *logical* contradiction, in which only two possibilities exhaust the universe and one of these must be false but, rather, to a condition of existential opposition between two or more

forces in which both do indeed exist but mutually inhibit or injure one another.

2. Svetozar Stojanovic reminds us of this in his *Kritik und Zukunft des Socialismus*, Munich, Reine Hanser, 1970. (Soon to be published in English by Oxford University Press.)

3. This compares most favourably with George Lichtheim's long-standing effort to weigh the effects of Romanticism on Marxism – an effort somewhat vitiated by Lichtheim's Goethian inclination to conceive of Romanticism as '*Krankheit*'.

4. George Lichtheim's well titled *From Marx to Hegel* (New York, Herder & Herder, 1971) deals directly with the conflict between Hegelian and anti-Hegelian Marxisms, as well as with the development of the former into the Critical or Frankfurt School in the work of Adorno, Marcuse and Habermas. Lichtheim always knows who the players are and situates them deftly. The very breadth of Lichtheim's scholarship, his even-handed treatment of conflicting standpoints, his insistence on clarity even from the Germans and his feeling for the historically concrete – all these are substantial virtues which make this book, with the exception of its last and very dated essay, essential reading for students of Marxism. Yet it is precisely these strengths that make us expect more than the book delivers – it lacks a depth corresponding to its breadth. In the end it remains a kind of Marxist reportage rather than an original contribution to the discussion itself.

Nicolas Lobkowicz's older *Theory and Practice* (South Bend, Ind.: University of Notre Dame Press, 1967) is in a class by itself, having a depth of analysis that its lucid style may lead one to underestimate. It is absolutely required reading for those who want to prepare themselves to assimilate the work of Jürgen Habermas which, while it exceeds Lobkowicz's in breadth, is often inferior to it in analytic directness. Lobkowicz's discussion of the dilemmas of Hegelian development and the way in which these influenced the young Hegelians has not, I believe, been surpassed even in the excellent and later work by David McLellan on the young Hegelians. W. J. Brazill's study of the same coterie had the bad luck of appearing shortly after McLellan's masterful study, and was thus unfortunately overshadowed by it. This is too bad, because Brazill's work is often more detailed and comprehensive and, at the same time, seeks to clarify certain general questions, such as the nature of 'critique'. (Wm J. Brazill, *The Young Hegelians*, New Haven, Yale University Press, 1970, and David McLellan, *The Young Hegelians and Karl Marx*, New York, Frederick Praeger, 1969.)

The work of István Mészáros, David McLellan and Bertell Ollman all now convincingly establish that a concern for alienation abides in the work of the older Marx, despite Louis Althusser's strenuous efforts to argue the opposite. In the 1971 *Socialist Register*, the Polish philosopher Leszek Kolakowski, one of the leaders of the East European renaissance of a humanist Marxism, deplored by Althusser, now in self-exile from Berkeley and Warsaw, formulates a biting critique of 'Althusser's Marx'. 'For anybody who knows the text of the *Grundrisse* to claim that Marx from 1845 onwards stopped thinking about society in the old "ideological" categories of "alienation" . . . is so obviously wrong that one wonders how to discuss it seriously.'

The *Grundrisse* (of 1857–8) was Marx's 1,000-page draft plan for the *Capital*. Indeed, there are those like David McLellan who regard it as exhibiting a larger framework of which even the *Capital* is only a partial segment (*Marx's Grundrisse*, New York, Harper & Row, 1972). The *Grundrisse* was translated into French in 1968, a translation which has been much criticized by Hegelian Marxists, and was not widely available even in German until the single-volume Dietz Verlag edition of 1953. There is no better case-history of the profound and often perverse effects of publishing practices on scholarship than the publishing history of the *Grundrisse*. A complete English translation is still to be completed by International Publishers, although McLellan's selections from the *Grundrisse* are excellent, clearly indicating the Hegelian continuities between the young and old Marx. Bertell Ollman's study of alienation also painstakingly establishes this continuity by a detailed examination of Marx's mature political economy, concluding that '*Capital* is a treatise on the law of value, and as such could only be a work about alienation'. (*Alienation: Marx's Conception of Man in Capitalist Society*, Cambridge University Press, 1971.)

5. Joachim Israel, *Alienation, from Marx to Modern Sociology*, Boston, Allyn & Bacon, 1971.

6. Albrecht Wellmer, *Critical Theory of Society*, New York, Herder & Herder, 1971.

7. Louis Althusser and Étienne Balibar, *Reading Capital*, New York, Random House, 1971. See also Louis Althusser *For Marx*, Allen Lane The Penguin Press, 1969, and New York, Random House, 1970.

8. Iring Fetscher's *Marx and Marxism* (New York, Herder & Herder, 1971) recounts these and subsequent developments with a lively understanding of the manner in which political and intellectual history interact.

9. cf. in Dick Howard and Karl E. Klar (eds.), *The Unknown Dimension: European Marxism Since Lenin*, New York, Basic Books, 1972.

10. For a similar point, see Karl Mannheim, *Ideology and Utopia*, New York, Harcourt Brace, 1936, p. 118.

11. *America and the Asian Revolutions*, Chicago, Aldine Publishing, 1970, p. 153.

12. *Monthly Review*, April 1972, p. 27.

13. ibid., p. 30.

14. ibid., p. 46.

15. *The Chinese Road to Socialism*, New York, Monthly Review Press, 1970, p. 221.

16. cf. M. Kosok, *Telos*, Spring 1971.

17. Quoted in Michael Ellman, *Soviet Planning Today*, Cambridge University Press, 1971, p. 188.

18. ibid.

19. ibid.

20. ibid., p. 189.

21. Quoted in the *Manchester Guardian Weekly*, 16 October 1971, p. 16.

22. 'Sartre Accuses the Intellectuals of Bad Faith', an interview with John Gerassi, *New York Times Magazine*, 17 October 1971, p. 38.

23. Guillain, quoted in the *Manchester Guardian Weekly*, 16 October 1971.

24. *New York Times Magazine*, 24 October 1971, p. 120.

25. Robert Payne, *Marx*, New York, Simon & Schuster, 1968, p. 414.

26. Frolic, *New York Times Magazine*, op. cit.

27. Kosok, op. cit., p. 207.

28. ibid., p. 135.

29. Guillain, *Manchester Guardian Weekly*, 16 October 1971.

30. ibid.

31. In Gerassi, *New York Times Magazine*, 17 October 1971.

Bibliographical Note

The articles gathered here have been selected with a view to clarifying the emerging vectors in my work, as well as those that have the closest bearing on my last book, *The Coming Crisis of Western Sociology*. They are not at all intended to be a true sampling of my work, let alone a full collection of my writings. Note, for example, that none of my work on organizational analysis is included. I have mostly left the articles here as they were originally published, although sometimes inserting an additional footnote.

1. 'Anti-minotaur' is here presented in its full and unabridged version. It has frequently been published in many anthologies in various abridged versions. It was first presented as my Presidential Address at the annual meeting of the Society for the Study of Social Problems, 28 August 1961, when, as an historical aside, I was introduced by Howard S. Becker. It was first published in *Social Problems*, Winter 1962.

2. 'The sociologist as partisan', first published in *The American Sociologist*, May 1968, has also been published in various shortened versions and is here printed in full. In one way, it is a clear foreshadowing of *The Coming Crisis*, having been written while I was working on the book. It is sometimes accused of being *ad hominem*, a criticism which works concerned with the historical conditioning of knowledge sometimes seem to deserve but have not always earned. The defect of this piece, in my present view, is not that it deduces anyone's intellectual weaknesses from an argument about 'personalities', but, rather, that it fails to do full justice to the view Becker represented by leaving implicit the rational dimension of his work and the useful contribution it makes to human emancipation.

3. 'Remembrance and renewal in sociology', published originally in *Psychology Today*, September 1971, is a transitional piece paraphrasing some of the main (and still commonly overlooked) theses of *The Coming Crisis*, and is thus backward-looking, while, at the same time,

beginning to articulate the importance of a community of social theorists for social knowledge.

4. 'The politics of the mind' is an expanded version of an essay originally published in *Social Policy*, March/April 1972, where the compact intimations of the previous essay are somewhat more fully adumbrated and the nature of the ontological and epistemological positions only implicit in *The Coming Crisis* are more fully explicated.

5. 'For sociology' was written in response to some of the critiques that appeared in the July issue of the *American Journal of Sociology*. Previously unpublished.

6. 'Some observations on systematic theory, 1945–55', published in Hans Zetterberg (ed.), *Sociology in the United States of America*, Unesco, 1955, is included here to establish that the many lines of criticism of Parsons' work, elaborated in the *Crisis*, were plainly present in my work almost twenty years ago, and that their full development in the *Crisis* represents no change in my estimate of Parsons' work or in the content of my critique of it. This small piece also does something that the *Crisis* fails to do, namely, it places Parsons in the perspective of Florian Znaniecki and P. A. Sorokin.

7. 'Reciprocity and autonomy in functional theory' was one of several efforts to develop a few of the theoretical possibilities opened in the previous essay. Originally published in L. Z. Gross (ed.), *Symposium on Sociological Theory*, Row, Peterson and Co., 1959, this piece is above all a critique of the notion of 'system'.

8. 'The norm of reciprocity', *American Sociological Review*, April 1960, continues to probe the flaws of functional analysis against the clear background of concern with problems of power and unequal exchange or exploitation. I have changed this in a few places.

9. 'The importance of something for nothing' was begun at the time when I was thinking through 'The norm of reciprocity' and, together with it, was the theoretical yeast that stimulated a number of interesting studies, which still remain dormant at the University of Illinois, including theses by Richard A. Peterson and Kenneth Downey. It was, however, only recently that I was persuaded to formulate this essay for publication and so it represents a contemporary formulation of earlier interests and commitments. Previously unpublished.

10. 'Personal reality, social theory and the tragic dimension', originally published as the Introduction to Gunnar Boalt's *The Sociology of Research*, S.I.U. Press, 1969.

11. 'Romanticism and Classicism' is part of my ongoing, larger commitment to the study of the origins of Western social theory. This essay

is the programmatic statement that has been guiding my joint work on Romanticism with Nedra Carp these last few years. Previously unpublished.

12. 'Émile Durkheim and the critique of socialism' was an introduction to the translation of Émile Durkheim, *Socialism and Saint-Simon*, Antioch Press, 1958. The dialectic between functionalism and Marxism that has long been central to my work is here made fully visible. It was written somewhat earlier than 'The norm of reciprocity'.

13. 'Sociology and Marxism' is a reply to a criticism of *The Coming Crisis*, made by a talented young Marxist and which is by far the most intellectually rigorous critique from the left. Originally published in *New Left Review*, January/February 1972.

14. 'The Red Guard', co-authored with Irving Louis Horowitz, was published originally in *Trans-Action* of November 1966, shortly after my return from an eighteen-month sojourn in Europe (which is probably one of the main roots of the changes that eventuated in *The Coming Crisis*). Some of the roots of this piece derive clearly from my work on Romanticism; some of its intellectual consequences may be explored in the second part of 'The two Marxisms'.

15. 'Comments on *History and Class Consciousness*' was originally a review of the American edition of Georg Lukács' important work, in the *New York Times Book Review*, 18 July 1971.

16. 'The two Marxisms' is, among other things, a development of some of the implications of the earlier pieces on Mao and Lukács. Of the several essays about Marxism here, this is most suggestive of the emerging tenor and direction of my still developing critique of Marxism, as yet far from finished; hence this should not at all be regarded as the fulfillment of a promise to write such a critique, which is still to come. Previously unpublished.

Concerning the title of this book: I have of course adapted it from Louis Althusser. This seemed especially fitting since I am *For Sociology* in very much the same sense, the same sublating and transcending sense, that Althusser is *Pour Marx*.